# LIBERIA

The Quest for Democracy

MAP 1  Liberia and Its African Neighbors, with County Boundaries, 1984–

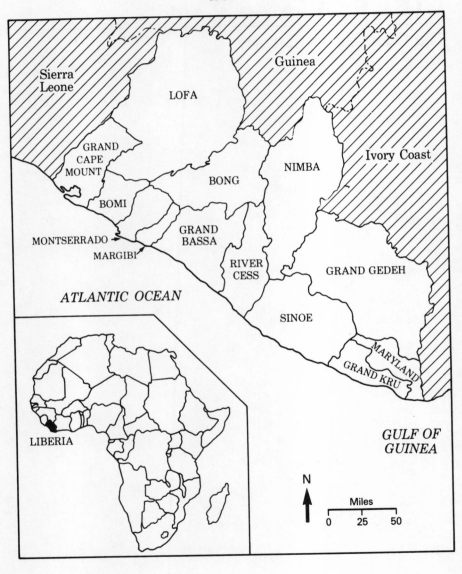

Sierra Leone

Guinea

LOFA

GRAND CAPE MOUNT

Ivory Coast

NIMBA

BONG

BOMI

MONTSERRADO

GRAND BASSA

MARGIBI

RIVER CESS

GRAND GEDEH

ATLANTIC OCEAN

SINOE

MARYLAND

GRAND KRU

LIBERIA

GULF OF GUINEA

N

Miles
0    25    50

# LIBERIA

## The Quest for Democracy

**J. Gus Liebenow**

INDIANA UNIVERSITY PRESS
*Bloomington and Indianapolis*

© 1987 by J. Gus Liebenow

Manufactured in the United States of America

**Library of Congress Cataloging-in-Publication Data**
Liebenow, J. Gus, 1925-
    Liberia : the quest for democracy.

Bibliography: p.
    Includes index.
    1. Liberia—Politics and government.    I. Title.
DT631.L53    1987    966.6'2    86-45956
ISBN 0-253-33436-5
ISBN 0-253-20424-0 (pbk.)

    1 2 3 4 5 91 90 89 88 87

*For Beverly*

# CONTENTS

Contents

# ILLUSTRATIONS

# ACKNOWLEDGMENTS

My scholarly interest in the substance and the style of Liberian politics remains as firm today as it was when I first started my study of Africa's oldest republic in 1960. For a social scientist interested in comparative analysis on the African continent, Liberia manifests all the contemporary problems relating to nation-building, overcoming poverty, and achieving popular control over government that are shared by neighbors who reckon their independence in terms of years and decades instead of roughly a century and a half. To that extent our approach has been to apply many of the accepted methods and methodology of social science by placing developments in Liberia within a continental (or even global) perspective. Yet, Liberia also represents a unique case of social stratification in which the vertical and horizontal crosscurrents based on race, ethnicity, response to modernization, and other factors have created a complex situation of caste and class divisions. Liberia also represents a significant laboratory for the analysis of the impact of economic growth without the concomitant reaction of the indigenous attitudes and infrastructures needed to sustain development. Finally, it represents not only the oldest model in Africa of a single-party state, but since 1980 has provided some critical data regarding the capacity of a military governing group to provide the mechanisms guaranteeing a restoration of popular control over government. While current social science tools are useful in analyzing the foregoing situations, a social scientist would certainly miss the essence of Liberian political behavior if he or she ignored the warmth, pathos, intrigue, contradictions, and sardonic humor that sometimes put Liberia in a political class with Italian city-states of the late Renaissance period.

My scholarly interest in Liberia has intensified over the years as the friendships that my wife and I have developed with Liberians in their own country as well as in the United States have grown both in number and in depth. We have shared with them their recent hopes as well as the ensuing despair regarding Liberia's prospects of realizing the long-denied right to the twin goals of democracy and development. It has in great measure been at the urging of our Liberian friends that I in 1985 and 1986 gave testimony on Liberia before the United States Senate and House of Representatives subcommittees on Africa, in hopes of changing American policy toward the Doe regime. Moreover, the frequent requests of Liberian friends have reinforced my resolve to produce this second book on Liberian politics.

During my initial and subsequent studies on Liberia, I found myself experiencing more than the usual share of self-questioning that properly confronts any social science researcher whose focus of inquiry concerns living human beings functioning in their own culture and society. I was, after all, a guest in the country and initially was permitted to do research in 1960–61 only after I had received personal clearance from President William V. S. Tubman. My inquiry and analysis could not have emerged had I not enjoyed the hospitality, cooperation, and friendship of many who did not ultimately appear in their most favorable light when my analysis was presented in print. The guest/host relationship in Liberia—as is true throughout Africa—creates very special obligations as well as privileges. In the final analysis, however, it has been Liberians themselves—both then and now; both before and after the fact—who have urged me to present my observations about Liberian politics with vigor and frankness, tempered with sympathetic understanding. Although my objective was a dispassionate social science analysis, I realized that I would have been guilty of condescension and done a disservice to many Liberians had I remained silent on key issues or glossed over events and situations which both young and old Liberians alike felt should be made explicit.

I realized, more with sobering humility than with pride, that my earlier writings as well as my first book on that country, *Liberia: The Evolution of Privilege*, had an impact upon the way that many Liberians came to perceive their own country. Despite rumors of an official ban of the book, thousands of copies were shipped to Liberia or "smuggled" back in the suitcases of returning students and even officials. Many Liberians visiting America during the 1970s made it a point to seek out not only me but also my wife and scholarly co-worker, who taught at Bromley Episcopal Mission School during our initial field research in 1960–61. Even though some Liberians disagreed with a statement here and there or with my interpretation regarding a specific situation or era, there seemed to be consensus regarding the thrust of my major theses. Surprisingly, even several of those who came out less favorably in my interpretation volunteered to help reinforce my argument or fill a gap in my analysis. I recognize, however, that Liberia is a complex country, and other researchers have had experiences in one region or another of the country that have led them to differing interpretations of the pace and direction of change. I respect their positions, but I do believe that my theses are historically sound.

During an extended absence from Liberia (I was rumored to be a "*persona non grata* to the *fourth* generation"!), I continued to write about the country, and assisted in putting Liberian studies in this country on a permanent footing by helping to found the Liberian Studies Association in 1968. Three weeks after the April 1980 coup, I elected to return to Liberia unannounced and without an official invitation, not knowing what my reception would be. I was pleasantly surprised by the warmth of my greeting and by the expressions of friendship by university faculty, officials in the new government, clerics, journalists, and others—many of whom I had met during their student days in America. Although my initial return visit was motivated largely by personal concern for my friends, I was impressed by those who argued that I had a moral responsibility to write about Liberia now that the iniquitous First Republic and its system of privilege had come to an end. Consequently, I not only extended that first visit but, with the generous support of the Universities Field Staff International,[1] I returned to Liberia for research purposes four times in the period from 1980 to late 1984.

This present book attempts to draw together my earlier studies of Liberian politics as well as my more recent observations on Liberia's renewed—although highly flawed—effort to pursue democracy and development. I am grateful to Cornell University Press for permission to draw liberally from my previously published materials in *Liberia: The Evolution of Privilege* (1969), and to the Universities Field Staff International for permission to use my analyses which appeared in "Liberia: The Dissolution of Privilege" (3 parts, 1980) and "Liberia: 'Dr. Doe' and the Demise of Democracy" (2 parts, 1984). I also wish to thank the *New Africa* magazine, London, U.K., for their kind permission in allowing me to reproduce Figure 6, on the Tolbert family tree, which appeared in their May 1980 issue.

Obviously, there are many to whom I owe a debt for having been permitted to do research in Liberia and to translate my thoughts into print. Without any hesitation, I acknowledge my wife, Beverly, who deserves first mention. She has been far more than a loving companion in our many trips to Liberia; she has been a treasured professional colleague who assisted me in research, helped compile the data on the political genealogy, became my sternest editorial critic, helped with the proofreading, and in countless other ways made my research efforts within a broader academic life possible and enjoyable. Also within the same galaxy—but for far different reasons—are my children, their spouses, and my grandchildren.

In thanking Liberians, I run the risk of overlooking many while acknowledging the few, and for that I apologize. But I am obliged, however, to acknowledge my official university hosts—Rocheforte Weeks and Christian Baker in 1960, and Mary Grimes Sherman in the period after 1980—for their extraordinary generosity. There is a special core of Liberians who were not only professional colleagues but true friends during the course of my research. These include Amos Sawyer, Jim Tarpeh, Patrick Seyon, Elwood Dunn, and Bai T. Moore.

There is also a group of Americans and other expatriates who have long been associated with us in our Liberian effort. On the very personal level are Mary and George Spratt and their children, the Fiore family, and my various doctoral students who have made significant contributions to Liberian scholarship. There are also academic colleagues-cum-friends who have sustained me in various ways: Warren and Cathy d'Azevedo, Jane Martin, Jeanette Carter, Father Ted Hayden, Ibrahim Sundiata, and Jyoti and Maya Chaudhuri. There is one in that latter category who deserves special mention for what he has done for the entire field of Liberian studies, both in Liberia and in the United States—Svend Holsoe.

I wish to acknowledge the institutional and financial support which made my research in Liberia possible over the years. This includes the Social Science Research Council of the American Council of Learned Societies; the Universities Field Staff International; Carnegie Foundation and Ford Foundation grants; and, of course, Indiana University.

I wish to give special thanks to Barbara Hopkins, who labored long and hard in the typing of the manuscript, and to Suzanne and Jim Hull of the I.U. Graphic Services Department, who prepared the tables, maps, and art work in a most creative fashion.

# LIBERIA

The Quest for Democracy

# I.

# The Liberian Paradox

Liberia is in many respects a paradox. In a continent which during the last quarter of a century has experienced the spectre of hunger, famine, and severe poverty, Liberia has not fared as badly as most. Indeed, just when the majority of African states were experiencing both their first fruits of political independence and their first realization of economic despair, Liberia in the late 1960s and early 1970s was experiencing a dramatic rate of economic growth and showing distinct signs of even greater potential for the future. The long-term optimism of both Liberian leaders and expatriate economists was based upon knowledge of the country's significant mineral reserves as well as rational estimates regarding the future prospects of Liberia's domestic and export agriculture. The World Bank then (as well as today) classified Liberia as a "middle-income oil importing country," ranking it 38 places up from the bottom of the list of less-developed countries (LDCs)—a promising contrast with the majority of new African states.[1] In the view of many economists, Liberia during the decade from the mid-1960s to the mid-1970s was considered one of the few fiscal success stories among the LDCs by virtue of its ability to generate revenue from its broad-based economic activities that significantly exceeded its public expenditures.[2] Its phenomenal 5.5 percent growth rate during that period—which included growth in agriculture (6.5), industry (6.2), and manufacturing (13.2)—put Liberia not only far ahead of most of its African neighbors but roughly on a par with the growth rates experienced by Japan, West Germany, and other developed states in the decades following the Second World War. Liberia is one of the few African states that have adequate rainfall, cultivatable land, and an underutilized pool of labor. Its potential resource base, moreover, is still unknown, for it has only been in the post-1980 period that a thoroughgoing and systematic geological survey of the country is being undertaken by the Liberian government, with the support of both private and public Western funding. The most significant asset of all, however, is Liberia's human talent. As a result of the strengthening of institutions of higher learning within Liberia during the last three decades, as well as a vast scholarship program financed by government, Christian missionaries, international agencies, and foreign donors, Liberia's pool of educated talent constitutes one of the higher per capita on the African continent.

By 1986, unfortunately, the optimism of the 1960s had turned to despair. Many economists view the Liberian economy as a situation of chaos in search of disaster. The once glowing economic growth rates had plummeted during the decade following the commencement of the 1973 oil crisis to 0.2 percent per annum in general, with across-the-board radical declines in growth rates in agriculture (2.0 percent), industry (-1.5 percent), and manufacturing (0.5 percent). Population growth rates, moreover, were well over the global average, going from 2.8 percent in the period from 1965 to 1973 to 3.3 percent by 1983. Many Liberians living in the depressed areas of Monrovia and the pockets of poverty in the rural hinterland have a standard of living approximating that of people living in the lowest income countries—the roughly forty states around the globe that are popularly called the Fourth World. Despite the strides at the university level, President Stephen Yekeson of Cuttington University College estimates that more than 75 percent of the Liberian population is illiterate, and only 50 percent of school-age children are enrolled in school. A sizable portion of its educated talent, moreover, lives in exile. Various tropical and temperate zone diseases are endemic to the country, and the roughly 54-year life expectancy of Liberians in the early 1980s was by a few years slightly better than that of most West Africans. The potential for industrialization is great; yet Liberia is one of the least industrialized states in Africa. Further complicating development, the rapid rate of rural to urban migration has created a food crisis, which has already had enormous political as well as economic and health consequences. Each year, there are fewer cultivators remaining in the rural areas and more unemployed urban mouths to be fed. Indeed, the percentage of Liberians who live in urban rather than rural areas went from 23 percent in 1965 to over 38 percent in 1985. To feed this burgeoning urban population, Liberia each year has had to import increasing quantities of grain and other foodstuffs. Rice imports alone went from 42,000 metric tons in 1974 to 126,000 metric tons in 1983.

The long-range nature of the economic crisis is revealed in the fact that almost a quarter of a century after the Northwestern University team conducted its early 1960s economic study, Liberia is still a case of "growth without development."[3] That is, the country has undergone a significant physical facelift and engaged in new and various economic activities, but the basic institutions and infrastructures needed to sustain development are either lacking or deficient. Many of the most significant beneficiaries of the economic growth of the period since World War II have, unfortunately, been either the privileged members of the political elite, who provided little real economic entrepreneurship, or the expatriate investors, bankers, advisers, and others. Many of the latter have repatriated sizable portions of their earnings to America, Europe, Lebanon, or elsewhere. These long-term economic programs are complicated today by the fact that Liberia's two principal exports, iron ore and rubber, are experiencing a depressed demand at the global level. Many of the rich iron ore lodes, moreover, have already been exhausted.

## The "Special Relationship" with America

Also in the realm of the paradoxical has been Liberia's relationship with America. Liberia is the only country in Africa which has enjoyed a sustained relationship with the United States over a period of more than 160 years. There is no suggestion that Americans and Liberians are obliged to regard the "special relationship" as reciprocal, even though Liberians and Americans, both individually and collectively, enjoy distinct advantages from the relationship in terms of commercial, military, security, navigational, transport, educational, communications, diplomatic, social, and other interests. Liberia, after all, is one among scores of countries to which the United States must relate. Yet Liberians continue to be offended by the fact that the average American knows far more about many countries in Europe, Asia, or Latin America which are remote from America's vital concerns than he or she does about Liberia, a country which was founded by Americans and whose capital is named after the fifth president of the United States, James Monroe. While Liberians are far more aware of the United States, they have not always viewed that "special relationship" in unambiguous terms, for it has had its shortcomings—if not actual liabilities—along with the benefits. This is certainly the case today when many Liberians at home and abroad regard the continued U.S. military support of the corrupt Doe regime as the primary instrument for keeping Doe in power. As one Liberian put it to this author, "It is the U.S. that is feeding our monster."

## The Political Paradoxes

The aspect of the Liberian paradox, however, that provides the main theme of this book is the comparison and contrast between Liberia and its African neighbors. At the heart of the anomaly is the fact that Liberia is Africa's oldest state; yet it is among the continent's newest nations. Technically, the fledgling colony, which was launched largely by private American efforts in 1822, declared itself independent from the founding American Colonization Society (ACS) in 1847. In turn, Liberia became a charter member of the League of Nations and of the United Nations. Despite Liberia's long history of independence, however, I was not surprised when visiting that country three weeks after the 1980 coup to have many young Liberians say to me, "This is our first year of independence." This view is shared by many within the majority of the population who consider themselves "tribal" (roughly 95 percent) rather than Americo-Liberians, the 5 percent who reckon their descent from the overseas founding of Liberia. Despite reforms in the last three decades, many tribal persons had existed in a quasi-colonial or caste-like situation vis-à-vis the Americo-Liberians until Master Sergeant Samuel Kanyon Doe and his colleagues toppled the government of the First Republic on 12 April 1980. Liberia's new leaders—many of whom are members of the Krahn, Gio, and other formerly subordinated ethnic groups—found themselves not only having to deal with the crisis of poverty, but also forced to address the two basic problems which have beset the leaders of those African states that only became independent in the last quarter of a century. Those two problems are the crisis of nation-building in the face of ethnic heterogeneity, and the crisis of popular control over government in a continent dominated by military coups.

As a consequence of the way in which the lines on the map of Africa were drawn during the nineteenth and twentieth century carve-up of the continent, Liberia, in common with its neighbors, has experienced a severe case of ethnic heterogeneity. The close to two million citizens of Liberia (in a country the size of Portugal or the American state of Ohio) find their loyalties divided between a commitment to the modern Liberian state and membership in one of the seventeen ethnic groups represented in the 1974 census. Being a Gola, a Grebo, a Krahn, or a Kru has often meant more to the individual than being a Liberian. Many of the tribal groups (a term still in use in Liberia despite its pejorative connotations elsewhere in Africa) have had intense, and often hostile, relations with the Americo-Liberian ethnic group over a period of more than 160 years. Many others, however, have only very recently come into systematic relationships with other Liberians, despite their nominal legal inclusion within the Liberian state.

Although the social and geographical boundaries of the various tribal groups are far from precise, at the core each group represents a distinct language, a different political authority system, and a unique way of organizing social, economic, religious, and cultural data relevant to their survival as a community. Within the broader Liberian state, moreover, there are discernible differences in skin pigmentation and physical type, which have had social and political consequences in spite of the external world's classification of all Liberians as Negroes or Blacks. Many of the social attitudes toward these differences in physical and cultural traits were consciously retained—sometimes as a matter of individual or group preference; sometimes as a matter of government policy, which was reflected in national programs and law. The specific problems that Liberian leaders both past and present have had to face in forging a "national society" in the face of heterogeneity on several planes will be explored in subsequent chapters.

The second political crisis, that of achieving popular control over government, is closely related to the preceding crisis. Almost from the point of initial contact in 1822—and persisting until the 1980 coup—the Americo-Liberian minority tended to occupy a position of political, economic, social, and religious superiority with respect to the subordinated tribal communities. In many respects the social stratification within Liberia during the First Republic resembled in form and spirit the caste relationship which long existed between the Tusi and the Hutu of Rwanda and Burundi. Many Liberians—including President William V. S. Tubman in his annual message to the Legislature in December 1960—described the relationship between Americo-Liberians and tribal people not in terms of caste, but rather as "colonial" in character. Indeed, in their expansion inward from the coastal enclaves, the settlers from the New World used many of the same techniques employed by the French, British, and other colonialists in their incorporation of African territory into their respective imperial systems. In any event—whether it be labeled a caste or a colonial relationship—a situation of dependency was created during the nineteenth century in which the authoritative allocation of values for the sixteen or more indigenous ethnic groups was increasingly performed by the settler minority from abroad and their descendants. In a dependency situation, the dominant group in the relationship tends to monopolize the use of force, establishes the primary goals for all parties to the relationship, limits the means for attaining group goals, and attempts to determine the nature and pace of any change in the situation of domination. The situation could, for example, remain indefinitely one of domination or it could, alternatively, lead either to full integration or to the eventual political separation of the several societies involved.

This, then, is the crux of the Liberian political paradox. Liberia was founded so that those who—on the basis of skin color alone—had been denied the rights and privileges of full participation in American society could enjoy the benefits of freedom in the continent of their ancestors. Yet, in the experience of securing the blessings of liberty for themselves, their treatment of the tribal people during the tutelary period under the American Colonization Society (1822–1847), as well as during the tenure of the First Republic (1847–1980), resulted in the systematic denial of liberty to others who were forcibly included within the Republic. There were many Americo-Liberians through the years who argued against a continuation of this iniquitous relationship between themselves and the tribal majority. It was not, however, until the Unification Program of President Tubman (1944–1971) that a concerted effort was made to remove many of the more odious distinctions between the descendants of the settlers and the indigenous population. The prospect of social, cultural, and political liberation being matched by economic betterment of the tribal majority was further enhanced by Tubman's Open Door policy. Under this policy, Liberian leaders boldly solicited foreign capital and expertise for the development of the country's mineral and agricultural resources. The improvements in the educational system, in health care, and in other aspects of life which accompanied economic growth under both Tubman and his successor, William R. Tolbert, unleashed unanticipated political and cultural responses by the tribal majority that could not be easily controlled or contained by the settler minority. This was certainly demonstrated by the ease and speed with which the legitimacy of the 1980 military coup (but not necessarily that of the military as a group) was established from one end of the Republic to the other. Till the bitter end, nevertheless, the central political core of the Americo-Liberian elite attempted to hold tight to the reins of power and to reap a disproportionate share of the benefits of economic growth.

The flawed nature of the Americo-Liberians' initial quest for a democratic society was further compounded during the latter part of the nineteenth century. Ironically, the same twin fears—tribal resistance, and competition from the European colonialists claiming the same territory in the interior—that had led to the establishment of the caste relationship between Americo-Liberians and the tribal majority also led to the principles of democracy being denied to the Americo-Liberians themselves. By ratifying a national constitution in 1847 for the fledgling republic, the leaders of the new society committed themselves to a democratic political system closely modeled after that of the United States.[4] In essence they accepted a political system that would encourage the fullest development of human talents unrestrained by governmental intrusion upon the rights of free speech, a free press, and freedom of worship. Limits upon the arbitrary exercise of governmental authority were nominally evident in the division of the tasks of government among the legislative, executive, and judicial branches, with each being separately constituted and buttressed with mechanisms for preserving its distinctive role within the national government. There was the implicit expectation, moreover, that free and open debate among competing electoral parties would not only guarantee a regular airing of the important issues of the day but also secure an orderly rotation in national leadership. Indeed, their emulation of the United States is further reflected in the parallel use of the terms "Republican" and "Whig" by two of the Republic's earliest political parties.

Unfortunately, the reality of political behavior during most years of the First Republic fell far short of the rhetorical commitment to democratic values and institutions. After a rather lively two-party competitive system during the first several decades, Liberia achieved the dubious distinction of producing the African continent's first single-party state. From 1884 to 1980 the True Whig Party (TWP) had no effective challenger to its monopoly over the Liberian political state. By the twentieth century, the internal limits on government authority atrophied as power increasingly gravitated from the legislative and judicial branches to an all-powerful executive. Intermittent denials of freedom of speech and of the press during the early years of the First Republic tended to become more systematic and all-encompassing during the twentieth century. Instead of a healthy pluralism, with many autonomous loci of influence and authority within the economic, religious, social, and other sectors of society, the Americo-Liberian political elite had co-opted leadership roles in the more significant structures of society and regulated those they did not directly lead.

The quest for democracy on the shores of West Africa reached its nadir in the late 1920s and early 1930s with the League of Nations inquiry into the Fernando Po scandal, during which the leadership of Liberia was accused of engaging in involuntary servitude with respect to the labor recruitment of Grebo, Kru, and other tribes. It took more than a decade and a half before relations between the settler minority and the tribal majority began to improve and at long last to move in the democratic direction that the Black and white founders of the west coast settlement had envisioned in the 1820s. President Tubman's Unification Program and his Open Door policy represented a dramatic reversal in actions and attitudes, which was matched later by the granting of suffrage to all adult citizens of Liberia and the extension of the county system of administration and representation to the tribal hinterland. The prospects that democracy was at last taking root in Liberia seemed bright indeed.

The potential as well as the glaring contradictions and shortcomings of the Tubman reforms only became apparent during the administration of his successor, William R. Tolbert (1971–1980). The unleashing of new popular forces, as well as the exposure of tribal persons to Western education, a cash economy, modern medicine, and a better standard of living, seemed to provide hope for a democratic future that would include the tribal majority. On the other hand, the more the central bastions of settler privilege were threatened, the tighter the restrictions imposed upon significant entry of tribal persons into the upper echelons of the executive branch, the True Whig Party, the Masonic Order, and the developing economic order. The costs of maintaining Whig privilege, moreover, created an even greater economic gap between the uppermost and the lowest strata of Liberian society. The fragile nature of the Tubman and Tolbert reforms was signaled by the Rice Riots of April 1979, and conclusively revealed in the military coup of 12 April 1980.

Thus, in the same week that Zimbabwe attained its independence from a form of settler-colonial domination, one of Africa's strangest cases of dependency rule also came crashing to an end in the western part of the continent. The struggle which culminated in the April 12 coup had been long in its gestation. Indeed, the depth of hostility that lay beneath the surface had been masked to the outside world by the very urbaneness and sophistication of those young diplomats and other officials who represented Liberia abroad during the past two or three decades. They radiated confidence and had projected the image of a stable, developing society. It was the coup itself and not only the incidents associated with it that surprised many of the leaders of other African states—particularly Liberia's immediate neighbors.

Despite the violence associated with the overthrow of the First Republic, however, there was a broad spectrum of support for Doe. It appeared that the 1980 coup—rather than the tentative starts under Tubman and Tolbert—provided Liberia with the first real opportunity to achieve fulfillment of its 160-year quest for democracy. The implicit nature of the commitment of the People's Redemption Council (PRC) to a return to civilian rule became explicit at the end of the first year of military governance. The launching of a very creative process of constitution-making, which involved the public en masse, reinforced the optimism that Liberia was at long last on the road to democracy. The flowering of pluralism in the religious, educational, social, economic, and other sectors brought forth talents and energies long suppressed. Despite the moratorium on political activity and discussion, there was hope that Liberia would embark on its first sustained experiment with freedom of the press and freedom of religion.

Unfortunately, by the end of the fourth year of PRC rule, the desire of Doe and the PRC to entrench itself permanently in office had become all too apparent. The flawed electoral process, the escalating violations of human rights and press freedom, and the transparent efforts to reestablish a one-party state undermined the legitimacy of the new government which took office on 6 January 1986. The fledgling experiment in Liberian democracy, which was reflected in the popularly supported constitution of the Second Republic, became a victim of infanticide. It was strangled almost at the moment of leaving the nest by the very man who had once given so many Liberian citizens hope that their aspirations for liberty were about to be realized—the usurper president, Samuel K. Doe. Whether the spirit of Liberian democracy can arise phoenixlike from its ashes is a matter of speculation. There are still countless numbers of Liberians both at home and in exile who firmly believe it can. It is to them and their hopes that I further dedicate this work.

# PART ONE

## Liberia's First Republic
### *The Evolution of Privilege*

# II.

# The Origins of the Modern Liberian State

The relationship between Africa and the West has been one of the more ignoble in the history of the human species. During most of the five and a half centuries since the Portuguese navigators rounded Cape Bojador in 1433, the Euro-African relationship was dominated by the impact of the transatlantic slave trade. By the time that infamous trade was finally terminated, during the third quarter of the last century, roughly 11.5 million Africans—with the full complicity of their fellow African middlemen—had been compelled to take the arduous, life-threatening sea voyage to the New World.[1] Although the institution of domestic slavery and other forms of involuntary servitude were not unknown to Africa before the European arrival, the practice of this institution on the western side of the Atlantic was a particularly degrading one. African slaves were in most instances divorced from their linguistic, religious, and other cultural roots and frequently deprived of the opportunity to establish familial and other social attachments on a systematic basis. Even the mulattoes, who were the products of illicit unions between white masters and female African slaves, and former slaves who had managed to achieve the status of free persons were pariahs in their New World environment. They were denied full participation in the political, economic, and social systems, which were dominated by whites. The ultimate demise of slavery and the slave trade was not the end of a bad relationship, for it occurred almost simultaneously with the emergence of still another negative aspect of the Euro-African connection: the imposition of colonial rule. Although the establishment of European dependencies in Africa did not gain momentum until the end of the nineteenth century, Africans living in a series of coastal colonial enclaves had as early as the sixteenth and seventeenth centuries found themselves relegated to the status of second-class residents in the lands of their birth. Europeans, in taking up the "white man's burden," succeeded in dominating all aspects of African life in the territories where the "European peace"—on occasion more insidious than slavery itself—prevailed.

It was in response to these adverse consequences of Western contact with Africa and Africans that the modern state of Liberia was launched. The Liberian experiment was not the only case in which "repatriation" to Africa was viewed as a just and humanitarian solution to interracial discord in the Americas and to the inequities of slavery and the persistence of the transatlantic slave trade. Indeed, one of the earlier examples of this approach, the 1787 founding of Freetown in Sierra Leone, also had American roots. Most of the initial settlers at Freetown were former slaves who had been freed by the first "emancipation proclamation" in North America: the promise of Sir Henry Clinton, the British commanding general in the South during the American Revolution, to guarantee the freedom of all slaves who deserted their rebellious masters.[2] Eventually, many of these freed slaves (later called Creoles) found their way to West Africa by way of Nova Scotia or Great Britain. Similar settlements for repatriated slaves and recaptives were established along the west and central Atlantic coast of Africa by the French, the Portuguese, and the Spanish.[3]

American slaves and even "free persons of color" lacked both the economic resources and the political and military clout required to bring about a successful repatriation project. Indeed, the founding of the modern state of Liberia was actually inspired by a number of prominent white Americans concerned with slavery, the slave trade, and the untenable position of "free persons of color" in the United States following the formation of the Federal Republic in 1787. Emigration or repatriation to Africa were not the only solutions offered to rectify the situation of racial conflict and injustice. Thomas Jefferson in 1784, Governor James Monroe of Virginia in 1801, and James Forten and other free Negroes of the Philadelphia Bethel Church in 1816 were among those who advocated various plans to establish "Black states" or territories in Louisiana, along the Missouri River, in the Pacific Northwest, or at other places in North America.[4] Ultimately the leaders of the colonization movement decided that the only feasible solution was to establish a colony on the west coast of Africa to serve as a refuge for freed American Blacks who desired repatriation to the land of their ancestors. The white founders felt that this could also provide an answer to the embarrassing question of what to do with the Ibos, Dahomeans, Congolese, and other Africans taken from slaving vessels intercepted by the United States Navy following the ban on importation of slaves after 1808 and the international agreement of 1819 to help suppress the slave trade on the high seas.

*Liberia's American Heritage*

The motives of those who organized the American Colonization Society in 1816 were decidedly mixed. Some saw emigration as a convenient device for ridding cities both North and South of a class that had not been successfully integrated into the American "melting pot." The free Black, moreover, had only a vague legal status in most states and was regarded as a constant source of social friction. Indeed, the concern of the "pragmatists" who advocated repatriation to Africa mounted as the ranks of the free Blacks grew from 59,466 in the first U.S. census in 1790 to 186,466 two decades later. By the onset of the Civil War their numbers had grown to 488,000—divided roughly evenly between North and South.[5] Southern planters, who figured prominently in the resettlement movement, were particularly interested in eliminating a class whose very existence—by setting an example of freedom and self-reliance among Blacks—constituted more than a symbolic and political threat to the institution of slavery. Other supporters of the Colonization Society—such as Robert Finley, a Presbyterian minister from New Jersey; William Thornton, a leading Quaker from New York; John Caldwell of the American Bible Society; and a host of Baptist, Congregationalist, and other Protestant spokesmen—had different motives. They saw the colony of American Blacks as a beachhead in West Africa for Protestant Christianity and Western civilization, not only spreading the Gospel to the "dark continent" but also implementing some of the fuzzy nineteenth-century ideas regarding pacifism, alcoholic prohibition, and other novel experiments in morality and social relationships. Finally, there were founders who were moved by more secular humanitarian considerations. They took what they assumed to be a pragmatic position, namely that free Blacks were capable of economic improvement and political self-government but that the entrenched prejudice of the white community as well as the recognition by Blacks of their political subordination made it impossible for them to compete on equal terms in a society dominated by whites.[6] Thus, by the humanitarian standards of that age, repatriation to Africa provided a morally just solution to the racial situation.

Whatever the motives of the American founders of Liberia, there was little doubt about their ability ultimately to translate their interest into political reality. Their membership included not only influential Protestant clergy but also a cadre of some of the most prominent names in American politics. The officers and sympathetic supporters of the American Colonization Society included Supreme Court Justice Bushrod Washington, nephew and heir of the late president; President James Monroe; four subsequent contenders for the presidency (Speaker of the House Henry Clay, General Andrew Jackson, Secretary of the Treasury William Crawford, and Congressman—later Senator—Daniel Webster of New Hampshire); and many prominent private citizens of the Revolutionary, Federalist, and Republican-Democratic periods of American history, including Francis Scott Key, John Randolph of Roanoke, and John Taylor of Caroline.

Although the American Colonization Society was not entirely successful in its endeavors to have the federal government underwrite the entire scheme, they did get the administration of President James Monroe to accept the Society's agent in West Africa as its own agent in the suppression of the slave trade and the resettlement of rescued Africans. Of even greater significance was the Society's victory in getting the United States Congress to appropriate $100,000—the first of a series of grants— to assist in the purchase of land, the construction of homes and forts, the acquisition of farm implements, the payment of teachers, and the carrying out of other projects necessary to the care, training, and defense of the settlers. The United States government outfitted the *Elizabeth*, which was accompanied by the U.S.S. *Cyane*, in

TABLE 1
*Political Leadership and Major Events*

| Agents of the ACS | | |
|---|---|---|
| | 1816 | Founding of American Colonization Society |
| | 1820 | First landing in Sierra Leone |
| 1821–24 Eli Ayres (intermittent) | 1821 | Purchase land at Cape Mesurado |
| 1822–28 Jehudi Ashmun | 1822 | First settlers at Cape Mesurado |
| 1828–29 Richard Randall | | |
| 1829–33 Joseph Mechlin | | |
| 1833 George R. McGill | | |
| 1834–35 John B. Pinney | | |
| 1835 Nathaniel Brander | | |
| 1835–36 Ezekiel Skinner | | |
| 1836–39 Anthony D. Williams | 1838 | Settlements unite, forming Commonwealth |

| Governors, Commonwealth | | |
|---|---|---|
| 1839–41 Thomas Buchanan | | |
| 1842–48 Joseph J. Roberts | 1847 | Declaration of Independence |

| Presidents, First Republic | | |
|---|---|---|
| 1848–56 Joseph J. Roberts | 1851 | Founding of Liberia College |
| | 1854 | Maryland becomes independent republic |
| 1856–64 Stephen A. Benson | 1857 | Maryland joins Liberian Republic |
| | 1862 | Lincoln extends U.S. recognition |
| 1864–68 Daniel B. Warner | 1865 | Arrival of the Barbadians |
| 1868–70 James S. Payne | 1868 | Anderson's journey to Musardu |
| | 1869 | True Whig Party founded |
| 1870–71 Edward J. Roye (a) | 1871 | Disastrous British loan |
| 1871–72 James S. Smith (b) | | |
| 1872–76 Joseph J. Roberts | | |
| 1876–78 James S. Payne | | |
| 1878–83 Anthony W. Gardiner (c) | | |
| 1883–84 Alfred F. Russell (d) | | |
| 1884–92 Hilary R. W. Johnson | 1885 | Gallinas annexed by Great Britain |
| | 1889 | Initial founding of Cuttington College |
| 1892–96 Joseph J. Cheeseman (e) | 1892 | French claim eastern areas |
| | 1893 | Grebo/settler conflict |
| 1896–1900 William D. Coleman (f) | 1900 | Gola victory over settlers |
| 1900–04 Garretson W. Gibson (g) | 1903 | Boundary with Sierra Leone fixed |
| 1904–12 Arthur Barclay | 1904 | Extension of citizenship to tribal sector; beginning of Indirect Rule |

TABLE 1—*Continued*

| 1912–20 | Daniel E. Howard | 1912 | Loan and customs receivership |
| | | 1918 | Monrovia shelled by German submarine |
| | | 1919 | Liberia enters League of Nations |
| 1920–30 | Charles D. B. King (h) | 1926 | Firestone Agreement |
| | | 1927 | Beginning of Fernando Po scandal |
| | | 1929 | League of Nations inquiry begins |
| 1930–44 | Edwin J. Barclay (i) | | |
| 1944–71 | William V. S. Tubman (j) | 1944 | Enunciation of Open Door policy and Unification Program |
| | | 1944 | Liberia enters Second World War |
| | | 1945 | Women suffrage amendment |
| | | 1946 | Suffrage extended to tribal Liberians |
| | | 1964 | Extension of county system to interior |
| 1971–80 | William R. Tolbert (k) | 1979 | Rice Riots |
| | | 1980 | Coup, assassination of Tolbert |
| *Head of State, PRC* | | | |
| 1980–86 | Samuel K. Doe | 1984 | Referendum on the Constitution of the Second Republic |
| | | 1985 | Elections, Quiwonkpa coup attempt |
| *President, Second Republic* | | | |
| 1986– | Samuel K. Doe | | |

KEY: (a) deposed; (b) filled truncated term of Roye; (c) resigned; (d) filled unexpired term; (e) died in office; (f) filled unexpired term, elected, resigned; (g) filled unexpired term, elected in his own right; (h) forced to resign; (i) filled unexpired term, elected in his own right; (j) died in office; (k) filled unexpired term, elected in his own right, assassinated.

an attempt in 1821 to settle American Blacks on Sherbro Island, off Sierra Leone. The settlement scheme proved abortive, and in the following year Lieutenant Robert F. Stockton of the U.S. Navy rescued Elijah Johnson and other survivors of malaria at Sherbro and carried them, as well as a new group of settlers from America, farther down what was popularly called the Grain Coast (named after the grains or seeds of the malagueta pepper, one of the principal exports of that area). The actual landing site of Cape Mesurado, near the present city of Monrovia, was selected by a young lieutenant named Matthew Perry, who later achieved fame as Commodore of the Africa Squadron and in the opening of Japan to Western influence.[7]

The negotiations at Cape Mesurado in December 1821—prior to the initial settlement on 25 April 1822—were protracted and heated. At gunpoint, Lieutenant Stockton attempted to convince "King Peter" and other minor Bassa and Dei chieftains that the settlers came as benefactors, not enemies. The American officer successfully negotiated the deeding of Cape Mesurado to the Colonization Society in return for $300 worth of muskets, beads, tobacco, gunpowder, clothing, mirrors, food, and rum.[8] This was the first of an endless string of transactions in which the tribal negotiators only belatedly realized the full implication of the "sale" of their land to the alien settlers from America. The settlers and their agent did not appreciate that the concept of "sale" of land had no meaning in societies where land was distributed communally on the basis of usufructuary right of occupancy rather than individual private freehold. Hostility intensified as the settlers later pressed tribal residents into service as field hands and household domestics and imposed American forms of speech, justice, and commerce in the area under their control. In some cases, such as the fragile settlement by the Mississippi Colonization Society in Sinoe, the settlers came into direct conflict with the indigenous Kru, who regarded them as competitors in the middleman and coastal trading which the Kru had earlier developed.[9]

The American relationship to its stepchild on the African west coast has been ambiguous during most of the century and a half since the initial settlement. As the ACS and the settlers extended their control over tribal land—often at gunpoint— it was only the timely intervention of American, British, and other naval forces that prevented the colonists from being thrown back into the sea. This is not meant to dismiss the Liberian navy (both during the ACS period and following independence) as being inconsequential. Although small and subject to more than its share of misfortunes, the Liberian navy was a factor in establishing Liberian territorial claims against both European and indigenous tribal challenges and in the suppression of the slave trade. It also provided a significant service in the coastal transfer of commodities to settlers along the Liberian littoral, in the delivery of mail, in the transporting of Liberian officials, and in collecting debts owed to the Liberian government by African traders.[10]

Despite official American assistance, however, the U.S. government stead-fastly refused to recognize the purchased areas as an official American colony, which created many international problems for the Colonization Society, the Americo-Liberian settlers, and the American government itself. This studied official aloofness assumed monumental proportions in the 1840s, when the British government, in support of European traders from Sierra Leone who ignored Liberian land claims and refused to pay customs fees, declined to acknowledge the sovereignty of the American Colonization Society. Although United States officials expressed to the British their concern for the rights of the settlers, it was the Americo-Liberians themselves—as they eventually came to be called—who resolved the impasse. In 1847 the Monrovia settlers issued a "Declaration of Independence," severing their ties with the founding Colonization Society and establishing Liberia as the first sovereign and independent Black republic in Africa. Similar action was subsequently taken by the settlers who had established themselves further down the coast near Cape Palmas in Maryland County. This settlement effort was fostered by the Maryland State Colonization Society, which broke away from the American Colonization Society in 1831 and started sending settlers to Maryland in Liberia in 1833. It remained a separate colony and republic until 1857, when it was annexed by the Republic of Liberia.[11] The almost immediate recognition in 1847 of the Liberian republic by Great Britain contrasted sharply with the American stance. Despite continued economic and military support, it was not until the administration of Abraham Lincoln, in 1862—when the Civil War had removed the principal objectors to the presence of a Black envoy in Washington, D.C.—that diplomatic recognition was extended.

A decided shift to dependence upon the British became very noticeable in the latter decades of the nineteenth century, despite conflicts with that country over land claims in the interior. In 1871, for example, the Liberian government turned to the British for a loan when it found itself in dire financial straits. Unfortunately, the results of this loan were disastrous for the Liberian people, for President Edward J. Roye (who was deposed as a result of having profited personally from the transactions), and indeed for everyone except the London bankers. British-Liberian ties were also manifest in the education of Liberian youth in England and Sierra Leone, in opening the first regular shipping schedule to Monrovia, in trade relations, and in the financial and other forms of assistance given by the British government in the reorganization of the Republic's administrative services and military forces. The British pound remained Liberia's official currency until 1943, when it was replaced by the American dollar. The European orientation of the Liberian republic was also evidenced by the fact that during most of the nineteenth and early twentieth centuries, Germany was Liberia's principal trading partner, with the Netherlands being a close second. Britain remained the primary supplier of imported goods and became even more important after the entreaties of Britain and the Allies succeeded in getting Liberia to break diplomatic relations with Germany—in return for the vague promises of the British to remove British restrictions on Liberian trade. The decision was an economic disaster for Liberia, since the Germans to that point controlled about three-quarters of Liberia's prewar trade and its demise brought not only a considerable loss of public revenues but a virtual collapse of commercial trade.[12]

Nonetheless, the American connection remained strong despite the lack of direct assistance from other than missionary sources during the first half century of independence. The United States was indeed influential in maintaining the independence of Liberia, even if it was not prepared to do more than admonish the British and French when they whittled away Liberia's extended territorial claims in the hinterland. In 1909, for instance, an American commission of inquiry, by its very presence and its recommendations (never officially accepted by the U.S. government), prevented both England and France from taking over the country as a protectorate as a result of Liberia's defaulting on the repayment of a series of European loans.

Liberian fears regarding British intentions were far from groundless. Indeed, in 1906 the British governor of Sierra Leone, Sir Leslie Probyn, suggested in a secret letter to the Colonial Office that Britain take over northwestern Liberia because the Sierra Leone Railway lay so close to the Liberian border. "It seems to me," Probyn wrote, "that a country owning a Railway in Africa is the natural overlord or suzerain of the country situated within say 50 miles of the Railway." He proposed that Britain "lease" Liberian territory along the model of the Chinese leaseholds extracted by European powers from weakened political authorities in imperial China. Probyn's chief desire, he insisted, was "that some method should be found whereby the interior of that part of Liberia which is adjacent to [Sierra Leone] can be properly governed."[13]

American diplomatic concern was also useful during World War I. In 1915 the United States forestalled British intervention in Liberia during an uprising on the Kru Coast by providing the Americo-Liberians with arms and military advisers to help crush the tribal rebellion. Fifteen years later, however, the American relationship once more took on an ambiguous quality during the League of Nations investigation of slavery in Liberia and the forcible recruitment of contract labor for service on the Spanish island of Fernando Po. Details of the League inquiry are discussed later in this volume. It is significant to note at this point, however, that although the American association with the League inquiry offended many Liberian officials, the United States action was instrumental in frustrating the efforts of the European powers to terminate Liberian sovereignty and to place Liberia under some form of international League of Nations mandate.[14] With the election of Franklin Roosevelt, relations between the United States and Liberia decidedly improved in the fields of economic development and foreign affairs as the Good Neighbor policy was extended across the Atlantic.

### The Condition and Aspirations of the Settlers

Despite the enthusiasm of the white founders of the American Colonization Society, and the subsequent efforts in Maryland, Pennsylvania, Mississippi, and other American states toward organized colonization in Liberia, emigration or repatriation to West Africa involved only a small fraction of the free Blacks and mulattoes, whose number had risen to over half a million by 1867.[15] The figures in table 2 indicate that less than twenty thousand persons were settled in Liberia, and close to six thousand of these had never been to America, for they were Africans rescued ("recaptured,") from slaving vessels on the high seas.[16]

The limited success of the colonization scheme was in part due to finances. The Colonization Society failed to get the U.S. government to underwrite the operation, and few liberated Blacks possessed the property necessary to pay their own way to Liberia and to survive until the first harvest there. The emigrants were thus dependent upon funds provided by former masters who had emancipated their slaves, the appropriations by various state legislatures in America, or the private fundraising ability of the Society. There were other reasons, however, for the poor showing. The abolitionists and antislavery people, for example, felt that repatriation actually undermined their case, since it removed from American shores the evidence that free Blacks could be industrious and gave support to the myth that the two

## TABLE 2.
### Liberian Immigrants, Nineteenth Century

#### Immigrants from 1822 to 1867

| | |
|---|---:|
| Born free | 4,541 |
| Purchased their freedom | 344 |
| Emancipated, to go to Liberia | 5,957 |
| Emancipated, for other reasons | 753 |
| Arrived from Barbados, 1865 | 346 |
| Settled in Maryland County, 1831–1862, origins not indicated | 1,227 |
| Recaptives, Africans taken from slave ships | |
| by the United States Navy, 1820–1843 | 287 |
| by the United States Navy, 1843–1860 | 5,457 |

#### Immigrants from 1865 to 1904

| | |
|---|---:|
| Origins in the United States | 4,093 |
| Total | 23,005 |

Adapted from Merran Fraenkel, *Tribe and Class in Monrovia* (Oxford University Press, 1964), p. 6; Peter J. Murdza, *Immigrants to Liberia: 1865 to 1904: An Alphabetical Listing* (Newark, Del.: Liberian Studies Association, 1971), Research Paper No. 4; and Tom W. Shick, *Behold the Promised Land: A History of Afro-American Settler Society in Nineteenth-Century Liberia* (Baltimore: The Johns Hopkins Press, 1977), pp. 66–68.

races could not exist in peace within a single society. This objection was voiced by many freed Blacks as well; the leaders of the Philadelphia Bethel Church in 1816 labeled the colonization scheme a slur upon their reputation and little more than a plan to dump free Blacks "into the savage wilds of Africa." It was, they claimed, "a circuitous route" back to bondage.[17]

The composition and aspirations of the group that settled in Liberia were mixed, and a form of social stratification emerged almost immediately within the group which paralleled the hierarchical relationship between the settlers and the indigenous tribal inhabitants.[18] At the lowest level within the settler grouping were the so-called recaptives, those Africans who had never seen the New World but had been rescued from slaving vessels by the British and American navies and deposited on the Grain Coast to start a new life. Whether their origins were present-day Nigeria, Ghana, or elsewhere, this lowest-status group within the Americo-Liberian fold came to be called Congoes. Curiously, "Congo" later became one of the terms that tribal people used to refer to all persons who claimed descent from the alien founders of Liberia.

The upper echelons of the Americo-Liberian group were the five thousand Black or mulatto immigrants who had been born free, who had been emancipated by their slave owners, or had been sufficiently enterprising in America to purchase their freedom. This was the group that provided the main thrust of dynamic leadership during the formative years. The settlers from the United States were augmented during the middle years of the nineteenth century by a remarkable group of West Indian Blacks who had become dissatisfied with British rule in Barbados, Jamaica, and other Caribbean islands. The ambitions of the Americo-Liberian elite collectively paralleled those of the white founders of the Society. Men like Lott Carey and Colin Teague, who were Baptist preachers, not only tended to the needs of the settlers but carried the Gospel as well to the tribal people along the coast. As Carey, a former warehouse hand from Richmond, Virginia, said: "I am an African. I wish to go to a country where I shall be estimated by my merits, not by my complexion; and I feel bound to labour for my suffering race."[19] So enterprising were Black and white missionaries alike that by 1838 there were over twenty churches along the Liberian coast, representing most of the major Protestant denominations.[20]

The church became a vital social institution to the settler in building new bonds in a strange land. Churches have borne (and continue to bear) a major educational burden in Liberia. By 1838 there were ten schools founded by church groups and staffed in most cases by Black settlers; the teaching profession was one of the few white-collar positions open to free Blacks in the pre-Civil War American South. The churches were equally important in launching newspapers in the colony, and the four presses in the early years were crucial in providing information on new groups, ship arrivals, market conditions, and other data about the environment. Later, several of the church presses became important political instruments. One editor, the Reverend John Seys, used his newspaper to supplement his pulpit criticism of the American Colonization Society and its administration of the colony.

Without the enthusiastic cooperation between the better-educated settlers and the white leaders who came out as the agents or governors in behalf of the American Colonization Society, the experiment in repatriation would have failed. A remarkable sense of dedication on the part of the white leaders was demonstrated by the first agents—Dr. Eli Ayres, a surgeon from Baltimore, and Jehudi Ashmun, a young Methodist minister—through the last white administrator, Governor Thomas Buchanan (brother of the future president of the United States), who died at his post in 1841. Despite the periods of crisis, the agents had generally high praise for the courage and endurance of many of the educated Americo-Liberians. Several of the settlers, such as Lott Carey, A. D. Williams, and the very gifted Joseph Jenkins Roberts, had taken over the administration of the Society's affairs during the temporary absences of the white agents from Liberia. Elijah Johnson, a survivor of the ill-fated Sierra Leone landing of 1820, had been the primary organizer of the defense of the settlements near Monrovia. Other Americo-Liberians had surveyed the farm plots and laid out the streets in the infant colony.

While cooperative in most instances, the settlers were far from subservient. They realized all too well their financial dependence upon the Society and their reliance upon the military support of the United States Navy in resisting tribal and

European threats to the life of the colony. Most of this group, however, had come to Liberia to escape white domination. Despite their vague legal status and lack of political influence, many—especially the offspring of illicit unions between slave women and white "gentlemen"—had received quality education, owned a certain amount of property, and even enjoyed a measure of social status. This group was restive under the tight reins of the Society's agents, and they occasionally rebelled. Even the quiet Jehudi Ashmun was forced to move temporarily to the Cape Verde Islands in the face of a revolt organized by Lott Carey.

Particularly annoying to the educated Americo-Liberian were the Jeffersonian ideals of many of the religious and philanthropical supporters of the Society who believed that the independent settlers should seek the serenity of a rural, agricultural existence and disavow the evils of urban commerce and industry.[21] Despite their origins in the rural South, many of the educated settlers had spent their adult years in the cities of the American North or the border states. They found that the rigors of life in Liberia took a significant toll in terms of both temperate zone and tropical diseases—particularly malaria, which accounted for a very high mortality rate in many of the settlements.[22] The settlers, moreover, associated agriculture with the life of servitude they or their parents had experienced. They did not adjust well to the diet of cassava, plantain, yams, and other foods to which indigenous Africans were accustomed. They preferred the more costly imported maize, wheat flour, pork, and ham, purchased with profits from petty trading. The educated Americo-Liberian would only associate himself with agriculture as the absentee landlord of a plantation of sugarcane, rice, or coffee cultivated by poorer settlers or African recaptives rescued from slave ships en route to the New World. Some of the late nineteenth century success of Liberia in exporting coffee, sugar, and other commodities can be attributed to the leasing of plantations to enterprising foreigners, although a few leading Liberian politicians did own successful farms. In any event, Liberian production was not able to withstand the global competition at the end of the century. For most Americo-Liberians, the role of dirt farmer was decidedly beneath their station.[23]

The disdain for agriculture, unfortunately, also spread to the second strata of Americo-Liberian society, the Blacks who had been emancipated with the express understanding that they go to Liberia. This group lacked the independent means of many in the upper strata, and being generally of "pure" African descent rather than "bright-skinned" mulattoes, they tended to be looked down upon during the early decades of Liberian settlement. Many in this second group had been household retainers or skilled artisans and were not used to the strenuous life of farming. Even those who had been farm managers or field hands, however, had assumed optimistically that a new life in Africa would hold forth something more than the hard calluses and sweaty brows of the past. Ironically, those compelled to till the soil in order to survive found farming in Liberia more difficult than in America. The torrential rain, which averages over 180 inches between April and October, often washed out the crops that had been planted using techniques developed in a more temperate zone. The rapidly leaching soils and the multitude of crop pests were unfamiliar to the immigrant farmers, and the strength they needed for their heavy chores was often drained by the fever of malaria and other tropical illnesses, since they or their ancestors had lost any natural immunity to these diseases.

Normally, only those Americo-Liberians who settled some distance from the commercial attractions of Monrovia persevered in agriculture. There were, for example, the band of freemen settled by the Mississippi Colonization Society at the mouth of the Sinoe River in 1838, or the dedicated cluster of Black Quakers who staked out farms near the mouth of the St. John River in 1835 and whose pacifist beliefs almost led to their total annihilation at the hands of hostile Africans. Curiously, the most successful farmers of all stood at the bottom of the Americo-Liberian social structure. This was the group referred to as "Congoes." These recaptive Africans lacked Western education, were unable to speak either English or the local indigenous languages, had been stripped of all their property and family ties, still adhered to their traditional religions and customs, and were entirely dependent on the mercy of the white agents and the Americo-Liberian settlers. Having been just a few days or perhaps months away from the yam farms in Nigeria or Dahomey, the Congoes were not at all disturbed by the conditions of agriculture in Liberia.

For reasons outlined in subsequent chapters, the preferred vocations of the uppermost strata of Americo-Liberian society continued until the 1980 coup to be politics and the law. At the outset of modern Liberian history, however, the prestigious callings also included the ministry, teaching, and commerce—with the last assuming increased importance during the first five decades of settlement. Despite the efforts of Ashmun and his successor to place legal and practical restrictions upon trade in favor of agriculture, the Americo-Liberian traders persevered. They gradually displaced the Mandingoes and even the European merchants and monopolized the trade between the coast and the interior. Among tribal persons and Westerners alike the Americo-Liberian trader enjoyed a reputation as a shrewd bargainer who exchanged the cloth, rum, and tobacco from America and Europe for the camwood, cane sugar, palm kernels, rice, and the occasional ivory tusk that tribal traders brought to the coast. Often the enterprising Americo-Liberian trader— at risk to his own life—ventured up the rivers in search of trade items.

Through trade with the interior, by serving as representatives of American and European trading firms, and through investment in the construction of schooners and direct engagement in the transatlantic trade, a number of Americo-Liberians attained substantial wealth and political privilege.[24] These included Francis Devaney, the former slave of U.S. Speaker of the House Langdon Cheves; Joseph Jenkins Roberts, the first president of Liberia; and Edward Roye, who in 1869 became the first person of entirely Black ancestry to be elected president of Liberia. By the mid-1870s, however, Liberian prosperity ended, and the country went into a steady economic decline. A number of factors contributed to the decline, including the worldwide economic depression, the sudden interest of European colonial powers to become more directly involved in the exploitation of Africa, the competition that European steamships provided the Liberian-constructed sailing schooners, the rise of the coffee industry in Brazil and the sugar-beet industry in Europe, and a series of disastrous government loans that wiped out the private fortunes of many public officials involved in the transactions.

Despite the economic decline of the better-educated fourth of the settler community, they continued to control the political, social, and religious standards of the entire Americo-Liberian group. Their standards were those of the antebellum American South. Far from rejecting the institutions, values, dress, and speech of a society that had rejected them, the free persons of color painstakingly attempted to reproduce that culture on an alien shore. What they had rejected, apparently, was a situation that denied them full participation in American society. Few, in fact, agreed with Lott Carey that Africa was their true home. The experiment in colonization was not the "in-gathering" of Africa's lost children. These were Americans, and their views of Africa and Africans were essentially those of nineteenth-century whites in the United States. The bonds of culture were stronger than the bonds of race, and the settlers clung tenaciously to the subtle differences that set them apart from the tribal "savages" in their midst. It was not unusual to hear tribal people refer to Americo-Liberians as Kwee, or "white" people, or to have them call Monrovia "the America place."[25]

The one American institution modified in the Atlantic crossing was the family. The extraordinary emphasis that the Americo-Liberian settlers placed upon family ties was undoubtedly a reaction against the cruel and recurrent disruption of the slave family and the status in America of illegitimacy for the products of mixed unions. The Americo-Liberian has from the outset emphasized family size by combining the bilaterialism of the American system (counting kinsmen in both the male and female lines) and the extended character of the African kinship system. Although rejecting the legality of polygamy, the Christian Americo-Liberian has increased his offspring by practicing what this author has referred to as "sequential monogamy," or having only one legal wife at a time. Divorce is a rather simple matter. Moreover, informal unions with "Congo" women and later with tribal women (for whom traditional bridewealth was paid to relatives) were socially countenanced. To the credit of Americo-Liberian mores, illegitimacy is a relatively unknown concept. The "outside children" have been invariably given full recognition within the family of the Americo-Liberian father.

In addition to the general acceptance of informal liaisons with Congo or tribal women, youngsters from these two groupings who had demonstrated intelligence and ability were fairly early assimilated into the Americo-Liberian family under the "ward" or apprentice system. This situation was legally recognized in 1838. In return for food, clothing, shelter, and often education as well, the ward helped out with the farming and other chores. When the system was abused, it differed little from domestic slavery. In many instances, however, a ward was fully adopted into the Americo-Liberian family and was permitted to bear the family name, inherit property, and enjoy the prestige of his "father." However deficient the system might have been, it provided one early avenue for assimilation on the part of Congo and tribal youth.

## Expansion into the Interior

Apart from the motives that prompted the white founders and the Americo-Liberians to establish the colony on the west coast of Africa, it early became apparent that Americo-Liberians themselves believed Liberia had a special meaning for all Africans.[26] Clearly borrowing a page from the contemporary American political scene, President Joseph Jenkins Roberts and other Liberian leaders declared that they had a "manifest destiny" to bring civilization to the tribal "heathens" of the hinterland. Less doctrinaire reasons were advanced to justify the expansion of Liberian influence and control beyond the original settlements in Monrovia, Buchanan, Harper, and other coastal points. Thus, it was argued that the defense and "natural growth" of the colony demanded that the Liberian state expand into the interior.

Americo-Liberian leaders seemed undisturbed by the fact that such expansion would further intensify their minority position within the new state. They were already outnumbered by an indigenous majority having no experience with the New World or Westernized slavery and differing markedly in culture from the immigrant community. Moreover, despite their official motto, "The Love of Liberty Brought Us Here," the Americo-Liberians seemed curiously unconcerned by the fact that the process of expansion created an anomalous relationship of political dependency between themselves and the members of more than sixteen ethnic groups indigenous to the Liberian hinterland. It was a relationship similar in most respects to that obtaining between whites and Africans in other sectors of the continent.[27] The distinguishing criterion for subordination, however, was not race—though differences in skin pigmentation between bright-skinned (i.e., persons of mixed ancestry) and dark-skinned Liberians continued to have important social and political consequences well into the twentieth century. Rather, the dependency relationship was based upon differences in culture and upon the barriers erected by the Americo-Liberians against either rapid or widespread assimilation of the dominant culture by tribal people.

The extension of political control by the Americo-Liberians over subordinate indigenous societies took place over a long period. In some areas the authority of the settlers and their descendants had been recognized only during the second or third decade of the present century. As a form of nineteenth- and twentieth-century colonialism in Africa, the Liberian case differed from most examples in which the essential imperial governing force was external. In this respect Liberia shared a parallel experience with the Amharic-speaking peoples of Ethiopia, the Afrikaaners of the Transvaal and the Orange Free State, the religiously inspired followers of the Muslim leaders Samori Touré and El Hadj Omar, and the military regiments of the Zulu King Shaka.[28] In each of these instances, a group which was basically internal to the continent had extended its political, economic, and social control over its less-powerful indigenous neighbors. In doing so, moreover, the locally based imperialists tended to manifest the same techniques of expansion and control as the external European colonialists, with whom they found themselves engaged in an armed competitive struggle. Thus, the Liberian settler group asserted its claims to sovereignty over an expanded area in West Africa based upon techniques which had been previously perfected in the European expansion in the Americas and Southeast Asia.

The initial Liberian acquisitions of land from the Bassa, Dei, and other coastal chiefs, for example, came through the "purchase" by the American Colonization Society of a strip 130 miles long and 40 miles wide in what is now Montserrado County. Since the "sale of land"—in the sense of a permanent transfer of ownership—was an unknown concept in that part of Africa, these transactions were questionable and a source of continuing friction. Despite the legal ambiguity, subsequent strips of land along the coast and in the river valleys were added between 1821 and 1845—often to forestall French or British incursions into the area. Similarly, much of the disputed area in the Gola and Vai territories later surrendered to the British as a part of Sierra Leone had been claimed by the Americo-Liberians on the basis of purchase (see map 2). Generally, diplomats in international quarters did not question the legal right of Liberian chiefs to sell land held in communal trust any more than they did the right of chiefs, lineage heads, and other political authorities to do so elsewhere in Africa.

An equally effective method of expansion which emulated the colonial strategies of the competing European imperial powers was the establishment of protectorate relationships over certain ethnic groups, based upon agreements negotiated between the American Colonization Society (or the successor Liberian government) and chiefs who feared their neighbors more than they did the strangers from America. In many instances the instruments of protection were broadly constructed—but nevertheless limited—treaties of friendship in which the chiefs agreed to end intercommunal warfare, submit quarrels to the Liberian government for arbitration, cooperate with the Americo-Liberians in ending the slave trade, and ban certain traditional practices, such as the use of poison ordeals in deciding the question of guilt in a court case. A treaty of this nature was concluded in 1839, for example, following the victory of Liberian General Joseph Jenkins Roberts over Chief Gatumba of Boporu, or Bopolu. This victory convinced the chiefs in the area northwest of Monrovia that the occasionally inept Liberian military forces could be effective. In other instances indigenous groups voluntarily accepted the protection of the Liberian government in the face of threats from neighboring ethnic communities or to avoid French or British domination. In addition to these treaties of friendship and protection, there were many treaties with only limited objectives, such as the development of commerce between the hinterland and Monrovia. Several commercial treaties were negotiated in the 1850s by President Roberts with the Vai, Gola, and Loma peoples. Whether the agreements were broad or limited in scope, however, the settler government rapidly converted the treaties of friendship into Liberian deeds of ownership to the territory of the people involved.

The immigrants also emulated their British and French competitors for control of the West Atlantic interior of Africa by considering that journeys of exploration provided the sponsoring state with a claim to any territory "discovered" by the traveler. Various Liberian presidents commissioned European trading firms to carry out such "journeys of discovery." Among the most exciting, however, were several undertaken by Americo-Liberians themselves. The chronicles of a young Liberian

MAP 2    Extent of Liberian Territorial Claims

SOURCES: Outward Bound Publishers, London, 1892, in *Liberia*, The Bulletin of the A.C.S, No. 14 (February 1899); Stefan von Gnielinski, *Liberia in Maps* (London: University of London Press, 1972), p. 11; and R. Earle Anderson, *Liberia: America's African Friend* (Chapel Hill: University of North Carolina Press, 1952), p. 89.

surveyor, Benjamin J. K. Anderson, who visited the western Mandingo city of Musardu in 1868, rank with some of the best literature in this genre.[29] Two other Liberians, Seymour and Ash, had earlier explored the area north of the St. Paul River and may even have reached Nimba Mountain and the headwaters of the Cavalla River in the northeast. Their purposes were probably more commercial than political.[30]

Finally, some Americo-Liberian claims to control were based upon conquest. Many of these military ventures in the early period against the Dei and Vai were only minor skirmishes in which the spears and knives of the tribal people proved unequal to the rifles and cannons of the Liberian troops. It was in the defense and expansion of the settler community, however, that some of the early heroes of Liberian history were created—such as Elijah Johnson. On occasion, however, the superior skill of the indigenous people in guerrilla warfare, enhanced by arms secured from outside sources, tipped the scales temporarily in favor of the tribal element. In such cases Liberian authority was established only after many years of fighting and considerable loss of life and property by both sides. The Gola people in the early period and the Grebo and the Kru as late as the early decades of the present century are outstanding examples of indigenous resistance to Liberian occupation.

### Resistance to Expansion

Indigenous resistance was not the only source of opposition to Liberian expansion. During the early colonial period Don Pedro Blanco, a mulatto from Brazil, and various European slave traders recognized the obvious threat to their activities posed by the American Colonization Society agents and the settlers, who had the support of the U.S. Navy in destroying the various slave factories, or depots, along the coast. Thus, the slave traders openly encouraged the Gola, Bassa, and others to attack the infant Americo-Liberian settlements. Although the combined efforts of the American and British navies eventually eliminated the slave traders, the lives of many Americo-Liberians and indigenous people were lost in the process.

Later, as the Americo-Liberians moved inland, they came into conflict with another entrenched element concerned with preserving its commercial interests— the Muslim Mandingoes.[31] The latter had established a fairly high degree of political and religious supremacy over the interior ethnic groups of the West Atlantic region. They had, moreover, effectively monopolized the trade among the peoples of the interior as well as the commerce between Europeans and others at the coast with the hinterland. Americo-Liberian merchants were determined to break this Mandingo monopoly, but the military and political organization of this group was much more sophisticated than that of the non-Moslem ethnic groups. Although the Liberians eventually won the struggle for supremacy, lingering animosity persisted into the present century. The Mandingo have been alternately discriminated against and given a favored position relative to the other people of the interior. They remain to this day, however, the most significant of the indigenous trading groups in Liberia and travel great distances across the Sahara and throughout West Africa in search of commercial opportunities.

Of another character was the opposition to Liberian expansion raised by the British and the French. The Europeans sometimes accomplished their objectives through outright encouragement of indigenous resistance. This was certainly the case in the Kolahun District adjacent to Sierra Leone as late as 1911. More frequently, however, the Europeans won their victories at the conference table. Liberia, with only token or moral support from the United States, often found that the rules for the game of "partition" during the nineteenth- and twentieth-century "scramble" for African territory changed at the whim of the European players. The British administration in Sierra Leone, for example, would not recognize the authority of the Liberian government to collect customs and otherwise regulate trade in the region west of the Mano River but, on the other hand, held the Liberian government responsible for not protecting the property of British traders against raids by indigenous people in the same region. In the Treaty of 1885, as a result of pressures, the Liberians conceded control of that area to the British. Two decades later the British extended their control over portions of the Kolahun District. Only because of belated protests from the United States was the British seizure limited to a small tract that was "exchanged" for a pocket of forest area east of the Mano River.

While the British were active in the area northwest of Liberia, the French pressed their claims to the north and east. In 1892 the French suddenly annexed to the Ivory Coast the fifty-mile stretch of coast between the Cavalla and the San Pedro rivers and much of the hinterland as well. Liberian protests were based upon treaties concluded more than fifty years earlier with the leaders of ethnic groups of that area; but the Liberians had major difficulties with the Grebo, who resided both in the disputed area and in Maryland County. Thus, they were incapable of resisting this French *fait accompli*. The final insult came over the deceptive wording of the treaty regarding the "right" and "left" banks of the Cavalla River. In the process the Liberians were tricked into accepting French control over the entire river. Furthermore, a boundary delimitation treaty in 1910 found the Liberians surrendering to the French their historic claims to a vast strip of land along the Guinea and Ivory Coast borders. In all, the British and French gained control of more than a third of the hinterland once claimed by the Americo-Liberians.

Not all the opposition to Americo-Liberian expansion was external. Elements within the settler community regarded expansion, especially by military means, with alarm. Not only did it curtail commerce and threaten the peace, but expansion might ultimately threaten the supremacy of the immigrant group in the new state. The intensity of internal opposition led to the resignation of at least one president, William D. Coleman, in 1900, and forced several others to modify substantially their interior policies. Vestiges of this conservative approach led many Americo-Liberians to oppose the programs of President Tubman which sought both national integration and the opening of the country to foreign investment and development. The "Old Guard" feared that this would open the political floodgates and swamp the descendants of the settlers in a tribal sea.

Despite the whittling away of Americo-Liberian claims to the interior, the settlers and their descendants eventually found themselves in possession of approximately 43,000 square miles of land, an area roughly the size of Portugal or the American state of Ohio.[32] Legal possession, however, was not the same as actual physical control. The Americo-Liberians, with only limited resources and limited technology at their command, found it difficult to build an effective system of roads into the interior. Indeed, the deep ravines that run at right angles to the coast, the tropical environment, and the extensive coastal mangrove swamps make contact even today among the Americo-Liberian coastal settlements a tenuous proposition. Forging inland beyond the forty-mile coastal plain required that one first penetrate a fairly dense tropical rain forest before reaching the interior plateau, a rolling expanse that averages approximately 800 to 1,000 feet in altitude, broken occasionally by small ranges of hills and outcroppings. The largest of the latter is Nimba Mountain (found in 1955 to be a major source of high-grade iron ore), which rises over 4,000 feet above sea level. The bulk of the Americo-Liberian population, then, remained clustered at the coast—much of it in the two focal cities of Monrovia and Harper. Despite the immense road and railroad construction of the Tubman and Tolbert periods, there are still vast areas in the interior where the writ of the Liberian government is very weak indeed. Nevertheless, the Liberian claims to sovereignty and effective occupation were sufficient at the beginning of the twentieth century for the European powers to recognize Liberia as a de facto colonial power in West Africa.

# III.

# Ethnicity and Traditionalism among the Tribal Majority

Given the history of the establishment of the First Republic, it was logical that the overseas origins and interests of the Americo-Liberians would be reflected in the symbols of sovereignty of the new political community. From a distance, for example, the Liberian flag resembles that of the United States. Instead of thirteen stripes, however, the Liberian banner has eleven alternating bars of red and white, signifying the eleven signers of the 1847 Declaration of Independence. The dark blue canton in the upper left corner is adorned by a single star, signifying Africa's sole independent republic in the nineteenth century. The most important national holiday, Independence Day, is in July (the 26th instead of the 4th), and its other holidays prior to the 1980 coup tended to reflect important days in the history of the minority elite—including Matilda Newport Day, honoring the settler equivalent of American Revolutionary War heroine Molly Pitcher. The national seal of Liberia is dominated by a square-rigger sailing ship—probably the *Elizabeth*—anchored off a tropical shore on which is depicted an agricultural implement obviously imported from the New World. The most pointed reminder of the alien origins of the Liberian state is the banner on the national seal announcing: "The Love of Liberty Brought Us Here." This patent exclusion of reference to the ancestors of the present-day tribal majority who were already there in 1822 was an issue which troubled both Tubman and Tolbert. Any efforts, however, to change the slogan or the other symbols of the alien origins of the First Republic were stoutly resisted by the Whig leadership until the very end of its tenure.

As will be noted later, the efforts of the military leadership following the 1980 coup to change the flag, cease the celebration of Independence Day, and alter other national symbols also failed. With respect to the national slogan, "The Love of Liberty Brought Us Here," the People's Redemption Council engaged in an interesting effort at social engineering, by retaining the label but altering its content.

As one PRC spokesman suggested in 1982 on the second anniversary of the coup:

The task of shaping and reshaping the world for the betterment of society is a no-nonsense responsibility which history has assigned to all generations of mankind based upon their respective cultures and geographies. Any generation that fails in this grave undertaking must therefore prepare to face the wrath of history, and vice versa.

The world watched, with interest, our fore-fathers when they made their exodus from the fallen kingdoms of West and Central Africa to the then "Grain Coast." The world watched because it wanted to ascertain whether or not these men would fulfill the historical mission which impelled them to trek to these shores. It also watched when they were later joined by their kinsmen from America who brought with them added tools to serve as a propelling force in advancing a common cause; namely, the desire to build "one nation indivisible, with liberty and justice for all."

Today the world is also watching us, the great, great, great grandchildren of those very men.[1]

Interesting as this selective rewriting of history may be, it is extremely doubtful that the "world watched" or was even aware of the earliest movements of Africans southward from the Sahel and thence from the plateau and forest regions north and east of present-day Liberia. For, despite the sporadic probes which took place over several millennia between the people of the interior and the prehistoric stone and iron workers of the West African coast, significant interregional contact did not begin until roughly the eighth century, when the forays emanating from the Western Sudanic trading empires brought the Sierra Leone–Liberian areas into the network of the emerging Manding peoples. It was not, however, until the second half of the sixteenth century that the developing relationship became a sustained one, marked by regular expeditions of Manding traders into the region.[2] Based on archaelogical, linguistic, medical, and ethnological data, recent scholars have suggested a general migration of the present-day Gola and Kissi into western Liberia at a fairly early period, roughly between the 1300s to 1700s.[3] This was followed by the movement of the Dei, Bassa, Krahn, Kru, and Grebo in a westward-southwestward direction out of their earlier homes in the Ivory Coast and beyond. The Dei, Svend Holsoe suggests, reached the Mano River on Liberia's present western boundary before 1500, followed closely by the Vai.[4] Migration, however, was a dynamic phenomenon and some early arrivals in the coastal region—such as the Belle and Krahn—moved northward, while others—such as the Kru, Bassa, and Dei—spread further out along the Atlantic littoral.[5] It is possible that four or five centuries ago much of what is today Sierra Leone and Liberia was largely uninhabited tropical rain forest. The great upheavals of the fifteenth and sixteenth centuries, associated with the rise, flourishing, and eventual collapse of the Songhai Empire on the Niger River, changed matters. A series of crises drove waves of non-Moslems into the forest region. The advent of European merchants at the coast further disturbed the political and economic balances in West Africa. Patterns of trade—especially with respect to human cargo—were dramatically reoriented.

While some groups, such as the Gola, migrated in search of salt, others sought new lands to cultivate. Still others, such as the Loma, the Mende, the Kissi, and the Gbandi people, were once again pushed southward as political refugees into

FIGURE 1    The Flag of Liberia

FIGURE 2    The Great Seal of Liberia

their present areas in northwestern Liberia by the Manding (Malinke) expansionism occurring several decades before the arrival of the Americo-Liberians in West Africa. This process of establishing Muslim-dominated theocracies to the north of modern Liberia continued at an accelerated pace toward the middle to the end of the nineteenth century as a consequence of the exploits of the great Malinke state-builders, such as Samori Touré, Mori Ule, and Sere Boureima Cisse.[6] Most of the nineteenth century was apparently marked by a constant series of movements, with stronger tribal groupings driving weaker ones farther into the rain forest or down the coast. Indeed, there has always been a certain amount of fluctuation of ethnic (tribal) boundaries. This process of migration on an individual basis has continued after the advent of effective Americo-Liberian rule under the First Republic as the constant search for new agricultural lands or the flight from tax collectors, labor recruiters, and arbitrary rulers have constantly driven people into previously uninhabited and uncharted sections of Liberia. Artificial and largely unregulated international boundaries have provided no obstacle to Mende, Gola, Kissi, and Vai who move back and forth to renew old ties with kinsmen in Sierra Leone; to Grebo, Kru, and Krahn who visit their relatives in the Ivory Coast; or to Loma, Kpelle, Mandingo, Mano, and Gio who have maintained their economic and social links with kinsmen in Guinea.

## The Nature of Tribal Identity

The question of who were the first inhabitants aside, the nineteenth-century expansion of the Liberian national community beyond the pockets of settlement at the coast created a highly complex political, social, and economic situation. It was not a simple case of one society dominating another. Rather, it was a relationship that ultimately subordinated sixteen or more ethnic groups (the words "tribe" and "tribal" are still acceptable usage in Liberia) to the Western-oriented community of Americo-Liberians. The dominated groups differed radically in culture, degree of political cohesion and organization, ability and resolution to resist Americo-Liberian domination, and responsiveness to modernization. Lacking both the personnel and the anthropological skills needed to carry out flexible and imaginative administrative policies in the tribal areas, the Americo-Liberian leadership was continually confounded by the character and variety of traditional ethnic institutions. In a period of rapid change, understanding of the nature of values and institutions of these ethnic groups by government leadership was a *sine qua non* for survival and continued domination.

It should be made explicit at this point that it has only been within the past three or four decades that Liberian scholars, joined by others from the United States, Western Europe, and elsewhere, have produced serious studies in anthropology, history, economics, and political science which deal with the Gola, Grebo, Kru, and other indigenous groups. We still lack definitive integrative studies which deal with tribal life in a comprehensive fashion but at the same time note the great variations and subtle nuances which differentiate the sixteen major ethnic groups from one another. There is a danger, thus, that our treatment in this brief chapter

MAP 3    Distribution of Major Liberian Ethnic and Language Groups

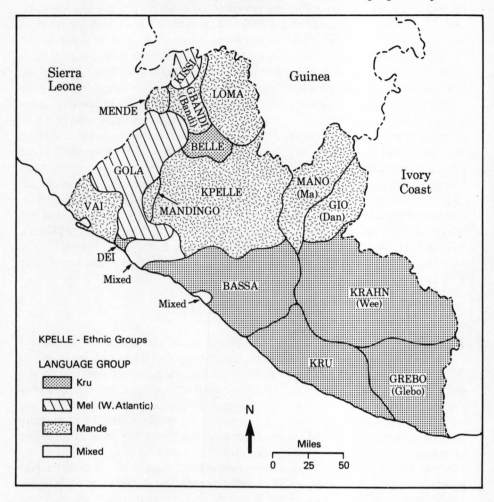

of those institutions, values, and behavorial patterns which in general set tribal
society apart from the Americo-Liberian community may create the impression of
greater homogeneity among tribal societies than the facts warrant. The reader should
bear this caveat in mind.

Although the relative size of Liberia's indigenous ethnic groupings has undoubtedly undergone constant change since the days of initial contact with the settler
community, an indication of the present-day numerical strength of the sixteen officially recognized ethnic groups will be useful.[7]

Only a few of the ethnic groups, such as the Bassa, the Belle, and the Dei,
are found almost entirely within Liberia. The majority of the sixteen straddle the
borders between Liberia and the neighboring states of Sierra Leone, Guinea, and

TABLE 3

*Ethnic Affiliation of Population, 1962, 1974*

| Ethnic group | Size 1962 | Percent | Size 1974 | Percent |
|---|---|---|---|---|
| Kpelle | 211,081 | 20 | 298,532 | 20 |
| Bassa | 165,856 | 16 | 214,143 | 14 |
| Gio | 83,208 | 8 | 130,360 | 9 |
| Kru | 80,813 | 8 | 121,414 | 8 |
| Grebo | 77,007 | 8 | 119,985 | 8 |
| Mano | 72,122 | 7 | 110,770 | 7 |
| Loma | 53,891 | 5 | 88,351 | 6 |
| Krahn | 52,552 | 5 | 71,177 | 5 |
| Gola | 47,295 | 5 | 67,819 | 4 |
| Kissi | 34,914 | 4 | 51,318 | 3 |
| Mandingo | 29,750 | 3 | 58,414 | 4 |
| Vai | 28,898 | 3 | 49,504 | 3 |
| Gbandi | 28,599 | 3 | 38,548 | 3 |
| Belle | 5,465 | .5 | 7,309 | .5 |
| Dei | 5,396 | .5 | 6,365 | .5 |
| Mende | 4,974 | .5 | 8,678 | .5 |
| Miscellaneous | 2,299 | .5 | 3,141 | .2 |
| Total tribal | 984,120 | 97 | 1,445,828 | 95.7 |
| No tribal affiliation | 23,478 | 2 | 42,834 | 2.9 |
| Alien African | 8,875 | 1 | 14,706 | 1.0 |
| Total population | 1,016,473 | 100 | 1,503,368 | 99.6 |

the Ivory Coast. In some cases, such as the Mende, the major portion of the group resides across the border.

The integrity of ethnic solidarity has been steadily eroding after more than 160 years of contact between the settler and the tribal population. Even today—despite the significant acceleration of social change under the Tubman, Tolbert, and Doe regimes—many (if not most) Liberians still identify much more strongly with their ethnic subcommunities than they do with the modern Liberian state. There are, however, considerable ranges in the degree of response to Americo-Liberian cultural norms. The Dei and the Bassa, who were settled behind Monrovia and Buchanan, early became involved in the settler economy during the colonial period as artisans, clerks, and domestic servants. The Vai, on the other hand, who also had early contact with the settlers in Cape Mount, proudly resisted submission to the taxing authority of the Liberian government until 1917. Individual Vai leaders, nevertheless, formed an aristocratic coalition with the Americo-Liberian leaders. By the beginning of the present century members of the Massaquoi, Fahnbulleh, and other Vai families (who skillfully moved from "pagan" to Muslim to Christian affiliations as the occasion demanded) were serving in the administration, the army officer cadre, and even the consular service.[8] Similarly, despite sporadic resistance offered by various sections of the group, mission-educated Grebo appeared as teachers, ministers, and even authors early in the 1900s.[9]

An ambivalent case was that of the Kru, who continued their resistance into the 1930s, yet were the most cash-minded group along the coast—far more so than those groups, such as Kpelle, who were primarily subsistence cultivators. Indeed, more than a century before the Americo-Liberian arrival the Kru (a term which covered a number of related groups) were trading with passing European vessels and serving as interpreters, middlemen, and coastal pilots. For many decades now the Kru have regularly served as crewmen and stevedores for European and African freighters plying the west coast of Africa.[10] The Gola and Mandingo, too, have had an ambivalent relationship with the Americo-Liberians.[11] Their long history of contact was constantly disturbed by the commercial rivalry between the settlers and these two groups, who had dominated the trade in slaves and legitimate items in northwestern Liberia. The unusual strength of the Poro secret society among the Gola (discussed later in this chapter) and the Islamic faith of the Mandingoes, moreover, served as barriers to rapid assimilation of these two ethnic groups.[12] And the existence of centralized state systems of authority among both groups was undoubtedly a factor in their being able to resist political domination by the Americo-Liberians for as long as they did.

In the remote hinterland of Liberia, Americo-Liberian official contact has been limited largely to the present century. Indeed, the Mano, Gio, Loma, and Krahn have really only had their traditional patterns of life substantially threatened during the years since the Second World War, as missionaries, new economic enterprises, and a network of roads and railroads have penetrated inland. The rich artistic traditions of the Gio and the Mano in the fields of wood sculpture, weaving, dancing, and music been giving way steadily to the enameled pots, ready-made shirts, and ''high life'' musical records brought north by the Lebanese traders. The Loma and Krahn, too, have been exposed to the Americo-Liberian political system through their involvement in the army. Perhaps the least acculturated group in the country was the largest—the Kpelle.[13] Even among these people, however, the pace of life was rapidly changing in this century as recruiters for the rubber plantations sought new labor markets and as iron-mining concessions were located within their midst and on the margins of their ethnic homeland.

### Significance of Tribal Membership

It is difficult to assess the historical contribution each ethnic group has made to the development of modern Liberia or the magnitude of the threat each posed to the Americo-Liberian settlers in the nineteenth century. Even the classification of Liberia's people into neat tribal compartments has been an extremely complicated task. Warren d'Azevedo notes the way in which neighbors of the Gola—viewing them as a superior group in many respects—attempted to "pass." Thus Kpelle men attempted to affiliate with the families of their Gola wives, and Kpelle women who married Gola men totally assimilated Gola culture. And among the Dei people,

TABLE 4
Linguistic Classification of Liberian Ethnic Groups

| Mande-<br>speaking peoples | Mel-<br>speaking peoples<br>(West Atlantic) | Kruan-<br>speaking peoples |
| --- | --- | --- |
| Mandingo (Malinke) | Gola | Bassa |
| Vai | Kissi (Gissi) | Dei (Dey) |
| Gbandi (Bandi) | | Grebo (Glebo) |
| Kpelle (Kpessi) | | Kru (Krou) (Klaoh) |
| Loma | | Belle (Kowaa) |
| Mende | | Krahn |
| Gio (Dan) | | Gbee |
| Mano (Ma) | | |

Based on U.S. Army, *Area Handbook for Liberia* (Washington, D.C.: U.S. Government Printing Office, Department of the Army, 1965), p. 51; earlier works of Joseph Greenberg, Deidrich Westermann, and Margaret A. Bryan; and John Duitsman, "Liberian Languages," *Liberian Studies Journal* Vol. 10 (1982-83), pp. 27–36.

particularly those where the Gola Poro society had become dominant, there was an increased use of Gola in preference to their own language.[14] Andreas Massing reports a similar tendency on the part of the Kissi to identify with their stronger, better-organized Manding neighbors.[15] Even where ethnic identity remains fairly constant, however, identity with one's larger ethnic group has not been coterminous with political affiliation. A major group such as the Kpelle, for example, has consisted of a great many relatively autonomous political units living on both sides of the Liberian and Guinean borders. On the other hand, the Condo confederation of the nineteenth century, which was headquartered at Bopolu in the interior, brought together people of diverse ethnic origins under the leadership of Sao Boso (called "Boatswain" by the settlers). The confederation stretched from the Lofa River to the vicinity of Cape Mesurado and from the coast far into the interior.[16] Thus, unlike the segmentary political systems based upon kinship and the mini-states which were characteristic of southeastern Liberia, the people of the northwest manifest many of the characteristics of state-like societies, with bureaucratic offices, distinct military roles, social stratification with respect to wealth and privilege, and explicit citizen obligations to political authority. Classification of Liberia's population into three language groups is of little value for political analysis, and it certainly does not tell us very much about the way people actually identified with one another for social, economic, and political purposes.[17] Finally, there is the problem of nomenclature, with a number of fairly distinct tribal people having the same group name, whereas a single grouping may refer to themselves by one name but be given other names by their various neighbors. The Loma people, for example, were formerly referred to by the pejorative term of "Buzi," which meant "wild person."

Perhaps the best that we can say is that tribal membership in Liberia has been a conscious state of "belonging," which has permitted a group of people to identify with each other and differentiate themselves from third parties on the basis of a broad configuration of common factors. Among the factors are language; the common occupation of some historical "homeland"; recognition of a set of mutual interests that are worth defending against both external and internal threats; solidarity and cooperation in a range of economic and social transactions; similar customs and ways of looking at the world; and even on occasion political centralization of authority. A given ethnic grouping may lack any one of these factors, but the broad character of the configuration permits the individual to give priority to the many overlapping and even conflicting membership groupings of which he or she may be a part.

Part of the establishment of ethnic identity involves the formation of stereotypes with respect to other similarly constituted groups with whom one comes into contact. The Liberian anthropologist Benjamin C. Dennis in his work on the Gbandi notes the way in which the Gbandi regard the Mende as "manipulators because they are perfectly willing to work for or against a particular person depending on the offer made to them." Another neighboring group, the Kissi, are "intelligent and brave (but are) very emotional and irrational in most of their behavior (and are) impatient and jealous over women." The Belle, according to the Gbandi, are suspected of being addicted to cannibalism in the past. A very positive stereotype has emerged with respect to the Loma, and Gbandi attempt to emulate their language, song, medicine, and other aspects of culture.[18]

### Parochial Character of Tribal Society

The most striking feature of traditional tribal society in Liberia has been the highly parochial character of social, economic, and political activity.[19] Aside from the Mandingo-dominated confederation of Kondo at Bopolu, Liberia had nothing resembling the complex trading kingdoms found elsewhere in West Africa. Even with government-directed consolidation under the Americo-Liberians, there were over 125 chiefdoms in the mid-1970s. With the exception of the Manding areas, there were no urban clusters of any consequence in the region until the arrival of the settlers from America. Apparently the problems of defense, limited technology, the extraordinary land requirements of shifting cultivation (which permits worn-out fields to lie fallow and revert to bush for several years in a pattern of rotation), and the difficulties of taming the tropical rain forest beyond the coastal strip mitigated against the concentration of people in urban settings.

The process of political and social decentralization of authority was most severe among the coastal Kru, among the Grebo and Krahn in the southeast, and among the Kissi. The most that could be found among these ethnic groups were clusters of villages or minor settlements, few of which numbered over several hundred inhabitants. Within these small units most of the political, social, and economic transactions of traditional society took place. Bonds of kinship were the most significant integrative force. The Gola, Mende, Vai, Loma, and Kpelle in the north and west, on the other hand, were organized into larger units under chiefs. As noted above, however, the ethnic group in each was broken into a number of relatively autonomous political units. The Vai, for example, are divided into nine chiefdoms, only four of which are located in Liberia. The Gola are distributed among five paramount chieftaincies. The political fragmentation among the larger Kpelle community is far greater.

Involvement in more cosmopolitan associations within a single ethnic group or even cutting across ethnic lines took place on a sporadic rather than a sustained basis, such as the loose confederacies among the Gola, organized to protect their middleman role against both the Americo-Liberians and the Mandingoes at Bopolu. Despite the typical parochialism, warfare brought people into contact with their neighbors for the purposes of resisting or committing aggression. Trading with itinerant Mandingoes gave a parochial community occasional vicarious economic contact with peoples as far away as the other side of the Sahara. George Brown, an American economist, reported in 1941 that an elaborate system of markets, involving the exchange of woven cloth and other commodities, had long ago developed among the Loma and adjacent northwestern ethnic groups. Although contemporary scholars have questioned the complexity of these markets, there was undoubtedly an exchange economy in which the twisted iron bars (called Kissi pennies) served as currency. Another cross-community tie was the journeys that tribesmen took to their parent villages to strengthen family and other bonds which had been permitted to lapse. Finally, the religious and mystical ties provided by the Poro, Sande, and other secret societies (discussed below) brought separate ethnic communities together for limited purposes.

Whether dealing with a state-like society or one based on kinship linkages, the basic building block of each ethnic society has been the nuclear family, consisting of a man, his wife or wives (polygamy has been the ideal, although not the norm), and his offspring. Also considered part of certain households in the past were the pawns, slaves, apprentices, and other people who had voluntarily or otherwise found themselves in the protective custody of important men in a community. The practice of pawning was widespread throughout West Africa. Under this system a man placed one of his relatives (and occasionally himself) in servitude until a debt had been paid. The greater the size of a man's retinue, the greater his prestige in the community.

Unlike many groupings in East Africa and occasional groups in West Africa where matrilineal rules of family membership and inheritance prevail, the ethnic groups of Liberia have largely adhered to a patrilineal system of reckoning social obligation. The family has been the most significant social unit for an indigenous Liberian, for birth into a particular patrilineal kinship group gives one legitimacy, support in time of crisis, and companionship. Throughout one's lifetime, however, an individual might be involved with more than one such kinship unit. Polygamy plus the rules of exogamy, which demand marriage outside one's own kinship group, established an expanding number of marital ties with women of other kin groups and even other ethnic groups. Thus, in the traditional period the overlapping and reinforcing ties of kinship created by marriage provided one of the mechanisms for resolving conflicts even in those political units without formal structures of government.

The family household was in many instances also the most important economic unit in indigenous Liberian society. The growing and processing of rice, cassava, and other staple crops has been a family enterprise, with the food produced being largely consumed by the family. Similarly, the products gathered in the forest, the meat and hides secured in the hunt, or the fish caught in the rivers or the sea have been processed by the family. There have been, however, certain exceptions to the parochial character of traditional economic activity. The bartering of the few surplus agricultural commodities and the sale of slaves did permit cultivators to acquire the hoes, cloth, and other commodities made by craft specialists or brought into the community by Mandingo traders. Among the Mano, Kpelle, and other groups in the northeast, labor cooperatives, or *kuus*, supplemented the basic family work group in larger villages.[20]

As economist David Blanchard has indicated for the Mano, a *kuu* consisted of households who combined

> for the purpose of working in rotation on the farms of members, because they believed that they worked harder and with more enjoyment when in a group. Kuus could be of men, women, or mixed. A household would contribute as many members as it was able. The number of days a kuu would work for each member was determined by a vote at the organizational meeting. Usually the kuu worked two full days for every member. Thus a household would receive two kuu days for every worker it contributed. Kuus were formed newly each season and were involved in such work as clearing forest, scratching and planting and harvesting. Only work which had a constant output could be organized into kuus. This ruled out all forms of production where an element of change was involved, such as hunting or fishing.

Just as the economic and social patterns have been both local and kinship-based, so have the patterns of political affiliation among groups in the southeast focused upon the family and the parochial community. Indeed, in certain instances in the past the family unit served double duty as the social and political unit. Migration or other action that severed the day-to-day ties of individuals with their parent villages permitted or compelled the heads of families to constitute their own political communities. Although initially ties might be maintained on an intermittent basis as migrants returned "home" to attend funerals, have their children initiated into the group, or claim an inheritance, eventually the hived-off community attained a political significance of its own, and the head of the family served also as the political head, or chief. The social scientist Amos Sawyer suggests that the relatively autonomous and isolated mini-states of the southeast encouraged to a greater degree than elsewhere the social values of individualism, competition, and achievement orientation. This stands in contrast to the ascriptive orientation, respect for authority, and other attributes of the state communities of the north and northwest.

Thus, it is not suggested that the family political community was either typical or normal outside the ethnic groups of the southeast (the Kru, Grebo, and Krahn) or the Kissi. The family-based chiefdom among the Kpelle or Gola did not usually remain small for very long. It would expand as the sons of the founders took wives from other villages or as migrating strangers were granted permission to farm upon their acceptance of the political authority of the founding headman or his heir, often referred to as the "owner of the land." Gradually a cluster of kin-related villages might be grouped with similar clusters to form "towns." When this occurred the original clusters would be regarded as wards, or quarters, each under the authority of a senior kinsman. The quarter chief would have special responsibilities for the safety and good order of the quarter; he inaugurated the agricultural cycle and was custodian of properties belonging to the corporate kinship group. One of the primary duties of a quarter chief among the Kpelle and Gola was the reassignment of land that had earlier been parceled out on a usufructuary right-of-occupancy basis. The quarter chief also organized community work projects and settled disputes involving not only his own kinsmen but also members of "stranger" kinship groups. The quarter chief had to be cautious in dealing with the interests of all groups in the community, and he was required to work through a council of elders, each of whom jealously guarded the rights and prerogatives of his particular family segment. Any elder who repeatedly became dissatisfied with the actions of the quarter chief could physically withdraw his family from the jurisdiction of the autocrat and establish a new political community.

At the town level, predominantly political institutions emerged, for impartial authorities were required to settle disputes among contesting kinship groupings. Succession to a town chieftainship was largely hereditary, but it often rotated among a series of leading families with equal claims of seniority, prestige, or wealth. Although town chiefs could act arbitrarily with respect to quarter chiefs and other subordinate officials, the council of elders attained a more structured bureaucratic character at the town level than it had achieved at the quarter level. Among certain groups the young men's age-grade societies also became more significant at this level of the political system, and a town chief had to contend with a corporate grouping that cut across kinship lines and shared his executive, legislative, and judicial functions. The young men's "house of representatives" played a vital role in some (but certainly not all) ethnic groupings in defense as well as in the control of the social behavior of its members. The primary sanction for the authority of the town chief probably stemmed from the belief that he was more impartial in his justice than the locally rooted quarter chief and yet not as remote from the affairs as the chief of the next higher level, the clan.

## *"Clan" Chieftainship*

The term *clan* in Liberian usage is deceptive, since it refers to a territorial unit rather than to a kinship grouping. The clan was typically the largest political entity among the various ethnic groupings of Liberia, even though larger, more ephemeral political communities did exist. The Americo-Liberians, moreover, undermined the supremacy of clan chieftainship by grouping various clan units into so-called paramount chieftaincies. In the traditional period the clan consisted of a number of towns, villages, and hamlets joined together for political purposes as a result of migrants having settled in the same area, as a consequence of defense alliances becoming permanent, or through normal expansion of towns where the common bonds of kinship and ethnicity were strong. In some cases, a noted warrior chief would be invited to assume the leadership of weaker chiefdoms incapable of defending themselves. The suzerainty of the warrior chief was invariably sealed by his marriage to the daughters of the leading town chiefs and of other "big men" of his area. Gola warrior clan chiefs, for example, often left the existing town and quarter structures intact, demanding only tribute in the form of rice, women, labor, and soldiers. In many instances, however, the warrior chief (as among the Mano) set up his own bureaucracy with a retinue of his relatives and mercenaries imported to administer the consolidated area.

The clan chief, or petty paramount chief, was the secular ruler of his area. He organized the defense of the clan, called the people out for work on major public projects, such as forest, bridges, and paths, and supervised the executive actions of the town chiefs. The clan chief heard cases on appeal, where an offended party did not feel that justice had been rendered by a town chief. For his efforts the clan chief was remunerated by tribute payments, court fees, and a share of the meat secured in a tribal hunt. He used his wealth to increase his stature in the community. This was done directly by sharing his rice, cloth, and even junior wives with a series of clients, who served as his claque and sang his praises. Indirectly, by giving the appearance of generosity and by meeting the needs of the community in times of crisis, a clan chief could establish a reputation that would attract new settlers into his chieftaincy. Thus, the base from which he could secure additional wealth as well as soldiers expanded in proportion to his patronage, and the chief's generosity was an important factor in community solidarity in traditional tribal society.

Succession to the office of clan chief seldom rigidly followed hereditary rules of succession, even though preference was normally given to the sons, brothers, and paternal cousins of the late incumbent chief. On occasion a son of the late chief's sister or even the sister herself could succeed to office. Experience did play a significant role in the actual selection by the elders, who sought someone who had displayed military skills, had demonstrated eloquence and impartiality in the settlement of a dispute, or could lead without resorting to force. Wealth also played a role, and a "big man" with a large clientage might get himself elected to the clan chieftainship. This was not really regarded as objectionable, since a chief was expected to display generosity, and the chief who lived poorly might be jealous of those who were more prosperous than himself.

The size of clan chiefdoms varied considerably and fluctuated as a result of normal increase and conquest. The size of a chiefdom might diminish as discontented elements hived off into the forest in search of new lands and freedom, as mercenaries switched their allegiances from a stingy and unsuccessful chief, or as traders and other specialists severed their client relationships with clan chiefs who became too demanding or could not furnish adequate protection for commerce. It was largely in western Liberia that the scale of the political community reached considerable proportions. There, a number of confederacies involving people from more than one ethnic group were brought into existence for purposes of warfare and trade. As enduring political units, however, they were relatively unstable.

*Religion and Social Control*

Not all of the restraints upon political leadership or upon mass deviant behavior were secular. There was a continual resort to supernatural mechanisms in controlling the operation of the political system. Magic, for example, has been a very persistent and effective means for securing social control or disruption. Furthermore, a chief might find his secular authority challenged by the religious authority of the "owner of the land." The latter was a descendant of the founder of the community and performed ritual functions in behalf of the whole chiefdom in time of crisis. The "owner of the land" also might be called upon to settle disputes between the secular chief and the officials of the secret societies.

Generally, those tribes, such as the Vai and the Gola, whose traditional religious system included a high god tended to regard the deity as benevolent and remote from the affairs of men. Man attempted to manipulate his fate, or had his fate manipulated, through the actions of either important ancestral spirits or nature spirits that inhabited the cottonwood trees, rivers, or rocks. Through sacrifice and rituals performed by paid specialists, called *zoes*, a man attempted to secure the success of his harvest or a journey and perhaps bring disaster upon his political, commercial, or matrimonial rivals. The position of *zoe* was normally inherited, and there were both male and female specialists. Other individuals sought prominence through their membership in the Baboon, Leopard, and other societies that practiced ritualistic murder. Although membership in such societies was supposedly secret, a person gained influence if it was popularly assumed that he belonged to such an organization.

Two secret societies constituted the greatest supernatural mechanisms for controlling both deviant behavior on the parts of the peasantry and autocratic tendencies on the part of the political leaders. The men's Poro and women's Sande societies represent a distinct cultural feature of the West Atlantic region.[21] The Poro is most highly developed among the Gola, and they are alleged to be the source of Poro authority among the Vai and Dei. Secret societies of varying strength are found among the Kpelle, Mano, Kissi, Gbandi, Belle, Loma, Gio, and Mende. The Mende claim to have brought the Poro to the tribes farther west, in Sierra Leone. Indeed, in the past the only indigenous Liberian people without the Poro in any form were the Bassa, Kru, and Mandingo. Among the Poro-oriented tribal groups, the rituals and sanctions of these secret societies took precedence over those of any other association or institution within the ethnic community. A chief often based his authority on his high rank within the Poro or on the backing of Poro officials. On important community matters, a chief would defer to the council of the Poro. The council consisted of old men who had attained the highest of the approximately one hundred degrees, or orders, of the Poro society. Meeting in the sacred grove, the council could reverse the decision of a chief who did not himself hold high status within the Poro.

In political terms, the Poro has been among the most significant of integrative forces within Gola, Kpelle, Mano, and Mende society. Its sacred bonds cut across the vertical kinship divisions within a community and bridged the geographic gaps separating various segments of a tribal community. Although loose in structure and only operating from time to time, the Poro could link otherwise autonomous chiefdoms within a single ethnic grouping. This occurred among the fragmented Gola, for example, as they expanded at the expense of their neighbors in the presettler period. There is also evidence that the Poro could provide a measure of cohesion that cut across even ethnic lines. Warren d'Azevedo, for example, commented that even today the Dei people await permission of Gola Poro officials before opening a new society. D'Azevedo also notes the significant role that the Poro has played in intergroup diplomacy in resolving conflict among rival Gola chiefdoms, as well as among Gola and neighboring ethnic groups. There has also been a great deal of interethnic exchange of ritual as young Poro members from one group have been apprenticed to powerful *zoes* of another. There is some disagreement, however, over the actual strength and breadth of the interethnic network of the Poro in Liberia. The late George Harley insisted that the highest officials of the various chapters of the Poro were bound together in some kind of supreme council. There is no historical evidence, however, that the transethnic links in Liberia reached the stage where the Poro could present a united indigenous front against Americo-Liberian penetration of the hinterland. In Sierra Leone, on the other hand, the Mende-based Poro was able to unite several ethnic groups in an abortive attempt to prevent British expansion into the interior of Sierra Leone in 1898 during the Bai Bureh War.[22]

For most purposes the Liberian Poro appears to have been effective largely at the local level.[23] The Poro societies, for example, were prominent during the traditional era in controlling such antisocial behavior as incest, murder, arson, and looting by warriors, as well as in ensuring positive cooperation in matters of defense, cultivation, house building, bridge construction, and other community projects. In cooperation with the Sande, the Poro controlled the behavior of women generally and of women"chiefs" in particular while the young warriors were absent from the community. The primary sanction of the Poro was the fear and awe that the visit of one of the masked figures instilled in the women, children, and uninitiated youths. The ultimate sanction of the Poro was the death penalty, which could be meted out to those who committed serious offenses against society or revealed the secrets of the Poro. Since the mask rather than the unidentified wearer was regarded as being directly responsible for the death sentence and execution, there could be no claims for compensation filed by the kinsmen of the victim; the mask, or the spirits presumed to reside in the mask, belonged to no kinship group, and its actions thus were ritually sanctioned. The rituals performed in relation to the pantheon of masks provided bonds of community solidarity far stronger than any secular bonds of mere economic or social cooperation.

The Poro and Sande societies, moreover, continue to be among the most important socializing agencies within the ethnic commmunity, and the Liberian government during the First Republic tolerated their activities if they did not interfere with Western-type schools, clinics, or other institutions. At extended intervals—frequently when a chief's young son reached puberty—the young boys and girls have been sent off to separate bush schools for four- and three-year periods, respectively. During their seclusion the children are instructed in the traditional lore and the secrets of the Poro or Sande. They are also taught marital responsibilities, the uses of herbs and other medicines, techniques of agriculture, and other matters relating to their adult roles in society. At the end of the confinement and indoctrination the initiate becomes in effect a new member of the community. This has been symbolized by the taking of a new name and in some groups by distinctive markings on the body. Although the boys have, in many instances, undergone circumcision prior to the bush school, clitoridectomy is usually performed on the young girls by an official of the Sande society during the period of seclusion.

Granting the positive aspects of the integrative and socializing functions of the Poro, the resort to the supernatural in controlling behavior casts some doubt on the proposition that traditional tribal government was essentially democratic. Caroline Bledsoe, for example, argues that the Poro and Sande were used as devices to maintain rather than mitigate social stratification.[24] George Harley argued, however, that the resort to masks and ordeals was a standby measure, which came into play only when the family structures, the council of elders, and other secular controls upon both autocracy and mass antisocial behavior failed. "In the last analysis," Harley said, "it was government by tradition, enforced by the fear of disapproval of the ancestors. Decisions were reached with the approval of the clan fathers both living and dead. The living merely used a technique, placing both the responsibility for these decisions and the blame for the administration of justice on the ancestral spirits."[25] Thus stability was maintained in a highly fragile and fragmented society.

*Summary*

To the Americo-Liberian district commissioner during the First Republic, to the American missionary, and to the Lebanese shopkeeper, an appreciation of the subtle distinctions in values and institutions among the sixteen or more tribal groups of Liberia spelled the difference between success or failure in their efforts to change traditional societies in the Liberian hinterland. It is impossible in this brief summary to do full justice to the great cultural variations among and even within the Gola, Kpelle, and other Liberian ethnic groups. Nevertheless, it is hoped that this synopsis has pointed out ways in which indigenous societies in general differ from (and resemble) the Americo-Liberian community that dominated their affairs during the period of settler rule. Perhaps the one outstanding feature was the small scale of the effective community within each ethnic group and the crucial role played by the extended patrilineal family in organizing the political, social, and economic affairs within the fragmented ethnic societies. Another feature that plagued the Americo-Liberians as they extended inland was the indigenous traditional attitude toward land tenure, which is based on use and need rather than upon private ownership. Furthermore, the religious and ritualistic base for political authority—especially among the northwestern tribes, where the Poro have been strong—provided a basis for conflict between traditional ethnic-based authorities and the Protestant Americo-Liberians.

Finally, some comment is required on the antipathy on the part of many ethnic groups toward change. Traditional society has been essentially concerned with consensus rather than conflict, even though intercommunity warfare was a fairly common event. No society is static. Nevertheless, traditional society often reacted to a major crisis by attempting through various mechanisms to restore equilibrium and to get things back to the way they were before the human or supernatural disaster disrupted the usual order of events. The extension of Americo-Liberian influence inland constituted a permanent challenge to the equilibrium of traditional society in the Liberian hinterland.

# IV.

# Class and Caste Stratification in the First Republic

## The Seeds of Discord

Hostility between the Americo-Liberian community and the tribal people had been a feature of Liberian society almost from the first settlers' arrival.[1] At the heart of conflict had been the issue of land. The initial misunderstanding was over the traditional African concept of land tenure, which is based upon use rather than ownership through purchase. This was compounded by the subsequent failure of the settlers or the American Colonization Society to pay even the low prices agreed upon; by the seizure of land for alleged insults against the colonists or for non-payment of debts; and by constant disputes over land boundaries. The land question was subsequently complicated by the policies and practices in the use of native labor on the farms of Liberian settlers. The outrageous wage differentials, the lack of amenities, the unregulated power of Americo-Liberian farmers to "fine" their tribal employees, and the abuse of the apprenticeship system under which tribal youths were assigned to Americo-Liberian families until they came of age were at the root of labor discord during the early period. Ironically, these actions created a situation in Africa not unlike the very one against which the repatriated Americo-Liberians themselves had rebelled in America. The indigenous African, moreover, was expected to give freely of his labor for road construction and other public projects as well as to pay taxes to an alien government. Despite the claims on tribal labor, neither initial Liberian legislation nor the Constitution of 1847 recognized the taxed tribal person as a citizen. Only the threat of European incursions into the hinterland compelled President Arthur Barclay in 1904 to extend citizenship to the tribal residents of the interior as proof of the "effectiveness" of Liberia's claim to the districts adjacent to Sierra Leone. It was another quarter of a century, however, before the issue of exploitation of tribal labor became a matter of international concern and threatened the independence of the Liberian republic. I refer to the Fernando Po scandal discussed later in this chapter.

In addition to conflict over land and labor, there were other points of controversy between the Americo-Liberians and tribal people. The Mandingoes in particular resented the Americo-Liberian disruption of the slave trade during the colonial period and their ultimate control over commerce in cloth, molasses, and other more legitimate items which the Mandingoes had tended to monopolize. The settlers' arrogance in their relations with the Vai, the Dei, and other indigenous inhabitants with whom they were in intimate contact created a climate of hostility which still persists today. Rulings during the early period against nudity, wage differentials between settlers and tribal persons, the reluctance of the settler males to marry— or provide dowry for—tribal women with whom they had established informal liaisons, continuing efforts at conversion to Christianity, and the patterns of segregation that emerged in housing and education demonstrated the settlers' contempt for the tribal person and his culture.[2]

Although over the years many of the abuses have been curbed and even a certain amount of assimilation has taken place across the settler/tribal line, the prescribed form of integration was decidedly on Americo-Liberian terms and conditional upon the acceptance by the tribal person of various facets of the settler culture, and not the reverse.[3] Curiously, the norms which the Americo-Liberians imposed were roughly modeled after those of the society across the Atlantic which had denied them full membership. Thus English, rather than one of the sixteen tribal languages, became the preferred medium of communication in official circles, in most mission schools, and elsewhere even though a Liberian version of English (pidgin) did emerge. Christianity—preferably a Protestant version of it—took priority over Islam or traditional forms of worship as the prescribed route to salvation. In the social realm, monogamy (or "sequential monogamy"), officially at least, succeeded polygamy in the organization of the family. To participate in national society, the tribal person had to accept political and legal institutions that bore at least a formal resemblance to those of the United States. Moreover, the tribesman had to accept—at least outwardly—the Americo-Liberian historical myth regarding the dominant role that the alien settlers (and the correspondingly negligible part that tribal people) had played in the founding of the Republic. To the extent that he was permitted to participate in the modern economic sphere, the tribal person seeking assimilation had to embrace the concept of private rather than communal ownership of property, engage in a cash economy, and assume a large measure of individual rather than collective responsibility for his own prosperity. Although changes in material culture flowed in both directions, in general, the tribal person had to accept the foods, dress, art, and architecture of the Americo-Liberians as the desired legitimate norm. The term "civilized" was invariably used to serve as a badge of class distinction separating the Americanized settler from the indigenous tribal person.[4]

Equally important to the maintenance of the caste relationship, the tribal person lacked rights as an individual citizen even after the formal extension of citizenship;

rather, he or she was a member of an ethnically defined corporate group. Social and other relationships of tribal persons in such groups were covered by a legal code distinct from that which applied to the settler citizen. A tribal person owned land only in the sense that he shared in its use as a member of an ethnic community. When representation and suffrage were extended in the Tubman era, the paramount chiefs cast the votes for the entire group. Even in the last decades of the First Republic, as a member of a corporate group, the individual was responsible for the actions of his tribal fellows and could sustain a group fine for some alleged violation of Americo-Liberian law.

## Augmentation of the Americo-Liberian Class

The tribal person who aspired to full participation in the new society found himself a largely unwelcome guest. The founding settlers of Liberia sought to swell their ranks not by converting the "heathen savages," as the indigenous Africans were frequently called, but by encouraging other alien Blacks to emigrate to their shores. The Congoes (recaptive Africans), for example, found themselves preferred to the indigenous Africans, and they gradually acquired the manners and aspirations of the dominant settler group. Their acceptance as full-fledged members of the Americo-Liberian community was far from automatic in the early years of settlement, when the recaptive Africans were assigned to living areas apart from those of the settlers from America and were expected to form a distinct community except for purposes of Christian worship. Unlike the settlers, who were permitted greater latitude in running their own affairs, the agent of the American Colonization Society exercised greater control over the recaptives—regulating their hours of waking and sleeping and taking greater care in their indoctrination with respect to Christianity. The recaptives were also directly instructed in agriculture, hygiene, and other aspects of Western life. Unlike the settlers, who were assigned land both in town and in the rural area, recaptives were long regarded as squatters or renters, rather than owners of land.[5]

By 1869 the subordinate and passive role of the recaptives in Liberian politics had been substantially modified with the rise of the True Whig Party, and for a considerable time they occupied a pivotal position in the factional arguments developing within the Americo-Liberian group. Their ultimate affiliation with the ruling True Whig Party under Edward J. Roye brought them to a position of near parity with the descendants of the American settlers, and today it is difficult to differentiate Congoes from other Americo-Liberians. The term Congo is loosely applied to all Americo-Liberians by many tribal persons today.

While the Americo-Liberians preferred to augment their ranks through recruitment from the New World, immigration fell dramatically after the abolition of slavery in the United States and the passage of the Fourteenth and Fifteenth Amendments, which nominally gave American Blacks citizenship and voting rights. Even the subsequent disillusionment with the degree and pace of the struggle for equality could not rekindle Black American hopes for Liberia as an answer to their problems.

In the four decades following the American Civil War, only 4,093 American Blacks were recorded as having emigrated to Liberia.[6] American Blacks largely rejected Marcus Garvey and other more recent advocates of a "back to Africa" movement.[7] In addition to Blacks from the United States, those who did make it to Liberia from the New World following the American Civil War included some notable emigrants from the West Indies. There was, for example, the band of 346 Barbadians who arrived in 1865. This group included the young Arthur Barclay, who ultimately founded one of the most remarkable family dynasties in Liberian history. Arthur Barclay served as president from 1904 to 1912, and his descendants included President Edwin Barclay, various justices of the Supreme Court, senators, and cabinet members, as well as Mrs. W. V. S. Tubman. The West Indies also was the origin of an earlier immigrant, Edward Wilmot Blyden, the scholar-statesman who contributed so significantly to the nineteenth-century history of both Liberia and Sierra Leone. Generally, however, immigration from Haiti, Jamaica, and other parts of the West Indies was steady but not numerically significant.

Further accretions to the dominant caste group resulted from a small amount of African emigration from Ghana, Nigeria, Sierra Leone, and other African states. The King family of Sierra Leone, for example, eventually provided Liberia with a president and other distinguished public officials. The majority of immigrant Africans, however, associated more closely with the tribal Liberians than with the Americo-Liberians, and they did not normally apply for naturalization. Indeed, African immigration has been to a considerable extent offset by the emigration of Liberians to other parts of the continent. Clusters of Liberians, both tribal and Americo-Liberian, can be found in Freetown, Lagos, and other cities along the west coast of Africa.

The curious feature in efforts to strengthen the Americo-Liberians' position within the Republic by adding to their numbers was that they so long rejected the notion of large-scale assimilation of the tribal people into their ranks. It was only within the present century—indeed, within the Tubman and Tolbert presidencies— that tribal persons were to have a realistic chance of participating in the governing of their own country.

## Control Strategy in Caste Maintenance

In analyzing and making explicit the control strategy employed by the Americo-Liberians in dominating the tribal majority, one runs the risk of suggesting that there was a logical pattern to the strategy in conformity to some "grand design." This was certainly not the case. Mechanisms which had been used with effectiveness in one period invariably gave way to newer and more sophisticated techniques of control in a later period. Tactics that worked well in Monrovia and other areas where the settler population was clustered could not be employed where the ranks of the Americo-Liberians were thin. The stereotypes that Americo-Liberians had evolved regarding the various ethnic groups also altered the application of control mechanisms.

## COERSION

One of the most obvious and persistent control mechanisms had been the negative sanction of force. This was perhaps inevitable, given the fact that the occupation of land by the aliens from America was not accepted readily by many of the indigenous groups, and it was only by the use of arms that the small, outnumbered settler groups maintained their precarious foothold on the Grain Coast of Africa. With some tribal groups the lesson of military superiority had to be demonstrated over and over again. In the earliest years the settlers survived under the protective eye of American naval forces, which played a key role in the initial settlement and subsequent survival of the group. As the American shield was gradually withdrawn, however, the Americo-Liberians themselves acquired the firepower and developed the military skills needed to bring under political control the members of the Vai, Bassa, Grebo, and other groups who had earlier threatened to throw them back into the sea.

Unfortunately, this reliance upon force as the primary sanction in maintaining control of some regions led to its general use in situations where force was not absolutely required. The history of the nineteenth and twentieth centuries is replete with incidents, moreover, in which the posting of a contingent of the militia or the Liberian Frontier Force to disturbed areas was all too frequently a measure of first, rather than last, resort in the maintenance of authority. Pathetically, if the area was not actually disturbed before the arrival of the troops, the prophecy of chaos was soon fulfilled. The remarks of President Arthur Barclay, in his 1904 inaugural address, that the militia—largely lower-class Americo-Liberians and tribal people drawn from areas other than those in which they were serving—was "tending to become a greater danger to the loyal citizen, and his property, which it ought to protect, than to the public enemy" had echoes in the pages of the government press during the Tubman and Tolbert eras and in the annual reports of district commissioners. The commissioner in Sanniquellie in 1960, for example, complained that the enlisted men, because of "lack of leadership, live an inebriated life, undisciplined, and mostly dishonest."[8] It had apparently long been the custom of the Frontier Force to live off the local community as much as traffic would bear.

In addition to direct physical force, obligations vis-à-vis the state had been imposed upon the tribal element that constituted at least a formal recognition of the superiority of the Liberian government. The hut tax, although only sporadically enforced in the early period, became a recurrent obligation. The tribal people also were compelled by law to render service to the central government and to the chiefs in the construction of roads and in carrying out other community projects. Furthermore, forcible recruitment into the Liberian Frontier Force was an ever-present threat to restive individuals within a tribal community.

Besides the legal coercive sanctions, extralegal exactions imposed upon tribal people by both officials and civilians drove home the lesson of Americo-Liberian supremacy. The convening of Executive Councils in the hinterland—which Tubman initiated and Tolbert continued—brought to light practices that in the previous administrations went unpunished and often unnoticed. The tribal people had previously felt powerless to complain when special unauthorized taxes were levied by the district commissioners or when they were forced to work for little or no pay upon the farms of officials and prominent private Americo-Liberians. Previously, they had no recourse, moreover, when officials acquired tribal consorts or wives without the payment of dowry. It was not until the Tubman and Tolbert eras that effective steps were taken to regularize and limit the use of compulsory labor.

## CONTROL OVER TRIBAL MOBILITY

Another category of negative sanctions calculated to maintain Americo-Liberian supremacy had been the control over residence and population movements. An extreme example was the deportation from their home areas of politically restive tribe members and their confinement in one of the more remote districts of the interior.[9] Of a more general character was the attempt to restrict intertribal contact during the nineteenth and early twentieth centuries by establishing tribal land units under traditional authority, similar to the reserve policy followed by the British in East Africa (and still used by the apartheid regime in South Africa under its Homelands policy). A member of a Liberian ethnic group had a right to acquire land in his tribal area, but a tribal stranger could take up residence only with the permission of the traditional leadership and upon the stranger's acceptance of the local chief's political authority.[10] Also to control population movement, the Liberian government even in the Tubman era would not tolerate the mass exodus of a community from its traditional ethnic area to avoid tax and labor obligations or to diminish the strength of an unpopular chief. The government took steps to discourage the flight from their families and farms of males wishing to take advantage of the gold and diamond discoveries of the period following World War II. Although the efforts to control the drift of tribal people to Monrovia and other urban centers proved to be largely ineffective (as well as counterproductive once the Open Door policy came into effect), there were moves attempted by the city courts to return tribal vagrants to the hinterland up to the period of the 1980 coup. Initially, tribal migrants to the urban areas were required to live in segregated areas, although in many instances it was a matter of individual or group preference that the Kru, Bassa, and other tribal migrants employed in Monrovia were organized into separate quarters or "towns" for administrative and judicial purposes.

## TRIBAL ISOLATION

In addition to restrictions upon the movement and residence of tribal people, the government attempted until the Firestone agreement in the 1920s to severely minimize contact between the indigenous population and external economic influences. This included even restrictions upon Americo-Liberians who attempted to head inland to "make farm" or engage in the interior trade. There was a fear both regarding the potential for conflict with tribal forces and regarding the "downward" adjustment in social relationships made by individual settler migrants to fit the tribal circumstances (sometimes called "going bush"), thereby diminishing the solidarity and prestige of the settler community. Contact was intended to be largely limited to official administrative or military personnel. Furthermore, even though isolation delayed the economic development of the country's resources, the Liberian government attempted during much of the nineteenth century to restrict legitimate foreign trade to a few coastal ports, and prohibit the travel of foreigners who might instigate hostility against the Americo-Liberians or lend credence to European colonial claims. Liberian government efforts often failed.[11]

The same hostility toward the undermining influences of aliens in the interior ironically applied to the activities of Christian missionaries. Here was an anomaly. On the one hand the Americo-Liberian elite used their commitment to Protestant Christianity as a way of enforcing group solidarity among the settler community. This is reflected in the way in which political leadership and religious leadership went hand in hand as will be noted in the next chapter). The settler elite, moreover, used proselytization as an explicit instrument for securing the acceptance of Americo-Liberian supremacy by both the Congoes (recaptives) and the tribal leadership alike—particularly at the coast. Beginning in the 1870s, however, the attitudes of the Americo-Liberian elites toward missionaries began to sour, particularly with respect to the activities of the Episcopal Church among the Grebo in Maryland County. The perception that the Episcopal leadership had been encouraging the Grebo revolts of the 1870s and the formation of a unified Grebo confederacy led to severe limitations being imposed upon Episcopal activities in Maryland County as well as in other parts of the country.[12] Hostility was also noticeable with respect to the Methodists and other mission groups, particularly where the use of African vernacular languages was encouraged at the expense of literacy in English. There was a generalized feeling during the later years of the nineteenth and beginning years of the present century that foreign missionaries were responsible for many of the reports that were circulated in Europe and America about Americo-Liberian mistreatment of indigenous Africans.

It was not only the settlers who manifested hostility toward the Christian missionaries. As a recent account by a member of a Kpelle family of converts testifies, many of the tribal people deeply resented what they viewed as the hypocritical attitudes and behavior on the part of many American and European missionaries. The missionaries saw little redeeming value in traditional socializing institutions, such as the Poro and Sande, and were actually destructive of tribal dance, sculpture, and other aspects of culture.[13]

This generalized hostility toward foreign missionaries made the religious, educational, and health work among the Kru, the Grebo, and others more difficult to accomplish. Even greater fears were manifest by the Whig leadership regarding activities of missionaries in the interior. Hence, the government refused, until well into the twentieth century, to permit Christian missionaries to establish churches and schools more than 50 miles into the interior despite the fact that they could be instrumental in imparting certain aspects of the culture the Americo-Liberians had established as the norm for the whole state. Indeed, the Christian mission stations at Bolahun, Ganta, and other points far in the interior were established not to

encourage Christian missionaries but rather as bulwarks against the southward penetration of Mandingo and other Muslim influences extending southward into Liberia.
Nevertheless, the teachings and actions of the European stranger potentially could
undermine the authority of the Liberian government, and until the Tubman era
Christian missionaries were generally restricted in their activities. While the positive
role of missionaries in education and health should not be minimized, there is
evidence that the fears on the part of the settler elite regarding the maintenance of
peace were perhaps justified. Disputes during the period of my 1960s research in
Liberia were observed between missionaries over proselytizing areas. There were
also physical attacks by the Swedish Evangelical Lutheran converts upon the Poro
and Sande secret societies which did pose real problems for the Americo-Liberians
in the maintenance of peace and order in the interior. Although aliens ultimately
were no longer required to have an authorized pass to enter the provinces, there
were still both legal and tacit restrictions upon the residence and activities of aliens
in the hinterland until well into the Tubman era.[14]

### INDIRECT RULE

The settlers and their descendants also hoped to maintain control over the tribal
majority through the development of an efficient administrative service. To that
end the Department of the Interior (restyled the Department of Internal Affairs) was
created in 1868 during the presidency of James Spriggs Payne. For many decades
the effectiveness of the department was blunted by the lack of qualified Americo-
Liberians interested in living in the hinterland as well as by the difficulties that
geography posed for the systematic departmental supervision of the activities of the
administrative officers themselves. There also was no explicit policy regarding both
the ultimate goals of the dependency relationship and the means whereby the relationship was to be maintained or transformed. It was only during the administration
of Arthur Barclay (1904–1912) that the Liberian government acknowledged that
the tribal people of the hinterland were citizens of the Republic. Not until then were
steps taken to establish a more efficient administrative service. Unfortunately, the
stimulus for these policy decisions was not internal politics but rather the charge
of the British and French that historic Liberian claims to territory could not be
internationally recognized in the absence of "effective occupation." Had the impetus for change come from within the Americo-Liberian community, the reforms
might have been more meaningful.

The administrative system introduced by Arthur Barclay was patterned along
the lines of the British colonial philosophy of "indirect rule": the utilization of
traditional tribal authorities as instruments of the central government in the maintenance of law and order at the local level.[15] In return for the maintenance of peace
in their area and the payment of taxes collected from their tribal constituents,
traditional authorities were given regular salaries, assured prestige, and license to
use or abuse the persons and services of their own subjects without the customary
tribal restraints on their actions.[16] Aside from the savings in money and personnel,
this policy had many advantages for the Americo-Liberian minority. In the first

place, by co-opting traditional tribal leaders as part of the national system of administration, it perpetuated the social division of the hinterland into more than sixteen ethnic groups and capitalized upon the existing political fragmentation of the majority of these ethnic groups into relatively autonomous chiefdoms. Even though the creation of consolidated paramount chieftainships reversed the process of fragmentation to a certain degree, only the Dei, Mende, Gbandi, Kissi, and Belle groups were separately permitted to organize themselves under single paramount chiefs. In the other groups, political authority within a group was divided among as many as five paramount chiefs. Morover, in drawing district boundaries, little respect was accorded to existing notions regarding ethnic territorial units. Thus, the Kpelle were dispersed among four administrative areas, whereas fragments of several mutually hostile ethnic groups were often incorporated within a single district. Curiously, in cases where chieftainship did not exist—as among the Kissi— the Liberians simply appointed paramount, clan, and town chiefs, whose only allegiances were to the Liberian government. In addition to representing the corporate political interest of the tribal constituents, the traditional and the appointed chiefs alike were the main contact points between the tribal people and the new society in terms of tax collection as well as labor recruitment for government, private settlers, or foreign entrepreneurs.

Notwithstanding the lack of respect for the integrity of a tribe as a social or political unit, indirect rule preserved the diversity of tribal customs and institutions regarding marriage, land tenure, and other matters. Where possible, tribal customs and institutions were preserved and used by the district commissioner in carrying out central government objectives. Thus, in many areas a modified form of hereditary succession to chieftainship has prevailed to the present day. Chiefs and elders at all levels administer customary law in the settlement of disputes concerning a wide range of social and economic relationships. Tribal membership has been further strengthened by the legalizing of the Poro and other secret societies, which in the early period were banned as potential political threats to America-Liberian rule. Corporate membership in the clan or other ethnic unit is emphasized not only by the system of land tenure but also by the practice during the First Republic of levying fines against a whole community in the settlement of boundary disputes or for failure to provide laborers for public projects. As will be described in the next chapter, the political stability that resulted from the policy of recognizing native traditions even prompted the Americo-Liberians until 1930 to countenance the institutions of domestic slavery and the pawning of persons in the tribal areas.

The Liberian commitment to indirect rule was of a pragmatic rather than a philosophic nature. No attempt was made, as Sir Donald Cameron had done in Tanganyika, to justify indirect rule as the morally best colonial system, the least damaging to the native personality in the transition from traditional to modern society. Tribal institutions in the Liberian hinterland have flourished only to the extent that they did not conflict with the interests of the Americo-Liberians. A chief, for example, might be chosen in a time-honored fashion; nevertheless, he held office only at the pleasure of the Liberian president. Similarly, the Poro survived only on sufferance. The expediency of the Liberian policy is revealed as well in the attitude toward "bush" schools, in which tribal youth were instructed in tribal lore and custom and initiated into the ethnic community. Once the central government took a more active interest in the educational programs of the interior, restrictions were placed upon the traditional system of ethnic indoctrination. The fate of the *zoes* and other practitioners of traditional medicine likewise became conditional upon the rate at which programs in modern medicine expanded into the hinterland.

## The Challenge to Caste Maintenance

The pacification of the tribal people through coercion or the seduction of its leadership and the subsequent emergence of a single-party system were fairly effective in maintaining Americo-Liberian control over Liberia during most of the nineteenth century and well into the twentieth. By the beginning of the twentieth century, however, it was apparent that additional modifications in the control strategy would be required to maintain Americo-Liberian supremacy. Continuing resistance well into the present century by groups such as the Kru led the Liberian leadership to call on Americans and other foreigners for financial support and for help in reorganizing the military and the hinterland bureaucracy. The need for government revenue in establishing effective control over the hinterland, in paying off foreign debts, and in implementing a modicum of social services in the settler areas, moreover, compelled the government in 1926 to sign an agreement with the American Firestone Company to develop the faltering rubber industry.

With nationalist movements slowly gaining momentum in neighboring West African colonies—particularly among those in the British dependencies—which threatened to dislodge Europeans from their dominant positions in neighboring states, it became apparent to the Liberian elite that more positive measures were required to secure the tribal people's acceptance of the legitimacy of Americo-Liberian rule. Indeed, three decades before Kwame Nkrumah's Convention Peoples Party of Ghana in 1957 displaced a colonial regime in Ghana (the former Gold Coast), the storm clouds of discontent among the Liberian tribal people were already gathering and threatening the continuation of Americo-Liberian supremacy in the Republic. The discontent that had been brewing during the administration of President Charles D. B. King (1920–1930) gave the settler elite clear warning that their control of the tribal majority was being seriously challenged.

The crisis that compelled the Liberian government to introduce drastic reforms in its interior policies and programs was the League of Nations inquiry of the late 1920s and early 1930s into the charges of abusive labor practices. (See table 1.) For a nation which was founded on the basis of liberation from slavery, it was ironic that the charges of slavery and indentured service should be hurled against the government of President King.[17] The inquiry confronted the Americo-Liberian elite with its gravest threat since the days of early settlement. Not only was there a brief recurrence of tribal rebellion along the Kru Coast, but the factor of external intervention was compounded far beyond the previous meddling of Liberia's colonial neighbors, Britain and France. This time the European menace was supported by the League of Nations. Moreover, the United States under President Herbert Hoover dramatically reversed two American policies. First of all, the United States government publicly rebuked the Liberian government, whose cause it normally championed against the colonial powers. Secondly, the United States indicated a willingness to cooperate with the League, which it had helped create but had refused to join.[18]

The League crisis, ironically, was in part a reaction to the increasing effectiveness of the elite in bringing the interior under military and administrative control and in collecting the hut tax. Most of the antagonism, however, centered upon labor practices, a matter in which the Americo-Liberians were not the only offenders. Both chiefs and influential Americo-Liberians had been involved in the abuses of the traditional pawning system whereby an impoverished tribal person could indenture himself or a relative until a debt had been repaid. In traditional society there were many safeguards for the system, but these had been weakened under the imposition of Americo-Liberian rule and the open collaboration between Americo-Liberian officials and tribal chiefs. There had been instances, for example, of pawns remaining unredeemed for forty years or more. Pawning, incidentally, was a fairly common practice throughout West Africa. One of the hypocrises of the League controversy was that the British government, which so sanctimoniously criticized the pawning system in Liberia, had only in 1928 overcome the resistance of Mende and other chiefs and abolished the last form of domestic slavery in neighboring Sierra Leone.

Some of the labor discontent was a direct reaction to government practices. There had been much abuse of the porterage system, under which Liberian officials could conscript able-bodied men to help carry them (in hammocks) and their supplies while on tour in the district. The requests for porters as well as the recruitment of both males and females for unpaid labor on roads and other public projects frequently came at the peak of the planting or harvesting seasons. The treatment of laborers on these projects by unsupervised gang foremen was apparently quite ruthless.

The most serious charges, however, concerned the forcible recruitment of labor to serve on private projects. Reference has already been made to the illegal use of native farm labor, recruited by chiefs for work on the farms of the district commissioners and other prominent Americo-Liberians. The signing of the agreement with the Firestone Plantations Company in 1926 aggravated this situation. The officers of Firestone acknowledged that, at least during the early years of their effort to produce rubber in Liberia, chiefs had directly assisted in the recruitment of involuntary labor.[19] What aroused the international community, however, were the "midnight" raids on tribal villages by Liberian soldiers seeking laborers for the cocoa and other plantations on the Spanish island of Fernando Po. What made the forcible recruitment particularly obnoxious was the active or at least tacit approval of many high Liberian officials, including Vice President Allen Yancy. It was even charged, but not definitely substantiated, that President King himself was involved in the lucrative enterprise, which brought $45 a head for each of 3,000 men exported and a bonus of $5,000 for every additional group of 1,500 recruited.

The plight of the tribal people gained international attention during a 1927 tour in the United States by Thomas J. R. Faulkner, who had been unsuccessful that year in his electoral bid to replace Mr. King. The American press, and ultimately the State Department, accepted Faulkner's charges regarding the King administration's role in condoning slavery, corruption, and "primitive" customs. In 1929, following a protest note by the U.S. State Department, Liberia agreed to request an international commission of inquiry to look into the charges. The Council of the League of Nations appointed a tripartite commission consisting of representatives from the United States, Great Britain, and Liberia, and headed by Dr. Cuthbert Christy, a physician with many years' experience in West Africa. The Christy Commission substantiated in 1930 many of the charges regarding the pawning system, the abuses of compulsory labor, the forcible recruitment of laborers for Fernando Po, and the complicity of Vice President Yancy and other high Liberian officials. They did not, however, find explicit cases of slavery in Liberia, at least as that term was defined in the Anti-Slavery Convention of 1925. Parenthetically, it might be noted that the Commission did not acknowledge that many of the practices criticized in Liberia were prevalent—in some instances in even more flagrant form— in certain European dependencies in Africa.

President King attempted to respond to the popular domestic criticism as well as to the Christy Commission's findings by banning the exportation of labor and the pawning system and by explicitly outlawing slavery. This tacit admission of Liberian guilt, however, so outraged many leading Americo-Liberians that both President King and Vice President Yancy were compelled to resign in December 1930, with Secretary of State Edwin Barclay assuming the presidency. This by no means ended the controversy. During the next four years a number of plans and counterplans were exchanged by the League, the Liberian leaders, and the British and American governments. Firestone also participated in the international discussions, much to its embarrassment. The most severe proposal came in 1932 as a result of the inquiry the preceding year by the Brunot Committee of the League, named for its chairman, a former French colonial governor. The Brunot proposal would have placed the fiscal and legal affairs of the Republic as well as its administration of the hinterland under an international supervisor—in effect making Liberia a League of Nations mandate territory. The refusal of the Liberian government to accept the proposal without serious amendment prolonged the discussions, and eventually the diplomatic delaying tactics paid off. An improvement in Liberia's economic situation through a rise in the price of rubber, followed by the more friendly attitude of the succeeding U.S. administration of Franklin D. Roosevelt, permitted the controversy to come to an inconclusive end in 1935. At that point American and Liberian diplomatic relations, which had been broken in 1930, were resumed.

President Barclay's efforts to reorganize the administrative services in the hinterland and to introduce a public health service and other programs of benefit to the tribal people were applauded by the international community. But the Barclay reform measures were to a great extent undermined by the obsession of certain Whig leaders with the desire to punish dissident Americo-Liberians and tribal people who had given testimony to the various League commissions. The ruthless suppression of unrest along the Kru Coast brought outward stability but undying hostility on the part of many tribal persons toward the Americo-Liberian leadership. Rumors of revolutionary activity cropped up repeatedly, and many individuals, including a recent secretary of public instruction, the late Nathaniel Massaquoi, were tried and imprisoned during the grim Barclay days for allegedly attempting to overthrow the Americo-Liberian ruling class by force.

## The Tubman Reforms: New Deal for the Hinterland

The election of President Tubman in 1943 signaled a change in the spirit as well as the substance of the caste relationship then existing between the tribal people and the descendants of the settlers. It also launched a new role for Liberia in the politics of the African continent. Although Tubman's credentials among the Americo-Liberian elite were of the highest order, and although he was Ernest Barclay's personal choice as his successor, it was obvious from the outset that Tubman intended to be an independent political commander. In addition to a very dynamic personality, he had a remarkable familiarity with the intricacies of the Liberian political system, which he learned from his father, who eventually became speaker of the House of Representatives. Even more significant, however, was the highly intimate knowledge he had gained of the political system as a legal defender of the Liberian officials involved in the League of Nations inquiry into the Fernando Po scandals. Tubman had thus come to know the sins of omission and commission of all the leading politicians of the day. He had, more importantly, developed an independent base of political power among both tribal people and the lower-class Americo-Liberians which permitted him to be something other than a mere defender of the traditional relationship between the Whig aristocracy and the tribal people. By the time he became a candidate for the presidency, he had acquired a considerable reputation as an eloquent lawyer who often took the cases of penniless clients even against prominent Americo-Liberian adversaries. For this reason, the Old Guard Whigs should not have been too surprised by the reformist posture assumed by the man who took office on January 1, 1944. Since Tubman had long served as a senator from Maryland County (1923–1937) and had accumulated four years of service on the Supreme Court at the time of his presidential nomination in 1943, the Old Guard had assumed that Tubman, like most of his predecessors, would ignore the fiery campaign rhetoric regarding reform of the political system once he had the reins of office firmly in hand. How mistaken they were!

### *The Open Door Policy*

Among the first of Tubman's programs to alter affairs in the tribal hinterland was the Open Door Policy. This policy was at base a calculated strategy of economic development which was designed not only to enhance the foundations of privilege for the Americo-Liberian elite but also to give them the revenues for maintaining a more modern and efficient system of control over the tribal majority. Indeed, the additional revenues which would accrue from exploitation of mineral resources as well as from the expansion and diversification of agriculture were absolutely essential to the control of the unintended or undesired consequences of economic modernization. Although social transformation of the tribal majority was secondary, nevertheless, the Open Door policy was an implicit recognition of the fact that the previous attempt to isolate the people of the hinterland from external economic influences and insulate them against the waves of both modernity and nationalism was no longer adequate. There was the danger that a further delay in the exposure of the tribal people to the twentieth century would build a time bomb under the archaic political, social, and economic structure that the descendants of the original settlers had inherited. While recognizing the potential dangers of exposing the tribal people to Westernization, industrialization, and urbanization, the Old Guard accepted Tubman's arguments that social reform could be controlled: change would be evolutionary rather than revolutionary.

The controlled change was to take place by opening Liberia to massive foreign investment in the exploitation of its natural resource potential.[20] Tubman had enacted laws at the outset of his presidency that gave foreign investors full freedom of entry and repatriation of their capital and profits. This legislation imposed few restrictions upon corporate structures or regulations regarding employment policies and practices. The alteration in domestic strategies was made possible largely through the systematic exploitation of Liberia's extensive deposits of high-grade iron ore. Many of the high-grade reserves at Bomi Hills, in Nimba Mountain, and in other locations had been surveyed long before the Open Door policy was implemented, but Liberian leaders lacked both the determination and the capital to exploit this resource. The dramatic consequences of the Tubman program are evidenced by the increase in Liberia's overall export earnings from a modest U.S. $30 million in 1953 (roughly the point of takeoff of the Tubman program) to an average U.S. $505 million during the last five years of the first Republic (1976–1980).

Through the early 1950s, the Liberian economic growth had been rigidly tied to one commodity—rubber—and largely to one foreign firm (or concession, as such firms are called in Liberia)—Firestone. Although rubber has continued to be an important export earner, the average yearly earnings for the last five years of the two decades from 1953 through 1972 were roughly what they had been in the first five years of that same period—U.S. $29 million. Rubber was subject to gross price fluctuations on the world market, particularly with the advent of synthetic rubber. It was not until the OPEC oil crisis of 1974, when there was an increase in the demand for sisal, rubber, and other plant products which had been displaced by the use of petroleum, that rubber once again became a significant revenue earner for Liberia (U.S. $102 million for 1980).

But as figure 3 indicates, the dominant role that rubber played in export earnings as late as 1957 (77 percent of the total) steadily gave way in relative, even if not in absolute, terms to iron ore. As the investments of the American, Swedish, German, and other firms came to fruition, iron ore accounted for as much as 75 percent of total export earnings (1967, and again in 1975). From the modest earnings of U.S. $5 million in 1953, export earnings from iron ore attained a peak of U.S. $328 million in 1976. At that point, iron ore earnings began a decline as the resources

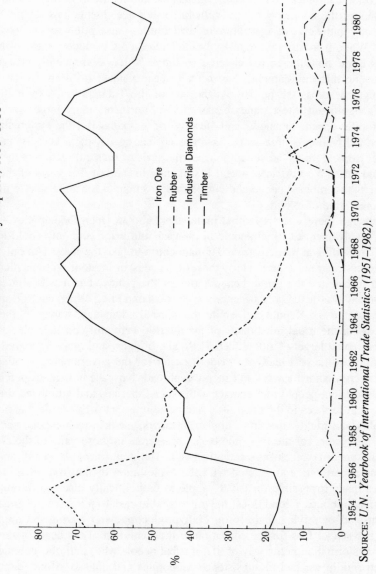

FIGURE 3  Liberian Commodity Exports, 1953–1981

Iron Ore
Rubber
Industrial Diamonds
Timber

SOURCE: *U.N. Yearbook of International Trade Statistics (1951–1982).*

at some mines—such as the one at Bomi Hills—were exhausted and as the recession throughout the developed world limited demand for iron.

There was one aspect of the Open Door strategy of economic growth which was slow in materializing, namely the diversification in natural resource exploitation. Diversification was to be a hedge against the dominance of a single commodity which makes the economy highly vulnerable to price fluctuations on the world market, or—in the case of agriculture or horticulture—susceptible to a serious plant disease. While it is true that industrial diamonds earned a modest share of export earnings throughout the period covered by figure 3, it was frequently charged by Sierra Leone that the diamonds had actually been panned in Sierra Leone rivers and smuggled across the border. At the end of the Tubman era, exploitation of Liberia's significant forest stands began to yield an increasingly larger harvest of timber for European, Japanese, and New World markets. But the systematic and sustained cultivation of tree crops—such as coffee, cocoa, palm kernels, papaya, and other tropical fruits—never approached the scale of such cultivation in the Ivory Coast and other West African states. It was only in the last five years of the First Republic that combined cocoa and coffee sales accounted for more than 2 percent of the total value of exports.

Although there were risks that under the Tubman Open Door policy the increased involvement of tribal people in the cash and wage economy could lead to demands for political participation, Tubman chose to take the risks. Not only were the Americo-Liberians—particularly those at the coast or in Monrovia specifically— destined to become the prime beneficiaries of the policy, but it was argued that development was actually a necessary tool in maintaining Whig control and supremacy within the Republic. Despite the skewed advantage, however, the consequences for the tribal inhabitants of the interior were still considerable, even if they represented largely "side effects." Roads, bridges, and other improved communications in the past had only made it easier for the government to collect hut taxes or recruit labor for work in Liberia or abroad. Now the new roads potentially brought the tribal people into contact with other Liberians and witnessed the flow of goods and services to the previously neglected interior. Albeit limited in number and quality and highly uneven in impact, teachers, medical technicians, and agricultural instructors for the first time began to operate in those parts of the country where the majority of citizens actually lived. The new forms of wealth and employment opportunities associated with the exploitation of the iron ore and other resources made it possible for tribal people to be politically placated through improvements in housing conditions, having available cash to purchase manufactured goods instead of relying entirely on craft production, and having the ability to accumulate school fees for the education of their children. Thus began a slow but steady transformation in the way of life of tribal people who, until the Tubman era, had been rigidly wedded to subsistence economies and able to afford few of the material luxuries of a modern society.

It took time for the transformation to occur. Indeed, initially many of the economic changes appeared to be a double-edged sword for tribal people. While providing benefits, the network of new roads, for example, also provided even more efficient means in collecting taxes and recruiting laborers and soldiers under less than voluntary terms. Improved transport, plus the weakening of tribal cohesion, moreover, made it easier for the Americo-Liberian elite to begin the systematic acquisition of land that had previously been reserved for the tribal people. It is estimated that the nominal purchase and outright theft of land in Liberia under both Tubman and his successor, Tolbert, constitute one of the major "land grabs" in African history, in a class with the land seizures by white settlers in South Africa, Zimbabwe, and Kenya during the colonial era.

A further consequence of the Open Door policy (see chapter 9) was the diversification of the trading relationships as well as the sources of foreign investment and personnel. This not only gave the Americo-Liberian leadership greater latitude in its foreign politics but reduced the threat of external intervention by a single dominant power in its domestic strategies of control. In particular, the Open Door policy diminished Liberia's inordinate dependence upon the United States and its relationship with Firestone, Goodrich, and other American-owned rubber firms. It made Liberia's economy less dependent upon the impact of global pricing mechanisms for this one agricultural commodity, which was already being affected by the development of synthetics.[21]

### Extension of Suffrage and Representation

The second plank in Tubman's program of reform—which complemented the Open Door policy—was the extension of legislative representation and suffrage to the tribal majority. Recalling that the granting of Liberian citizenship to the tribal people at the turn of the century had cost the Americo-Liberians almost nothing in terms of real power (but had been notably successful in forestalling British encroachments along the northwestern frontier), the Tubman regime attempted to eliminate many of the formal legal barriers to participation by the tribal element in the affairs of the Republic. A property qualification for voting did remain, but it had been revised downward to extend the ballot to the owner of any hut upon which taxes had been paid. Suffrage, moreover, became an individual right, in contrast to the past, when a chief, acting in his corporate capacity as the holder of title to tribal land, could register and vote on behalf of the members of his community as a unit.[22] Later, in the spirit of electoral reform, Tubman extended the vote to women, and under Tolbert the age limit was lowered to 18.

Along with the changes in suffrage qualifications, the form of representation for the tribal people had been altered. In the past any tribe that paid one hundred dollars had the privilege of electing one of its members as a delegate to the House of Representatives. Delegates had the opportunity to discuss and vote upon all matters relating to tribal interests. In 1944 the regular membership of the House of Representatives was increased to permit the provinces (see map 4) as well as the tribal areas within the coastal counties to have regular informal representation. This process was brought to its logical culmination in 1964 with the elimination of the provincial system of administration and the creation of four new counties in the interior, each of which was given full representation in the House and permitted to

MAP 4    Political Boundaries before 1964

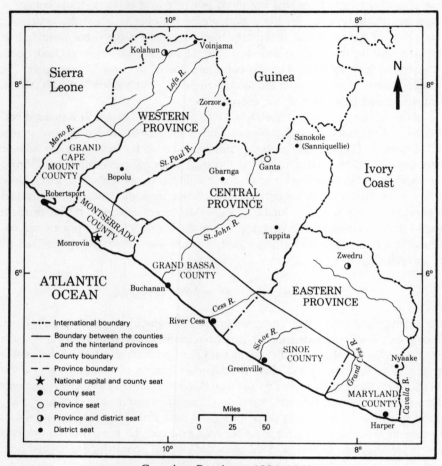

Counties, Provinces 1904–1963

elect two senators to the upper house of the Liberian Legislature (see map 5). Finally, Tubman and Tolbert publicized the appointment of persons with tribal backgrounds to positions of prominence at the executive cabinet and judicial levels as well—albeit their numbers were limited.

### The Unification Program

Even greater than suffrage and representation, the more comprehensive complement to the Open Door policy was Tubman's Unification Program, which was designed to reduce or eliminate the legal and other distinctions between tribal and settler descendants and to give a new appreciation to tribal culture and social norms. Some of the archaic laws in the pre-Tubman era had prevented tribal people from acquiring

MAP 5   Changes in County Boundaries, 1964

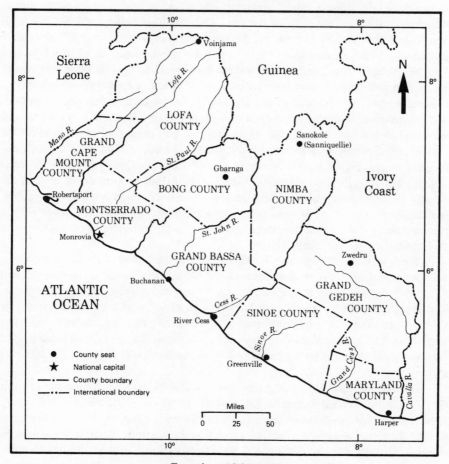

Counties, 1964–1984

land on a freehold basis or suing and being sued in a national court. More important than any particular act of legislation or executive decree, the Unification Program represented a creative posture that permitted the tribal majority to identify with the Liberian nation through the personality of the president. Under Tubman's administration—and for the first time in Liberian history—the doors of the Executive Mansion were open to tribal persons who had suggestions or petitions of grievance to present to the president. Moreover, Tubman developed in a more systematic fashion the device of personal intergroup diplomacy in the hinterland initiated in only a sporadic fashion by President King. It was an innovation that Tubman's successor, William Tolbert, not only used but—in certain cases—actually perfected.

Tubman made it a point to visit each of the main headquarters in the interior during a three-year period. There he held extended sessions of his Executive Council in which the people and chiefs sought correction of wrongs, requested new programs in health or education, secured executive arbitration of boundary disputes, and in other ways solicited the help of the president. Without being burdened by legal restrictions or bound by precedents, the president meted out a form of substantive justice which had a tremendous impact upon the tribal people, most of whom had long felt isolated from Liberian politics and had never had the opportunity of seeing a Liberian president. The summary dismissal of errant district commissioners (including a very close relative of the president), the immediate granting of justice, and the promises to extend benefits of new economic development to the hinterland were significant factors in almost eliminating violent organized opposition on the part of tribal people to America-Liberian rule. Tubman's Executive Council decisions, moreover, frequently struck at one of the most tender spots in the relationship between the two elements, namely, the illegal acquisition of land in the interior by leading members of the Americo-Liberian community. The fines, public rebuke, forfeiture of crops, and other stern treatment accorded the latter helped reassure the tribal people that there would be some restraints upon violation of traditional land tenure rights.

There were other ways, too, in which Tubman attempted to eradicate the legal, economic, and other distinctions between the members of the two communities and to indicate that the tribal people had a right to be proud of their traditional heritage. The president often appeared in tribal dress on civic occasions, took a series of tribal names, and encouraged the appreciation of native dancing and art forms. The employment of anthropologists to study tribal customs, law, and social organization was also evidence of a new appreciation of the indigenous culture of the Liberian masses.

Perhaps the most promising sign in the entire picture was the sense of guilt that Americo-Liberians began to have when it came to differentiating in public speeches and writings between themselves and the tribal element. The official efforts to drop the term "Americo-Liberian" as well as the resort by officials to ambiguous expressions such as "the natives and the other element" or the "civilized people and the other element" constituted evidence that the self-assuredness of the settler aristocracy had been undermined. Moreover, frontal attacks on the image of the early settlers were being made by prominent members of the Americo-Liberian community themselves. During the commencement address at Bromley School for Girls in 1960, for example, the sister of an important cabinet official referred to the founding fathers of Liberia as the "ill-prepared, ill-informed, and illegitimate offspring of the union between master and slave." After Tubman came to power, it once again became respectable for someone named Caine to call himself Kandakai or for a Freeman to resort to the tribal form of Fahnbulleh. This was very important for Liberian students and others who went abroad and wanted to emphasize their ties with Africa rather than the West. Thus, County Superintendent George F. Sherman became G. Flama Sherman upon his appointment as ambassador to Ghana. In many respects, however, the most positive contribution of the Unification Program was psychological. Tribal Liberians could at last take open pride in their cultural identities, could wear lapas and other traditional dress in public, and could openly acknowledge conversion to Islam. The expanding educational system of the Tubman years permitted people of tribal background to occupy posts in the bureaucracy once monopolized by Americo-Liberians. Educated tribal youths were, in increasing numbers, employed by Monrovia-based law firms to run their branch offices in the interior. New government offices, moreover, were being created as the county system of government was extended into the interior.

It was, however, another example of the appearance of reform being far greater than the reality. This was particularly the case after the political changes of 1964 when—as one significant participant-observer of the Liberian scene suggested—the Tubman engine of reform ran out of steam. Without denigrating either Tubman's or Tolbert's efforts at national integration, it was clear that the overwhelming thrust of integration during the last decades of the First Republic was still in the direction of accepting settler rather than tribal norms of behavior. Detracting from the benefits to be derived from the extension to the tribal hinterland of suffrage and representation in the Legislature was the fact that elections had actually become almost meaningless exercises within the single-party state. Real power had gravitated even more effectively from the Legislature to the President and to those influential Americo-Liberians who surrounded him. Although education provided more bureaucratic jobs for tribal youth and lower income Americo-Liberians, the really significant executive, legislative, judicial, and ambassadorial positions were retained by the leading families at the core the the Americo-Liberian elite.

Many analysts had been too enthusiastic regarding the social impact of the new employment opportunities in the private sector which had increased dramatically under the Tubman program—and even more so under Tolbert. The Americo-Liberian leaders, however, still preferred to leave it to Americans, Europeans, Lebanese and other non-Blacks to provide the main sources of capital and entrepreneurial talent. Since the 1847 Constitution prevented non-Blacks from becoming citizens, the foreign entrepreneurs operated in Liberia on sufferance and could be deported if they became a direct factor in domestic politics. Rather than being intimately involved in private business, Americo-Liberian officials until the Tolbert era largely "poached on the periphery." That is, either they served on the boards of foreign corporations that had concession agreements with the government, and thereby had access to salaries, trips abroad, and scholarships for their children, or the politicians used their positions to acquire businesses, rubber plantations, and other enterprises that were managed by Nigerians, West Indians, and other foreigners. Thus, there was no divorce between politics and control over economic power in Tubman's Liberia, even though Liberian entrepreneurship was poorly developed.

## The Sources of Change

The roots of Tubman's Unification Program were various, and it would be unfair to attribute the change solely to a desire on the part of the Americo-Liberian elite to insulate itself from the wave of nationalism undermining alien rule in other parts of Africa. Many Liberians had traveled to Europe, America, and other African territories and returned convinced that the lot of the tribal people should be improved. Many in the upper class had familial and other personal ties with tribal communities and were sufficiently indignant about tribal discrimination to advocate reform long before Tubman arrived on the scene. Nevertheless, it was clear that the nationalist unrest mounting elsewhere would one day touch Liberia; if the settler element did not lead the tribal people to modernity and grant them political and social rights, the latter would one day try to achieve these things on their own. Thus, if the Americo-Liberians could not prevent change, they could at least attempt to control it.

What forces prompted the changes of the first two decades of the Tubman era? Certainly the events of World War II, and in particular the presence of over five thousand American troops, both white and Black, had a marked impact not only upon the monetizing of the economy but also on the social attitudes of the tribal people and the poorer element within the Americo-Liberian community. The free-spending as well as the free living of the American troops had a dramatic (if somewhat disruptive) effect on the Liberian economy and tribal social codes. The presence of the Americans also drove home the idea that a life of poverty need not be accepted blindly. Moreover, ideas of a political and social character inevitably emerged from this new cultural contact.

Economic development, which had been tentatively launched in the 1920s when Firestone Plantations Company took over the operation of the abandoned rubber plantations near Monrovia, had an even more sustained impact in breaking down traditional tribal relationships and increasing economic demands that would eventually seek political solutions.[23] Firestone punctured the myth of the lack of economic motivation on the part of the Liberian tribesmen, and the myth was dealt its death blow by the iron ore companies and other foreign concessions brought into Liberia by Tubman's Open Door policy in the postwar period. The tribesman took readily to a money economy and to the new status that material wealth could bring to one in his tribal area as well as in the new urban centers. The influx of foreigners under the Open Door policy also exposed the tribal people to individuals from several continents and reversed the longstanding attempt by the Americo-Liberians to insulate the tribal people against alien influences.

Another sustained contributor to social change has been the education of tribal youth, a responsibility assumed almost entirely by the Christian missionaries prior to the Tubman administration. Education produced a corps of tribal youths who no longer were satisfied with a second-class status in their own country. Higher education, either at the University of Liberia or through foreign scholarships, had been the virtual monopoly of the Americo-Liberian class. The first significant break for the tribal people came in the period following World War II when the Episcopal Church, with the assistance of the Methodist and Lutheran missions, re-established Cuttington College (now University College). The institution was at that stage far more practical in its orientation to the development needs of the country and more insistent upon maintaining high academic standards than had been the case with the University of Liberia. Since Cuttington was located at Gbarnga, over a hundred miles into the interior, it was long regarded as a ''country people'' college by the

Americo-Liberian youth, who preferred either education abroad or the political and social dynamism associated with the University of Liberia—located literally a stone's throw from the Capitol and the new Executive Mansion.

The development, use, and impact of radio and the press were not as significant as instigators of change in Liberia as they were in other parts of Africa, and in a sense the government missed a ready-made opportunity for the political indoctrination of the tribal masses by not having a strong AM radio station under government control. Until the Tolbert period, the national broadcasting station (ELBC) in Monrovia could only be heard in pockets of the country under the best of atmospheric conditions unless one had a very expensive set. The inexpensive transistor radios that were being widely distributed throughout the country did pick up the Voice of America (which in the 1960s built a transmitter outside Monrovia) and the English and tribal-language programs of ELWA, the Sudan Interior Mission radio station in Monrovia. In certain sectors of the country, however, it was easier to receive broadcasts from Guinea or Radio Peking than it was to receive Western interpretations of the news.

Similarly, the printed word was not the critical source of revolutionary change in Liberia that it had been in Asia or even in Nigeria and Ghana. The history of the opposition press in Liberia was a checkered one at best, with editions of a dissident publication seldom going on beyond a year, a month, or even a single issue.[24] Lack of funding, or outright government suppression and harassment of journalists and editors, frequently brought the antiestablishment critics "into line." There were few with the courage of inveterate pamphleteer Albert Porte, who persevered as a nettle in the sides of four True Whig presidents and continued his attacks against the regime of Samuel Doe until his death in March 1986. In the 1960s there was not a single bookstore of note in the whole of Monrovia. The government-controlled newspapers and private publications which supported the settler position (such as the *Daily Listener*) had to be hawked along the sidewalks and highways. Foreign periodicals such as *Time* and *West Africa* were sold, but they experienced occasional banning of issues with articles which the Whig regime regarded as offensive, and in any event they had a limited Liberian readership given the state of illiteracy in the country.

A much older and more effective means of communication remained, of course: the carrying of news by the steady flow of people moving back and forth across the artificial boundaries separating Liberia from Guinea, Sierra Leone, and the Ivory Coast. The efforts of the late Sékou Touré in Guinea and of Félix Houphouët-Boigny in the Ivory Coast to organize mass-based parties had not gone unnoticed by the tribal people of Liberia. Of even greater significance to the Americo-Liberians was the chain of events in Sierra Leone that brought the tribal people to political power years before the achievement of independence in 1961. There the Creoles, who as descendants of British-released slaves had alien roots overseas paralleling those of the Americo-Liberians, were compelled by British colonial authorities to accommodate themselves to a minority political role within the newly emerging state.

The success of President Tubman's Unification Program in changing conditions in the hinterland and in altering tribal attitudes toward the Liberian political system was best underscored by the very real personal popularity that Tubman seemed to enjoy whenever he journeyed in the interior. Nevertheless, a group of leading True Whigs during the middle years of the Tubman era acknowledged quite frankly that ''the lines of cleavage are beginning to lessen somewhat, but the distinctions still remain. . . . It would be inaccurate to say that at this time members of the tribal groups are not at a disadvantage. . . .''[25] Despite the substance and the appearance of even greater reforms in the relationship between America-Liberians and the indigenous population under Tubman's successor, William R. Tolbert, the changes were too little and too late—as the 1980 coup demonstrated.

# V.

# Primacy of Politics in the First Republic

One of the critical factors in maintaining settler control over the processes of change in the First Republic was the priority given within the Americo-Liberian group itself to politics at the expense of other kinds of social interaction. Exceptions obviously existed, for no political system is watertight, but a Liberian under the First Republic rarely could enjoy great prestige or pursue his professional goals without some political base. An individual enjoyed a position of influence in a church, a business, a charitable organization, or a fraternal society because he held, or had held, office in the Liberian government or the True Whig Party. Prominence in a nonpolitical structure, then, was a reward for excellent performance in the political arena. The monopoly of the political leadership over religious, economic, and other institutions guaranteed that these structures would not fall under the sway of those not committed to the preservation of the distribution of political power that guaranteed settler supremacy. Anyone who attempted to gain a position of influence in national society without first gaining political sanction within the established party or government was regarded with suspicion.

The consequences of this primacy of politics in terms of the rapid modernization of Liberian society were depressing. The independent, nonpolitical entrepreneur survived only with great difficulty. He either was crushed by a series of legal or informal obstacles, or he ultimately survived by "getting into line." In conforming to the norms of administrative behavior peculiar to Liberia, any young Western-educated Liberian soon found his professional ethics and his textbook skills shelved and his reforming zeal diminished as he attempted to navigate the intricate political maze and learn the expediencies necessary for occupational survival. The fruits of cooperation soon made the reforming zealot a defender of the status quo. He developed in time the politically sensitive antennae of his seniors and helped perpetuate a situation that made the Liberian political system a modern equivalent of a Renaissance Italian city-state.

## Economic Structures

**TRIBAL INVOLVEMENT**

Obviously, the Whig leadership at the onset of the Tubman Open Door policy was mindful of the nineteenth-century history of economic challenge posed by the Gola, Mandingo, and other indigenous middlemen, and mindful as well of the persisting military and political threat posed by the Grebo and Kru even within this century. The major economic challenge to the Whig system of supremacy that the Old Guard feared most, however, was the one posed from within their own ranks. The tribal majority, after all, were still somewhat remote from the Tubman economic revolution in the mineral and industrial sectors. Not only were most members of the tribal majority still engaged in agriculture (roughly 90 percent in 1950, 80 percent in 1960, and still 70 percent in 1980), but most were primarily devoted to subsistence cultivation or wage employment on the foreign-managed estates. Very little of the expansion of agricultural production for export described in chapter 4 (see figure 3) took place on smallholder plots; it was almost entirely in agribusiness on foreign-owned plantations.

The Americo-Liberian elite displayed an ambivalent political concern toward the involvement of tribal people in traditional forms of economic association. Certain traditional work societies, such as the *kuus* among the Mano and Kpelle of the interior, were permitted—if not actually encouraged—to flourish. Indeed, as Seibel and Massing have demonstrated, all ethnic groups in Liberia had some indigenous forms of work, savings, producing, or building cooperatives, although they differed remarkably in their complexity, strength, and recency of origin.[1] It was not until the late 1970s—when some of the traditional cooperatives, with the encouragement of the political movement called MOJA (Movement for Justice in Africa; see chapter 12), became assertive regarding better prices and marketing facilities—that the True Whig regime under Tolbert became obstructive with respect to the functioning of *kuus*.[2] The government was equally indulgent with respect to the burial associations, as well as the thrift and improvement associations—often called *susu*—so popular among the Bassa, Kru, and other tribal people who had gravitated to Monrovia and other urbanized centers.[3] The limited economic and social objectives of these groupings had been rigidly maintained by government-appointed leaders who regulated the conduct of their fellow tribesmen in the urban areas. Also controlled by the urban tribal leaders were the syncretistic religious societies, such as the Bassa Community Church, which could challenge the orthodox Christian leadership of Liberia.

The involvement of tribal people in more modern forms of economic associations, on the other hand, was viewed with open hostility by the Whig leadership. Aware of the role that the cocoa cooperatives of Ghana and the coffee cooperatives of Tanganyika played in the rise of nationalist movements, this writer was not surprised to hear President Tubman in 1960 indicate to me that the people of Liberia were not yet ready for cooperative societies. In the absence of government support of cooperatives, the cash-crop economy was destined to remain under the control of foreign entrepreneurs and leaders of the Americo-Liberian class, with little competition from peasant cultivators. Very little was actually changed when Tolbert in his second year of office announced that the government would finance the creation of agricultural cooperatives in an effort to increase production of rice and other staples. The sincerity of his pledge was undermined by the hostility of the government toward the support which a political movement in the late 1970s gave to the modernization of traditional cooperatives, or *kuu*, among the Kpelle, the Krahn, and other groups in the interior.

The animosity of the Whigs toward tribal entrepreneurship even extended to the growing number of urban migrants who attempted to involve themselves in the money economy by "making small store" (establishing themselves as sidewalk peddlers). Tubman and Tolbert alike took action against the Lebanese traders who were supplying these small entrepreneurs with their razor blades, shoelaces, and chewing gum. Apparently the Lebanese found themselves in competition with Liberian officials, such as Stephen Tolbert, the brother of the president and his minister of finance, who wanted to monopolize petty trading.

TRADE UNIONISM

Superficially at least, the tribal people of Liberia made some progress in at least one sector of the economy. Since 1949, a year after Liberia signed the international treaty regulating Freedom of Association and Protection of the Right to Organize, trade unions began to operate in Liberia with assistance and encouragement from United States and Western European labor organizations. The government passed a labor code, and from time to time went on record expressing support of collective bargaining, an "active and free labor organization," and improvement in the conditions of labor in the agricultural, mining, and transport sectors of the Liberian economy.

How did one account for government encouragement of structures that could be—and indeed with increasing frequency were—used to challenge the existing power distribution in Liberia? The answer could be found largely in the Whig leadership's concern with its external image. Painfully aware that abuse of Liberian tribal labor brought about external intervention and toppled a government in the Fernando Po scandal of the late 1920s, the Tubman and Tolbert regimes attempted to avoid criticism by the International Labor Organization (ILO), and by the leaders of the American labor movement in particular. One of the cardinal techniques for Whig survival was the neutralization of a potentially hostile international environment.

Thus, the Liberian government did not oppose unions *per se*; they opposed only *effective* unions. One device for keeping unions ineffective was control of their leadership. The two major unions in the industrial sector during the Tubman period were the Labor Congress of Liberia and the Congress of Industrial Organizations (CIO) (assisted by, but not formally affiliated with, the American AFL-CIO). The former had long been under the control of T. Dupigny-Leigh, a member of the House of Representatives and formerly President Tubman's social secretary. Du-

pigny-Leigh's commitment to labor principles was curiously revealed in his statement in the 1960s that he did "not favor strikes." The larger organization, the
CIO, during much of the 1960s was under the leadership of William V. S. Tubman,
Jr. Without his sensing any conflict of interest on his part, the president's son had
also been in charge of labor and public relations for Liberian American-Swedish
Minerals Company (LAMCO), one of the principal foreign employers of Liberian
labor. He thus was able to use his leadership talents to work both sides of several
streets. The major union in the agricultural sector, the Firestone Rubber Tappers
Association, was formed only after a severe strike in 1966, and its officers were
either selected by Firestone or elected under company supervision. Moreover, to
prevent the possible consolidation of union power, the government in 1966 specifically forbade the formation of unions that would represent the interests of both
agricultural and industrial workers. Thus, the reforming zeal of President Tubman
considerably diminished in the face of the most blatant economic challenge to Whig
authority till that point. The precedent of elite control and co-optation persisted into
the Tolbert period, as A. B. Tolbert, the favorite son of the president, became head
of the Liberia Federation of Trade Unions (the reorganized CIO) and Emmett Harmon, a scion of one of the old Whig families and Tolbert's ambassador at large,
became president of the United Workers Congress. Efforts on the part of the rank
and file to oppose its own political leadership—as happened in the 1978 LAMCO
strike—revealed the true nature of the unholy linkage between management, government, and top union leadership in Liberia.[4]

In addition to controlling the leadership and organizational structure of unions
in Liberia, the government attempted to emasculate unions by outlawing their ultimate weapons: strikes and boycotts. Prior to the enactment of the Labor Code in
1963, all strikes were illegal until the dispute over wages or conditions of labor
had been submitted to a labor court. Inasmuch as no labor court had ever been
established, all strikes had been in fact illegal. The subsequent requirement that no
strike could be called without a decision by the government-established Labor Practices Review Board also frustrated union leadership. The board during the past has
been criticized by the ILO for either failing to meet when faced with a strike threat,
failing to issue a decision, or unreasonably delaying the announcement of its decision. Even when the board decided in favor of the workers, there seemed to be
no means for enforcing a judgment against a company.[5]

Legal or not, strikes by both organized and unorganized laborers had been, in
fact, increasingly frequent during the two decades preceding the 1980 coup. The
spate of a dozen or more strikes in 1961 alone almost equalled those for the entire
period from 1949 to 1960. The general strike of September 1961 occurred shortly
after President Tubman's son had gone abroad on his honeymoon, thereby leaving
the union leaderless. That strike set the pattern of unorganized violence on the part
of workers, followed by the use of government troops against strikers and the arrest
of union leaders on charges of sedition, and followed ultimately by the charges of
a "foreign" conspiracy. This scenario was repeated in subsequent strikes at the
Firestone and Goodrich rubber plantations, as well as at the LAMCO iron mining
operation at Nimba. Strikes also occurred with increased frequency at firms which

had no union representation at all. In 1976, for example, nine of the twelve major strikes occurred at companies that lacked unions.[6] The growing number of strikes prompted the Legislature to give President Tubman and his successor, William Tolbert, emergency powers on an annual basis to deal with unions and strikes, to mobilize for defense, and to take other extraordinary measures. Clearly, the Whig leadership feared the creature it had been compelled to spawn, and its actions in dealing with the striking unions indeed brought on the very international criticism by the ILO it had hoped to avoid by fostering unions in the first place. In any event, organization of industrial and agricultural workers during the Whig era did not substantially disrupt the labor recruitment tactics of the "Liberian ruling class which," as Mayson and Sawyer contended, "has always regarded the rural population as a large reservoir of cheap labour to be hired out to European capitalists, for public works and porterage duties, and for employment (almost gratis) on the farms of members of the ruling class."[7]

## COMMERCE AND THE AMERICO-LIBERIAN

The circumspect posture of the Whig leadership extended even to economic associations whose membership was limited largely to Americo-Liberians. In part, however, the explanation for the failure of the Americo-Liberians to involve themselves in major economic undertakings was historical. The disdain of the upper ranks of the Americo-Liberian community toward commerce and industry had been commented upon by observers of the Liberian scene since the middle of the last century. Much of it can be accounted for as responses to the paternalism of the American Colonization Society or to the attitudes against commerce imparted by some of the radical missionary groups. The distrust of commerce can also be traced to the circumstances which became painfully apparent in the last decades of the nineteenth century, as the once-prosperous Americo-Liberian shipping and "merchant princes" suffered almost total collapse. From a peak of 139 vessels from 1847 to 1871, the merchants saw their fortunes wither as a consequence of the depletion of camwood reserves, the development of aniline dies, the onset of global depressions, and the failure of Liberian frigates to compete with steam-propelled European freighters, making Liberian sailing ships obsolete. From that point onward at the end of the nineteenth century, commerce as a vocation declined and politics became "king."[8] The reputation of Liberia as a "maritime" nation emerged once again in the twentieth century, but in this case foreigners, rather than Liberians, flew the Liberian "flag of convenience."[9]

As part of the Tubman Open Door policy the Liberian government has been able to secure both revenues and development funds without having to make a significant investment in Liberian entrepreneurial skill in the registration of foreign ships under the Liberian flag. In serving as an "international Delaware," the West African republic has ranked among the seven largest maritime powers during the period since the 1950s, along with the United States, Britain, Norway, Japan, the Soviet Union, and Greece. The system of Liberian registry was actually created at the urging of the U.S. Joint Chiefs of Staff to encourage the building of ships which might be needed by the United States during wartime. The registration agency is an American-based corporation with headquarters in Reston, Virginia.[10] In 1982, despite the grave threat posed to the registration system by the uncertainties related to the 1980 coup, Liberia had the largest merchant fleet registered under its flag— twice the tonnage of its nearest rival, Japan. The Liberian government still secures a considerable revenue in this fashion from American and European shipowners, who take advantage of Liberia's lax laws on employment, unionization, safety, fees, and taxes.

The historical disdain of the Americo-Liberians for commerce could further be explained by the prestige that the legal and political professions had over business in the defense of the Republic against the external European colonial threat. Finally, the low status of commerce can be rationalized in terms of the inevitable politics of a small state. The system permitted the political leadership to control the economy to its personal advantage through its manipulation of tariffs, the granting of franchises and subsidies, and the letting of contracts. The rule for the ambitious businessman was to follow Nkrumah's later advice: "Seek ye first the political kingdom." The marked failure, for example, of the Liberian National Businessmen's Association in the last decades of the First Republic to constitute an effective force in Liberian politics was all the more curious when viewed against the remarkable growth which was taking place in the national economy during the Tubman and Tolbert eras. The fact is that few Liberians were permitted to become wealthy as a result of direct involvement in the management of agricultural, industrial, or commercial enterprises. Aside from petty trading, any significant economic involvement of the Americo-Liberian group came as a consequence of the influence and access that rewarded those holding political office. If they reaped the benefits of economic development, they did so as a by-product of their involvement in the affairs of the True Whig Party. They became part of what Sawyer and Mayson have referred to as "the false bourgeoisie," which comprised the administrative and para-administrative higher government officials who were not directly involved in the process of production and lacked real economic power—since that was still in the hands of expatriate managers.[11] Independent Liberian entrepreneurs who might create patron/client or other types of relationships with tribal traders or cultivators were severely discouraged since they posed a threat to Whig supremacy. This strategy, of course, antedated the Tubman and Tolbert eras. The high value placed upon politics by the Americo-Liberian elite had been recorded by many observers of the Liberian scene. Professor Frederick Starr in 1913, for example, wrote: "In Liberia there is a general desire to feed at the public trough; it makes no difference what a man is or what he has accomplished, every one is ready to go into politics; neither trade, agriculture, nor professional life restrains a man who has political opportunities presented to him; everybody of ability wants office."[12] Lebanese and other foreigners—who could be "controlled" through threats of deportation—filled the commercial void. Under both the Firestone agreement and the Tubman Open Door policy, the real economic entrepreneurs in agriculture, mining, and industry have been expatriate Americans, Europeans, and other foreigners.

Thus, instead of using his economic position as a base from which to make particularistic demands upon the political system, an Americo-Liberian leader exploited his political position to gain a greater share in the productivity of the economy. He became a politician first and a businessman second. An Americo-Liberian who attempted to reverse the procedure or who tried to remain entirely aloof from the political system was usually doomed to failure. The maverick was invariably driven out of the business or coerced into conformity by a series of devices: the refusal of the government to grant a visa or an export license, the harassing visit of a government auditor, or the strict enforcement of a long-dormant tax law. The obvious antipathy of the government toward both Americo-Liberian and tribal businessmen was acknowledged by several officials, who publicly agreed that as a "rule the government does not do business with Liberian businessmen."[13] More accurately, the government did not do business with *independent-minded* businessmen. Nominally, at least, the number of Liberian businessmen and rubber farmers seemed to grow significantly during the Tubman period. Invariably, however, the legal owners were the absentee national political leaders. The actual managers of these "private" concerns were, in many cases, West Indians or even alien Africans, from Sierra Leone or Nigeria, who were more subject to manipulation than were Liberian citizens.

Admittedly, a massive infusion of external capital had been required to get development under way. Americo-Liberians were quick to point out that their country did not have the "advantages" of the British Colonial Welfare and Development Act or the comparable French schemes, which stimulated postwar economic development in other African states. Nevertheless, the wealthier and better-educated Americo-Liberians could have invested both their talents and their money to a considerably greater extent in the development of their own country. Few were interested in the launching and practical management of new economic enterprises. Although they may have been prepared to underwrite foreign management, they were reluctant to lend funds to Liberian small businessmen. Similarly, despite much talk about cooperative societies and a development loan corporation for small businessmen, the Liberian government under the Whigs did not choose to disperse its patronage among Liberian small businessmen.[14]

The trend continued from the Tubman era to the Tolbert era as the following comparison of two surveys of Liberian businessmen will demonstrate. An analysis this author did of 386 companies registered in Montserrado County in the 1960s revealed that only 63 were owned by either Americo-Liberians or tribal persons. The Liberian-owned enterprises fell into two categories: petty businesses, such as a florist shop, a bar, a gift shop, a hostel, or a barbershop, run by a small entrepreneur who lacked real political stature; or a series of major firms owned—but not actually managed—by officials such as the secretary of commerce, the undersecretary for agriculture, the former secretary of state and adviser to the president on foreign affairs, and several members of the Legislature. Moreover, of the firms financed by Swiss, Swedish, and other European investors, the more successful ones included prominent Liberian officials on their boards of directors or retained lawyer-legislators to represent them in their negotiations with the government. One of the Liberian officials who was most deeply involved in the so-called private sector of the economy from the late 1950s until his death in 1975 was Stephen Tolbert, who held the office of secretary of agriculture and commerce under Tubman and minister of finance under his brother, President Tolbert. Both positions were crucial with respect to acquiring business interests—legally or otherwise. I was not startled in my interview with him, in 1961, when he stated that the government was considering subsidizing Japanese fishermen to establish an industry based in Monrovia instead of encouraging Liberian fishermen to expand their operations. Tubman himself had similar views. When asked about the larger number of Lebanese doing business in the country, Tubman responded that Liberians had no business acumen and should learn how to trade from the Lebanese.[15]

The continuity of the trend is revealed in a survey conducted by the Ministry of Commerce under Tolbert—a decade after my 1961 survey—which showed little change in quality of ownership. Of the 2,535 businesses identified in 1972, seventy-two percent (1,825) were owned by foreigners, and this included most of the major concessions, import firms, and other significant enterprises.[16] Sawyer and Mayson estimated that the year before the coup, five out of every seven firms were foreign-owned and even a business which was owned by government invariably had both foreign capital for its operations and was foreign-controlled through lucrative management contracts with expatriates.[17] The situation in the commercial and light-industrial sectors of the economy also applied to agricultural production: the major effort was under the direct control of Firestone, Goodrich, and other foreign concessionaires. Of the eleven leading independent rubber producers in my 1961 survey, all but two of the farms were owned by families of previous presidents of Liberia or by individuals who had served in the Tubman administration at one stage or another. Prominent in the top twenty-five producers were members of the cabinet, leading legislators, and even district commissioners. In many cases the district commissioners owned farms in the districts where they were serving, despite the explicit ban in the Liberian Code of Laws on conflict of interest with regard to the Department of Internal Affairs.

THE ALIEN SAFETY VALVE

How, then, does one account not only for the economic survival of Liberia but for its postwar economic boom? Aside from the tribal people, who were in the past employed on various projects on a compulsory labor basis and who still are employed largely at marginal wages, the economy of the Americo-Liberians was to a great degree subsidized by external sources. American and other missionary societies from the outset provided funds, equipment, and personnel for the bulk of the education and health services in Liberia. The capital and managerial skill required to exploit Liberia's agricultural and mineral resources were secured from foreign sources, with Firestone Plantations and various mining and other concessions owned and operated by Americans, Germans, Scandinavians, Swiss, and other non-Liberians. In the view of some analysts, the presence of expatriates associated with the multinational firms had little direct affect on Liberian culture, inasmuch as the expatriates tended to live in tight enclaves and refused to transmit their managerial

and other skills to the local population.[18] One researcher suggested that the Grän-
gesberg Company ("Gränges"), the company that operates LAMCO, did make an
effort to apply Swedish welfare policies in its Nimba mines. Its sincerity, however,
was called into question during the handling of the 1965–66 LAMCO strikes.[19] At
an earlier stage the major concessionaires in the absence of existing talent, felt
obliged to train Liberians for management or skilled technical posts in their enterprises. This gradually ceased when the government continued its practice of hiring
away the better-trained personnel at the end of the training course to perform jobs
in government. In the long run, moreover, the failure of the government to insist
upon a Liberianization of the economy worked to the detriment of the Americo-
Liberian ruling class and foreign economic interests. The Whig elite could not
forever insulate itself against a violent nationalist reaction to this situation by both
the tribal element and the lower ranks of the Americo-Liberian community.

The Liberian control over the concessionaires appeared to become firmer in the
Tolbert years. Each renewal of an agreement, for example, set up more stringent
regulations regarding the exact areas for exploitation, the type of production allowed,
the conditions of labor, the extent of taxation, and other details. The government
also insisted upon ownership of a considerable fraction of the company shares and
extra provisions regarding scholarships, positions on the board of directors for
Liberians, and other benefits. Needless to say, the benefits were often monopolized
by the Americo-Liberian ruling group, and very little trickled down to the masses.
For their part, the concessionaires raised their demands by insisting that labor union
activity be curtailed or that workers' compensation legislation not be enforced.
Firestone, whether inadvertently or by design, ensured itself against future nationalization by distributing free rubber seedlings to the "honorables." The processing
of the rubber still remained a Firestone enterprise, however, and thus a strong
coalition was formed between the concessions and the leading politicians.

The exclusion of Liberian small businessmen was further evidenced in the field
of merchandising of commodities. This activity during the Tubman period remained
largely in Lebanese hands, although in the Tolbert era their numbers were augmented
by Indians, West Indians, Nigerians, and other "alien" Africans. Even the taxi
trade, in actual practice, became at the end of the First Republic an increasingly
non-Liberian occupation, with Guineans and others operating the cabs, which may
have been owned directly by Liberian politicans or indirectly by Lebanese who used
Liberians as "front men." Except for some very small shopkeepers and the Mandingo traders ("Charlies"), the commercial activities of Monrovia and other urban
centers have remained dependent upon the Asians and alien Africans. As indicated
above, their presence serves as a safety valve against revolutionary change. Yet
each year the price of their presence in Liberia continued to rise as new devices
were erected to redirect some of the profits into government revenues or the pockets
of Whig officials. One measure enacted in the late 1960s required all shopkeepers
in the country to deposit $10,000 in Monrovia banks as "caution money" to cover
any commercial dishonesty. Most Lebanese and others continued to do business,
and the higher costs of operations were simply passed on to the tribal and lower-
class Americo-Liberian consumer.

This tendency of the True Whig leadership to rely on an "alien" safety valve persisted during the tenure of the First Republic despite the various foreign aid programs of the American and other friendly governments which were providing capital, technical skill, and education on an increasing scale since the end of the Second World War. The consequences of this were as true on the eve of the 1980 coup as they were when first noted by the economic survey team of Northwestern University in 1962. The Northwestern study suggested that:

> It is only a slight exaggeration to say that the professional, managerial, and entrepreneurial labor force in Liberia is divided neatly into two groups: Liberians work for government, are owners of rubber farms, transport facilities, and buildings, provide legal services, and to a small extent medical and commercial services. Foreigners are overwhelmingly predominant in staff positions in iron ore, rubber, and timber. When Liberians are employed by concessions, they most frequently act as nonresident advisers in law, public relations, and advertising.[20]

This heavy reliance upon alien personnel led the Northwestern group in 1960 to refer to the economic experiment in Liberia during the Tubman era as a case of "growth without development." A decade later, in 1970, roughly 40 percent of all payments in wages, salaries, and benefits in the Liberian economy went to the 50,000 workers in the foreign concessions.[21] Since not only the managerial staff were predominantly Americans, Europeans, and West Indians, but many of the workers were from neighboring African countries, much of the wealth generated from these enterprises left the country in the form of repatriated salaries, money orders, and purchased goods, and the country lost the advantage of any skills which had been developed in Liberia when the expatriates departed.

Obviously, the alien supporters of Liberia felt that there were worthwhile goals to be achieved by their continuing to buttress the economy. Each venture, however, brought an exaction for the Americo-Liberian leadership. Even the missionaries, whose goal had long been the winning of converts to Christianity, were required by law to establish schools before the missions could pursue their calling. Each new concession agreement or renewal of an old agreement brought increased benefits to the Whig-controlled government or new positions and enterprises that would accrue to the Whig leadership. The advantage for the Whig Party in dealing with alien entrepreneurs rather than middle-class Liberians was that the former were in the country on sufferance. As aliens (and in the case of non-Blacks this meant permanent aliens, for they are still ineligible for citizenship), the twenty thousand Americans, Lebanese, Europeans, and Israelis were not able to own real estate, engage in certain reserved occupations, or become involved in the political process as members of a political party or pressure group. The depoliticization of the most significant groups in the Liberian economy thus appeared to serve as a safety valve for the Whigs against a tribal-based revolution achieving its goal via the economic route.

Few Liberians—particularly those identified as lower-status Americo-Liberians or tribal persons—were permitted to develop significant economic careers independent of a prior role in the True Whig Party. The poorer settlers and tribal persons could participate in the new economy, but largely as unskilled or semiskilled laborers. In contrast, the leading political families within the Americo-Liberian class reaped some of the major internal benefits of foreign development. They did so through acquisition of shares in the foreign companies; through membership on the boards of directors (including all the perquisites but few of the real responsibilities); through scholarships for their children to study abroad; and through outright extortion of the Lebanese merchants and other more vulnerable expatriates.

## Religious Structures

As with economic structures, the primary concern of the Americo-Liberian elite was focused on the potentially divisive role of Christianity within the settler minority itself. Other than their fear of the Poro (discussed below), the settlers gave relatively little thought to the traditional religions (that is, non-Christian or non-Muslim) which were still vital to roughly 60 percent of the tribal people. These were locally based religious systems and presented no particular political challenge. Americo-Liberian concerns regarding the roughly 20 to 25 percent of the citizenry who were Muslims, on the other hand, were quite explicit during the nineteenth and early twentieth centuries, and efforts were made until the Tubman era to contain Islamic penetration of the hinterland areas. A persistent and more threatening concern was the potentially independent role of Christian religious associations and syncretistic churches in the Liberian political process under the First Republic. Curiously, despite the suspicion concerning foreign missionaries noted previously, a loose form of interlocking directorates ensured that the clergy of most Protestant churches, the lay organization within the Episcopal and Roman Catholic churches, and the officers of the YMCA and other semireligious societies remained under Whig Party control. It was possible for a small community preacher to use his pulpit as a springboard for political advancement, or for a very prominent religious leader, such as Bennie Warner, who was at the time the presiding bishop of the Methodist Church, to be tapped as the vice president under William Tolbert. In most instances, however, the process was reversed. Almost by right, prominent political figures could claim high office in a religious organization. Thus, William Tolbert, who in 1966 was serving as Tubman's vice president, also served as international president of the Baptist World Alliance. Earlier he had been elected president of the Liberian Baptist Missionary and Educational Convention, emerging victorious over a competitor who was only a member of the House of Representatives. Another Tubman era member of the Legislature, Representative J. J. Mends-Cole, was elected head moderator of the Presbyterian Church. In fact, many of the Protestant ministers, to maintain a decent standard of living, divided their time between their congregation and a government job. Hence, their lack of reforming zeal was reflected in both their religious and their political roles. In addition to churches, it is worth noting that incumbents in the post of Worshipful Grand Masters of the Masonic Order in the last several decades before the 1980 coup included three presidents, one vice president, a speaker of the House, a chief justice and an associate justice of the Supreme Court, an attorney general, and other leading Whig officials. The head of the YMCA in the 1960s was the then-powerful secretary of the treasury.

Religious office undoubtedly reinforced the political standing of an individual, for the style of Liberian politics demanded that officials attend church and even preach sermons or read the lesson. The speeches of President Tubman, who was himself a Methodist preacher, were invariably laced with biblical references. When, for example, he was asked in May 1962 about his intentions regarding a fifth term, he sent reporters to their Bibles to discover the message of Isaiah 49:8 ("Thus saith the Lord: In an acceptable time I have heard thee, and in the day of salvation I have helped thee. I have preserved thee and given thee to be a Covenant of the people.") Certain churches, such as the First Methodist Church and Trinity Episcopal Cathedral, were regarded as "political" in the sense that some of the leading figures in the "honorable" class were members. A younger political leader, attempting to establish an independent base for movement upward in the political scale, would attempt to become the person of influence in one of the smaller churches in Monrovia. The correlation between religious and political office was certainly made evident to this author during his attendance at a meeting of the vestry of Trinity Episcopal Church in Monrovia. In a blatant fashion a man who only a few days previously had been removed from political office by the president found himself stripped by the vestry of his post as senior warden in the church.

The tendency to emphasize the linkages between Protestant Christianity and Americo-Liberian politics persisted until the end of the First Republic. As noted earlier, Tolbert, in seeking a vice president to succeed the late James Greene, who died in July 1976, turned to a cleric whose political sermons had been laced with attacks on official corruption and abuses of authority and who had led the campaign on rejecting a bill to legalize gambling. Thus, Bennie Warner, the presiding bishop of the United Methodist Church, was tapped as Greene's replacement.

No particular effort was made by the Americo-Liberian elite to control the Bassa Community Church and other syncretistic religious groups. There was, however, great concern in the 1920s about the spread of Islam into Liberia, but it was apparent during the Tubman and Tolbert eras that the Mandingo and other Muslims did not attempt to secure political objectives at variance with the objectives of the Americo-Liberian elite. It is significant that the "Muslim" leader who presented a petition for Tubman to run for a fifth term in 1960 was Momolu Dukuly. Five years earlier, when Dukuly was the Liberian secretary of state, he had traveled abroad to represent his county at the Methodist General Conference!

Despite the official posture, which insisted that Liberia observe a strict separation of church and state, this was obviously not the case. The Jehovah's Witnesses, for example, were arrested and harassed for failing to salute the flag. The members of the syncretistic Harris Church were also intimidated by authorities. Far from being neutral, indeed, the political leadership of Liberia regarded the churches as instrumental to the continuation of the existing caste relationship. In turn, reciprocity was expected: a good political leader was obliged to "raise the offering" in support of church activities. President Tubman's effort in this regard during one session of the Maryland County National Executive Council illustrated both his effectiveness and his "impartiality." It was reported that

> . . . in his hometown he sponsored a rally for Mount Scott Methodist Church of which he is a member and raised $15,000 in less than an hour. At the Mount Tubman Methodist Church built in 1899 under the pastorage of the late Reverend Alexander Tubman, his father, he assisted in raising $2,531.91. At St. Mark's Protestant Episcopal Church he raised $500. Whilst in Grand Cess he and his suite contributed $800 toward the Christian and educational efforts in that area. Of this amount the Catholic Church received $300 and the Robertson Memorial Methodist Church got the $500 balance.[22]

Finally, it might be noted, the Masonic Order, with President Tubman as chairman of its building committee, never really doubted that its splendid new temple on Mamba Point in Monrovia would be completed.

## Social and Charitable Organizations

Next to involvement in politics, membership in social organizations was the most dominant characteristic of Americo-Liberian public life. Indeed, membership in such organizations, as was true of religious participation, advanced and reinforced a political career. Conviviality and "running with a crowd" were marks of a successful politician. Advancement went to one who shared his good fortune with his fellows, who gossiped and publicly speculated instead of being introverted and secretive about his affairs, and who capitalized upon the friendships and knowledge he had gained through social interaction in securing his own position. In this way the elite preserved the kind of society in which the Americo-Liberians could continue to dominate. Most of the social clubs were small, a dozen or so members at most, and brought together a cluster of individuals of approximately the same age and from the same community. Many had ties which were formed in school. To a certain degree the members of a group rose together in the political system. Among the more important groups were several with such quaint names as the Crowd 15, the Hungry Club, the Saturday Afternoon Club, the Triple Six, the Crowd Three Times, Crowd 13, "Coba," and the Moonlight Sonata Club.

Involvement in charitable organizations served other functions. Participation as a sponsor of the Boy Scouts, the Girl Guides, the Red Cross, and other groups provided a political leader with a base from which he could demonstrate publicly his personal concern for the plight of the poor. One political leader in the Boy Scout movement was quite cynical about the benefits the office brought him. "People *do* contribute to the Scouts, you know," he said. "And I have gone abroad twice to present our case to the international headquarters [on recognition of this chapter]." Hikes, campouts, and the usual activities associated with the Boy Scout movement, however, were nowhere apparent. A leading officer of the Red Cross (a wife of a former president of Liberia), moreover, made a considerable personal profit from the sale of potatoes donated for relief purposes by an American naval vessel on a goodwill visit.

Thrift, credit, and social clubs similar to the Monrovia "crowds" were formed among lower-stratum Congo people and even among some tribal people who migrated to the urbanized centers. A Liberian War Veterans Association—largely tribal in membership—flourished in Monrovia. Such groups were permitted and even encouraged, provided that the leadership of lower-strata organizations abstained from using the group as a vehicle for political pressure. The Americo-Liberian rulers were far less permissive with respect to various associations involving the tribal inhabitants while still resident in the interior. The creation of social clubs involving only educated tribal youths in an area constituted prima facie evidence of subversion. An absolute ban prevailed with respect to traditional groups, such as the Leopard Society, which were organized to commit murder, cannibalism, and other crimes. Equally proscribed was the Mende tribe's Baboon Society, which in the immediate pre-Tubman era was implicated in an alleged plot to destroy the Americo-Liberian aristocracy.[23]

The most prominent and prevalent of tribal traditional organizations—the men's Poro and the women's Sande societies—were, however, permitted to function once they were assumed to have been brought under government control. The historic fears of the Americo-Liberians regarding the power of the Poro were not exaggerated. It was the Poro societies, after all, which fomented the Bai Bureh uprising of 1898 in neighboring Sierra Leone against the extension of British and Creole influence into the tribal hinterland of that dependency. The alliance launched in Liberia during the last century between the Whigs and the traditional chiefs, the political and administrative fragmentation of some of the larger tribal groupings, and other measures have been employed in emasculating the political powers of the Poro leadership. The licensing of *zoes* and other Poro officials and the naming of the Liberian president as the head of all Poros were assumed to have given the president an added popular base, as well as a measure of supervisory control. As educational, health, and other facilities of the national government were extended to the interior during the last decades of the First Republic, the functions of the Poro became more and more reduced. The recognition of the Poro societies became an important element in the Unification Program, similar to the pride in the Vai script, which the Liberian government was taking great pains to publicize as an example of indigenous African writing.[24] Once the Poro had been brought under a degree of political control, its bush schools, medicine, and community dancing were assumed to have kept the tribal people contented. The Americo-Liberians thus felt they could view the Poro with indulgence.

## Students and the Educational System

In the long run, students were to provide one of the key elements in accelerating the pace of genuine social reform in Liberia. This was evident in the Rice Riots of 1979 discussed in a later chapter. The confrontational role of students during the Tubman and Tolbert eras was a decided reversal of function for the Liberian educational system. Before the Tubman regime, formal education served as a significant reinforcing mechanism for the maintenance of the caste-like relationship that characterized the First Republic. Education had long remained the monopoly of the elite. Although the schools were staffed and financed to a great extent by American and other foreign missionaries, broad political control over the educational system remained largely in the hands of the upper strata of Americo-Liberian residents at the coast.[25] Missionaries, in obtaining the privilege of recruiting new members, had been required by the government to provide school facilities. Political intervention by the Americo-Liberian "honorables" was so strong that the missions were obliged to give preferred admission to the children of settler families even when the schools were located outside Monrovia or the other coastal towns. It was only in the period following the Second World War that missionaries were permitted to stake out new territories in the remote interior, in such places as Ganta and Bolahun. Only then was a tribal child given even a fair chance of a modern education. In some areas, such as the Kpelle districts in Bong County, the Lutherans, Methodists, and Episcopalians at the time of the 1980 coup were training the third generation of modernized Kpelle youth. This had a significant impact upon the quantity and the quality of Kpelle participation in the administration of the county.

There are dangers in overstressing the modernizing role played by foreign technicians and educators. Nevertheless, foreign aid groups such as the American Peace Corps have constituted dynamic forces for change, and it was probably only the prodding of the U.S. AID program with regard to the construction of new schools in the interior that partially corrected the gross educational imbalance between the coast and the hinterland. The Peace Corps volunteer provided one of the few examples to tribal children of a dedicated and impartial teacher who had no ulterior vested political or religious interest to pursue. The volunteer served as a full-time instructor rather than one who had to "moonlight" (often at the direct financial expense of his students) to secure a living wage. The Peace Corpsman's use of standardized English better prepared the student for his advanced studies at the university level. Significantly, the impact of the Peace Corps presence was frequently as strong upon the Liberian teachers as it was upon the students.

Although professionalism engendered a measure of social class solidarity among primary and secondary schoolteachers, political control over the school system remained fairly secure until the middle years of the Tolbert era, when opposition to crass politicization became pronounced. Until that time, the appointment of a teacher constituted a political act, and assignment to a particular institution was based upon the influence and political loyalty of the teacher's family. As with all other government employees, teachers were required to surrender a month's salary each year to the support of the True Whig Party. The eagerness with which school superintendents and principals left their posts to run for office or accept a nonacademic post in government was some measure of the low level of pay and professionalism even at the upper reaches of school administration.

The conservative and limited character of the educational system at the university had also been long apparent. The University of Liberia, founded as Liberia College in 1862, was almost entirely limited to the Americo-Liberian group prior to the 1950s. The curriculum was weighted overwhelmingly in favor of politics and the law, and prior to Tubman, almost no attention was given to practical matters such as agriculture, engineering, forestry, veterinary science, or commerce. Even during the period of my earlier research, in 1960–61, university lecturers in many instances "moonlighted" from elective or appointive offices in government, and the university's board of trustees included five senators, five representatives, and seven appointees of the president. Neither the faculty nor the board could be expected to challenge the fundamental structure of Liberian society. The students as well were largely products of the Establishment, and the graduation roster of the University of Liberia in the past read like a "Who Will Be Who" of future governments of Liberia. Friendship ties forged during their college days were directly responsible for the political success of members of a given graduating class, and this was a factor in maintaining Americo-Liberian elite solidarity. The four graduates of the class of 1944, for example, had by 1968 come to play a critical role in Liberian politics, holding the posts of secretary of state, director-general of national public health services, president of the University of Liberia, and ambassador to an important African state. Indeed, 80 percent of the surviving members of the graduating classes of 1934 through 1949 held significant posts in the cabinet, the Legislature, the more important ambassadorial positions, and the senior ranks of the bureaucracy in 1968. Regardless of subsequent educational experience abroad, attendance at the University of Liberia until the middle of the Tubman era, had been an essential stepping-stone for political success in the First Republic.

As long as the educational system remained small, it was possible to control its output in terms of preserving the status quo. The expansion of the primary and secondary school network into the interior called for a complementary expansion of the pool of teachers. This meant recruitment from one of three sources, each a potential threat to the regime: the tribal element; expatriates, who might be committed to idealism, materialism, or some other philosophy disruptive of Whig supremacy; or lower-economic stratum Americo-Liberians. The last group was viewed as constituting the greatest threat. Resentful of being deprived of their "heritage" and regarding posts in the interior as a form of exile far removed from the political and social rewards of Monrovia, the lower-class Americo-Liberians were frequently charged with exploiting the tribal people more than did members of the ruling aristocracy. Less interested in preserving a system that denied them their "just due," they tended to be less restrained in their arrogance toward tribal people.

Although the rising tide of student discontent did not crest until the Tolbert years, it was apparent even earlier that expansion of the foreign scholarship programs of the American, West German, Israeli, and other governments broadened the opportunity for tribal, as well as for Americo-Liberian, youths. The sheer magnitude of the scholarship programs made it difficult to limit the opportunities merely to deserving members of the upper strata of Liberian society. Increasingly, too, the terms of the grants emphasized training in engineering, agriculture, and other fields that contributed to the development of a pool of nonpolitical technocrats opposed to the inefficiencies of the existing political system. With this potential threat in mind, the Liberian government, beginning in 1962, insisted that all foreign fellowships were to be channeled through, and awarded by, the Liberian government.

Like those who went abroad, however, students who received their secondary or higher education within Liberia also constituted an equally disturbing element. In fact, by creaming off the progeny of the Whig elite for study abroad, the foreign fellowship programs increased the prospects of tribal youth and poorer Americo-Liberians securing admission to the University of Liberia and Cuttington College (now University College). Beginning with the late 1950s, strikes at Cuttington College and at the Seventh Day Adventist Academy at Konola provided some index of student restiveness. By 1963, Tubman had become so alarmed by the strident demands of students that he attempted to link the faculty and students at Cuttington, the College of West Africa (a Methodist high school), and the University of Liberia with an alleged military plot against his government. He labeled these institutions breeding grounds for "socialistic and subversive ideas" and put the leadership on notice that the institutions would be closed down if passions were not controlled. Tubman stated that he could not object to the socialist tendencies of his African neighbors (presumably Nkrumah and Touré), but that Liberians would "fight to the death any attempt to impose or force upon us what we consider a mystical illusion."[26] Thus, the student challenge to the Whig structures, which coincided with the confrontation with trade unions, was an additional factor in explaining why Tubman's posture on reform became less enthusiastic during the last seven years of his administration. By 1972 the strike became a political weapon in the hands of students wishing to make a symbolic point—such as the demand that Mrs. Tolbert's cousin be removed as President of the University of Liberia.

The crescendo of student dissent over the existing political and economic systems reached deafening proportions during the final year of the Tolbert regime—as will be noted in the chapters on the 1980 coup. Five years later—once the post-coup ban on politics had been removed by the military government of Samuel Doe—the political role of university students, faculty, and administrators manifested itself in a dramatic confrontational fashion. Student and faculty dissent was destined to be a long-term factor in shaping the politics of Liberia during the Second Republic.

# VI.

# The Single-Party System and Americo-Liberian Privilege

In defending their claims to govern the tribal people of the hinterland, the Americo-Liberian leaders had to concern themselves not merely with the twin threats posed by resistance of the tribal people and by the competing claims of the British and French in the neighboring colonies. Of equal danger to settler minority rule was the possibility of dissension within the ranks of the Americo-Liberian community weakening it during a moment of crisis. Thus, means had to be found to control the intense interest in politics and the tendency toward factionalism that have characterized Americo-Liberian society. The ultimate political solution to this problem was the emergence of a single dominant party, which maintained the solidarity of the settler community in the face of both internal and external threats. The True Whig Party monopolized politics during the period from its contested victory in the election of 1877 (made definite by the unchallenged triumph of R. W. H. Johnson in 1883) until the 1980 coup. Although dramatically different in its purpose and ideology from other contemporary dominant parties in Africa, the True Whig Party of Liberia inadvertently became the prototype for what is now a fairly typical institution in postindependence Africa.

### The Passion for Politics

An all-absorbing interest in politics and the organization of protest along factional lines had been evident in settler society almost from the establishment of the colony in 1822.[1] The Remonstrance of 5 December 1823, regarding the allocation of house plots in the settlement at Mesurado, provided the American Colonization Society with concrete evidence that the settlers were not entirely content with paternalistic government. The Remonstrance compelled the Society to publish the Plan of Civil Government of 1824, which set forth the powers of the Board of Agents with respect to the colonists. During most of the first decade, however, the acceptable political activity of the Americo-Liberians was limited to the right of assembly and petition and to the election of a vice-agent and two councilors, who were to advise the agent in the administration of the colony. The election of settlers to fill these three posts turned largely on the personal qualifications of the candidates.

In the election of 1830, a decided split in the settler community arose between those supporting and those opposing the Colonization Society's administration of the settlements. This tendency of elections to revolve more and more around issues rather than personalities became even more apparent as the number of elective offices increased. By 1835 a cleavage of interest became manifest between the more conservative agricultural groups in the upper settlements and the more liberal and commercial elements in and around Monrovia. It was not until the Commonwealth period (1839–1847), during which the settlers achieved a measure of self-government prior to independence, that a rudimentary party system actually emerged. The Reverend John Seys, who had been personally offended by Governor Buchanan's policy on the entry of duty-free goods for missionaries, organized an opposition party that conducted its attack on a number of fronts: in the legislative chamber, in public meetings, and through the columns of Seys's newspaper, *Africa's Luminary*. Seys criticized the administration for its policies and actions in the fields of health, relations with the tribal chiefs, foreign commerce, and taxation. Despite Seys's fanatic following and its occasional resorts to violence, the Seys faction found itself unable to dislodge the Monrovia group from control of the Commonwealth Legislature. Buchanan's successor, Joseph Jenkins Roberts, and other members of the pro-administration group remained in control during the transition to republic status in 1847. Although the opposition party apparently concurred in the decision of 1847 to break the ties binding the settlers to the American Colonization Society, it vigorously opposed the ratification of the proposed constitution and threatened to have Grand Bassa secede from the new state.[2]

Like the American Constitution, upon which it is modeled, the Liberian Constitution of 1847 made no specific reference to political parties or interest groups. "Factionalism" and "politics," moreover, seemed to have had the same negative connotations associated with these words that were held by James Madison in his tenth *Federalist* paper and George Washington in his Farewell Address. Interest groups and parties, nevertheless, were found to be as necessary to the functioning of the First Liberian Republic as they had been to its American antecedent. At the time of independence, the True Liberian, or Republican, Party had been launched by President Joseph Jenkins Roberts, and it managed to retain control of the national government until the election of 1869. The Anti-Administration Party, which rallied under the banner of Samuel Benedict in opposition to ratification of the constitution in 1847, never seriously threatened the Republicans. Although the Anti-Administration Party did not constitute a serious opponent, divisions arose within the Republican Party itself regarding the alleged domination by Monrovia and Montserrado County of the rest of the country. Curiously enough—given the origins of Liberia as a reaction against racism—the most divisive issue within the Republican Party concerned racial extraction. Roberts, an octoroon, was rejected in his bid for a fifth term in 1855 in favor of Stephen A. Benson. The latter was also of mixed ancestry, but he was considerably darker in complexion than was Roberts. Benson had the support of the poorer Americo-Liberians and the Congoes, who were the descendants of Congolese, Nigerian, and other Africans who had been taken from slaving vessels intercepted en route to the New World. Both the lower-class settlers and the Congoes felt discriminated against by those of "brighter" skin color.[3]

By the election of 1869, issues of skin pigmentation and ancestry split the solidarity of the Republican ranks and brought to power the True Whig Party, which had been formed to oppose the lighter-skinned aristocracy. The candidate of the True Whigs, Edward J. Roye, was Liberia's first full-blooded Black president. His birth in America, his superior education, and his meteoric rise in Liberian commerce, as well as his distinguished service on the Supreme Court, made him sufficiently acceptable to the "brighter skinned" Republican leaders to bring about a peaceful transfer of party control. His promise of a program of national integration and his pledge to extend education to the tribal youth could have created a very different Liberia.

Roye, however, was a tragic figure. His personal involvement in the disastrous British loan of 1871 and his attempt that year to extend the presidential term of office from two to four years led to his ouster and to his subsequent death under mysterious circumstances. Whether he was executed or died escaping to a British vessel remains a matter of legend. A Republican junta forced his vice-president, James S. Smith, to accept the truncated term of office and ultimately brought ex-President Roberts back to the presidency. The Republicans were victorious in the next two elections.

*The Emergence of Single-Party Dominance*

With the electoral triumph of Anthony Gardiner in 1877 came the first of a series of Whig victories that continued unbroken until the 1980 coup. Whig domination, however, was not really assured until the election in 1883 of Hilary R. W. Johnson, the son of Elijah Johnson. The latter was one of the founding settlers and a military hero in the Americo-Liberian struggle against tribal resistance. Hilary Johnson, who was born in Monrovia, thus became Liberia's first "son of the soil" president. Although he actually had been nominated in 1883 by both the True Whig and the Republican parties, Johnson declared himself a Whig after the election.

Thus during the last quarter of the nineteenth century Liberia arrived at the pattern of one-party rule that became the political norm in most of the African states upon the achievement of independence in the 1950s and subsequent decades. Until the threat posed in the late 1970s by the Progressive Alliance of Liberians (PAL) and the Movement for Justice in Africa (MOJA) against the abuses of the Tolbert regime (discussed in chapter 12), the era from 1848 to 1883 was the only period of intensive interparty competition in Liberia during which the opposition had more than merely a theoretical chance of unseating the ruling party. Thereafter, Americo-Liberians found themselves captives of the very situation they had created. The expansion of the Republic into the hostile tribal hinterland beyond the coastal counties increasingly brought them into sustained conflict with the British and French, who were coveting the same inland areas. The need, then, for solidarity in meeting the dual threats of tribal rebellion and European incursions convinced the Americo-Liberian leadership of the value of the single-party system. Periodically, incidents such as the Kru uprising during the First World War or the League of Nations inquiry regarding charges of slavery in Liberia during the early 1930s reinforced the Americo-Liberian faith in the wisdom of this decision. When pressed to the wall, the party leadership made tactical retreats and jettisoned its standard-bearer, as it did with President William D. Coleman in 1900. It did so again with President Charles D. B. King and Vice President Allen N. Yancy in 1930 during the Fernando Po scandal. The strategy of using the True Whig Party as the vehicle of Americo-Liberian supremacy and solidarity remained intact until the 1980 coup.

The success of the True Whig Party as an institution stemmed not only from the fact that it maintained solidarity within the Americo-Liberian community but that it also—at least until the Tolbert period—adapted itself to changing circumstances. The Unification Program and the various political reforms introduced by the Tubman regime in response to rising pressures for change within West Africa in general found the True Whig Party manifesting both continuity and flexibility. Patronage, for example, continued to remain a primary weapon in keeping the party faithful in line and in undermining potential opposition by seduction of its qualified leadership. Under Tubman and Tolbert, however, the net of patronage was selectively thrown to bring in potential dissidents from the tribal sector as well as the younger, restive and politically ambitious Americo-Liberians. The creation of new county offices in the hinterland under Tolbert accelerated this process. If only to satisfy Liberia's many external critics, the True Whig Party had to provide the appearance, at least, of democratic reform.

It was the last-named consideration that compelled the leadership of the True Whig Party to provide more than perfunctory observance of the cardinal procedural norm of party systems in Western democracies, namely, elections. An election in the United States, Britain, France, and other Western democracies provides the victorious party with the popular mandate which it needs to govern as the legitimate spokesman of the people. During the course of an election the candidates, policies, and programs are subjected to severe scrutiny by the opposition party or parties which seek to gain the right or privilege of governing by displacing incumbent political party leaders. In most cases, the electorate has a viable alternative. The very vigorous nature of the election thus not only legitimizes the victorious party but it validates the political system itself by demonstrating the enthusiastic commitment of the populace to the existing arrangement for selecting a government.

It was for the foregoing reasons that elections during the Whig reign were more than perfunctory exercises. The elaborate and extended ritual of petitioning the president and other candidates to seek re-election, the lively nominating conventions, the campaigning that carried candidates into the smallest backwater communities, the colorful and often humorous political posters, and the element of suspense regarding the counting of votes on election day were designed to convince the casual observer that the results of the election were actually in doubt and that the opposition party had an outside chance of unseating the Whig candidates.

Little, however, was actually left to chance. The party feared that the license permitted the opposition during an election might encourage them to regard a substantial electoral showing as a precursor of better things to come. By being given free rein to exploit the cleavages within the ranks of the Americo-Liberians, an opposition party might have been encouraged to resort to violence to achieve its objectives. The assassination attempt against Tubman in 1955 revealed that violence had actually been resorted to on occasion when the opposition felt that the channels for orderly change of government personnel were closed.[4] This attitude surfaced again in the months preceding the 1980 coup.

The mechanism of control over the electoral system under the True Whig Party began with the naming of the elections commission. In theory the commission was nonpartisan, and the facade was maintained by the requirement that members were required, when appointed, to renounce all party affiliations. True Whig dominance, however, was assured by the proviso that the president not only name the chairman and the Whig Party representative to the commission but also select the third member from a list of candidates submitted by the opposition parties. One of the key duties of the commission was the determination of whether a candidate or a party was entitled to a place on the official ballot. In 1951, for example, the Reformation Party was declared an illegal group by the commission and denied the right to contest Tubman's bid for a second term. The Reformation Party had been formed by dissident Kru under the leadership of Didhwo Twe, once considered a close friend of President Tubman. In 1955 the Legislature made the decision easier for the commission, outlawing by statute both the Independent True Whig Party and the Reformation Party "because of their dangerous, unpatriotic, unconstitutional, illegal, and conscienceless acts. . . ."[5] Both parties supported former President Edwin Barclay, who had decided to challenge the successor whom he had hand-picked for the post of president in 1943.

## *Restrictions on Public Dissent*

Even if an opposition group were permitted a place on the ballot, the Whig Party's near-monopoly over the principal channels of communication had the opposition at a decided disadvantage. Under the Tubman and Tolbert regimes, the government-owned *Liberian Age* and *Liberian Star* as well as the privately owned but government-subsidized *Daily Listener* had observed almost a conspiracy of silence with respect to opposition parties that threatened to be even moderately successful in their appeal.[6] Journalists who worked for the government press, moreover, found themselves on occasion being held "in contempt of the Legislature" or in other ways punished by any unsanctioned criticism of government policy or a member of the "honorable" class. Many journalists—even those with credentials from some of the leading schools of journalism in the United States—complained about the low prestige accorded the Fourth Estate in Liberia. Even the government-employed newsmen were treated with suspicion and disdain by the central core of the True Whig elite. Indeed, in 1966 the editor of the government-owned *Liberian Star* was imprisoned for "improprieties" which were never clearly defined. Imprisonment was an even more vehement and frequent fate of opposition editors who found themselves running afoul of the highly restrictive and capriciously enforced libel law, which gave the president and other leading officials of government immunity from ordinary criticism.

Liberian political history during the First Republic was checkered by the suppression of private newspapers, but historian Svend Holsoe suggested to this author that the suppression only became systematic during the administration of Edwin Barclay (1930–1944). This may have been an overreaction to the domestic turmoil which followed the Fernando Po scandal. In any event, the trend of oppression continued under Barclay's successors with the suppression of independent newspapers such as *The Friend* (1954) and the *Independent* (1955) and the arrest of their staffs. The editor of the *African Nationalist* lingered fifteen years in prison before his release in 1966. Albert Porte, who died in 1986, was an inveterate and irrepressible pamphleteer in Montserrado County. Because of age, family esteem, and the political utility of some of his criticism, Porte was able to escape with little more than a brief jail sentence, dismissal from his job, or public rebuke by the press or the Legislature during the Tubman era. It was only during the Tolbert period that more severe measures—including a massive civil damages suit brought by Stephen Tolbert, President Tolbert's brother—were taken in an effort to silence this "eloquent gadfly."[7] There are other pieces of evidence, too, which suggest that a certain amount of "loyal" criticism was permitted in the editorials, letters to the editor, and even straight news stories, providing that the political leader criticized was not of very high rank or the policy too vital to the stability of the regime. Indeed, it was strongly suggested in Machiavellian terms that Tubman and Tolbert often encouraged press criticism as a circuitous means whereby the president could put a miscreant official "on notice" without having to do so directly.

In addition to governmental censorship, the opposition party and its leadership found itself subjected to various forms of harassment. Didhwo Twe, the Kru leader who challenged Tubman in the election of 1951, was obliged to flee the country on the eve of the election.[8] In his final election speech, Tubman charged that Twe's hands were "stained with the blood of treason, rebellion and sedition. He has been unfaithful and recreant to his trust as a Liberian citizen."[9] Twe fled from Liberia and remained in exile in Sierra Leone until 1960, when Tubman granted him "pardon and freedom from prosecution."[10] His major sin, apparently, was to emphasize too strongly his Kru antecedents. Tubman's next opponent, ex-President Edwin Barclay, found the efforts of his coalition of Independent True Whig and Reformation parties in 1955 also equated with treason to the Liberian state. He found his campaign impeded by an official investigation, with a vague charge of attempted murder being leveled against him.

Finally, throughout every campaign the activities of the opposition partisans were reported to the president by his "liaison and relations officers," who were stationed in every county and territory in the Republic. The duty of these officers, according to the Liberian code, was to provide for "the prevention of subversive activity and dissemination of dangerous propaganda."[11] The secretary of the treasury had a statutory mandate to provide for their salaries.

Public criticism of the True Whig Party was regarded as a threat to the solidarity of the Americo-Liberian community, exposing it to challenges from the tribal majority. Public disagreement raised the spectre of a dissident settler group tipping the political scales in its own favor by forming an alliance that crossed the cultural line dividing the Whigs and the tribal element. Public dissension also tarnished the image of the "New Liberia" which the leadership was attempting to project in its intra-African relations. It was especially offensive when criticisms of Liberia were made abroad. Former Attorney-General C. A. Cassell found himself disbarred for life for having criticized the Liberian judiciary at the Lagos Conference of Jurists in 1961. His remarks, oddly enough, were less offensive than the indictment against the same judiciary by A. Dash Wilson upon assuming the office of chief justice a few years previously.[12] The continuing official sensitivity to critical remarks made by Liberians abroad is reflected in the harsh treatment that the Doe regime meted out to a former minister of finance, Ellen Johnson-Sirleaf, following a speech which she made in Philadelphia during the summer of 1985, in which she referred to some Liberian officials as "idiots."

## The Function of Elections

If an opposition party perservered till election day under the First Republic, there was still no assurance that its partisans would be permitted to vote or that their votes would even be counted. In the 1955 election the ballots cast for the Independent True Whig Party were counted in only two counties. If the ballots of an opposition party were counted and a majority were recorded, there was no assurance that the victory would be officially recognized. After the 1931 election in Maryland County, for example, the Legislature, in a naked display of power, simply refused to seat the candidates of the People's Party, who had defeated the True Whigs by 1,676 votes to 367.[13]

Nonetheless, Liberian elections under the First Republic were not entirely meaningless. There was, first of all, the observance of constitutional norms, which apparently had a high value to the legally minded Americo-Liberians. Secondly, it did provide for at least a biennial discussion of the party's goals and permitted new generations to be socialized to the purposes and leadership of the party. Not only politics but the personnel of government did change as a result of this active discussion. Following each election the president considered that he had a new mandate and shuffled executive appointments without having to justify dismissals and additions as he would have had to do if he reorganized his administration in midterm.

The most significant function of elections in Liberia under the First Republic, however, was the maintenance of a good image abroad. Despite Whig trepidations about elections and despite the measures taken to emasculate the opposition, Whig leaders publicly insisted that opposition was healthy for the Republic. On the eve of both the 1955 and the 1959 elections, for example, President Tubman indicated that he was going to vote for his opponent, "even though it may not be in accordance with the law. . . ."[14] His opponent, Circuit Court Judge William O. Davies-Bright, was a True Whig running as an Independent on the policy of "sincerity, purity, and peace." He stated after the election of 1955 that had he known of Mr. Tubman's voting for him, he would have voted for Tubman. With only 16 votes for Davies-Bright and 244,937 votes for Tubman, the former had very few to spare! In the election of 1959, Davies-Bright increased his constituency to 55 voters to Tubman's 530,566. As the judge stated, he only ran in response to Tubman's call for "fair and friendly competition." (Not inappropriately, the party symbol on the ballot for Davies-Bright was a sheep). Largely in response to a suggestion from President John F. Kennedy, Tubman permitted token opposition—at least during the campaign stage—in 1963 in his fifth bid for the presidency. By 1967 he no longer felt it was necessary to continue the ritual, or else he felt that an opposition campaign could be a threat to stability in view of the wave of strikes in 1966. Similarly, Tolbert ran unopposed in the election of 1975, feeling that he had no need to engage in the charade of an opposition—so sure was he of his popular support.

Despite its almost complete annihilation of opposition party movements, the Whig leadership abhored overt violence and extended controversy. Indeed, the rancor following the election of 1955, which led ultimately to an assassination attempt against President Tubman as well as the subsequent indiscriminate prosecution of members of the opposition, was rare for Liberian politics.[15] Typically, the "hand of forgiveness" was extended to dissident Whigs who led opposition movements. This was a well-established pattern in Liberian politics. In Liberia's first election as a republic, Joseph Jenkins Roberts named his defeated opponent as the first chief justice of the Liberian Supreme Court. In 1912, following a bitterly contested election of the preceding year, President Daniel Howard named his opponent president of Liberia College and subsequently chief justice. Again, during Tubman's first administration he went so far as to establish a coalition cabinet by naming leaders of the Unit Whig Party and the People's Party to executive posts, including the very important position of secretary of the Department of Interior (later restyled Internal Affairs). The experiment was short-lived, however, for it had the undesired effect of giving second parties public status and access to patronage. In 1966, Tubman personally went to the prison cell and pardoned one of the individuals convicted in the 1955 assassination attempt. One of Tolbert's first actions after succeeding to the presidency upon the death of Tubman was to free all political prisoners. Several were even appointed to high office.

## Structures of the True Whig Party

### INTERNAL PARTY ORGANIZATION

The True Whig Party, from 1877 until the 1980 coup, was the only political organization in Liberia that functioned on a continuing basis. From the foregoing commentary, it seems obvious that opposition parties were highly personalized affairs, organized to compete in specific elections and rally under the banner of a dissident Whig. In at least four instances in this century, the opposition leader had been a former president. The hastily contrived campaign staff was disbanded once the party had met its inevitable defeat, and a new band of dissidents took up the dissident cause in a subsequent election. Although there was a measure of continuity in leadership in the People's Party between 1923 and 1927, the repeated use of popular opposition labels gave a false impression of continuity between, for example, the Republican Party of 1883 and the Republican Party of 1911; the People's Party of 1927, of 1943, and of 1979; the Unit Whig Party of 1935 and of 1943; or the Reformation Party of 1951 and of 1955. The informality of opposition party procedures was illustrated by the "convention" of the Independent True Whig Party, which was formed in 1955. A hundred or more dissident Whigs met in the home of ex-President Edwin Barclay to nominate him for the presidency. So pressed was Barclay for fellow partisans that the convention nominated candidates for the Legislature without receiving their approval.

Opposition politics was normally an affair of the more politically alert counties: Montserrado and, occasionally, Maryland. In the remaining areas dissent was subject to greater restrictions by the ruling families, who were very much aware of their minority position vis-à-vis the tribal people. Normally, too, the opposition party concentrated upon the main political prize, the presidency. For this reason the opposition parties seldom made an appearance in the biennial elections for the Legislature.

In contrast to the ephemeral organization of the renegade Whigs, the apparatus of the True Whig Party survived more than forty-five national elections since its founding in 1869. There were various principles of organization evident in the party effort. During the Tubman regime, for example, various specialized wings, based upon age or sex, were formed to give additional foci to party activities. The primary principle of organization, however, was geographic. The extension of legislative representation and almost universal suffrage to the people of the hinterland meant that potentially every voting precinct within the Republic could be organized into a local chapter of the True Whig Party. The local chapters were loosely affiliated into what were, in effect, two separate Whig parties. The first was the National Whig Party, which met every eight or four years to nominate presidential and vice-presidential candidates. The second was the county or territorial Whig Party, which met at least every two years in convention to nominate candidates for the Legislature. The autonomy of each convention was revealed in 1959 at the county conventions, which met after the national convention had renominated President Tubman. Proposed resolutions endorsing the nominations made by the national conclave were objected to by various delegates as an attempt on the part of the county party to "review the decisions of the National party."[16]

THE NATIONAL CONVENTION

The national convention met every eight or four years, depending upon whether the president was in his first or a subsequent term. Normally, the meeting was held in Monrovia during January, more than three months in advance of the May elections and more than eleven months before the beginning of a new administration. A symbolic break with this practice came in the national convention of 1975, which nominated Tolbert for what was to be his first term in his own right. Since it cost the party little in terms of real power but demonstated Tolbert's much-advertised concern for the development of the hinterland counties, the convention was held in Lofa County. During the present century, the choice of a national convention regarding a "standard-bearer" was seldom an issue, inasmuch as only twice since 1912 was "lame duckism" a problem for the First Republic. The principal open question for the convention was the nomination of a vice-presidential candidate. The "dumping" of a vice president by the president did give the convention a greater choice in the selection of this candidate than it had in the naming of a national standard-bearer. Only four times in the present century had an incumbent president decided to retire and permit the convention to name a candidate. In fact, nomination was a pro forma ratification of the incumbent president's choice.

At least publicly, the conventions of 1919 and 1934 seemed to be lively affairs, with several contenders competing for the votes of the delegates. In 1943, Clarence Simpson, S. David Coleman, James F. Cooper, and Louis A. Grimes were actively considered, and various individuals were placed in nomination. Actually, the *African Nationalist*, a leading paper during the Barclay administration, provided a clue regarding Barclay's possible choice through its detailed reporting of every movement of Associate Justice William V. S. Tubman during 1940 and 1941. More than fifteen months before the convention in 1943, the editor picked Tubman as the leading aspirant and noted that Tubman "has the whole of Maryland County, and not a minor part of Montserrado, and everywhere his name is heard, it has a captivating charm, because he is a natural mixer of men, good manners, and some persons say—liqueurs."[17] Although the convention choice was apparently determined in advance, the intraparty struggle at the convention compelled Tubman to accept Simpson as his running mate and to name members from the opposition party to his first administration. Thus, a latent function of the national convention at the time of a succession was to reveal the lines of factionalism within the party.

The ineffectiveness of the national convention as a constituent body that made decisions independently of those arrived at by the party leadership was revealed by the flexible rules regarding membership in the convention. There was no allocation of a fixed number of seats to county and territorial units of the party. There was an informal understanding regarding those whose Whig credentials were in order and who therefore should be permitted to attend the convention. The number of delegates could run from as low as three to four hundred, as in 1959, to several thousand, which was the case in 1955, when Tubman wanted to undercut the threat posed by the candidacy of former President Edwin Barclay.

The national convention performed other, less-publicized tasks. The party platform, for example, was formulated by leaders of the party and presented for approval. The relative unimportance of the platform was revealed in the failure of the leading papers to report its contents. Finally, the conventions elected the officers of the True Whig Party, who assisted the president in the management of party affairs between conventions. The national chairman, the vice national chairman, the general secretary, the general treasurer, and the other elected members of the executive committee not only constituted the trusted friends of the president but also tended to represent the Old Guard within the party.[18] The executive committee of the party also included the president, leading members of the cabinet and the Legislature, and influential private citizens who the president felt should be included from time to time. The committee was loosely structured and its proceedings and significance varied according to the whim of the president, the de facto head of the True Whig Party.

## THE NATIONAL CHAIRMAN

Following an occasional American pattern, the national chairman of the True Whig Party was frequently given the office of postmaster general, although a recent chairman was president pro tempore of the Senate and the incumbent at the time of the 1980 coup had served in various executive posts. The national chairman of the party under both Tubman and Tolbert did not, however, possess the same power in the field of patronage and other essential party matters that chairmen and general secretaries enjoyed before the presidency of Arthur Barclay (1904–1912). The resignation of President Coleman in 1900, for example, was in great measure forced by the public stand taken against Coleman's hinterland policies by T. W. Howard, who was national chairman of the party and treasurer of the Republic, and his son, Daniel E. Howard, who was at that time party secretary and governor of Montserrado County. Daniel Howard, in turn, was national chairman at the time of his election as president in 1911. His knowledge of patronage allocation and party decisions permitted him to consolidate his position as president quickly against the attempt of the strong-willed and very popular former President Arthur Barclay to exercise power behind the scenes following his retirement. It was Howard's experience, undoubtedly, which brought about the eclipse in the power of the national chairman and left the office in the hands of those who demonstrated a strong personal allegiance to the president. Aside from his role in the investment and allocation of party funds and in the mediation of contests over candidacies for seats in the Legislature, the chairman's duties related largely to the organization of the national convention, the management of the presidential campaign, and the appointment of registrars and other election officials.

## GEOGRAPHIC UNITS OF THE TRUE WHIG PARTY

The constituent body for the county and territorial units of the True Whig Party was the biennial convention that nominated candidates for the Legislature. In the case of the hinterland counties and territories, the selection of representatives was accomplished quickly. The county conventions at the coast, on the other hand, were much more active gatherings. This emerged from the absence of clearly demarcated senatorial or representative districts, which compelled the convention to adopt a single at-large slate for the county—a device which prevented opposition inroads being made at the polls. Certain principles evolved to limit the intraparty struggle. In the case of senators, there was, until the mid-1960s, a fairly rigid rule that ''each side of the river'' within the county was to be represented. Secondly, there was an unwritten rule that each senator and representative was entitled to a second term, so that the issue of succession was foreclosed for eight or four years, respectively. Although the tacit counterpart of this second rule was that no legislator was entitled to more than two terms, Speaker of the House Richard Henries actually continued in office from 1944 until deposed by the 1980 coup. Other influential legislators also served for more than a decade, and Tubman made it explicit to a group from Montserrado County in 1962 that ''there is no limit to the number of times a legislator may be re-elected to the House of Representatives.''[19]

One electoral issue that regularly generated intraparty conflict was representation in the House of Representatives for the various geographic areas within the coastal and hinterland counties. Letters to the editor of the *Liberian Age* reflected the general discontent over this problem, which had implications of intertribal animosity in the interior and interfamily struggles for supremacy among the Whigs at the coast. As a consequence, it was not always possible for an outsider to predict the outcome of a county convention. In 1959, for example, at the Sinoe County preconvention caucus, Representative William Witherspoon turned back the challenge of H. C. Williamson, the inspector of mines, by 223 votes to 84. Although Witherspoon's name was supposed to be the only one presented to the county convention to represent the precincts involved, the convention ended up nominating Williamson.[20] Although the appearance of decisional autonomy was thus maintained, contradictory evidence suggests that in this and other instances the national party leadership maintained a firm hand over the county convention proceedings and actually crushed attempts at rebellion on the part of the rank and file. There was, for example, the statement in the 4 March 1955 issue of the *Daily Listener*, which was owned and edited by Charles C. Dennis, nominee for the House of Representatives of the Montserrado County Convention. The *Listener* stated that the ''result of the nomination was a bedrock conclusion that had been reached a day previous when shrewd politicians of the True Whig Party met at a caucus held at the Executive Mansion, the seat of the TWP standard bearer.''[21] There was also the Grand Bassa Convention of 1959, whose unanimous choice of a senatorial candidate was vetoed by the national party leadership. A second convention had to be held to renominate the incumbent senator, who had irritated his constituents by his failure to visit Grand Bassa between sessions. Tubman justified the reversal of the convention's original decision on the ground that there had been a violation both of the two-term rule and of the stipulation that both sides of the St. John River were to be represented.[22]

There was no established pattern in the election of officers for the county organizations. The chairman could be the senior senator or senior representative or could hold an executive position, such as county superintendent. The chairman as well as the secretary and other key officers were usually acceptable to the leading families within the county. In the case of Montserrado County, which occupied such a pivotal role in Liberian politics, the confidence of the president was a key factor in selecting party officers for the county organization.

At the lowest level of party organization was the local branch, which could either be limited to a single town or embrace all of the towns and precincts included within the vaguely defined representative districts. The most obvious function of the local branches was to pass resolutions supporting presidential and legislative candidates. A new aspirant to office usually made his case to the national leadership on the basis of the number of resolutions he had received from local branches of the party within his area. Certain local chapters of the party constituted very powerful units of the national and county party, and control over the organization was essential for the future of key politicians. Speaker of the House Richard Henries, for example, maintained his national influence through his chairmanship of the vital Monrovia local party, a position that he assumed in 1944 and held until the 1980 coup.

## SPECIALIZED UNITS OF THE PARTY

In the last years of the Tubman era, geographic units of the True Whig Party were supplemented by the establishment of specialized units to mobilize the energies of individuals who might not be adquately represented in the county or national parties. In 1959, for example, the Young People's Political Association of the Whig Party was formed in Maryland County and spread to the other counties. The youth association held its own convention shortly after the national convention met in 1959 and was active in legislative elections. There had been little likelihood that the association would become a focal point for opposition to the Old Guard. President Tubman's personal secretary (and reputed illegitimate son), until his death in 1962 in an auto accident, was the first national chairman of the group.

A second specialized organization was the inevitable outgrowth of the granting of female suffrage during the Tubman administration. The Liberian Women Social and Political Movement was formed in the 1950s by Sarah Simpson George, the sister of Tubman's first vice president and wife of one of the more influential representatives from Montserrado County. The chairman of the movement at the time of the 1980 coup was Doris Banks Henries, the wife of the speaker of the House. Its primary goals were those of interesting the women of Liberia in politics and agitating for greater representation of women in the government of Liberia.

## PARTY FINANCES

The method of financing the True Whig Party remained substantially the same for several decades, although the details changed. Raymond Buell in 1928 reported that the treasurer of Liberia automatically deducted 10 percent of the monthly salary of every government employee until the expenses of the preceding presidential campaign were met.[23] Doris Duncan Grimes, the wife of the former secretary of state and daughter of a former cabinet officer, indicated in the 1950s that a yearly "tax" was levied upon every public employee to the extent of one month of his salary collected over a two-month period.[24] There were other ways in which the party coffers were replenished. Following his nomination, a candidate was expected to make generous contributions to the national and county parties. The loser in a bitter party struggle could also make a public offering to the party to heal the breach and retain his True Whig Party membership in good standing. Finally, the Lebanese businessmen and other foreign entrepreneurs were expected to contribute to the party in the form of cash or by picking up the tab for party and official entertainment. There had never been a public accounting of party funds. Various sources indicated that a European trading company in Monrovia served as the bank for the party.

In contrast to the True Whig Party, the patronage-poor opposition party had to be financed largely out of the personal fortunes of its leaders. Every effort was made by the Whig leadership to drain the opposition of its limited resources by constant litigation. In 1955, following Edwin Barclay's attempt to have the Legislature investigate the conduct of the election, the Legislature decided that Barclay should pay $19,000 as the estimated cost of the farcical and futile special session.

It is apparent that throughout much of Liberia's history under the First Republic the True Whig Party's monopolization of the electoral process served as a strong bulwark of Americo-Liberian supremacy within the state. The techniques of controlling the machinery of organization, the procedures of nomination, and dissemination of information were learned well by the founders of the modern Liberian state. The facade of democracy and adherence to legalistic norms were maintained without surrendering to the possibility of open conflict within the ruling group—a situation that could only benefit the tribal majority.

This facade of democracy and the monopoly over the political process so long enjoyed by the descendants of the settlers were under seige in the late 1970s. Ironically, those who challenged the system were the very tribal youth and lower-strata Americo-Liberians and Congoes who had been the beneficiaries of Tubman's creative economic and social response to the changing political climate in West Africa.

# VII.

# Family Linkage and Elite Solidarity

Nominally, the Tubman reforms that introduced almost universal adult suffrage and extended the principle of direct legislative representation to the hinterland area created a potentially open political system. Even though electoral competition was effectively limited to a single party, in terms of identity and some form of participation, the True Whig Party had been converted from an elite to a mass-based party, with membership open to every adult citizen of the Republic without regard to cultural, ethnic, or religious origins. Even the property qualification for voting was largely ignored until the contested 1979 mayoralty election in Monrovia. The only residents of the country excluded from politics were the twenty thousand aliens, many of whom had come to Liberia to engage in religious, educational, and economic activities. The majority of the aliens came from other African countries or the West Indies, and thus even they were eligible to vote once they had become naturalized citizens. The 1847 constitution denied citizenship only to persons who lacked African ancestry.[1] (This was one clause, incidentally, that was retained in the 1984 Sawyer Constitution.)

On the face of it, the Liberian precoup political system was highly democratic. The procedures whereby one became a member of the True Whig Party, and thus eligible for participation in national politics, were purposely vague. Although individuals were in some cases formally "read out" of the party by a local or national convention of the party due to the commission of certain "disloyal" acts, the more positive action of affiliation was apparently not signaled by any formal step on the part of either the member or the leadership. Any person could call himself a member on the basis of his or her participation in precinct or other local meetings of the party, by contributing funds to the organization or to individual candidates, by marching in parades, by voting even in uncontested elections, and by providing other outward signs of partisanship.

## Circles of Involvement

Like participatory political systems anywhere, the Liberian political system can be viewed as a series of concentric circles, in which the outermost ring is least influential and the circles closer to the core have greater influence over the course of events and the actual decision-making process. Universal suffrage and the extension of the representative principle to all regions of Liberia in theory made each participant in the outermost circle of political involvement (adult male citizens) equal in the election of a president and members of the Legislature.

Qualitative differences between residents of the coastal areas and those of the interior continued to exist, however, despite the fact that under Tubman and Tolbert the tribal residents were permitted to elect members to both the House of Representatives and the Senate. Despite nominal equality, many of the legislators from the four interior counties of the tribal hinterland were either Americo-Liberians or had strong family, political, or legal links with the members of the Whig elite. The extension of the county system in 1964, which supposedly eliminated any subordinate administrative status that might have resulted from the former provincial system of rule in the hinterland, nevertheless found settlers with disproportionate political and economic influence in the inland counties.

Discrimination continued, moreover, due to the fact that the four interior counties, which had been created out of the three hinterland tribal provinces, possessed 54 percent of the population in 1962 but were given only eight senators, as opposed to the ten controlled by the Americo-Liberian residents of the original five coastal counties. The disparities in representation were even more apparent in the lower house of the Legislature. With 54 percent of the population, the interior counties had only 20 percent of the representation. Montserrado County, which includes Monrovia, was a special case of overrepresentation, with 23 percent of the seats (nine of forty) despite having less than 16 percent of the population. Moreover, Montserrado County (along with Maryland County during Tubman's administration), tended to monopolize the important committee assignments and chairmanships in the Legislature.

The second circle of political involvement was narrowed to those who participated in the nominating conventions for members of the Legislature. Although in theory a county convention of the True Whig Party was open to all who could make the journey to the county headquarters, the conventions were often limited to the elected and appointed officials of the Liberian government, former officials, prominent private citizens, and the camp followers of the leading committed candidates. Although the semblance of decisional autonomy was maintained, for the most part the nominations were agreed upon by the True Whig leadership in advance of the convention. In the selection of representatives from the interior counties, the "conventions" frequently consisted of informal gatherings of leading chiefs, influential Americo-Liberians who had farms in the counties, and representatives of the Department of Internal Affairs who collectively decided upon "safe candidates." Unfortunately for the tribal people included within the newly drawn boundaries of the original coastal counties in 1964 (when the county system was extended through-

FIGURE 4    Circles of Political Involvement during the Tubman-Tolbert Eras
of the First Republic

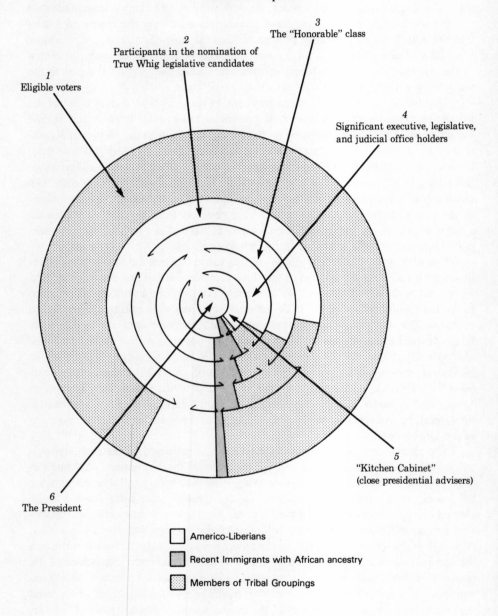

out the Republic), their influence was even less than that of their kinsmen in the hinterland and led to demands that the Gola, the Kru, and others have separate county status. This was a cause which only came to fulfillment in the post-1980 coup period. One irritant in the post-1964 system of representation was the abandonment of the traditional practice of dividing the Senate seats within each of the coastal counties between the towns and the less-developed areas. The rural areas tended to be even more underrepresented.

The third circle of involvement consisted for the most part of those who held, had held, or were "eligible" to hold important posts in the government of Liberia. This was the main bulwark of the True Whig Party and of the Americo-Liberian class, even though access was permitted to some few not born into that class. This group tended to monopolize civic deference, and entry into the circle was indicated by the use of the title "Honorable" on public occasions or in the local press. Another outward and visible sign was the "knighting" of outstanding citizens by the president, a practice initiated by Anthony Gardiner in 1879 with the establishment of the Humane Order of African Redemption. The most recent addition to these odd trappings for a republic was Tubman's creation in 1955 of the Most Venerable Order of Knighthood of the Pioneers of Liberia.

The actual holding of office under the First Republic (the fourth circle) was not merely important for the prestige of members of the "honorable" class. Public office provided access to the important sources of patronage: government jobs for one's relatives, attorney's fees for representing the government in cases and contracts, the "forgiveness" of taxes and payments for services of government, and the payment of a "dash" by any citizen who received a service or favor from a public official. Even more significant forms of patronage, however, appeared in the period of rapid economic growth under Tubman and Tolbert. Free housing and automobiles, frequent trips abroad on government business, preference in the awarding of foreign scholarships, access to the president's favor in the acquisition of land in the tribal hinterland, and the privilege of receiving exorbitant tax-free rentals on private buildings leased by the government were all part of the patronage system that enabled the Americo-Liberian class to maintain a higher standard of living than could the rank and file members of the tribal majority.

Passage from the outermost to the second circle of political involvement was essentially a transition in culture. It indicated movement from a circle in which the majority of individuals were still largely committed to tribal loyalties and traditional norms to a circle dominated by those who had accepted the cultural standards and the political, economic, and social structures of the Americo-Liberian community. Passage from the second to the third circle, however, was based upon much more narrowly ascriptive grounds. Participation in the third circle was monopolized largely by those identified by birth, marriage, or lifestyle with the nineteenth-century pioneer founders of the Liberian state.

## The Significance of Family Ties

The significance of the extended family in the politics of the tribal societies of Liberia has been dealt with previously. Prior to the publication of my *Liberia: The*

*Evolution of Privilege*, there were only brief references in the ethnographic and historical literature on Liberia with respect to the importance of the family as a political, economic, and social institution within the more Westernized sector of the population. Indeed, it was my contention that an understanding of family ties among the Americo-Liberian class was crucial to the understanding of the national political system. An Americo-Liberian attached great importance not only to the bilateral ties that he acquired at birth, but also to those he later acquired through his own marriage or even the marriage of his siblings and his children. There was a decided tendency within the leading members of the Americo-Liberian community to adhere to the principle of endogamy, or marriage within the larger settler group. As a consequence of birth or marriage one became a member of a series of corporate family groups that not only imposed obligations but also provided political allies in times of crisis or advanced one's standing in the community. Family allies, moreover, provided information regarding changes in the political climate and access to the spoils available to the True Whig leadership.

Detailed knowledge of his own ties and the family ties of others became a *sine qua non* for the social and political survival of an ambitious individual. Birth and marriage were political events as much as they were social or economic ones and established broader bonds than those among two or more individuals. Americo-Liberians interacted not solely as individual personalities but as representatives of family groupings. On the basis of the affiliations of an acquaintance, one cultivated his friendship, avoided his company, or regarded him as a political neutral. Knowledge of family ties also played a peculiar role in maintaining the supremacy of the nontribal over the tribal community. Only occasionally was entry to the Americo-Liberian inner circles of influence permitted to naturalized Liberians and to Gola, Grebo, and others who had undergone a measure of acculturation. The self-conscious efforts in the waning decades of the First Republic to publicize "mixed" marriages only served to emphasize the exceptional character of the act.

Obviously, romantic love was certainly a factor both in marriage and in the establishment of informal liaisons. Marriages within the "honorable" class were not mechanistically arranged in the Oriental manner. Attachments formed in school, both at home and abroad, in church gatherings, and in other social settings could actually be stronger considerations than class identification and family loyalty in choosing a mate. Nevertheless, an examination of the genealogies of the leading personalities of the political hierarchy in Liberia in the 1960s demonstrates that connubial ties constituted an important element in the political advancement of the ambitious individual. Although a certain amount of permissiveness across class lines was tolerated in premarital and extramarital situations, the marriages of an "honorable" and of his siblings and children provided formal political alliances undertaken with an eye to the future. Thus, when the son of a cabinet member married the daughter of a senator or an ambassador, he was assured two patrons who would be concerned with his political advancement. The corollary to this situation was that divorces and remarriages were as much instruments of political realignment as they were of social readjustment. There was a strong correlation between the severance of marriage ties and the decline in the political fortunes of the family of one of the parties concerned. Divorce became one of the weapons of group conflict, and the "sequential monogamy" practiced by many of the leading political personalities bore a rough approximation to the rise and fall in the political fortunes of the families of past, present, and prospective marriage partners.

An analysis of the genealogies of the political leadership of Liberia over a period of years provided the objective observer as well as the active participant in the First Republic with an explicit map of the Liberian political terrain, plotting not only the immediate strength of a given family and its patrons but also a history of the upward and downward movement of various families in the political scene. A political genealogy for 1960–1961, for example, indicates that there were three primary pockets of national strength, each dominated by a dominant patron: President William V. S. Tubman, Vice President William R. Tolbert, and Secretary of the Treasury Charles B. Sherman.[2] In the case of the first two, a significant link was forged in 1961 with the marriage of William V. S. Tubman, Jr., to Wokie Rose Tolbert, the daughter of the vice president. By 1968, however, the Cape Mount Shermans (as opposed to the Grand Bassa Shermans) were noticeably absent from the roster of the political elite, and they seemed destined to join the ranks of the Cassells, the Colemans, and others whose political fortunes had waxed and then waned during earlier stages of the Tubman presidency. By 1968, President Tubman was more firmly entrenched than ever (see figure 5). A cluster of his own relatives (the Barnes, Yancy, and Brewer families of Maryland County) and his wife's (the Padmore, Grimes, Wiles, and other families associated with the Barclays) dominated the executive, legislative, and judicial branches of government and controlled a good portion of the diplomatic posts as well. Although the Tolbert group at that time had been affected by the removal of Stephen Tolbert to a position of influence outside the formal government apparatus, it remained strongly entrenched in a number of key financial offices. Similarly well placed in the area of finance and economic planning were the relatives of Richard S. S. Bright, a former diplomat who used his political influence to acquire a considerable share of the independent rubber market. Scattered throughout the chart on family and politics were representatives of families that had always played a substantial role in Liberian politics (the various branches of the Cooper, Dennis, and Gibson families) as well as smaller families whose influence was on the rise or decline. Space did not permit me to include several very significant new family clusters that in 1968 had been gathering strength during the preceding decade: the relatives of Postmaster General McKinley DeShield, Secretary of the Treasury James Milton Weeks, and Speaker of the House Richard A. Henries, for example.

With the accession of William R. Tolbert to the presidency in 1971 upon the death of William Tubman in an English hospital, the rules of family succession persisted. All that had changed were the names of the central actors in the political system, many of whom were the offspring, siblings, and cousins of the new president and his wife. The one significant difference, as figure 6 indicates, was the more direct involvement of the president's family in the new Liberian economic enterprises, many of which enjoyed monopoly status as a consequence of government patronage.

FIGURE 5   Family and Politics, the Tubman Era (1967–68)

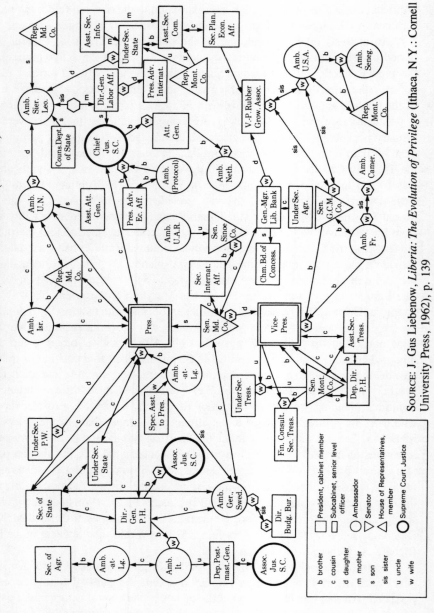

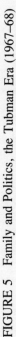

SOURCE: J. Gus Liebenow, *Liberia: The Evolution of Privilege* (Ithaca, N.Y.: Cornell University Press, 1962), p. 139

FIGURE 6   Family and Politics, the Tolbert Era (1971–79)

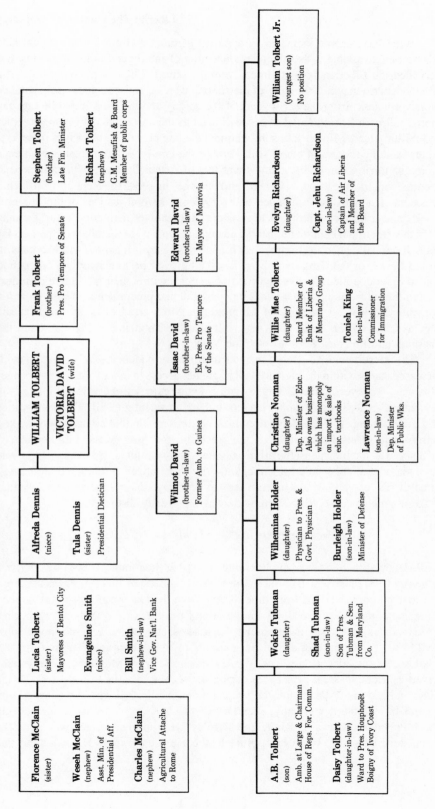

SOURCE: The Tolbert family tree and office-holders: an example of deep-rooted nepotism. Courtesy of *New African* magazine, May 1980 issue.

What has become increasingly apparent as more and more genealogical data has become available is that the interconnection of family and political interest has pervaded the Liberian system almost from the outset. There is no suggestion of a Great Scenario in which the rules of matrimony were established and rigidly adhered to; nevertheless, from the early years of the colony and the First Republic one can literally discern "presidential dynasties" such as the descendants of pioneer settler and military leader Elijah Johnson, who include one president, the wives of several others, and the in-laws of others still. Perhaps the family with the greatest resilience on the national scene in this century was that of Arthur Barclay, who emigrated to Liberia from the West Indies in 1865 and became, in 1904, the Republic's fifteenth president. His heirs have included two presidents, several justices of the Supreme Court, and a host of diplomats, legislators, and cabinet members. Mrs. Tubman and other important cabinet ministers and ambassadors were members of the Barclay clan. Regionally, certain families such as the Grigsbys in Sinoe, the Morgans in Grand Bassa, or the Gibsons in Maryland had greater prominence than others and tended to monopolize elective and appointive posts within their respective counties. Several families, on the other hand, enjoyed national preeminence. These included not only the leading families of Monrovia or Montserrado County, such as the Barclays, the Grimes, and the Kings, but also the Tubmans of Maryland and the Sherman and Freeman families of Cape Mount.

The recruitment of one's kinsmen to office provided the Whig patron with increased status within the party as well as greater access to other forms of patronage. This was, however, a double-edged sword, for it increased the vulnerability of the key patron vis-à-vis other family leaders and the president himself. The possibilities of a minor member of the clan committing an indiscretion that embarrassed the key patron were great. The position of the president, too, was considerably enhanced by his role as the indispensable arbiter of interfamily conflicts. He could, moreover, put a major challenger to presidential authority "on notice" indirectly by removing some of his lesser kinsmen from office. In this way, the equilibrium so essential to the maintenance of Whig supremacy was not greatly disturbed.

### New Entrants to the "Honorable" Class

While leadership in the third circle of influence (the "honorable" class) was derived primarily from those who had links with the early settlers of Liberia, it was apparent that new blood was added from time to time from the lower ranks of the Americo-Liberian community, from Black immigration from the New World or neighboring African states, and even from among the tribal sector of the Liberian population itself. Two of the earliest significant entrants to the "honorable" class from the tribal sector included Henry Too Wesley, a Grebo from Maryland County who served as vice president (1924–28) during the second term of President C. D. B. King; and Momolu Massaquoi, the Vai chief and intellectual who served as consul general in Hamburg, Germany, secretary of the interior, and postmaster general under Presidents Howard, King, and Barclay. His political career was abruptly terminated, however, when he aspired to the presidency in 1931, following the

League of Nations scandal. His initial rise in the settler-dominated society was facilitated by having married into the family of J. Jenkins Roberts and Hilary Johnson, two of Liberia's nineteenth-century presidents.[3] Thus marriage was not strictly endogamous with respect to the Americo-Liberian "ethnic group." Indeed, even prior to Tubman, the exclusion of the indigenous population from power was far from total. There were at least three ways in which persons of tribal origin could be accepted as members of the "honorable" class. For example, under the "ward" system, talented tribal youths who had been given to prominent Americo-Liberian families for care and training found one avenue to cultural assimilation. Although there were instances of abuse in which the ward differed only slightly from a domestic servant, there were also countless cases in which tribal youths had been adopted in the fullest sense and given all the privileges of education and access to politics afforded a full-fledged Americo-Liberian youth. One of the long-serving members of the Legislature was a tribal ward of former President Edwin Barclay. Also significant in this respect was the political career of Jackson Doe, who challenged Samuel Doe for the presidency in 1985. As a youth, Jackson Doe had been the ward of former Chief Justice Louis Grimes.

A second precursor of Tubman's Unification policy was found in the liaisons that Americo-Liberian males (and occasionally females) established with tribal persons, frequently without benefit of clergy. Fortunately for the offspring of such unions, neither illegitimacy nor the mixed character of one's parentage had social stigma attached to it in Liberia. Indeed, several leading members of the Tubman and Tolbert cabinets and of the ambassadorial group found it advantageous to stress the tribal backgrounds of their parents, and at least one appeared to be quite proud of the fact that he was considered a "wild oat."

A third form of assimilation of tribal persons into the Americo-Liberian elite came through co-optation of leading tribal personalities who were instrumental in establishing Liberian authority in their respective areas during the first century and a half of Liberian national history. These tribal leaders shared in the patronage available to Americo-Liberians, gained prominent posts in government, and had their children educated abroad. Although it had been politically expedient for these individuals to maintain their traditional connections, for all practical purposes they accepted the settler culture. The Mandingo tribesmen deserve special mention, since they had ultimately been made an auxiliary of the Americo-Liberian community despite their early opposition to settler expansion into the interior. Their talent in commercial enterprises had been appreciated by President Tubman, who encouraged them to emigrate from Guinea and other West African states. They enjoyed exemption from compulsory tribal labor, and they were not normally subject to the jurisdiction of local tribal courts but had been given their own chief and judges.

In addition to accretions from the tribal ranks, the Americo-Liberian community during most of the First Republic had a small but steady infusion of new blood from other African countries, the West Indies, and the United States. The Liberian government waxed and waned in its attitude toward Black immigration from the United States. The immigrants, who were frequently better educated and accustomed to more modern amenities, often tended to be hypercritical of conditions in Liberia.

Frequently, for them residence in Liberia was a temporary matter, and they often became disillusioned with affairs and moved to one of the newer African states or returned to the New World. Some of the fears held by the Americo-Liberians were revealed in October 1967, when a special commission was established to supervise the settlement of new immigrants from the United States. At a presidential news conference, Tubman indicated quite pointedly that the immigrant community from the New World should not be too large to be integrated into the existing framework of society. He noted further—with obvious reference to potential Black Muslim and Black Power immigrants—that Liberia would not tolerate any racial hatred or animosity, and that it would require the immigrants to pledge themselves to uphold the principle of separation of church and state.[4] During U.S. Vice President Hubert Humphrey's visit to Liberia in 1968, Humphrey greeted leaders of a group of 160 Black "Hebrews" who had settled at Ghabartella, 50 miles inland from Monrovia. They had emigrated from Chicago and regarded themselves as children of Israel who had come home.[5] Although my genealogical charts of 1968 indicated a number of West Indian Black males who had attained fairly high political office, I was unable to locate any American Black male immigrants in the upper reaches of the political hierarchy. Many of the Americo-Liberian officials, however, were married to Black American wives. It is highly significant that in 1962 the census takers identified only 231 of the 10,268 citizens of foreign birth as coming from the United States. The majority of new citizens came from Guinea (4,469), Sierra Leone (2,601), Ghana (1,359), and the Ivory Coast (754).

Under the Tubman regime, the elevation of persons of tribal origins and persons from the lower strata of the Americo-Liberian society into the "honorable" class had been steadily accelerated. The expansion of the bureaucracy, to cope with the vast economic changes and the creation of diplomatic posts in various quarters of the globe, placed a marked strain upon the limited pool of talent available from the list of the top fifteen or twenty families. The lack of French-speaking Americo-Liberians, for example, led the regime to recruit young, educated tribal persons whose homes were near the Guinean or Ivory Coast border for assignment to Liberian embassies in Haiti or the French-speaking countries of Africa. Other talents, such as a gift for oratory—so characteristic of the Liberian elite political style—became a prime factor in the political advancement of some tribal youths and poorer Americo-Liberians who were eager to leave their professions as teacher or preacher.

In a society which was increasingly concerned with technology, moreover, performance in a skilled role brought a measure of advancement for many tribal youth, members of lower-class Americo-Liberian families, and the descendants of the "Congoes." Indeed, not having the automatic assurance of a job or the access to privilege available to the "honorable" class, these individuals took their studies in Liberia or overseas far more seriously and tended to emphasize performance in securing and maintaining their jobs once they had returned home. The Congo or tribal youth acquired a more modern and broader world view—not one based narrowly on Liberia and its archaic system of elite privilege. The demands for skilled manpower meant that their numbers in the upper levels of the economy and the governmental bureaucracy were expanding relative to those who were the guardians of Whig hegemony. Given the increased complexity of society and the commitment to technology evident in government, the new industrial enterprises, and the private sector generally, these individuals became indispensable to the continued operation of the new Liberian society. Advice from this quarter of the bureaucracy was becoming increasingly necessary to the successful performance of Whig officials in dealing with their foreign counterparts, in negotiating with the foreign concessionaires, and in other matters. Increasingly, it was this group that was involved in the effective (rather than the formal) decision making. As will be noted later (chapters 10 and 11), the failure on the part of the Whig elite to recognize this new role and to reward it was one of the factors leading up to the social ferment prior to the coup of 1980 and the ready acceptance of the coup as legitimate.

Instead of rewarding merit, there was a persistence of the elite notion that those who advanced on the basis of merit alone or in spite of their tribal or alien background constituted potential threats to the regime. Advancement from outside the third circle not only constituted an attack upon the rules of political preferment but also invited the possibility of the new entrant's gaining a following among the tribal majority. This accounts for the early and occasionally ruthless political demise of officials who unduly emphasized their tribal antecedents and as a consequence achieved mass appeal. Several cabinet members during both the Tubman and Tolbert regimes suffered such a fate. The threat posed by the new entrant diminished if he was "legitimized" by the establishment of marriage ties with the leading families. This was obviously of value to him. It also helped maintain the system, for he acquired a vested interest in the preservation of the privileged status of the ruling group, as well as a group of in-laws who attempted to ensure that his newly acquired loyalties took precedence over his loyalties to his former tribe, kinsmen, or country. On balance, however, the appearance of change did not match the reality of the situation insofar as enjoyment of real political power was concerned. The members of Tolbert's cabinet, for example, in the last days of the First Republic still were dominated by settler names such as Dennis, Phillips, Sherman, Bright, Holder, Townsend, Tucker, Neal, Smith, and Clarke. The only ministry which had a fairly regular succession of persons with tribal antecedents as chief administrator was the Ministry of Education, with G. Flama Sherman (a Grand Bassa, not a Cape Mount, Sherman), Bernard Blamo, and Jackson Doe serving in all but the brief period when the post of minister was held by Advertus Hoff, a cousin of Mrs. Victoria Tolbert. One other minister with tribal links was permitted to hold the relatively apolitical portfolio of Information, Cultural Affairs, and Tourism—Dr. Edward Binyah Kesselly, who ran for the presidency in 1985.

Ironically, the very success of the Tubman and Tolbert efforts in expanding economic growth and the extension of public services to the hinterland entailed a dramatic increase in scale of the national bureaucracy. The global foreign policies pursued by Presidents Tubman and Tolbert further required a vast enlargement of Liberian official representation abroad. It was early recognized that the leading members of the Americo-Liberian elite alone could no longer provide the men and women needed to staff this enhanced governmental structure. Thus, the allocation of jobs inevitably involved not only those from the lower rung of the Americo-

Liberian social ladder but also the growing pool of tribal youth who had been educated both at home and abroad as a result of mission or government scholarships. Where possible, the Americo-Liberians attempted to reserve the key posts for themselves. It was undoubtedly a factor in the acceptance of the 1980 coup by so many educated Liberians that the allocation of jobs prior to the coup to those who were not members of the "honorable" class fell far below their expectations and such opportunities as were made available usually lacked the salary, fringe benefits, and job security accorded an identically trained offspring of an "honorable." A few more persons of tribal background did appear in the Legislature, the courts, and the cabinet of the Tolbert regime as well as in the second echelon in many departments. Lacking patrons, however, they might be removed for a trivial infraction of a rule while a scion of an "honorable" would suffer no more than a slap on the wrist for corrupt practices on a grand scale.

### The Cores of Greatest Influence

In analyzing the characteristics of the Whig Party leadership that stood at the fourth circle of political involvement—the significant officeholders in the executive, legislative, and judicial branches of the national government—the corporate "property" of the elite included far more than family ties. As a group, Liberian officials under the Tubman and Tolbert regimes had a greater per capita exposure to higher education than most of the leadership groups in the newer African states. The establishment of Liberia College (now the University of Liberia) around 1858–1862 gave Liberia a considerable educational lead over its neighbors. Its advantage in university graduates had been supplemented in the postwar period by the establishment of Cuttington College (now University) in the interior and Our Lady of Fatima College in Maryland, as well as by a veritable exodus of Liberian youths to study in the United States, Western Europe, Israel, and Asia under missionary, American government, and other types of scholarships. Although Tubman (and more recently Samuel Doe) did not receive university education, the use of the title "Doctor" indicated the high value placed upon even an honorary degree from the University of Liberia (or South Korea, for Mr. Doe). Increasingly during the decades from 1960 to 1980 the majority of the officials holding cabinet or subcabinet ranks not only had at least one college degree, but also had received some graduate education abroad.

One was impressed, too, with the youth of those holding key government posts under the Tubman and Tolbert regimes. Admittedly, many of the Old Guard continued to exercise influence in the party behind the scenes or even while holding government office. Speaker of the House Richard Henries, who was executed in 1980, demonstrated the latter point. Inevitably the occupants of government offices tended to monopolize patronage and hence power within the party. In 1962 the cabinet members in charge of the Departments of State, National Defense, Education, National Public Health Service, Public Works and Utilities, and Justice ranged between thirty and forty-two years of age. In 1968 the average age of the new cabinet was the lowest in this century. This situation was only slightly altered during the nine years of President Tolbert. The same youth and vitality were evident in the diplomatic personnel dispatched to the four corners of the globe to represent Liberia's growing economic and political interests.

Finally, as was suggested earlier, the innermost circle was characterized by a high degree of full-time commitment to politics. The preference for politics and the legal profession was clearly reflected in the degrees received by Liberian students at home and abroad and in the almost immediate pursuit of political office even by those whose scholarships had compelled them to take courses in geology, engineering, medicine, and other professions. There was, moreover—as indicated earlier—a decided antipathy or disdain for commerce and agriculture as one's primary occupation, although involvement in business increasingly became an expected by-product of one's political career.

The latter tendency was blatantly demonstrated during the Tolbert administration when members of the president's immediate family were heavily involved in corrupt business practices. The president's brother, Stephen, who served intermittently as secretary of agriculture and commerce under Tubman (1960–65) and minister of finance under William Tolbert from 1972 until his death in a plane crash in 1975, was a prime example. He used his official position, with all the instruments of persuasion and obstruction, to gain substantial control of many foreign and domestic businesses. Indeed, any private Liberian entrepreneur who seemed to be succeeding in a business that Stephen Tolbert coveted could be sure that export licenses would be delayed, government auditors would pay surprise visits, and that he might even be the victim of outright sabotage. The Tolbert family—through the Mesurado Group of companies—had almost monopolistic interests in the fishing industry, housing, food distribution, transport, catering, and even the sale of charcoal to the urban poor. The Tolberts had acquired tribal land in the hinterland with a vengeance.

It was at the core of political involvement, the innermost circles of presidential advisors and the presidency itself, that we discovered the real key to the future direction and tempo of change in Liberia during the First Republic. For at the center of all things political, social, and economic in Liberia under the First Republic stood the president. Under Tubman the institution had undergone a remarkable transformation, with the previous bases for presidential authority being irretrievably altered. His successor, William Tolbert, continued and extended this accumulation of power and authority in the office of the president.

# VIII.

## The Cult of the Presidency
### *The Tubman Imprint*

The subordination of economic and other interests to politics, the True Whig Party's monopoly on the electoral system, and reliance upon family ties as an instrument of political recruitment served as effective mechanisms in maintaining the supremacy of the Americo-Liberian community in a changing Liberia. The ultimate line of defense during the twentieth century in preserving an island of privilege in a sea of hostility had been the emergence of a strong president, who stood at the center of the circles of political influence (see figure 4). While the presidency continued to serve as a guardian of privilege, however, it also became, under William Tubman, the most dynamic factor in determining the pace, character, and direction of change. It was a trend that continued during William R. Tolbert's nine-year presidency. Tubman's predecessors defended the status quo by resisting change. Tubman—and to a certain degree Tolbert as well—preferred to manipulate the champions of the status quo in making a positive response to inevitable demands for change.

Tubman's long tenure in office (1944–1971) gave him an advantage over his predecessors in terms of making a significant impact upon the office, and this created problems as well for Tolbert, whose every act was measured in terms of how it fit the transformed image of the presidency established by Tubman. Tenure alone, however, cannot explain the dramatic changes in the institution after Tubman assumed office in 1944. His remarkable personality, his full knowledge of even the most minor detail of the political terrain, his pursuit of imaginative policies in the face of what had initially been a wall of opposition on the part of the Old Guard, and his ability to disguise tactical retreats as victories all became part of the story. Most important, he was the first chief executive of Liberia who attempted to be the president of Liberia instead of merely the servant of the Americo-Liberian community. This was the model that Tolbert attempted to emulate—indeed, *had* to emulate—during the final decade of the First Republic.

The emergence of the president as the dominant figure in Liberian national politics, with the consequent subordination of the other two major branches of the national government, was neither desired nor anticipated by the founding fathers of the Republic. Indeed, despite the long tenures of Joseph Jenkins Roberts (1848–1856, 1872–1876), Hilary Johnson (1884–1892), and other strong-willed presidents during the first fifty years of independence, this pattern did not crystallize until well into the present century. (See table 1.) In fact, until the 1930s, precedent suggested the contrary development. Of the eighteen men who held the office during twenty presidencies (two were elected for second, nonconsecutive terms), only seven (Benson, Roberts in 1876, Johnson, Gibson, Arthur Barclay, Howard, and Edwin Barclay) retired voluntarily. In an eighth case (Cheeseman) and that of Tubman himself, the president died in office. Of the ten remaining presidents, three (Roberts in 1855, Warner, and Payne in both 1869 and 1877) were defeated in their bids for reelection; one (Russell) lost the support of his party and was not renominated; one (Roye) was forcibly deposed; three (Gardiner, Coleman, and King) were compelled to resign under the implied or explicit threat of impeachment; and one succeeding vice president (Smith) was forced to accept a truncated term of several months until a new election could be held. Tolbert was the only victim of assassination, even though several attempts had been made on the life of Tubman. In addition to the eleven who lost power, at least one more—Garretson Gibson—was threatened by a mob calling for his resignation. He failed, however, to panic.

## The Growth of Presidential Power

A number of factors accounted for the growth in the powers of the president. Partly it was the result of a series of constitutional amendments to the 1847 provision that required the president to seek reelection every two years. It was only much later that—following an initial term of eight years—a president was permitted to run for any successive number of four-year terms. This not only freed the executive from recurrent intraparty struggles and campaigning, it also permitted him to launch long-range programs and to consolidate a personal following in the various branches of government. The president, too, had become one of the prime beneficiaries of the increasing effectiveness of the central government's administrative and military services and the improvement in transportation and communications. The regional administrative appointments of the government were increasingly subject to his firm control. An elaborate system of surveillance, including the employment of "personal relations officers" who reported directly to the president; *ad hoc* reviews of specific situations by the president or one of his subordinates; and the penchant of Tubman, in particular, to scrutinize vouchers of more than $250 also strengthened the president's hand in the political system.

The expanding dimension of governmental operation in Liberia as a result of foreign investment and United States government aid also became a significant factor. In a country where few offices were elective, where the civil service system existed largely on paper, and where the government was one of the largest employers of personnel, the power of appointment provided the president with a powerful political weapon. The expansion of governmental operations meant not only more jobs to distribute but also more perquisites of office that could be dispensed to reward the faithful, seduce the doubtful, and entrap the powerful opponents of the regime. Moreover, in a country in which the extended family had become an important political group, the executive did not limit the use of patronage to entrenchment of his own family. He used patronage to keep the leading families in a state of equilibrium so that no single group constituted a threat. This accounted for the "rapidly changing face" of the bureaucracy. When one contender and his family appeared to be gaining patronage and prestige, the family was actually increasing its vulnerability with respect to the president and other leading families. In this situation the president became indispensable as the arbiter of interdynastic disputes.

*The Presidency under Tubman*

The presidency became an indispensable institution in still another crucial respect. The external and internal threats posed to Americo-Liberian supremacy in the First Republic forced the descendants of the settlers to accept the solitary leadership of the president rather than that of the pluralistic and locally oriented Legislature. Indeed, the resignations of Presidents Gardiner (1883), Coleman (1900), and King (1930) were forced precisely because the incumbent president's actions exposed the settler community to foreign or tribal threats to the Republic. (See Table 1.) The critical importance of the president to the Americo-Liberian community became even more apparent during the administrations of Tubman and Tolbert. Tubman felt compelled to emulate some of his West African neighbors by casting himself in the role of a charismatic leader who could breach the social and tribal schisms within Liberia. There is little doubt that he had greater popularity with the tribal people than any president before him. Tubman's accessibility and his dispensation of personal justice, his respect for tribal customs, the ceremonial aspects of his Unification policy, and his informality on public occasions had a decided appeal to the indigenous element. It is questionable whether these things justified the erection of statues of Tubman around the country or whether they were sufficient to offset some of the obvious deficiencies of the Unification policy. Nevertheless, there was no other Americo-Liberian who had as popular a following among the tribal people, and, therefore, tribal challengers to the president's leadership were effectively denied their potential constituency.

Despite Tubman's prophetic announcement in January 1968 that this term in office (his sixth) would be his last, few people in Liberia really took him seriously. Indeed, he had made similar statements in 1964, 1960, 1956, and 1952. There were no individuals on the scene who could match Tubman's broad base of support within both the Whig and the tribal communities. The Americo-Liberians, for example, appreciated that their initial fears regarding the Open Door policy had not as yet materialized. Indeed, the policy had yielded considerable financial benefits for the elite without unduly mobilizing the tribal people in political terms. The descendants of the settlers appreciated, too, that Tubman's activist approach to international politics shielded Liberia from the pressures of neighboring African nationalism. Thus, long before Tubman's death the Old Guard had come to accept the new status quo.

## The President as Manager

While he became the dominant authoritarian figure in Liberian national politics, President Tubman was not a totalitarian dictator. A more accurate description would be that he had become the presiding officer of the Americo-Liberian ruling class and that at least until the political reforms of 1964, the president assumed the role of managing director of a moderate social revolution. Although Tubman manipulated the leadership of various family, regional, tribal, and other groups, he also depended upon them for support. The continuing problems of transportation and communication and the inefficiencies of administration (especially with respect to postaudits) left many independent pockets of political power throughout the system. The relative political autonomy of these groups forced the president constantly to placate his political opposition. The hand of forgiveness was always extended, and even those removed from office on serious charges or imprisoned for grievous offenses found that the gates of patronage were never completely closed. With luck, after a due period of grace, the penitent would be appointed to an even higher post in government. The president could not rely too strongly on his personal popularity as a weapon with which to control the political opposition. The insecurity of Tubman's charisma was certainly evidenced by the fact that much of what passed for expressions of popular support was either highly subsidized by government or was the result of legal and unofficial coercion. Any unpopularity was masked by the absence of an independent press and by the severity of the libel, slander, and sedition laws when it came to criticism of the president or his family.[1] Indeed, the very thin-skinned reaction which he manifested to any hint of criticism during his last seven years in office suggests that his reformist zeal had flagged and his popularity was increasingly on the wane.

## Adulation of the Presidency

Despite the remarkable imprint that Tubman made upon the Liberian presidency in terms of humanizing it and projecting the office into the pivotal role of balancing forces within the Liberian political system, there were two significant weaknesses that developed at an equal pace with the strengthening of the office. Both of these turned out to be troublesome to Tubman; they were literally and figuratively fatal to his successor. The first flaw was the cost to government and the private citizens of the adulation associated with the president. Sycophancy permeated the Tubman and Tolbert presidencies. It was marked by the erection of presidential statues at various points in the country; the naming of bridges, streets, and public buildings after the president or members of his family; the requirement that the president's picture be displayed in every commercial establishment; and the observance of public holidays to commemorate significant events in his life. At times the clamor that preceded the president on every public occasion bordered on blasphemy in its attempt to emphasize the extraordinary character of the president. With respect to Tubman, for example, the *Liberian Age* frequently published such contributions from its readers as the "Ten Commandments of Tubmanism," and its own reporters dutifully reported that during one of Tubman's appearances "blue heaven sent a light shower of blessing upon the partisans."[2] The adulation extended occasionally to Mrs. Tubman, who was greeted upon her return from a trip to Europe in 1960 by a huge banner in downtown Monrovia proclaiming: "Welcome Back Our Blessed Lady Antoinette." Victoria Tolbert was similarly given almost saintlike status.

Criticism of the high cost of presidential adulation began to mount in the 1960s and 1970s. One of the more onerous aspects of such adulation was the recurrent annual deduction made from the salaries of teachers and other public employees to provide increasingly more spectacular birthday presents for Tubman every November. In 1959 the celebrations were still of manageable proportions, with a few thousand citizens and foreigners attending a picnic given in the president's honor by Vice President Tolbert. The next year the president was presented with a new car, the following year a yacht, then a plane, and finally a series of public buildings: a library, a cultural center, and then a military academy. The site of the birthday celebrations rotated around the country, and each county vied to outdo the others. The people who suffered most were the public employees, who continually found their monthly paychecks depleted.[3]

Tolbert's "Rally Time" campaign in 1972–73 threatened to surpass even the efforts of Tubman in extracting pledges from the citizenry in an attempt to raise private funds for development. Although some of the projects reflected the president's stated objective of "self-reliance," the burden on the average citizen and public employees as well as the corruption associated with the handling of the Rally Time funds gave it a short life indeed.

The greatest single example of presidential adulation during the Tubman era was the new Executive Mansion. Perhaps it was indeed time that the Liberian government owned an Executive Mansion, for the previous one—like most public buildings in Liberia, including schools—was "rented" to the government by the "honorable" family (the Barclays) that owned it. Nevertheless, for a government with an annual budget of $27 million in 1960, it was somewhat questionable whether the country could afford one building that ultimately cost around $15 million. Tubman's instructions to the architect were simple: "It should be awesome." When faced with criticism, Tubman responded: "It is too fabulous for a country with economic and financial resources such as ours. . . . It is too good for me to live in, but not too good for a president of Liberia."[4]

Under Tolbert the scale of public adulation became more outrageous as birthday gifts from the nation ate heavily into the limited resources of low-paid government workers and the rural peasantry. Despite, however, his great start in continuing the humanizing of the presidency which had been initiated by Tubman, Tolbert seemed incapable of sustaining the momentum. His initial populist posturing gradually gave way to all the trappings of royalty, including the processions of limousines, the long lines of schoolchildren along his route of return from the airport, and the erection of statues and other monuments in his honor. Increasingly he became more guarded in his public appearances, and the huge fences surrounding his properties and the Executive Mansion were signs of a growing paranoia he had developed in his relationship with the people. He mingled less and less with the crowds. Increasingly, too, his rhetoric regarding the need for reform of the system seemed patently insincere, particularly when the observable realities differed so drastically from the sycophantic praise heaped upon Tolbert by the government-controlled news media, by the never-ending tribal delegations, from the interior, and by the pulpit pronouncements of Whig politicans-cum-pastors. Evidently sensitive, Tolbert lashed out quickly at public criticism of himself and his family. In response to pamphleteer Albert Porte's cataloguing in 1974 of Minister of Finance Stephen Tolbert's efforts to "buy the country," the president permitted his brother to bring a crippling civil damages suit against Porte.[5] In typical fashion, the presiding judge for the trial was Chief Justice James Pierre—Stephen Tolbert's father-in-law. Equally repugnant was Tolbert's failure to muzzle the arrogance of his son, A. B. Tolbert, who had dynastic ambitions. Indeed, on the CBS "60 Minutes" television show taped in Liberia in December 1979 (and brought back to Liberia in the form of video cassette tapes), A. B. Tolbert claimed not only that he would be the next president of Liberia, but that he hoped to become the president of *all* of Africa someday!

In more visible terms than the cold statistics that indicated a growing gulf between the Whig elite under Tolbert and the tribal masses was the aristocratic style of life adopted by the Tolbert family. The Executive Mansion was at least assumed to be the property of the Liberian people; "Bentol" was another matter, and it epitomized the blatant arrogance of the Tolbert family. When I first visited the Tolbert ancestral home in 1960 it was still called Bensonville. Located a few miles from Monrovia, it was then a humble village with a dirt road serving as the main street. The houses were built on stilts and constructed of wood and corrugated iron, with shutters instead of glass windows. It had probably changed little since the 1860s, when Tolbert's grandfather and other immigrants from South Carolina and the West Indies had settled there. During the nine years of Tolbert's presidency, however, Bentol—renamed to honor the incumbent president—had taken on all the negative imagery of a Palace of Versailles in the days of the Bourbons. Bentol had become a city with more than a score of opulent villas lining the well-lighted, carefully manicured boulevards. Each member of the Tolbert clan had his private estate with a high, steel picket fence and an elaborate security system designed to keep out the poor. Bentol came complete with a private zoo and an artificial lake for motorboat racing and waterskiing. The scale of the new post office and other public buildings of what had become the new county seat of Montserrado County was out of all proportion to the small elite population to be served. The stark contrast between the splendor of Bentol, on the one hand, and the squalor of Monrovia's slums and the general poverty of any up-country village, on the other, could—in the words of one of my Liberian friends—"be described in a single phrase: *utterly obscene!*"

## The Issue of Rotation in Office

The second major concern of the Tubman presidency was whether his transformation of the office had made it virtually impossible for any other person adequately to fill the role and whether the constitutional rules of presidential succession would have to be abandoned in the event of a vacancy in the office. The issue of continuity and stability versus a healthy rotation in political leadership is one that troubles not only most African states today; it is one that concerns even societies that are more expressly committed to democratic norms. Few strong chief executives encourage competition for the mantle of office, preferring to have weak colleagues serve in the standby role of vice president or deputy head of state.

Despite historical efforts to limit the tenure of Liberian presidents and the number of terms an individual could serve, the constitution during the present century at least never stood in the way of a strong incumbent succeeding himself indefinitely. Indeed, the style of Liberian politics in the twentieth century seldom permitted the question of succession to be raised. It was assumed that a president would attempt to succeed himself even when the constitution seemed to deny him this privilege—as it did during Edwin Barclay's second term and William Tubman's first term. From the outset of his term of office, the incumbent was besieged with resolutions from local chapters of the True Whig Party urging him to seek reelection. Indeed, the first resolution urging Tubman to run for a *fifth* term came two weeks after his renomination by the party convention in 1959 for a *fourth* term.[6] During his final term he had already received a petition from the women's branch of the party asking him to stand for a *seventh* term in 1972.

A further lesson of the twentieth-century presidency in Liberia was that presidential authority was not divisible. This was a lesson that ex-Presidents Arthur Barclay, Daniel Howard, and Charles D. B. King learned to their sorrow as they failed in their efforts to control the actions of their successors once they themselves had left office. Hence, once a strong president voluntarily surrendered power, he had to be prepared to be permanently relegated to the sidelines. If the incumbent felt that no person had the stature or commitment to continue his policies and programs, he literally had to be carried from office in a coffin—which was what happened to President Tubman, who died in July 1971 while undergoing surgery in a London hospital.

It was at that point that the full impact of the Tubman legacy on the First Republic's presidency became apparent. William R. Tolbert succeeded Tubman on 23 July 1971 not because the 1847 Constitution provided for the vice president to succeed a deceased or incapacitated president; Tolbert succeeded because he recognized that he was obliged to accept the institutional changes that his predecessor had made in the office. Indeed, during much of the speculation during the 1960s regarding a possible successor to Tubman, few focused their attention upon Tolbert, who had been regarded as the "invisible vice president" who quietly and obsequiously served with Tubman during five of his six terms in office. At best Tolbert was regarded as a possible interim president, but nothing more. Speculation instead focused on some of the old stalwarts of the True Whig Party (such as former Treasury Secretary Charles Sherman), on some of the rising young stalwarts who had both Americo-Liberian and tribal antecedents (such as Foreign Minister Rudolph Grimes), or on "Shad, Jr.," Tubman's son by his first marriage, whom Tubman, Sr., made chief of the cabinet in 1964 and later senator from Maryland County (a post once held by Tubman, Sr.). Shad, Jr., had both youth and an American education at both Harvard and Rutgers. Prior to holding public office, moreover, he served as president general of the Congress of Industrial Organizations and thereby became identified (as his father had before him) with the lot of those who pose the greatest threat to Whig supremacy: the lower middle classes and the tribalized elements of Monrovia. He appeared to be attempting to build the popular image that his father had had years ago as an attorney in Maryland County when he took without fee the cases of the destitute. Shad, Jr., used his position to advantage in speaking before civic clubs or at school exercises. A recurrent theme was that the enemy of the working class was not the True Whig Party leadership, but rather the Lebanese and other foreign entrepreneurs in Liberia.[7] His marriage to the daughter of Vice President Tolbert in 1961 was taken by several observers to indicate that Tolbert's possible succession would constitute a mere holding operation for Tubman's son. Although this turned out not to be the case, it was apparent later that the Tubman name still had a magic ring to it not only during the Tolbert presidency but during the period of military government as well. Relatives of the former president, such as his nephew Winston Tubman and Robert Tubman, and son-in-law Gabriel Tucker, have been considered part of a dynastic legacy by the Doe regime, which has used them to bolster its crumbling legitimacy. Those officials who were not related but who were most closely identified with the Tubman—as opposed to the Tolbert—regime continued to have legitimacy during the early days following the 1980 coup.

### The Tolbert Succession

Given the changed nature of the Liberian presidency in 1971, there were few who regarded William Tolbert as anything more than an interim successor who would quickly have to be shunted aside in favor of a stronger, more astute political craftsman who fit the radically altered image that Tubman had imposed on the office. The Tubman transformation appeared to require at a minimum that the incumbent president had to be acceptable to both the Americo-Liberians and the tribal element without being too closely identified with the primary interests of either one. He must have, so conventional wisdom dictated, the appreciation of pomp and ceremony that the aristocratic-minded Whigs demanded of their leader and yet have the human foibles—indeed, the ability to establish an empathetic joking relationship with the masses—that enhanced Tubman's reputation with the tribal people.

On most counts, before 1971, Tolbert failed to measure up to the Tubman image. His immaculate three-piece suit and his impeccable use of American English made him a sharp contrast to the rough-and-tumble Tubman. His greatest strength was also his greatest liability: namely, his close identification with the Americo-Liberian community, which was bound to raise suspicions among the recently involved tribal leadership that Tubman had cultivated. When interviewing him in 1960, I found him to be reserved, humorless, and a bit of a "stuffed shirt" who was ill at ease on social occasions. Tolbert, moreover, was viewed with contempt by other Whig politicians—such as Speaker Richard Henries—who regarded him as little more than Tubman's errand boy. There was, of course, already the liability of his family's rapacious greed. In addition to Secretary of Agriculture and Commerce Stephen Tolbert, his other brother, Frank Tolbert (later president pro tempore of the Senate), had "purchased" large tracts of land in Bong County.

Despite his apparent shortcomings, William Tolbert surprised everyone by his willingness and ability to respond to the new institutional imperatives that Tubman had established for the office. As one elder Liberian commented to me about William Tolbert, "There was one leopard that did change his spots." Laying aside the tuxedos and Fifth Avenue business suits which had been his trademark—as well as the silk top hats and long-tailed grey morning coats which had been the official uniform of the "honorable" class on ceremonial occasions—Tolbert appeared at his inauguration in the open-necked, short-sleeved cotton jacket worn by Nyerere, Kaunda, and many other African heads of state. Abandoning his austere style of speaking, he succeeded in appearing folksy with tribal and other leaders. His performance even rivaled that of Tubman by his surprise repetition of his inaugural speech in Liberian English (a form of pidgin) and his tendency to lace his official pronouncements with the biblical references so dear to the hearts of the Whig aristocracy. Exceeding the energy of Tubman, Tolbert became a frequent visitor to every county in the Republic—often driving (in the early years at least) in the Volkswagen car he had surprisingly substituted for the official black Mercedes at his inauguration.

More than had been true of Tubman, the national development schemes under Tolbert were not only more avowedly oriented to transformation of the rural hinterland, but they had a highly populist ring to them. The program which he laid out in 1972 called for "total involvement for higher heights," with an emphasis on self-reliance, decreased dependence on foreign aid, and Liberianization of the economy. The "Rally Time" contributions referred to previously stressed the obligations of the expatriates and those who were employed by government to share their good fortune with the poor by contributing a portion of their salaries to national development targets. The slogan which was designed to encourage increases in food production, modernization, and mechanization of agriculture, and the use of capital to increase urban employment was expressed as a pledge to move Liberians from "mats on the floor to a mattress on every bed."

Tolbert also attempted to support populist goals in the area of education by promising during his inaugural address in 1972 that the government would provide free secondary education to any Liberian desiring it. To accomplish this goal there had to be an acceleration of school construction, particularly in the rural hinterland, as well as an enlargement of the pool of schoolteachers. Unfortunately, teachers' salaries remained low, and schools were often short of textbooks and other needed supplies, since the government did not always pay its overseas bills. In one area, however, Tolbert did deliver. He came through on his promise to advance the University of Liberia from the somewhat reduced status it enjoyed in the 1950s and 1960s to that of a vital, respectable institution of higher learning. Considerable funds and energy were spent in upgrading its faculty, administration, laboratories, and other physical facilities. During his later years a new campus was being created at Fendel, roughly ten miles from Monrovia. This physical removal of the campus from the center of politics bode well for academe. Also in a calculated gesture toward the youth, Tolbert in 1972 urged that the nine new seats being created for the House of Representatives be reserved for True Whig candidates between the ages of 18 and 28.

Tolbert attempted, moreover, to out-Tubman Tubman by carrying forward the Unification Program, which had tended to lag in the last years of Tubman's rule. Tolbert downplayed some of the more odious symbols of the caste and class divisions within Liberian society. These symbols included the national holiday celebrating the 1820s heroism of Matilda Newport, as well as the motto on the official seal: "The Love of Liberty Brought Us Here" (see figure 2). To address all of the historic actions and symbolism which had divided Liberia since its founding, Tolbert created a national commission which was to evaluate the continued use of the existing motto, flag, and national anthem. Some of the language of the constitution which was offensive to the tribal majority was also being considered for elimination at the time of Tolbert's assassination.

A further effort which appeared to address both the problems of rural development and the enhanced participation of tribal people in national affairs was the creation of new county government positions and a series of modern (rather than tribal) courts for the resolution of conflict. These actions in turn provided new job outlets for educated tribal youths—particularly those who apprenticed themselves to Monrovia-based lawyers. Also popular with the educated tribal youths was the decision of Tolbert in 1971 decreeing that paramount, clan, and town chiefs were henceforth to be subjected to electoral choice for limited terms instead of being administratively appointed for indefinite tenures. The chiefs were also to be put on fixed salaries rather than being permitted to keep a portion of the poll taxes collected in their areas. It should be stressed with respect to all these reforms that the national government—and the president in particular—continued to enjoy real power in contrast to the feeble authority of local officials.

The Tolbert populist image was also projected by a series of moves early in his assumption of power which gave Liberia the appearance of a democratic golden age. One of Tolbert's first gestures after Tubman's death was to release all political prisoners, and in the traditional Liberian style of extending the "hand of forgiveness" he appointed several to high office. One former detainee, James Gbarbea, who had been released just prior to Tubman's death, was appointed minister of lands and mines, while former Ambassador Henry Fahnbulleh, who had been convicted of sedition under Tubman, was appointed assistant minister for presidential affairs. An even more telling gesture was Tolbert's abolition of the system of "public relations officers," which had financially rewarded Liberians for "informing" on one another with regard to any deviation from political orthodoxy. This was at the core of the numerous political detentions and trials which had marred the preceding administrations. Equally surprising was Tolbert's pledge, shortly after taking office, to guarantee freedom of the press. During the early years the students in particular took advantage of his pledge, as did the editors of the government-owned *Liberian Age*. The latter, for example, in 1973 criticized the Legislature for having granted the president broad emergency powers which included the authority to suspend the right to a writ of habeas corpus. Most press criticism during the early years of Tolbert's administration was concentrated upon economic issues, such as inflation, Liberia's use of the American dollar as its official currency, urban unemployment, changes in traditional land tenure, and the shortages of rice, petroleum, and other products from time to time. The lifting of the tight hand of the censor did permit a series of privately funded newspapers to emerge. Some of them even survived the reintroduction of press restrictions later in the Tolbert era.

By 1975 there was little doubt in the minds of most Liberian leaders that Tolbert had skillfully shed his Old Guard Americo-Liberian image and had actually improved upon the model of the assertive national leader developed by Tubman. Despite the call by former Attorney General Abayomi Cassell for the formation of a second party, no opposition group registered, and Tolbert ran unopposed in the October 1975 elections. Still unsure of his full control over the office, however, Tolbert had to engage in a series of "pork barrel" negotiations with local party leaders at the coast as well as in the hinterland guaranteeing his support for local pet projects. Undoubtedly, however, one factor in his being elected in his own right was the fact that Tolbert cleverly dealt with the issues of presidential tenure and succession before the election. Tolbert persuaded the Legislature to amend the constitution by limiting future presidencies to a single eight-year term with no possibility of succession. Thus, the almost indefinite tenure of Tubman, and even the twelve-year term which Tolbert would have enjoyed had he lived till 1984, would have been a thing of the past. The routinization of democratic norms, which requires rotation in office, would have been accomplished.

### Presidential Ascendancy and Legislative Decline

Like the U.S. Constitution, after which it was modeled, the Liberian Constitution of 1847 assumed that the legislative branch of the national government was to be superior to the executive, or at least that the separation of powers and the pattern of checks-and-balances would make them coequal branches of government, sharing power with the third branch, the judiciary. Liberia in the nineteenth century had witnessed, however, the gradual—albeit intermittent—eclipse of legislative power with a corresponding increase in the exercise of presidential authority. By the early decades of the present century, this tendency accelerated; during the Tubman era, the capitulation of the Legislature was all but complete.

It remained true that in furtherance of many Whig objectives the speaker of the House, the president pro tempore of the Senate, and other leading legislators personally exercised considerably greater influence over the course of affairs during the First Republic than did members of the president's cabinet. As an institution, however, the Legislature had been decidedly eclipsed by the presidency. This subordination had become apparent during the administration of Edwin Barclay (1930–1944) and was intensified under the administrations of Tubman and Tolbert. None of the author's informants could point to one significant measure that had emerged from the Legislature without presidential approval, nor could they point to any major legislation that failed in the face of concerted and sustained support from the Executive Mansion.

This did not mean that the House and Senate were completely under the domination of the president, for the membership of the Legislature included some of the leading figures in the hierarchy of the True Whig Party. These men had bases of political support that were independent of the president. The speaker of the House, the vice president, the president pro tempore of the Senate, as well as the senior men in the county delegations, were powerful figures within their own geographic areas. Consultation behind the scene and surveying the opposition in advance were required to spare the president public political defeat. The president in most instances got his way eventually and substantially, if not always completely or immediately, on measures submitted to the Legislature by the executive. One of the few exceptions recalled by informants occurred during Tolbert's administration when a bill—introduced in 1974 as a pet project of the minister of finance, Stephen Tolbert (the president's brother)—would have authorized a national lottery and the building of an international casino in Liberia. Prompted by editorial criticism in the newspaper *Revelation* and spurred on by the young members of a new political organization, MOJA, Bishop Bennie Warner of the Methodist Church and other clerics condemned the gambling projects. At that point, many of the legislators suddenly began to voice their opposition as well. Executive pressure did compel the Legislature to adopt the measure by a narrow margin; public pressures, however, in turn forced the president—himself a religious leader—to veto his own measure. Beyond this, there were a number of cases in which leading senators or representatives were permitted to place a personal imprint upon certain types of legislation and even to object to the passage of a measure.

The expression of legislative independence, however, was often illusory. Delay in passage of a bill in many cases actually indicated the lack of presidential intent to do more than publicly espouse a reform that he had no intention of putting into effect at that time. Similarly the senatorial rejection of a presidential nomination for the Supreme Court was useful largely as a device for creating an impression of legislative independence. One celebrated case during Tubman's reign was openly acknowledged as a facade for a change of heart on the part of the president. The senator who led the assault on the presidential nomination for an important executive position was himself immediately nominated for the same post. The subordinate role of the Legislature was clearly expressed in the remarks of then Vice President William Tolbert to this writer in 1960 at the opening of the Legislature. Mr. Tolbert stated that the House and the Senate could not consider any measure during the first month inasmuch as the president was still in Europe and "we don't know what his thoughts are." Significantly, the $27 million annual budget introduced on 23 December 1960 was passed into law on the following day, without amendment.

Although as a body the Legislature did not initiate legislation or provide a public check upon presidential power, it did have an educative function to perform. Its debates were lively, if highly rhetorical, and helped to educate the local leadership and the general public regarding the significance of a new policy decision. The debates often exposed defects or pitfalls in a proposed measure, which helped the executive branch in reformulating its proposal and the drafting committees of the Legislature in presenting a final version of the measure.

The Legislature's representative function, however, was poorly served by the tendency to make decisions outside the legislative body and by the policy of the True Whig Party to derogate pressure-group activity to a minor role in the political process. Party representation, moreover, exaggerated the strength of the True Whig Party, which had enjoyed a virtual monopoly in the Legislature since the party's ultimate capture of the presidency in the 1880s.

Despite the lack of significant power in the matter of legislation, the office of senator or representative was eagerly sought. Membership in the Legislature automatically gave one the informal title of "honorable" as well as the perquisites due to the very few elective officials in Liberia. In addition to the other forms of patronage available to party members in good standing, a high proportion of the legislators received attorney's fees for representing the foreign concessionaires and the more prominent private Liberians. Speaker of the House Richard Henries, for example, had the most flourishing law practice in the country. If a legislator was not a lawyer at the time of election, he quickly found himself studying for the bar. The Legislature, moreover, was regarded as a very attractive forum for the establishment of a national reputation. With success a young man could go on to the Supreme Court, an ambassadorship, the cabinet, or even the presidency. In any case, the two-term tradition of the True Whig Party assured the senator at the end of six years and the representative at the end of four years that his term of office would be renewed without a contest. Indeed, in the election of senators in 1973, the five incumbents and the four newly nominated candidates ran unopposed. Some legislators were able to extend their tenure indefinitely, and, in effect, had lifetime tenures. Part of the hatred directed against Speaker of the House Richard Henries—who was among the officials executed on the beach shortly after the April 1980 coup—was that his decades in office had permitted him to accumulate a storehouse of inside information on the sins of omission and commission of most of the other Liberian leaders. Extended tenure in other cases stemmed from the fact that some legislators felt that their regional and family alliances both required and permitted them to use the Legislature as a long-term independent political base for defending their groups' corporate interests—even if that meant opposing the president on policy matters. In 1962, for example, the Senate—out of "senatorial courtesy"—secured modifications in various provisions of the proposed Mount Coffee Hydroelectric Agreement, which had offended the vital interests of one of the senators from that county.[8]

*The Subordination of the Judiciary*

The judiciary was very much the third branch of the national government during the First Republic. Despite the constitutional provision upholding the independence of the judiciary, the judges of the Supreme Court and subordinate courts were in fact subject to the control of the other two branches of government. The removal of judges by joint resolution of the Legislature was a fairly common occurrence. Two justices of the Supreme Court, for example, were removed in 1957. The occasional display of independence by the judiciary was treated with indifference by the more obviously political branches. A case in point was the classic decision of 1919 (referred to by Tubman in his famous 1960 speech to the Legislature) in which the Court declared that the existing system of "colonial" administration of the interior was unconstitutional. That pattern of administration, nevertheless, continued in effect until 1964.

The lack of previous judicial experience or even legal training was apparent at all levels of the court system. This was compounded by the lack of certainty with respect to what the law actually was—given the lack of a systematic codification of the law prior to the 1950s.[9] Chief Justice A. Dash Wilson, upon taking office in 1958, delivered a caustic lecture to the whole judiciary that noted the persistent bias on the part of the judges with respect to litigants, the many improper instructions to juries, and the lack of courage on the part of the courts in dealing with unscrupulous lawyers. In 1966 the chief justice announced that the collection of fines, costs, and fees by judges and clerks of the court had resulted in such a flagrant distortion of justice that judges were required to turn this function over to administrative officers.

Perhaps the greatest problem concerning the judiciary was the delay in bringing cases to completion. The first judicial circuit in Montserrado County in one year, for example, was able to dispose of less than 7 percent of the 1,297 criminal cases on its docket.[10] Similar situations prevailed in the other tribunals, especially those dealing with civil cases. For a community that placed a high value on litigation, this was indeed a serious problem. Litigation, in fact, was one of the most effective weapons for keeping the politically and socially dissident Liberians in line. The expense, the loss of business time, the neglect of family and friends, as well as other by-products of protracted court cases dampened the enthusiasm of the social mischief-maker and the political reformer under the First Republic.[11]

*Control over the Bureaucracy*

Supremacy of the presidency in the national government came not merely through the subordination of the other two major branches; it was equally a consequence of increased presidential control over the bureaucracy. Presidential control, however, did not mean greater administrative efficiency. As the central government expanded its agencies throughout the Republic, the failure of the national government to address itself to the problems of the civil service reform became increasingly apparent. Indeed, administrative inefficiency and dishonesty undermined the very system of control the Americo-Liberians were attempting to expand and perpetuate. The deplorable state of the Liberian bureaucracy even under the Tubman and Tolbert reforms has been commented upon by many expatriate analysts and confirmed in an insightful study done by a Liberian of Kru background in the late 1970s.[12]

In theory Liberia under the First Republic was a highly centralized unitary state. There was relatively little legal autonomy enjoyed by the major political subdivisions—the five coastal and four interior counties—or by the districts, territories, and municipalities into which the counties had been subdivided. Prior to 1964 the tribal hinterland was divided into three provinces under provincial commissioners and administered in a colonial fashion. In 1964 the boundaries of the coastal counties, where the majority of Americo-Liberians resided, were extended inland before the establishment of four new counties in the interior (see map 5). In fact, only the counties and municipalities had a basis in the constitution, whereas the other units remained creatures of the Legislature. Administrative officials at all levels were appointed by the president or by the president with the advice and consent of the Senate. Decisions regarding policies, problems, and the expenditure of funds were also made largely at the national level. Revenue collection, moreover, was virtually a monopoly of the central government, even though the fines and fees collected by chiefs could be spent for local projects under proper central government supervision. The political division of the country tended largely to be disregarded by the departments of the national government in the planning of programs in agriculture, health, education, and other fields. Thus, the superintendents of counties and territories and the district commissioners were "chief executives" of their respective areas in only a limited number of government functions. The counties and territories existed largely as electoral areas for the national legislature or, together with the hinterland and coastal districts, as units for the maintenance of order and the collection of taxes.

Unfortunately for the Whig theory of administrative organization, a number of factors militated against the assertion of central government authority in many areas of the Republic under the Whig regimes.[13] Most significant were the geographical barriers to an inexpensive and effective system of transport and communications, the emergence along the coastal strip of satrapies under the control of leading families, the resistance of the tribal people, and the historic trepidation or indifference of the Americo-Liberians to the establishment of control over the hinterland. As a consequence of these things, in many areas of the Republic little got done by way of positive governmental programs or what was done was accomplished in a highly inefficient manner with a maximum amount of coercion from the top and scant initiative or enthusiasm at the grass-roots level.

New highways, the airplane, and the radio did provide the means for centralizing administrative control over field services. Much more needed to be done, however, to improve the system of public administration at both national and local levels. It did no good to hold the field officer responsible for implementing national government policy directives if he had almost no trained staff, was indifferent to the need for adequate reports and records, and had only sporadic supervision of his work by higher officials. Nor was central government direction feasible if the executive branch had only recently recognized the value of planning or data collection, if the president ignored the legal chain of command from chiefs up through the secretary of internal affairs and insisted upon being accessible to all, or if the president rigorously studied the preaudit expenditures but almost ignored postaudits. Indeed, all the problems of public administration both in developed states and in other African countries appeared to be compounded in Liberia under the First Republic. To make matters worse, often some relatively inconsequential gesture was assumed to constitute monumental and fundamental reform, such as the 1971 change in titles of cabinet officers from secretary (borrowing the American terminology) to minister (following the pattern in Europe and most of Africa). Tolbert's other highly significant "reform" that year was to bring Liberia into the modern era by adhering to GMT instead of stubbornly remaining 16 minutes off GMT!

Perhaps the heart of the problem was personnel. In terms of per capita exposure to university training, the Liberian upper class was among the best educated of any African state. This appeared to give the government of Liberia a decided advantage over its neighbors. But this was not the case. Partly this failure resulted from the inadequacies of the education received at the University of Liberia prior to the late 1960s or at many of the smaller colleges of the United States where Liberian students in earlier days were sent on scholarships. It was also a product of the overemphasis upon legal and political studies to the neglect of agriculture, engineering, accounting, business administration, and other subjects that form the substance of governmental programs or are essential to the efficient operation of government. Even if a Liberian student did pursue a technical course, there was no guarantee that his talents would be put to the best use. Sheer inefficiency in allocating personnel, the student's own recognition that politics would be the most rewarding profession in the long run, and the operation of the patronage system all contributed to the waste of human talent by the government.

The patronage system pervaded all administrative practices. Although in some instances appointment and promotion were based on merit alone rather than influence, this usually happened only when a particular skill was required in a hurry. As the civil service commissioners testified in their annual reports, the senior executives regarded with scorn such notions as the competitive testing and certification of candidates, the establishment of impartial criteria for the promotion or firing of employees, and the need for preservice or in-service training for posts in government. Only the Department of State (later restyled Ministry of Foreign Affairs) attempted to regularize its testing and training programs for foreign service officers and thereby reduce some—but certainly not all—of the evils of patronage. This effort attested to the critical importance attached by Liberia to good public relations in international politics.

In patronage terms the government employee under the Whig regimes had a dual obligation. The obligation to the president and the True Whig Party was satisfied by attendance at rallies, by voting, by public displays of loyalty to the president, and by the annual "contribution" to the True Whig Party, which was automatically deducted from his salary. The second obligation was to his patron or patrons, whom he supported in their struggle for power with other influential members of the political hierarchy, including perhaps the employee's administrative superiors. The spread of patronage ties, which were in many cases synonymous with blood and marriage ties, provided the president with a useful mechanism for maintaining control over the political system. There was a built-in watchdog system, with each bloc reporting the sins of omission and commission of the competing bloc. Patronage rivalry, however, took its toll on administrative boldness in launching new programs and generally played havoc with a superior's control of his subordinates. A simple executive directive could easily be converted into a contest for power at a higher level in the bureaucracy. The authorized lines of command were often jammed. Action frequently took place only by means of circuitous communications, and the consequent delay was often fatal for programs.

In addition to its inefficiencies, the Liberian bureaucracy was clearly too large. Expansion of government into areas that might more efficiently be left to private hands was but one of the factors. Lack of planning, inadequacies of training, and cultural insistence upon a rigid division of labor also contributed to a multiplication of the number of workers required if administrative programs were to be accomplished at all. Expansion of the bureaucracy increased the need for the general service staff and contributed to a reduction in salary scales at the lower level. This in turn perpetuated the demand for "dash" or petty gifts in return for any service rendered by a public employee.

At higher levels of the bureaucracy, inadequacies of training were not so apparent. Although in 1961 several senior members of the government were only high school graduates, at the beginning of the Tolbert era, in 1971, this had become the exception. A good many leaders in the upper echelons of government had advanced degrees from the best universities in America and Europe. Indeed, articulateness of Liberian leaders regarding the problems of government was disarming to the outside observer, who later discovered a great chasm between the expressed desire for reform and any positive evidence that administrative and political energies were being directed toward that end. Some of the most vociferous critics of patronage stood at the heart of a vast patronage empire. On the slightest provocation, moreover, agency heads with major responsibilities for new programs undertook extended trips to visit community development schemes in the Negev Desert or clinics for midwives in the Soviet Union. Often the primary reason for a senior official venturing into the interior of Liberia was to visit his rubber farm or to attend a ceremonial function. There was apparently no notion of a conflict of interest when a government official reaped personal financial profit from his position by securing a monopoly for his company or by receiving retaining fees from foreign concessions. Such behavior was not inconsistent with the moral standards of the Americo-Liberian community, and, indeed, it was compatible with the efforts of the ruling class to control economic developments so that neither a tribal nor a settler middle class emerged to challenge the existing order. Whether it stimulated or inhibited rapid economic development is an arguable matter. It did compromise the official's objectivity, however, and detracted from the performance of his duties. Ultimately, it had the unintended result of undermining the very social and political system it was designed to perpetuate.

To compensate for inadequacies of training and to overcome some inefficient practices, the Liberian government under Presidents Tubman and Tolbert placed increased reliance upon foreign advisers from the United States, Great Britain, and other developed countries. The American Agency for International Development (and its predecessors) and United Nations specialized agencies provided most of the external advisers. The fact that European and American financial and other advisers had been imposed upon Liberia as international supervisors at various points in its past made the task of the foreign adviser a difficult one indeed. Some advisers found the inertia and lack of cooperation too much to bear and quit in disgust. Others attempted to deal with their frustrations by assuming an operational rather than an advisory role. On the whole, the Liberian government usually did not get its money's worth from its foreign advisers, but it is not certain that the government intended to. In certain cases the foreign adviser was even made the unwitting scapegoat for the institution of a new program that encountered public opposition.

Many signs indicated that Presidents Tubman and Tolbert were finding it more and more difficult to control all phases of bureaucratic activity. The increasing frequency of either dismissal or rotation to new posts of fairly senior officers of the national government was continuing evidence of a loss of trust between the chief executive and some of his major subordinates. The ability of the president and the cabinet to continue to control the character, pace, and direction of change was certainly being challenged by the increasing scope of governmental operations, not only on the domestic scene but in international affairs as well. Without a dramatic change in the philosophy of bureaucratic growth, the national administration found its talents strained beyond the point where it could cope with the various programs facing a modern government.

Under President Tolbert this inability of the president to control the bureaucracy was underscored by a number of incidents—many of which were intended to demonstrate the strength of the Liberian executive but instead underscored its weaknesses. Early in his presidency, for example, Tolbert in 1973 sacked the minister of education—G. Flama Sherman—and other officials who were not at their desks by eight o'clock in the morning during Tolbert's heralded surprise visits. Others were publicly admonished for some trivial error in judgment. Often these gestures were efforts to persuade the International Monetary Fund (IMF) and other external groups of the growing efficiency of the Liberian bureaucracy. In most instances, however, it perpetuated the image of a national president who meddled in the details of administration while failing to come to grips with the greater issues of economic planning, fiscal conservancy, and rampant corruption within official circles.

There is no doubt that the presidency in Liberia had undergone a dramatic change during the quarter of a century of Tubman's rule. Whether he was largely a creature or a molder of events is a subject of continuing debate among his critics and admirers. Certainly, however, for the first time in Liberian history the office of president had become a national institution rather than the peculiar plaything of the Whig minority. The ground rules of succession had been irrevocably altered, and a successor to Tubman who ignored this fundamental change in the political process did so at his peril. Whether the institution could continue to adjust to the mounting pressures from within and from without and bring off an evolutionary rather than a revolutionary transformation of the social fabric was a question that faced the Liberian nation in 1971. Part—but only part—of the answer to that question came in the coup of 12 April 1980.

# IX.

# A Place in the Sun
## *Foreign Policy as an Instrument of Social Control*

Liberia's relations with the outside world have not always been of its own choosing. Cast adrift on alien shores, the Americo-Liberian settlers were compelled as a matter of survival to devise effective means for neutralizing their relatively hostile environment. Immediately behind the coastal settlements were the Vai, Grebo, Kru, and others with whom they came into constant conflict over questions of land, trade, and cultural identity. Their other adversaries—the British and French colonialists, operating out of bases in Sierra Leone, the Ivory Coast, and Guinea—challenged the extended claims of the settlers not only to the interior but to the coastal areas as well. (See map 2.) Occasionally, too, the Americo-Liberians found their suzerainty challenged by freebooting slave traders, such as Pedro Blanco, who incited the tribal people to rebellion whenever the settlers made inroads into the slave-raiding areas of the Europeans and Brazilians. An effective foreign policy then was vital for the survival of the settlers and their descendants against a variety of threats.

*Liberian/American Relations*

Considering the history of Liberian settlement, it was perhaps inevitable that Liberia's external orientation during much of the history of the First Republic should be stronger toward the United States than toward any other state or dependency. The "special relationship" has been a significant factor in foreign affairs and continues to be so under the Second Republic of Samuel Doe. Even during the nineteenth century, when the long-delayed official recognition of Liberia was followed by only token or merely moral support to the settlers in their disputes with Britain and France, the American connections were firmly maintained through a range of non-official channels. Not only, for example, did the activities of Protestant missionaries provide organizational and friendship ties between Americans and the colonists, but they were also responsible for most of the educational and health programs in the country. On a very personal level, too, the family linkages that spanned the ocean remained strong and actually increased as Liberian students and visitors to the United States acquired American spouses.

The twentieth century witnessed the expansion of a variety of nongovernmental connections with the United States. Significant in this respect was the decision by the Firestone Plantations Company in 1926 to buy out previously flawed attempts to grow rubber in Liberia and, in the process, pioneer the economic development of the country. Firestone's action was followed by the involvement of a host of other American investors and commercial firms. Until that point, Germany and the Netherlands were Liberia's best customers. American universities, too, became involved in the development of Liberia during the period between the two World Wars. Only the Nigerians accounted for a higher percentage of African students in the United States. Cornell University, Texas A. & M., Northwestern University, and Harvard became even more directly involved by providing assistance to the Liberian government and to educational institutions in that country. Other private foundations, such as Rockefeller and Eli Lilly, have been actively combating the problems of disease, illiteracy, and economic underdevelopment.

At the official level as well, contacts between the two republics expanded in the twentieth century. The military assistance the United States gave Liberia in 1915 to quell an uprising on the Kru Coast was continued in a more or less sporadic manner until the period following World War II. From the latter point onward, the training and equipping of Liberian troops by the United States was put on a permanent basis. In 1959, Liberia became the first—and thus far the only—African state to conclude a mutual defense pact with the United States. In terms of economic assistance, too, Liberia became one of the leading African beneficiaries of lend-lease aid, technical assistance programs, and loans from the Export-Import Bank and AID (Agency for International Development). The independence of Nigeria and other new African states in the 1960s was expected to diminish Liberia's special role in African-American relations. Relatively speaking, this did happen, but in absolute terms the American interest in Liberia continued to expand at a significant rate with respect to both governmental assistance and private investment in iron mining and other enterprises. In addition to emergency measures, such as the sale of rice in 1966 at low cost under the Food for Peace Program, the United States provided technical assistance in the fields of road construction, agriculture, forestry, veterinary science, fish production, public administration, and mapping and geodetic survey. The greatest technical assistance, however, was in the field of education, and especially since the Peace Corps in 1962 began sending more than two hundred new volunteers to Liberia each year on two-year contracts.

The Agency for International Development was one of the most significant continuing sources for needed investment funds for the Tubman and Tolbert regimes. Either through direct loans or through guarantees of private investment, the United States was instrumental during the Tubman and Tolbert period in securing a $5.3

million modern teaching hospital for Monrovia, several hundred school buildings at the coast and in the interior, a $27 million hydroelectric plant on the St. Paul River, a $7.2 million expansion of the capital's sanitation system, and major improvements in Liberia's overall transportation and communication network.

Liberian officials under Tubman and Tolbert, however, became increasingly ambivalent about the relationship of their country to the United States.[1] On the one hand, they felt that American aid had been too small in relation to need and had "too many strings attached." There was undoubtedly a sincere conviction in the constant repetition of the theme that the United States had a debt to Liberia stemming from Liberia's origins as a quasi-American colony and from the injustices that the ancestors of the Americo-Liberians suffered at the hands of Southern slave-owners. This attitude regarding the policy of benign neglect was summarized in 1957 by Liberia's ambassador to the United Nations (who was himself a son of a former president of Liberia) during the celebration of Ghana's independence. In an ironic twist, Ambassador Charles T. O. King remarked that in contrast to Ghana, Liberia had not "reaped the advantages of colonialism."[2] With the exception of the Hoover period (1929–1933), U.S. policy toward Liberia was "characterized by caution, apathy, paternalism, and nonintervention." Indeed, it was private Americans—philanthropists, Black activists, missionaries, and business interests—who attempted to secure greater official involvement.[3]

A more recent American debt was felt to have been incurred as a result of Liberia's following the lead of the United States in entering both World Wars against the Germans. In World War II, Liberia provided the Allied forces with land for an important military base, was the major source of natural rubber following the fall of Malaya, and made many sacrifices it need not have made had the country remained neutral. Both Tubman and Tolbert, moreover, provided diplomatic support for the American position during the struggle in Viet Nam. Liberia has also given the United States a considerable advantage in the continuing propaganda war with the Soviet Union by permitting the construction near Monrovia of a Voice of America transmitter powerful enough to cover the entire African continent. The American linkage was further reinforced through the opening in 1976 of the OMEGA navigational station in Liberia, a system which provides worldwide assistance to shipping in all weather conditions, 24 hours a day. Although American-financed, it is staffed by Liberians and is, of course, of benefit to Liberia directly in view of the Liberian registration of ships owned by other nationals.

At the same time that Liberian officials were stressing the "special relationship" with the United States and claiming, thereby, the American obligation of economic support, both Tubman and Tolbert were explicitly attempting to move Liberia away from America and closer to a pro-African, pro-neutralist role in foreign affairs. Liberian leaders were sensitive to the fact that the U.S. State Department often took Liberia's U.N. support for granted. Symbolic of the longstanding policy of "benign neglect," it was not until the 1978 visit of Jimmy Carter that an American president had paid an official visit to Liberia (Franklin Roosevelt's landing at Robertsfield during World War II was merely a transit stop en route to the Casablanca conference). Liberian leaders have also been sensitive to the country's lack of an official currency, making it susceptible to the African and European charge of being the "slave and enclave of the dollar."

The efforts on the part of both Tubman and Tolbert to distance themselves from the United States through diversification of their foreign contacts were evident in a broad range of fields. The Liberian government, for example, sought and received an increasing number of scholarships and bursaries for Liberians to study in Western Europe, Canada, Israel, and even Eastern bloc countries. Encouragement was given to missionaries from Sweden, West Germany, Britain, and other countries to broaden the foreign base of support for both educational and health services in Liberia. Liberian participation in a whole range of private or quasi-governmental conferences in Europe and other parts of Africa also helped to broaden Liberian perspectives beyond a narrow focus upon the United States.

A very definite effort to broaden the range of economic linkages with the global community was apparent in the area of international trade. In analyzing Liberia's relationships with its major trading partners during the more than three decades from 1948 to 1981, it is clear that despite minor fluctuations there was steady growth in both imports from and exports to the United States.[4] Imports from the United States rose from U.S. $6.4 million in value in 1948 to an annual average of U.S. $123.8 million during the last five years of the First Republic. Exports to the United States experienced a similar expansion, from U.S. $12.6 million in 1948 to an annual average of U.S. $110.4 million during the last five years of the Whig era.

Figure 7, however, indicates quite another story with respect to the relative position occupied by the United States in trade with Liberia during that same 34-year period. Although the United States continued to be the single most important country in terms of providing Liberia with machinery, consumer goods, and other imports, its position relative to other nations and groups of nations experienced a dramatic change, with West Germany being a close rival and Western Europe as a whole (including West Germany) outdistancing the United States in exports to Liberia. A similar relative expansion of exports to Liberia occurred collectively with respect to Asia (Japan, Hong Kong, South Korea, China, and Malaysia) and the Middle East (Israel, Iraq, and Saudi Arabia).

Even more significant was the relative reduction in significance of Liberian exports to the United States, with West Germany actually surpassing the United States as a single country destination during the last six years of the Tolbert administration. Western Europe as a whole (including West Germany) surpassed the United States as the major export area for Liberia's iron, rubber, timber, and other commodities in 1961, and in the last decade of the First Republic the United States was eclipsed in a ratio of roughly three to one by the European Economic Community and other West European states receiving Liberian exports.

A similar pattern of disengagement has occurred with respect to sources of foreign investment since the implementation of Tubman's Open Door policy, even though the nature of ownership of multinationals and the manner in which Liberia reports data to the United Nations make it difficult to document these changes with any degree of precision. American domination of the heights of economic growth in Liberia prior to the Second World War was evidenced by the role played by one primary source of revenue: the rubber produced at Firestone Plantations Company. By 1967, with Liberia encouraging diversified foreign investment, there were over forty major foreign concerns and many minor ones at work in Liberia, with a total investment of $750 million. Although the Americans still constituted the largest single group of foreign investors, each year the proportion of Swedish, West German, Swiss, Israeli, Canadian, and Lebanese contributions to development increased at the expense of the American share. By skillful manipulation of the various foreign investment groups, the Americo-Liberians gained rather firm control of the general direction of economic growth.

In addition to achieving a measure of economic independence from the United States, Liberia under both Tubman and Tolbert expanded its diplomatic horizons far beyond the "special relationship" with the United States, by establishing a complex of bilateral and multilateral agreements with countries in all quarters of the globe. Even before 1960 Liberia had embassies in most countries of Western Europe and the Near East as well as in Haiti and Taiwan. With the attainment of independence by neighboring states, Liberia made it a policy to establish direct diplomatic ties with each new African country.

The determination of the Tolbert regime to forge an even more independent role in international politics, however, led to the appearance of a dramatic break with the American and Western camp. This came during the gradual warming of Liberian relations with the Communist bloc countries in 1972, when a series of informal bilateral contacts led to the establishment of formal diplomatic links with the Soviet Union and Romania, followed in the next year by exchanges of diplomats with each member of the Warsaw Pact. Although initially Tolbert followed his predecessor's policy in the United Nations of denying Peking the right to take the Security Council seat reserved for China, ultimately, in 1977, he chose to risk the loss of the significant economic and technical assistance provided by Taiwan in recognizing Peking (against the advice of his more conservative supporters). A year before his assassination, Tolbert made a ten-day official visit to the Chinese mainland. Given the changes by that time in American attitudes toward China, this could hardly have been considered a violation of the special Liberian-American relationship. More challenging to that connection, however, was Tolbert's recognition in 1976 of Cuba, followed closely by an exchange of diplomats with Colonel Qaddafi's Libya. The latter country was openly courted as a pet project of President Tolbert's son, A. B. Tolbert, who used Libyan financing in advancing some of his private construction and other interests. In the pursuit, moreover, of a more pro-African foreign policy—particularly where the issues more directly affected Liberian concerns—Liberia under Tolbert found itself parting company with the Americans in the United Nations on an increasing number of key votes.

*Relations with Europe and Asia*

Although the American shield had been useful in guaranteeing Liberia's survival in the past, Tubman and Tolbert increasingly made the entire globe an arena for

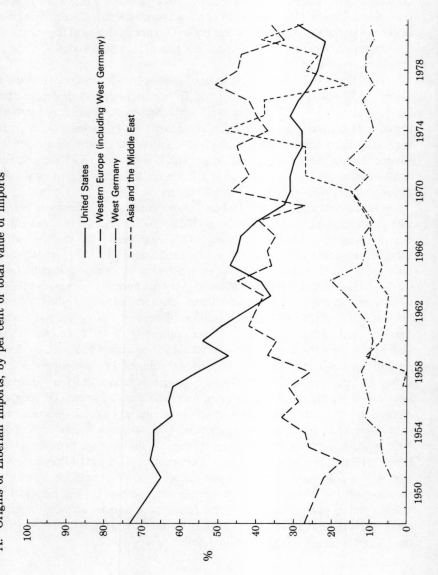

FIGURE 7  Liberia's Major Trading Relationships, 1948–1981

A.  Origins of Liberian Imports, by per cent of total value of imports

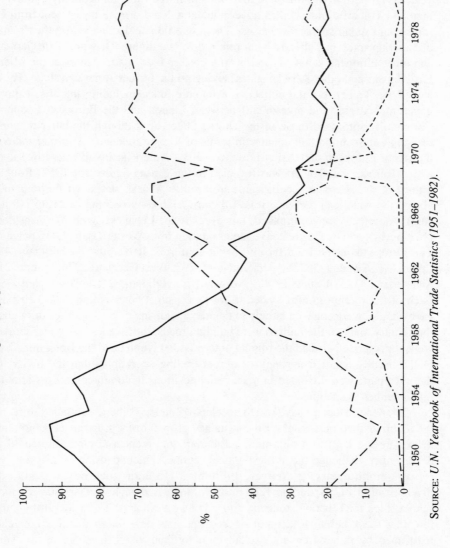

B. Destination of Liberian Exports, by per cent of total value of exports

SOURCE: *U.N. Yearbook of International Trade Statistics (1951–1982).*

Liberia's diplomatic action. Membership in the United Nations—Liberia is a charter member—had provided an obvious channel for this purpose, but it was not until other states in Africa achieved independence that Tubman and Tolbert began fully to use this forum. Liberia increasingly found it more profitable, in terms of securing economic and political goals, to engage in a series of bilateral arrangements with European and Asian states. Although the American presence remained strong, each year the proportion of American involvement in the Liberian economy under Tubman and Tolbert diminished as governmental aid and private investment from European and Asian sources increased. The proportionate decline in America's share of Liberian trade has already been referred to (see figure 7), with West Germany and other European states, as well as the Eastern bloc, Latin America, the Middle East, Japan, and other African states, taking up the former American share. By the end of the Tolbert era the collective economic links (including imports, exports, governmental aid, and investment) between Liberia and the European Economic Community surpassed those of the United States even though the latter remained the single most important country in terms of foreign linkages. A further index of the rising European and Asian presence versus American involvement in Liberia under Tubman and Tolbert was revealed in the census figures for 1962. Roughly a third of the aliens in Liberia came from other African states. Of the remaining aliens, the American presence was still considerable—1,645 out of 21,365 (8 percent). Americans were outranked, however, by the Lebanese, with 2,077 residents (10 percent), and by the collective representation from Western Europe (15 percent). The Europeans came from the following countries: Italy, 699; Netherlands, 481; Spain, 470; Sweden, 383; United Kingdom, 293; West Germany, 275; France, 210; Switzerland, 125; Denmark, 47; Norway, 28; Belgium, 24; undesignated, 198. Each of the foreign groups tended to make a distinct contribution. The Lebanese, for example, were engaged largely in the merchandising of commodities throughout the country; most of the Italians were building roads; the Swedes and West Germans were concentrated around the mining enterprises at Nimba and the Bong mines; the Dutch usually handled the major external trading operations; and the Swiss, for the most part, were involved in managerial positions in commercial firms or at the major rubber plantations.

The Open Door policy, which accelerated under Tolbert, continued to recruit the required alien personnel for the sustained growth of the Liberian economy, and in the process kept to a minimum a Liberian entrepreneurial class that could independently challenge the Whig political regime. The expansion of Liberia's external commitments, moreover, brought in foreign governmental aid, the diversification of its trading relationships, increased technical assistance, more scholarships for Liberian students, and private investment. There was little doubt, too, that the Liberian leadership banked upon its new international agreements, reaffirmed by rather frequent exchanges of official visits, to shore up its world prestige. Like Israel, Liberia under Tubman and Tolbert felt that it must have friends to defend its interests in a world it still regarded as relatively hostile. Although it largely avoided strong economic ties with the Communist bloc (beyond exchanges of diplomats), Liberia from the 1950s to the 1980 coup forged significant economic links with many of the neutralist states such as Austria, Switzerland, India, and the Scandinavian group and with countries that were not always popular with Liberia's more nationalistic and socialistic friends in Africa. Included in the latter list have been Belgium, Nationalist China, Spain, South Korea, and Haiti. There was also the strong relationship which Liberia—along with several of its African neighbors— had established with Israel and which had resulted in significant technical assistance as well as investment in Liberia. Yielding to the pressure of other African states as he attempted to capitalize upon and strengthen the leadership role in African affairs forged by Tubman, Tolbert in 1973 capitulated and broke the twenty-year diplomatic and economic connection with Israel.

### Intra-African Relations

It was in the efforts of Liberia to cast itself in a leadership role in intra-African affairs that the foreign policies of Tubman and Tolbert made the most decisive break with Liberia's isolationist past. It has been noted previously that Liberian leaders initially viewed the impending liberation of Liberia's African neighbors with some trepidation. First of all, it provided an unwelcome example of colonial liberation which the suppressed peoples of Liberia's hinterland might attempt to emulate. Even more important, the now benign European colonial presence in neighboring territories was about to be replaced by independent regimes whose ideologies and policies might be inimical to the Americo-Liberians. This was particularly the case with respect to the socialist regime of Sékou Touré in Guinea. Official apprehension regarding Liberia's own well-being in a continent of independent states was clearly stated by the secretary of defense in his *Annual Report for 1960*:

> With the attainment of independence of our sister African brothers [sic] contiguous to our borderline, problems which we never thought of are arising and have to be grappled with [with] every degree of efficiency and alertness. Not only are the problems of the crossing into our territories of citizens of other states involved but also the question of national ideologies, some of which are divergent to ours and destined to threaten and uproot the very foundation upon which our democratic institution was founded. To ensure that the situation just referred to will be averted and not permitted to take a foothold in Liberia we have to strengthen and increase our border control units and give more attention to border problems as they arise from day to day.

Despite the intensification of intra-African contacts during the Second World War and its aftermath, Liberia still found itself largely isolated from continental affairs on the eve of Ghana's independence in 1957. The continued heavy reliance of Liberia upon American support was only one of the factors contributing to this isolation. Geography was another, for the rough terrain made it difficult for the Liberians to build roads and bridges connecting Monrovia with its own hinterland, let alone reaching the French and British territories beyond. European politics was also a factor, inasmuch as Liberia was excluded from the British and French colonial systems, which at least had led to some interterritorial cooperation, for example, between Nigeria and Sierra Leone, or Senegal and the Ivory Coast. The critical attitudes Europeans assumed with respect to the ability of the Americo-Liberians to govern themselves were frequently adopted by African leaders as well.[5] Isolation, however, was also a product of choice by the Americo-Liberians, who rejected their African heritage in favor of an emphasis upon their Western background.

Such contact as did take place between Liberians and other West Africans before the 1960s was largely personal in character. Family ties, for example, between the Creoles of Sierra Leone and the Americo-Liberians remained strong, as did those among the tribal peoples separated by the arbitrarily drawn international boundaries.[6] The parents of Americo-Liberian youths in many cases recognized the superior standard of schools in the Gold Coast and Sierra Leone and sent their children there for education. Better employment opportunities lured the Kru people as well as many Americo-Liberians to Nigeria and Senegal.

The achievement of independence by Ghana in 1957 and Guinea in 1958 had a profound impact upon Tubman and other Whig leaders. Not only was the Republic permitted for the first time to establish direct official relations with other West African governments, but such ties were recognized as vital for Americo-Liberian survival. The rising wave of African nationalism posed a threat both to the supremacy of the settler community within the Republic and to Liberia's claim to a major share of the technical and other forms of assistance given throughout the United Nations to developing countries in Africa. This is a plausible explanation for the almost frenzied efforts of the Liberian government to establish ties with the new states, to assume a role of leadership in the United Nations and at the various conferences of African states, and to intensify its role as the champion of African liberation.[7] The drain upon Liberia's financial resources (roughly one-tenth of the national budget) and upon its pool of educated talent as a consequence of Liberia establishing embassies in each new African country was considerable. Exchanges of visits between Tubman and Tolbert with other African heads of state were frequent and often led to signing of bilateral agreements on trade, cultural exchanges, and other matters. Liberian officials each year attended an average of fifty conferences on African problems or the general condition of developing societies.

In the two decades preceding the 1980 coup, Liberia served as the host country for many conferences which had historic significance for the African continent as a whole. A largely unheralded meeting which took place in the remote interior at Sanniquellie in 1959—just prior to the "Year of African Independence"—had a profound impact in scuttling Kwame Nkrumah's version of Pan-Africanism, which entailed a political union of African states at the continental level. The Sanniquellie Conference (attended by Tubman, Nkrumah, and Sékou Touré of Guinea) was a victory for Tubman's regional and economic approaches to Pan-African unity.[8]

Another famous conference of the Tubman period was the Monrovia Conference of 1961, which signaled the deepening cleavage between the more revolutionary socialist-oriented states (called the Casablanca bloc) and the more moderate or conservative powers (which came to be called the Brazzaville and later the Monrovia bloc). The Monrovia Conference was of critical importance in shaping the outlines of the future Organization of African Unity.

Liberia's claim to speak for other African states in the United Nations was given more than symbolic recognition in December 1960 by its selection as the first African state to be seated on the Security Council and by the election in 1969 of its U.N. delegate, Mrs. Angie Brooks-Randolph, as the first African president of the General Assembly. Under Tubman, and increasingly so under Tolbert, Liberian delegates within the various organs of the United Nations seized the mantle of leadership within the African caucus, mounting a steady campaign of criticism against South Africa for its policy of apartheid and its administration of Namibia, against Portugal for its repression of African nationalism in Angola and Mozambique, and against Britain for not having taken a more vigorous stand in Rhodesia-Zimbabwe. Why Tubman and his successor were allowed to assume the leadership role in the African camp was a mystery to many, given the preindependence hostility of many Nigerian, Ghanaian, and other African nationalists toward Liberia. In part, it may have been purely practical considerations: Liberia, among all the states in Africa, appeared to have the financial means and the educated personnel to spare for the diplomatic advancement of African causes. Its special relationship with the United States—obviously a distinct disadvantage in many instances—did nevertheless give Liberia diplomatic and other forms of access to the most powerful member of the international community. Finally, deference to Tubman's seniority spared many African leaders in the early postindependence era from having to recognize the self-acclaimed leadership role of Kwame Nkrumah. This was particularly important to the leaders of Nigeria, Sierra Leone, and most of the French-speaking states, who regarded Nkrumah's international role as a threat to domestic stability within their own countries.

Whether or not the leadership of Tubman and Tolbert was appreciated by other African heads of state, Liberia's leaders felt that the new posture was vital for that country's survival. Unless it magnified its importance in intra-African affairs, even its special relationship with the United States was likely to be diminished, with more and more foreign aid directed to Nigeria, Ghana, and other larger and more activist states. Unless Liberia took positive stands on issues, African leadership would be monopolized by the radical group at the opposite ideological pole from Liberia. This explains why Liberia during the Congo crisis provided troops for the United Nations efforts and involved itself diplomatically in the undermining of Lumumba and Gizenga. It accounts, too, for the rather ubiquitous presence of Liberians in most of the United Nations specialized agencies. Liberia under Tubman and Tolbert used its membership in the World Health Organization, in UNESCO, and in other bodies not only to expand its own channels for technical assistance but to advance more general African causes as well. With the exception of the International Labor Organization (ILO), where it was occasionally attacked for its own labor practices, the Liberians in the United Nations had been highly successful in their attempt to capture the role of spokesman for Africa.

Despite the vigorous stance on southern African questions, Liberia's vital interests within the broader context of continental affairs under Tubman and Tolbert tended to be focused on the more conservative and pro-Western states of Africa than with those countries that tended to take more radical positions on world prob-

lems, relations with the West, Pan-Africanism, and development of socialist economies. Tubman and Tolbert alike, for example, went out of their way to establish
very special links with the late Emperor Haile Selassie I of Ethiopia, President
Habib Bourguiba of Tunisia, the leaders of many Francophone states of West and
Central Africa, and even with Malawi's president, Hastings Kamuzu Banda, who
committed the cardinal sin in the eyes of many by establishing diplomatic relations
with South Africa. Tubman also took relatively bold and unpopular stances in
defense of Moise Tshombe, both during his leadership of the Congo (Zaire) in 1964
and during his detention in Algeria in 1967. On the other hand, Tubman's relations
with Ghana during the Nkrumah period and with Mali, Algeria, and Nasser's Egypt
ranged from studied correctness to outright hostility. At various points in the Tubman
era, Nkrumah's and Nasser's diplomatic personnel were expelled for alleged interference in Liberian internal affairs.

Of particular concern to the Tubman and Tolbert regimes was the relationship
between Liberia and its more immediate neighbors. Potentially, Sierra Leone might
have constituted a threat to the Americo-Liberians, for that state, even before its
independence in 1961, had come under the control of the tribal people of the
hinterland. Despite the potential for conflict arising from the cross-boundary ethnic
ties of the Mende, Gola, Kissi, and others and the links between the Americo-
Liberians and their Sierra Leone counterparts, the Creoles, relations between the
two governments remained cordial. The military regime that took over in Sierra
Leone in 1967 appeared to be as conservative as the preceding governments of Sir
Milton and Sir Albert Margai. The ascendancy of the more liberal Siaka Stevens,
however, caused some concern in Monrovia. The only major source of irritation
between the two states during the Tubman and Tolbert period, however, appeared
to be the substantial revenue loss that Sierra Leone sustained as a result of diamond
smuggling. Many of the diamonds that entered the world market through Monrovia
apparently had been mined in the Kono District of Sierra Leone. Relations with
Sierra Leone took a more favorable turn under Tolbert with the discussion of bridge
and road construction linking the two countries as well as the establishment of a
joint customs union. Both developments came to pass, and the birth of the Mano
River Union in 1973 provided the groundwork for a common market which eventually would include Guinea (and eventually possibly even the Ivory Coast) within
the broader framework of the Economic Community of West African States
(ECOWAS).

Liberia's eastern neighbor, the Ivory Coast, also generally maintained good
relations with the Tubman and Tolbert governments, inasmuch as President Félix
Houphouët-Boigny shared Tubman's and Tolbert's views of Pan-Africanism, capitalism, and relations with the West. Indeed, highly personalized links between the
leadership of the two states were forged with the marriage of the Liberian president's
son, A. B. Tolbert, to the niece (ward) of Houphouët-Boigny. A joint Liberian-
Ivorien commission on cooperation was established under Tolbert. The one major
issue dividing the two countries prior to the 1980 coup was the Ivory Coast's efforts
to market its coffee in the United States—a move which threatened the tenuous
foothold that Liberia enjoyed as a result of its share of the American market. One

latent source of concern to Liberia was the continuing hostility between Liberia's mutual neighbors, the Ivory Coast and Guinea, which raised the spectre of military disorder near Liberia's borders. Thus, Tolbert was committed to continuing the work of his predecessor in bringing the parties to that dispute—as well as the dispute between Guinea and Senegal—to the conference table. Tolbert's peacemaker skills ultimately achieved an accord among the various parties following the April 1978 peace conference in Monrovia.

In the late 1950s the greater cause for regional concern was neither Sierra Leone nor the Ivory Coast; it was Guinea. As the successors to the French, the Guineans inherited the series of boundary disputes with Liberia, especially those relating to the ownership of the iron-rich Nimba Mountain. The more threatening problem, however, was the ideological chasm separating the True Whig Party and Sékou Touré's Parti Démocratique de Guinée. The latter, in seeking the rapid political, social, and economic mobilization of all elements within society along socialist lines, stood in sharp contrast to the True Whig Party. As a result, moreover, of the ruthless fashion in which de Gaulle withdrew from Guinea at the time of independence, Sékou Touré was forced to search for other friends at the global level in order to stave off economic collapse. The Soviet bloc eagerly stepped into this void. Thus, the major protagonists of the Cold War—the United States and the Soviet Union—found their respective major spheres of influence in Africa face to face at the Guinean-Liberian border.

Nonetheless, Sékou Touré and William Tubman ultimately arrived at a harmonious modus vivendi. Strangely enough—given the differences in age, background, ideological orientation, and other factors—a rather remarkable friendship developed between these two West African leaders during the last decade of Tubman's rule, and friendship between the two countries actually intensified under Tolbert. Indeed, when the Tolbert regime, in April 1979, seemed to be on the verge of collapse in the face of the rice rioters, it was Sékou Touré—under a previously signed defense agreement—who sent MIG planes and a contingent of troops to buttress the shaky regime. A significant consideration in the development of close Guinean-Liberian relations has been the dependence of Guinea upon Liberian roads and the Free Port of Monrovia in getting its goods from eastern Guinea into the world market. The longer route to Conakry and the general shortage of fuel in Guinea have made the Liberian route to the sea vital. Moreover, the agreement permitting Guinea to use the new railroad from Nimba to the port of Buchanan has made it economically feasible for Guinea to mine the iron ore found in its portion of the Nimba Range. Hence, there were sound reasons for Sékou Touré's implicit self-restraint in exporting revolution to Liberia. There were few restrictions on the movement of Liberian and Guinean nationals across their frontiers for social or economic contract.

### Pan-Africanism

Perhaps the oddest element in the Tubman-Touré friendship was the acceptance by the Guinean president of Tubman's viewpoint on Pan-Africanism, despite Touré's earlier collaboration with Nkrumah. Indeed, in a sense, Tubman and Touré were thrown together by Nkrumah.[9] It is true that Nkrumah's electrifying announcement in November 1958 that Ghana and Guinea had united (in what quickly turned out to be a union on paper only) provided Touré with the kind of psychological boost he needed at that moment both at home and abroad—given de Gaulle's efforts to "quarantine" the newly independent state. Gradually, however, Touré found Nkrumah's embrace somewhat suffocating. Tubman, for his part, found the prospect of Nkrumah as his next-door neighbor a direct challenge to the Liberian political system. In opposition to the Nkrumah posture that Pan-African unity had to be achieved immediately, politically, and on a continental plane, Tubman gradually evolved a counterversion of Pan-Africanism that emphasized gradualism, economic and cultural cooperation as a precursor to political discussion, and regional rather than continental cooperation.

I regard Tubman's diplomatic victory in his discussions with Nkrumah and Touré at Sanniquellie in 1959 as one of the landmarks in the history of the Pan-African movement. Tubman effectively undermined the Nkrumah approach and in the process loosened the bonds between Touré and the Ghanaian leader. Indeed, by the time of Nkrumah's overthrow in 1966, the political experiment represented by the expanded Guinea-Ghana-Mali union was in ashes, and Guinea found itself in a regional customs union that linked it with three of the more conservative states of West Africa: Sierra Leone, Ivory Coast, and Liberia. Although the Organization for West African Economic Cooperation did not function as effectively as its advocates hoped it would, its creation was important. It demonstrated once again the manner in which Tubman had been able to use his remarkable talents in international diplomacy to reduce a clear and present ideological threat to Liberia's domestic stability.

At the continental level as well, Liberia's posture on Pan-African cooperation was welcomed by many African leaders who viewed Nkrumah's activities as unrealistic, if not threatening. The Monrovia Conference of May 1961, the Lagos Conference of 1962, and the Addis Ababa founding conference of the OAU were stamped "Made in Liberia." In its functioning since 1963, the Organization of African Unity has failed to be the dynamic force in African affairs which Nkrumah had hoped, and Tubman had feared, it might be. Despite Liberia's initial hesitancy and doubt, the full recognition of the role Liberia played in the formation of the OAU and of Liberia's leadership role in Africa came in 1978 with the selection of Monrovia as the site for the 1979 OAU head of states meeting, with Tolbert automatically becoming the presiding chairman of the OAU at the conclusion of the conference. Tolbert's role in projecting Liberia as the spokesman of the African continent had been cultivated over a long period and was a far more bold attempt than even Tubman had dared. Tolbert cast himself in the role of mediator of intra-African disputes and achieved some measure of success in relieving tensions between Guinea and its African neighbors, Senegal and Ivory Coast, and also helped delay the inevitable military confrontation between Uganda's Idi Amin and Julius Nyerere of Tanzania. Not all of Tolbert's efforts in this regard were as skillfully executed as his ill-timed secret midnight flight to Biafra at the height of the Nigerian civil war—an act which offended the ultimately victorious forces of the Nigerian federal government.

Tolbert also vigorously pursued what Tubman had earlier attempted in the form of regional economic cooperation within Africa. He moved from the successful launching of the Mano River Union to hosting, in January 1975, the founding meeting of the Economic Community of West African States, which attempted to transcend linguistic, historic, and other barriers to cooperation among the fifteen states of that region. Although its ultimate goal of creating a homogeneous West African political community is still far from being realized, ECOWAS has broken down some of the obstacles to trade, migration, and the flow of goods and capital among the 170 million inhabitants of the region.

What ultimately garnered Tolbert the OAU chairmanship, however, was his advocacy of a militant stance against the white regimes in Angola, Mozambique, and Rhodesia-Zimbabwe and his demands for the independence of Namibia and the dismantling of South Africa's system of apartheid. Liberian delegates were energetic and vocal on these issues in the United Nations and in the councils of the Organization of African Unity. In his earliest efforts Tolbert was bumbling and vacillating on the question of South Africa. After having chided Houphouët-Boigny in 1972 for suggesting that the Black African states should engage in dialogue with the white South African leadership, by February 1975 Tolbert startled most of his Black African colleagues in the OAU by quietly inviting South African Prime Minister John Vorster to Monrovia.[10] The two leaders reportedly discussed the independence of Namibia, the end of South Africa's support of the Ian Smith regime in Zimbabwe, and the eradication of the Homelands policy and apartheid within South Africa itself. Since this act gave the Vorster regime the appearance of legitimacy (without accomplishing positive results), it was roundly criticized in African circles. Few were placated by Tolbert's explanation that he had "cleared" his invitation with SWAPO leaders in Namibia and with notable Black leaders in South Africa. It was only the persistence of Tolbert's vocal efforts as well as the generous financial contribution of the Liberian government and the expatriate community in Liberia to southern African liberation that permitted Tolbert to command respect on this issue. In all fairness, Tolbert's southern African stance helped the liberation cause, if only because it broke the ranks of conservative states that had long remained mute on the subject.

During the Tubman and Tolbert decades, Liberia managed to execute almost complete reversal of its relatively isolationist stance. Without abandoning its ties with America—even increasing them in terms of economic, cultural, and military assistance—Liberia forged an independent, activist role in international politics. New links with Asia and Europe gave it more maneuverability in resisting demands from the United States. Its new ties with its African neighbors reduced the dangers of ideological threats closer to home. From a position of low repute in the attitudes of African elites elsewhere on the continent, it was permitted to claim the mantle of leadership in pressing African causes. Thus, by pursuing an activist foreign policy, Liberia managed to neutralize the potentially hostile environment in which it had formerly found itself. In a curious way, too, the activist foreign policy provided yet another hedge against revolution by providing an outlet for the pool of young educated Liberians who had had their aspirations and professional talents intentionally thwarted insofar as the domestic economic transformation of Liberia was concerned.

# PART TWO

## The 1980 Coup
### *Prelude and Perspective*

# X.

# The Gathering Storm

The quarter of a century during which Tubman ruled Liberia and the decade of the Tolbert era provided the Americo-Liberians with new and more effective techniques for the art of political survival. In many respects the twentieth-century threats posed to the Whig autocracy by African nationalism in neighboring states constituted even greater challenges than the hostility of the physical environment, tribal resistance, and the machinations of the European colonial powers that had to be overcome by the founding settlers in the nineteenth century. Although Liberia as a whole undoubtedly gained, it was the decidedly good fortune of the Americo-Liberian class that the modern challenge to its supremacy found its hero. Tubman—frequently over the strenuous opposition of those whose interests ironically prospered—displayed a talent for political imagination and manipulation far exceeding any of his predecessors. Tolbert—with uneven results—attempted to follow in his footsteps.

The Open Door policy, for example, ingeniously expanded the financial means for the continued subsidizing of the system of Americo-Liberian privilege. At the same time, the revenues from iron ore, rubber, and other resources provided the financial and technical means for the suppression, seduction, and control of dissent of the tribal majority. The foreigner in the nineteenth century was considered an overt threat to Americo-Liberian supremacy in the tribal hinterland; in the Tubman and Tolbert eras the foreigner became the witting or unwitting partner in the exploitation of the tribal masses. President Tubman's and President Tolbert's foreign policies, moreover, skillfully injected Liberia into world affairs and ended Liberia's isolation from its African neighbors. As a result, both presidents managed to neutralize the potential hostility of neighboring African leaders, who had committed themselves to a different kind of political, social, and economic revolution for the people of their respective countries. Finally, the extension of suffrage and representation to the tribal hinterland and the implementation of the Unification Program provided to the external world at least the semblance of greater access for the tribal people to the citadels of political, social, and economic power in Liberia.

*The Limits of the Unification Program*

The key to the continued success of Tubman and Tolbert's evolutionary approach to change lay largely in the future of the Unification Program. There is abundant evidence that in official circumstances at least, the many historic barriers to legal, political, and social equality between the tribal masses and the descendants of the founding settlers were being eroded. Public arrogance on the part of Americo-Liberians toward tribal people—still blatant during the administration of Edwin Barclay—became rarer, and the most flagrant abuses of basic substantive and procedural rights were largely curbed during the Tubman and Tolbert eras. In more positive terms, the Unification Program encouraged the tribal people to take a measure of pride in their antecedents, their art and language, and even their traditional names. Foreign and Liberian anthropologists, folklorists, historians, and other scholars were being invited to portray more accurately the tribal contribution to the making of modern Liberia. Finally, the tribal people at last came to realize that the president of Liberia was also their president. As a popular political figure who evidenced warmth, humor, and the ability to render substantive justice, Tubman did much to bridge the gap separating the two communities in Liberia. And Tolbert attempted to emulate, if not surpass, Tubman as a role model.

For the national society in general, however, the cultural integration of the settler and tribal communities was far from complete even though education abroad had started to create common bonds among a growing cadre of Americo-Liberian and tribal youth who were raising serious questions about the continued course of political, economic, and social development of their country. Yet the gulf between the two communities remained. Although public abuse of tribal people had diminished, covert discrimination in governmental service as well as in social relationships continued. Even after the 1980 coup many—if not most—tribal people still tended to regard themselves as Bassa, Kpelle, or Loma, reserving the title "Liberian" for the Americo-Liberians. While the national legal code was purposely vague on the point, it was apparent that a legal distinction had been perpetuated between the two communities in matters of marriage and divorce, jurisdiction of tribal and statutory courts, and the occupation of land in the interior. Oddly enough, when legal distinctions had been eliminated, the situation usually worked to the monetary and political advantage of the corps of Monrovia-based lawyers and their young tribal protégés. Conversely, it worked to the decided disadvantage of the illiterate tribal peasant, who found himself trapped in the unfamiliar procedures of the Liberian national court system, which was spreading throughout the hinterland counties.[1] Frequently, moreover, the Westernized tribal youth found himself in the frustrating position of having his claim to "civilized" status rejected both by his tribal kin and by the Americo-Liberian elite.

Until the 1980 coup, there were still serious obstacles to the easy acquisition of the certificate that exempted a tribal person from compulsory labor, porter service, and the jurisdiction of tribal courts. Thus, the kinsmen of a Western-educated tribal youth continued to hold him responsible for the traditional obligations with respect to his family and to tribal political leaders despite his superior education, his acceptance of Christianity, and his involvement in the money economy. Without denigrating efforts at national integration, it is clear that the overwhelming thrust of integration was still in the direction of accepting settler rather than tribal norms of behavior.

As suffrage was extended, moreover, elections within the single-party system became mere ratifications of the status quo. By the time hinterland citizens were accorded representation in the national legislature, power had already gravitated to the executive branch. And as posts in government were allocated to tribal persons in growing numbers, control over the key positions in society remained ever more firmly in the hands of those families who would guarantee continued settler control over the changing political community. As was noted in chapter 7, neither Tubman nor Tolbert had more than one or two token tribal persons in the cabinet, and more often than not the one token representative was named to the Ministry of Education or to Information and Tourism, which were felt to be nonthreatening posts with respect to Americo-Liberian privilege. In some instances a tribal person who attained high office had very close links with some of the Americo-Liberian families. Jackson Doe—whom Tolbert had selected as a deputy minister of education and who in 1985 challenged Samuel Doe (no relation) for the presidency—had been reared by the family of former Chief Justice Louis Grimes.

Although in relative terms the material lot of the tribal people was substantially improved by the rapid economic exploitation of Liberia's resources, in absolute terms the gains of the tribal people were small when contrasted with those of the Americo-Liberian elite. By the Tolbert government's own admission, each year the gap between the extremes of income became greater, while restraints upon training opportunities and the upward mobility of tribal people in the economy were eased only slightly. Only the rigorous and persistent prodding of American and other foreign advisers persuaded the government to take into account the urgent needs of the tribal areas for new schools or hospitals, government scholarships, and welfare programs. Although the Peace Corps effort in particular led to some correction of the gross imbalances, much still remained to be done.

### The Issue of Land

In the long run the greatest continuing irritant was still the initial source of antagonism between the founding settlers and the indigenous tribal leaders: land. Quietly but steadily, as the new roads penetrated the hinterland, the "honorables" and others who had the ear of the president engaged in one of the most extensive programs of private land acquisition outside of South Africa, Rhodesia, and the Portuguese dependencies. The actual extent of the transfer of title from tribal land to freehold land was not a matter of public record, for only the least consequential registrations of title were published in the press. So outrageous was the covert acquisition of land that President Tubman himself, in his inaugural address of 1964, commented on the situation. He noted that several citizens—including the chiefs allied with the Americo-Liberian ruling class—had acquired estates of up to twenty thousand acres, for as little as fifty cents an acre. "One day," Tubman warned, "the growing educated population in the rural areas might find themselves without land, which would have been bought up by Monrovia folk."[2] It was a self-serving comment, however, for it was President Tubman's office which authorized the transfer of titles, and the president's own family holdings were substantial, even if not highly visible or publicized. Under Tolbert the acquisition of land by members of the Tolbert family became blatant.

### Self-Interest, Group Interest, and Political Stability

It remained a troubling question whether the evolutionary pace of change that still left the Americo-Liberian ruling class firmly in control would give way under Tolbert to a more revolutionary approach that promised a more egalitarian society. The answer to that question depended ultimately upon the attitudes and actions of the young generation of Liberians—both Americo-Liberian and tribal—who had been the beneficiaries of changes in the economic order.

One of the striking features of Liberia in the post-Tubman era was that few of the beneficiaries of the system of privilege entered the jobs that were most critical to the maintenance of continued True Whig control. For example, the role of district commissioner in the hinterland areas had become a position of increasingly strategic proportions relative to settler dominance. New roads, the growth of trading centers inland, the fluid migration of tribal people, and new economic enterprises called for more rigorous surveillance in maintaining Whig domination of Liberian politics. But being posted to the hinterland as a district commissioner—far from the bright lights and the vital center of politics in Monrovia—had little appeal to the sons of the more prominent Americo-Liberian families. By default, then, the job of district commissioner often went to an individual who had perhaps only a rudimentary education and who came from a family whose origins were either lower-class Americo-Liberian or even tribal (assuming that his loyalty to the regime had been demonstrated). The consequence was that the district commissioner was not particularly committed to the perpetuation of a system that gave greater favors and rewards to the urban aristocracy at the coast. To the lower-class Americo-Liberian from Monrovia, the remote interior district took on all the attributes of a "punishment station." He attempted where he could to compensate for his low political status and overcome his sense of personal frustration. He tended, for example to emulate the "honorables" by engaging in extensive purchasing of land (despite the specific legal provision against such conflict of interest), to use local labor for his farm, and to perform other acts that advanced his own personal interests but further antagonized the tribal masses toward the system of government he represented. Indeed, lacking the kind of family connections that both sustained and restrained the Americo-Liberian official through good fortunes and bad, the lower-status district commissioner felt compelled to make the best of his opportunities while he could.

Ironically, this situation was magnified by the 1964 political reform—namely, the extension of the county system to the former provinces. A whole new layer of county jobs was created. Although some of the senatorial and house seats were assumed by bona fide members of the Whig elite, the rest went to Western-educated tribal persons, as did many of the new administrative and legal posts in the new system. Thus, the educated tribal person who had demonstrated his loyalty to the regime was given the chance of actively involving himself in local politics, forgoing, for the time being, his ambitions to participate at the national level. If he came from one of the tribal groups, such as the Gola, which has an individualistic and somewhat capitalistic orientation, he could play the game of exploitation in the same way as his Americo-Liberian counterpart. In the absence of strong family, tribal, or regional affiliations which could serve as social restraining mechanisms in the politics of the interior, the exploitation of the uneducated tribal masses by their young evolved kinsmen often became even more relentless than the Americo-Liberian exploitation of the past.

A similar process, but with sharply differing effects, occurred in the network of government schools which were steadily reaching some of the remotest areas of the Republic. The assignment of teachers to Monrovia and other coastal school systems was made strictly on a political basis, with the teachers from the leading families having prior claims. Being in Monrovia, they could frequently hold down a second job, which permitted them to compensate for their low teaching salaries. On the other hand, the teacher posted up-country tended to be less dedicated to the existing order of privilege than his coastal counterpart. Covertly, and even overtly, the teacher in the hinterland became an advocate of a more rapid change in the political, economic, and social system. Experiencing fewer of the rewards of modernization, despite a significant investment in time and tuition, he or she resented and opposed the many involuntary salary deductions for the True Whig Party and other projects. The teacher tended, too, to resent the unpredictable intrusions into professional affairs made by Monrovia politicians as well as by local private Americo-Liberian residents. Feeling cheated by the social system, the teacher in the interior could not avoid conveying a sense of frustration to the students. The characterizations in Fletcher Knebel's novel *Zinzin Road* (which was based on Liberia) were not far from the mark.[3]

Furthermore, the ruling elite's disdain of commerce and industry contributed to its undoing. Given the scale of economic growth and the discovery of new deposits of iron ore, it was possible to continue for some time the uneconomic use of foreign personnel to manage the burgeoning economy. At a certain point, however, higher wages, housing, and other perquisites made the recruitment of non-Liberian personnel a costly enterprise. Coupled with this development was the fact that the expanding scholarship programs for higher education had already created a pool of skilled talent that the regime simply could not absorb en masse into governmental sinecures and yet could not permit to become part of an unemployed intellectual group, clustering in Monrovia and other urban communities. Hence, it was inevitable that educated tribal youth eventually began displacing the foreign managerial personnel. This group did not long remain content with the slow pace of change in the 1970s.

The migrant worker as well no longer continued to be satisfied with the unskilled or semiskilled jobs offered him when he left the security of his tribal area. So rapid was the pace of change that by 1970 approximately one-fourth of the tribal people were involved in some phase of the money economy. A decade later one-third to one-half were actively involved, and many had migrated to the coastal cities or the new urban areas around the mining compounds. The percentage of Liberians who were urban residents went from 23 percent in 1965 to 38 percent two decades later. As the migratory laborers traveled from place to place, the mixed message of despair and hope became ever more difficult to stifle with the rhetoric of progress and free enterprise mouthed by the leaders of society. Returning to his rural home-land, the migrant, who had seen the life that prosperity had brought to other Li-berians, found it more and more difficult to accept the mounting taxes, the extortions from itinerant soldiers, and the illegal demands for labor made by officials and private Americo-Liberians alike. Indeed, the level of agitation was raised by such acts as the revolutionary step LAMCO took in 1967 in agreeing to pay its mechanics as high as $1.20 an *hour*—twice what Firestone and Liberian rubber growers were paying unskilled laborers per *day* just a few years previously.[4]

Unorganized discontent among the masses elsewhere in the world, however, had never been a sufficient factor in itself in bringing about revolutionary change. Political movements require leadership, and until the Tolbert era all the leadership talent had been monopolized, seduced, or suppressed by the Americo-Liberian class. The disaffected peasant or mineworker was not likely to find the leader for his cause among the Old Guard of the settler elite. Many of the latter had been frequent critics of Presidents Tubman and Tolbert, but their criticism was against the reforms that had weakened rigid settler control over politics. Radical leadership was slow in emerging from among the group of "new" Liberians, the young, educated, and polished officials who surrounded the president. Having just eased the Old Guard from the stage, this group was eager to enjoy its inheritance. Equally delayed in protecting the system were the Western-educated tribal youth, many of whom were busily developing entrenched private interests in the "new politics" of the hinterland counties. At the national level, moreover, the tenure in the past of either young or elderly officials who had too openly paraded their tribal origins had been brief, and occasionally brutal. Indeed, the tribal person who succeeded in gaining prominence on the national scene often became almost a caricature of Old Guard Americo-Liberian manners and mores.

## Formalism and Reform

One of the fundamental flaws in the Unification Program conceived by Tubman and further advanced by Tolbert is that it did not result in a substantial sharing of political power between the Americo-Liberian elite and the tribal masses. Neither president could act without the cooperation of his main source of support within the settler community. Before the assumption of office by Tubman, the Americo-Liberian settlers and their descendants had survived for a century and a quarter, and the Old Guard at least was not about to surrender tried and accepted techniques of survival without a struggle. Where they had not frontally attacked the president and his policies, the more conservative Americo-Liberians accepted the rhetoric of reform without feeling obliged to give it substance. Indeed, in this respect the opponents of change continued the tendency toward *formalism*, a dominant characteristic of Liberian policies almost from the outset. It is against this background of formalism as a political philosophy and as a way of life that one must attempt to evaluate the reality of reform under the Tubman regime.

The tendency toward formalism was readily apparent in the constant emphasis upon constitutionalism, adherence to legal technicalities in the courts, and the charade of conducting elaborate electoral campaigns when there were no opponents to the True Whig Party candidates. Indeed, when a forceful individual violated the expectations of formalism—as Amos Sawyer did in boldly opting to contest the Monrovia mayoral election in 1979 and pit himself against the slated candidate (see chapter 12)—the election was canceled. The emphasis upon proper form and procedure pervaded almost all aspects of social intercourse in Liberia during the First Republic. The tendency to emphasize form and style at the expense of substance, moreover, was not limited to the upper strata of the Americo-Liberian community; it infected the poorer element of that society as well as the tribal person who had only recently migrated to Monrovia. A casual and impatient visitor to Liberia frequently failed to comprehend or appreciate the rigorous attention to detail regarding dress and other items of protocol on state occasions, the exacting fashion in which a preacher adhered to the Order of Worship in a church service, and the almost stylized ritual that had to be observed in completing a transaction with a trader or in circumventing a demand for a "dash" on the part of a traffic policeman. A hinterland court clerk would take great pains to make an exact transcript of a case without any attention being given to the matter of keeping, let alone compiling, the records in any systematic way so that they could constitute a guide for the more efficient administration of a district.[5] The act of making a record had a logic and mystique of its own almost unrelated to improving government procedures. The historical basis for this emphasis upon formalism may perhaps have been that Liberia was founded by men and women who were in, but not part of, an antebellum southern society in America where the propriety of an act was given great value.

Formalism was highly evident in the political sphere. Campaign rhetoric, letters to the editor, church sermons, and debates in the Legislature were replete with demands that politicians must observe both the letter and the spirit of the Constitution of 1847.[6] It mattered little that the elaborate description in the Liberian Constitution of the ways in which power was distributed among a president, a bicameral legislature, and a supreme court bore even less resemblance to the actual distribution of power than it did in most other societies with written constitutions. The absence until recently of a collected code of laws or a compilation of Supreme Court decisions, however, had not prevented Americo-Liberian lawyers from arguing eloquently and at great length about the fine points of law and legal precedents. The constitutional arrangement, which rejected both federalism and the creation of meaningful structures of local government, placed a high emphasis on centralization of power in Monrovia. Yet, in the management of local affairs, prominent families in each of the counties and the urbanized communities exercised a considerable degree of local autonomy, while the formalities of centralized control over the administration of national programs were still rigorously adhered to.

   While we cannot dismiss the formal structures of government and the formal allocations of authority as unimportant, we must appreciate that they had relevance largely to the problem of legitimacy of the existing leadership group. Despite the fact that neither Tubman nor Tolbert in their respective last bids for office had no opponents, they were required to go through the formality of campaigning. Earlier, no one doubted that either could continue to run for office for an indefinite number of terms even though the 1847 Constitution had to be changed specifically to accommodate the imcumbent president. Despite this obvious violation of the spirit of the Constitution, each felt obliged to have the Constitution formally amended.

   I have dealt with the problems of formalism at length in order to stress the fact that the constant revision of suffrage requirements, the extension of the principle of representation, and the changes in the administrative framework of the national government did not bring about an actual realignment of political power. The mechanisms devised by the Americo-Liberian elite during the last four decades of the First Republic were intended to ensure that the changes in the Liberian political system would be evolutionary rather than revolutionary in character. Although a facade of mass participation in the political process was being presented to the outside world, the decision-making process within the True Whig Party remained firmly under the control of the Americo-Liberian minority.

# XI.

# Economic Stresses in the Tolbert Era

Many of the anomalies of economic, social, cultural, and political change in Liberia only came to a head toward the end of the Tubman era. It fell to the man who succeeded Tubman in 1971, William R. Tolbert, to reap the wild winds of change. The physical transformation of Liberia which brought many improvements in the quality of life unfortunately also brought disruption of previous economic networks and institutions, and—in particular—a diminished capacity of Liberia's agriculture to meet the country's demands for food. These problems of the domestic economy were compounded by falls in the international prices of iron and rubber—Liberia's main exports—in the face of rising prices for imported oil. Thus a severe balance of payments situation for Liberia had developed by the mid-1970s.

On balance, the economic record of the Tolbert administration was curiously mixed. In sheer physical terms, for example, the construction of new schools and hospitals, the completion of a new stretches of highway and bridges throughout the interior, and the building of many new multi-storied office structures and of private homes in all of Liberia's cities had taken place at a more impressive pace under Tolbert than had been true even under Tubman. Liberia's new national and international image under Tolbert had been a key factor in attracting at an accelerating rate the foreign capital needed for economic expansion in the mineral, agricultural, and forestry sectors. While it is true that the growing middle class in Monrovia and other cities was suffering from a severe spiral of inflation, it is also true that their burden was a far cry from what citizens of Ghana, Nigeria, and other West African states were experiencing. The very scope of the expansion of governmental and private enterprises meant that the previously neglected tribal youth and lower-income Americo-Liberians acquired new skills, new employment opportunities, and other benefits.

In the field of education, progress was evident everywhere, despite a high incidence of illiteracy among the adult population (roughly 75–80 percent for the country as a whole). The enrollment of children in primary schools had doubled from 31 percent in 1960 to 66 percent at the time of the 1980 coup, while secondary school enrollments had leaped from 2 to 20 percent for that same period. Although still dependent upon traditional Christian mission support as well as new foreign sources—such as the Peace Corps—the government itself had undertaken a more direct responsibility in that important area of training educated manpower for development. The textbooks, moreover, were written with the problems of Liberia and a developing society in mind, and a similar shift in emphasis was noticeable in the curriculum from a classical to a development-oriented bias. As has been noted elsewhere, the University of Liberia, for example, had become a respected institution of higher learning. Another index of modernization with respect to education is that in 1960 I could find only one bookshop in Monrovia, while in 1980 I counted over twenty bookshops, many well stocked with paperback books on literature, science, practical arts (language, bookkeeping, beekeeping), and other fields—including, incidentally, a large display of very explicit "adult" books.

*Transport and Development*

Perhaps nowhere was Liberia's physical transformation more apparent than with respect to transportation. Before the Tubman era, not only was Liberia remote from the rest of the world (including its immediate neighbors), but both limited means and a conscious policy of insulating the tribal hinterland against divisive alien influences had kept the coastal strip relatively isolated from the rest of the country. During the Tubman and Tolbert periods there had been a dramatic reversal of the previous situation with respect to establishing both improved road, sea, and air links to the outside world and an effective road and bridge network that was systematically covering the entire Republic. There were now rail links connecting the coast with the key mining areas in the interior.

These transport developments not only promoted expanded production and distribution of commodities, but also facilitated political integration and control, which perhaps accounted for the high priority given this phase of economic growth. The construction of artificial harbors at Monrovia, Harper, Buchanan, and Greenville resulted from the Firestone investment, Liberia's role in World War II, and Tubman's Open Door policy, which facilitated exploitation of agricultural potential and mineral resources. Previously all passengers and produce brought into Liberia had to be discharged to small surf boats from ships anchored a mile or more from shore. The many cataracts and shifting sandbars in the rivers of Liberia had made them useless for anything other than local internal trade. In the period following World War II the airplane diminished the isolation of Liberia, and Roberts International Airport became a major field serving a number of American, European, African, Middle East, and Latin American airlines. The airplane, however, did not alleviate the problem of internal transportation, especially where bulk commodities were concerned. The Bomi Hills, Nimba, and other iron-mining operations led to the construction of several railroads connecting the interior with the coast. In the critical area of road construction, however, Liberia for a long time lagged considerably behind most countries in West Africa. In 1945 there were only 206 miles of all-weather roads in the country—most of it built by Firestone—and even Monrovia lacked macadamized streets. With the help of U.S. AID (Agency for International Development) loans and other forms of external assistance, by 1981 the number of miles of all-weather roads increased dramatically to 6,218 miles. Only less than 8 percent was macadamized; most roads were laterite surfaced. The road network at long last connected Monrovia with the major settlements in the interior and knifed through large tracts of previously inaccessible forest areas. The main routes were still often devious, the branch-road system was still primitive, and even the "all-weather" roads were frequently impassable during the torrential rains. But the transformation was nevertheless dramatic.

There was another side to the Tolbert coin, however. The new roads which provided enhanced education and employment opportunities to tribal persons, for example, also provided better access to the collectors of that odious regressive hut tax. The new roads also made it possible for the "honorables" to accelerate their "purchases" of tribal lands—which constituted one of the greatest land grabs in modern African history. The roads, moreover, accelerated the recruitment of rural labor for the mining and plantation enterprises of both foreigners and the Americo-Liberian politicians. The net effect was that the roads and their aftermath broke up the traditional rural family as a social security unit. Since farmers no longer had an assured claim to the land they cultivated, they neglected both subsistence and cash crop agriculture in favor of wage employment in the enclave sector of the economy. This in turn meant that Liberia had to import rice and other basic foodstuffs, which not only aggravated its balance of payments problem but also forced urban Liberians to pay more for the less nutritious imported foods.

## Creation of New Jobs

It is true that many new jobs in both government and the private sector were created during the Tolbert era. As one group of economists observed, economic growth from 1960 to 1980 "provided relatively high-income wage employment for over one-third of the adult male population in the country—a higher proportion than in most low-income LDCs."[1] It is equally true, on the other hand, that the ranks of the urban unemployed in Monrovia and elsewhere had swelled dramatically as cultivators and often their families as well drifted to the city in search of what were often nonexistent jobs in the hopes of offsetting their loss in family farm income.[2] The loss of farm income was a consequence of the government's policy of holding down prices paid to farmers as a way of subsidizing the food bill of the urbanites. The urbanites included not only the privileged class itself but the politically volatile unemployed and marginally employed, who were at the very doorstep of the elite. Liberia's rate of urban growth was accelerating, and by the end of the Tolbert era over a quarter of Liberia's population was urbanized—most of it concentrated in Monrovia, but some in the new centers at Sanniquellie, Buchanan, and other cities which had expanded as a result of the iron industry. Unemployment, plus the changes associated with social dislocation, meant a rise in urban crime and prostitution, the spread of slum housing conditions, and a general demoralization.

The jobs that went to the educated portion of the tribal sector and to the lower-rung Americo-Liberians inevitably fell far below their expectations and usually lacked the salary, fringe benefits, and job security accorded an identically trained offspring of an "honorable." A few more persons of tribal background did appear in the Legislature, the courts, and the cabinet as well as in the second echelon in many departments. Lacking patrons, however, they might be removed for a trivial infraction of a rule while a scion of an "honorable" would suffer no penalty for even greater offenses.

Frequently Tolbert appeared to be on the verge of recognizing the deep-seated inequities in Liberian society and especially the plight of the tribal poor. In the final analysis he substituted rhetoric for action or retreated in the face of greed and pressure from the Old Guard. With great fanfare, for example, Tolbert launched a program to increase public housing in Liberia. Indeed, from 1973 to 1980, five new housing projects were completed. Only one of these, however, actually was made available to low-income families; the remainder were allocated to middle-class occupants or made available for private purchase, with the "honorables" reaping the profits from rentals.

## Storm Signals in the Mining Sector

The economic difficulties at the micro-level mirrored the problems at the macro-level. Despite all the intense discussion in the 1960s about the diversification of the economy, Liberia at the time of the 1980 coup was still largely dependent upon the export earnings of two commodities, iron ore and rubber, which accounted for 52 and 14 percent of export earnings, respectively. The difficulties with respect to agriculture will be dealt with subsequently, but the danger signs were even more startling at the end of the First Republic with respect to mining—that aspect of the Open Door policy which had made the dramatic physical transformation possible and which had been the key to the economic miracle of the 1960s and early 1970s. Prior to Tubman's Open Door policy, no one even suspected the magnitude of Liberia's potential in iron ore production. By 1967 Liberia had become not only the leading producer of iron ore in Africa, but also the third largest exporter of iron ore in the world. Beginning in 1951 with the Bomi Hills operations of the Liberian Mining Company (a subsidiary of Republic Steel), iron ore production increased rapidly as five new companies came into production during the 1960s. Although the Mano River site of the National Iron Ore Company (consisting in large measure of Liberian stockholders) and those of DELIMCO (a German consortium) in the Bong Range were impressive, the operations of LAMCO (Liberian American-Swedish Minerals Company) and of Liberian Iron Ore, Ltd. (a Canadian company organized in 1966) at Nimba Mountain proved to be the most impressive and accounted for a radical transformation of the Liberian economy. The 4,000-foot-high Nimba Mountain, the site of the LAMCO operation, was practically a solid block of very high-grade iron ore. Exploitation of the ore involved the labor of several thousand workers from Liberia and neighboring states. Building a 170-mile railroad to the port facilities at Buchanan employed many more thousands of laborers. New roads and the railroad brought about the social and economic transformation of vast reaches of the country that had only nominally been under the jurisdiction of the Liberian state during the preceding century.

The Americo-Liberian elite had apparently little concern about the eventual depletion of the Nimba reserve and other new ore deposits in the Kitoma Mountain area and the Bong Range. The government was optimistic that even greater profits—as well as a modicum of industrialization—would come from an iron-ore washing and pelletizing plant that LAMCO had opened at the new port of Buchanan. The plant permitted the various grades of ore to be separated, with the immediate marketing of the high-purity pellets, which can be reduced to metallic iron faster than iron ore in its natural state.

This optimism had a rude awakening in the mid-years of the Tolbert era. Even before the blithe illusion about the inexhaustible nature of its iron reserve was shattered with the closure of the once bustling Bomi Hills operations of the Liberian Mining Company, the global recession was sending up storm signals regarding Liberia's future as one of the world's leading iron ore producers. Liberia's economic future was complicated by the fact that to finance its expanding economy the government had borrowed heavily in the commercial money market. Its rising debt, unfortunately, coincided with a drop in world prices for both rubber and iron ore as well as with a phasing-out of the infrastructure stages of mineral exploitation: foreign investment was reduced and workers were laid off as the harbors, roads, and other supporting facilities were completed. Liberia's public debt (from both official and private sources) went from $158 million in 1970 to $642 million a decade later. Substantial and repeated assistance from the International Monetary Fund was required to ease Liberia's adverse balance of payments position.

The financial crisis over global pricing arrangements was merely the "tip of the iceberg." Instead of optimism about the growth potential of Liberia, it was the conclusion of the Northwestern University economic survey team as early as 1962 that the government should have grave concern for Liberia's economic future. According to the Northwestern group, Liberia was an extreme case of "growth without development."[3] That is, observable economic change was not complemented by structural changes in lines of production, by adoption of more efficient techniques in the private sectors or government, by the significant involvement of domestic personnel in anything other than the unskilled labor category, or by new social achievements and new levels of economic aspirations. In fact, if the foreign entrepreneurs and investments were withdrawn, the modern sector of the economy would virtually cease to function. The Northwestern team contended that the failure of true economic development was traceable ultimately to the political and social system, which left the tribal majority firmly under the control of the Americo-Liberian minority. Having made this indictment, the survey team suggested that "under present political and social arrangements, offering economic advice to Liberian leaders was rather futile.'' It is against that background that some of the more significant defects of the Liberian economy came to a head during the last days of the First Republic in 1979 and 1980.

### Absence of Rational Planning

Among the more critical problems that contributed to the condition criticized by the Northwestern group was the lack of a serious and sincere commitment to planning. Curiously enough, one of the severest critics of both the Northwestern team and of this author on that point—Elliott Berg—himself acknowledged this to be a continuing deficiency in Liberia two decades later.[4] The relevance of systematic record-keeping and the need for statistical data and comprehensive surveys in carrying out development schemes only recently became apparent to Liberian officials. Few economic priorities had been established, with the result that scarce capital was dissipated on a host of projects that were never completed, or was squandered on prestige enterprises that added little to the basic infrastructure of a developing society. As the Northwestern group pointed out in the 1960s (and this was still true in 1980), what Liberia needed was better schools and low-cost public housing rather than first-class highways and presidential palaces; it needed not merely physical capital but improved institutional procedures and labor skills.[5]

The planning of industrial growth under the First Republic had been extremely chaotic. The tremendous development of rubber and iron-mining enterprises, which in 1968 accounted for over 90 percent of Liberia's export earnings (and 66 percent in 1980), had taken place within enclave situations: there was very little interdependence between the foreign concessions and other sectors of the economy. Few satellite industries had been created in response to the presence of the foreign concessions, other than some small enterprises such as an explosives plant, a nail factory, a cement firm, an oil refinery, an umbrella factory, a rice mill, and an aluminum-frame window factory. Moreover, while one could not deny the long-range value of things like palm kernel oil mills, fish canneries, shoe factories, and starch-reducing plants, some questions could be raised about the earlier priorities given to the establishment of a gin distillery, a brewery, a marble tile factory, and a television industry. Many of the raw materials for these enterprises are imported, thus undercutting the idea of import substitution industries. Although the introduction of heavier industries might have been awaiting the full utilization of Mount Coffee hydroelectric power, by 1980 there was little evidence that industrialization was being carried out with the principles of development planning in mind. Development planning involves, as the Northwestern team noted, ''deliberate, reasoned, and orderly measures to achieve stated economic goals in determined sequence.''[6]

### Crises in Agricultural Production

A general deterioration in agricultural production was also glaringly evident in the later years of the Tolbert period, despite the fact that roughly 70 percent of Liberia's work force was still engaged in agricultural labor. Overall growth in this sector had declined from a 3.3 percent growth rate in volume in the 1960–70 period to 2.1 percent for the Tolbert decade. Although agriculture still accounted for 35 percent of the gross domestic product (GDP) in 1981, it was difficult to gauge agricultural output precisely since roughly 60 percent of the labor force was still engaged predominantly if not exclusively in subsistence cultivation. There have, of course, been exceptions. Long before the Americo-Liberians arrived, some of the hinterland tribes had established market centers in which various types of crude currency were employed. There existed also a rather sophisticated form of intertribal production and exchange of arts and crafts. During the decades since the Open Door policy, individual tribesmen have been brought into the cash economy in increasing numbers as wage earners on large estates or at the mines, as participants in tribal communal enterprises, or even as small farmers. Typically, however, the food that the rural tribal family consumes is the food that the family and neighbors collectively produce. Little is left over for exchange beyond the village. The diet is high in starch, since rice and cassava are the principal staples as well as plantain, eddoes, and sweet potatoes. Some balance is secured through the production of okra, groundnuts, and a range of fruits, including papaya, mangoes, avocadoes, and various citrus fruits. Despite the success of the Green Revolution elsewhere in the Third World, Liberian yields of rice (92 percent upland or dry rice as opposed to swamp varieties) are still low—roughly 1,000 pounds per acre. As the Northwestern University team suggested two decades ago, "even the most eloquent advocate of economic progress cannot demonstrate the advantages of growing two grains of rice where only one flourished before if the prospective grower knows that both grains will go to someone else."[7]

Most subsistence agricultural plots are small—roughly four or five acres—and must be numerous to accommodate the fallow system of rotation and the slash-and-burn technique of bringing new land under the hoe. Although there is still no scientific agreement over the utility of traditional techniques of agriculture, one sure cost is the estimated annual destruction of roughly 30,000 acres of timber to accomplish shifting cultivation. Farms are for the most part held under usufructory right of occupancy, with only a small percentage of the tribal people opting for freehold titles. The intrusion of Americo-Liberians into the hinterland in terms of land purchases has already been noted and was a contributing factor in the rural-to-urban migration that accelerated during the Tolbert period. Rather than be tenants on the lands of their ancestors, tribal people simply "threw in the towel" and elected to join the urban unemployed or marginally employed.

With respect to export estate cultivation, several negative aspects became decidedly pronounced during the last years of the Tolbert period, although they were present throughout the preceding decades. First of all, despite government- and donor-assisted research on a whole range of new crops which are well adapted to Liberia's soil and generous rainfall conditions, and in spite of the constant campaigns to diversify agricultural exports, large-scale agricultural production continues to be dominated by one crop: rubber. Fluctuations in Liberian production of coffee, cocoa, papaya, and other tree crops were undoubtedly a reflection of the dramatically fluctuating prices of these commodities on the world market and increased com-petition from the older, more efficient world producers of these commodities. In-variably, when farmers have turned their attention to other tree crops or to sugar and tobacco, they have lacked the technical advice, qualified labor, transport fa-cilities, and systematic marketing arrangements to make their enterprises commer-cial successes. The only promising area of diversification came not with respect to agriculture directly, but with respect to the export of timber, which witnessed a steady rise from the 1960s onward. That, too, unfortunately came to a virtual standstill in the late 1970s as a result of the global recession.

The second negative aspect of export agriculture was the dominance of foreign-owned concessions in all fields, particularly rubber. Despite the politically sound program of Firestone in the 1960s in encouraging the establishment of private farms (most of which were owned by absentee politicians, who hired non-Liberians as managers), and despite the government's and the World Bank's similar encour-agement in the late 1970s, foreign concessionaires continued to dominate. Not only did they account for the major share of direct production, but they also monopolized the processing of latex into exportable rubber products. The two Firestone plan-tations and the six other foreign firms were better able financially to withstand the steady fall in global prices for crude rubber during the 1960s and 1970s, and were able, through their employee benefit programs, to out-compete the private producers for the needed labor force. Declining prices for rubber on global markets had resulted in a dramatic cutback in Liberian production and sales. This was complicated by the use of synthetic rubber and the employment of substitutes for rubber in many industries in the developed countries.

The most serious problem of Liberian agriculture, and one which had direct political consequences in 1979, came with respect to food production. In spite of the statistics which showed Liberian food production becoming *more* efficient (going from −2.7 percent average annual growth rate of total production per capita in 1960–70 to −0.5 in 1970–82), in fact the food import needs rose dramatically during that same period. Indeed, just in the period preceding the coup, Liberia went from a required 1,300 metric tons of imported food grains in 1978 to 26,300 metric tons by 1981. Thus, under the Tubman and Tolbert eras Liberia found itself in the embarrassing position of having to import rice, the mainstay of the Liberian diet, despite the fact that Liberia had unused land, underutilized labor, and a population primarily committed to agricultural production. Various presidentially orchestrated campaigns under the Tolbert administration to help correct this situation failed miserably, as did the coercive tactics of his predecessor in fining chiefs $2,000 if their respective areas failed to meet assigned quotas of increased food production.

## The Absence of Distributive Justice

As long as the economy of a developing society is expanding, one can ignore some of the discrepancies in distribution of the benefits of growth; when the economy slows down, this can be ignored only at one's peril by those in control of the reins of political power. Indeed, one of the serious flaws in the Tubman and Tolbert economic "miracle" was the absence of distributive justice. While exploitation of the tremendous natural resources had brought wealth to the country and had managed to affect the lives of all except those in the remotest reaches of the interior, the benefits were dispersed in a highly inequitable fashion. The Northwestern team in the early 1960s estimated that the 97 percent of the population classified as tribal or lower-class Americo-Liberian received only 25 percent of the share of national income, and the Northwestern team predicted that "this share is not likely to expand in the years to come unless deliberate action is taken to alter both the structure of the economy and the distribution of aggregate earnings."[8] The remaining 75 percent of the national income was distributed to the foreign households and business firms and to the 3 percent of the Liberian population that constituted the political elite.

Seeking an analogy for the dramatic economic growth that benefits only the ruling elite, the Northwestern team concluded that it "was as though a country club has suddenly expanded its revenues."[9] In contrast to the general poverty of the tribal masses, the standard of living of the "honorable" class had been immeasurably altered as a result of the rapid growth of the economy and the government subsidization of the Whig class discussed previously. In itself, Liberia's system of preferential treatment and graft did not differ radically from that of other countries of the world. What made the Liberian case so critical was that the benefits accrued to a very close-knit minority while the wages for the tribal people involved in the highly inflated money economy seldom exceeded fifty cents a day. Moreover, efforts of the tribal people to enhance their bargaining position through cooperatives and trade unions had been crassly discouraged. Indeed, the most striking result of the dramatic change in the Liberian economy was that the new roads made it easier for the Americo-Liberians—officials and nonofficials alike—to exploit the tribal hinterland through labor recruitment, the imposition of extraordinary taxes, and the constant requisitioning of crops and livestock. One can readily agree that "roads that bring good government to backward areas are clearly a blessing; roads that bring bad government may be a curse."[10]

The unequal distribution was compounded under Tolbert by the rising scale of corruption, which proved to be enormous for a small state. Each new mineral resource or each new economic opportunity escalated the involvement of public officials in bribes and other forms of coercion. Flagrant abuses of the public trust often brought only a slap on the wrist to the offending official whose deeds had been publicized. In many instances the miscreant may have actually received a promotion to another position. What contributed in particular to the fall in Tolbert's domestic stock was the centrality of his own immediate family in the mounting system of avarice. As noted earlier, Tubman had carefully avoided having his family so personally conspicuous. In contrast, Tolbert and the members of his family engaged in corruption in a most blatant way. The control of the political system by a few key patrons had been ingeniously perpetuated under the Tolbert regime. The rules of the game were the same as under Tubman; all that had changed were the names of the central figures, many of whom were the offspring, siblings, and cousins of the president and his wife.

The 1961 predictions of the Northwestern University team, unfortunately, understated the case. Even leaving out corruption, the economic maldistribution of the Tolbert regime on the eve of the 1980 coup was amply indicated in the cold statistics produced by Tolbert's own Ministry of Planning and Economic Affairs, which revealed the growing distance between the elite and the masses in Liberia: 4 percent of the population owned more than 60 percent of the wealth! In more visible terms, the socioeconomic distance was epitomized in the miraculously transformed ancestral home of the Tolbert clan at Bentol, the former Bensonville (described in chapter 8). Bentol's blatant arrogance mocked the creeping squalor of the slums of Monrovia in a manner reminiscent of Marie Antoinette.

What finally undermined both Tolbert and the Whig aristocracy was the inability of the system to cope with the need for substantial political change. Initially, the successor to consummate politician William Tubman appeared to be a remarkable political craftsman in his own right who surprised the experts with his ability to adapt to the requirements of the presidency as modified by the charismatic Tubman. Despite Tolbert's promising start in adjusting to the new realities, the adulation of the presidency ultimately blinded him to the rise of dissent which was growing under his very nose. He seemed to be incapable of handling reform in a timely way. Indeed, Tolbert's greatest weakness with respect to reform was his constant vacillation. What he graciously conceded one day, he ruthlessly took away the next. In the process, he not only alienated the Old Guard of the Whig aristocracy, who regarded concessions as a sign of weakness; he outraged the young dissidents, who felt that he was not a man whose word could be trusted.

In any event, the euphoria which international economists had expressed in the 1960s regarding Liberia's 5 to 6 percent growth rates was steadily vanishing as the rate fell below 1 percent on the eve of the 1980 coup. Difficulties arose for Tolbert even in the one area in which he prided himself for attracting foreign investments as well as fulfilling Liberia's proper leadership role as Africa's oldest republic—an activist foreign policy. Perhaps the new international image of Liberia made it easier for World Bank and International Monetary Fund representatives to ''sell'' Liberian requests to their bosses because Liberia had become a force of international significance. The final bill for Tolbert's massaging of his own ego through international adventurism will ultimately be paid by future generations of Liberians. Included in this reckoning will be not only the high cost of diplomatic representations, which Liberia enjoyed out of all proportion to its size, its resources, and its vital interests. Even more burdensome will be the repayment of the loans for the construction in 1979 of the OAU center in Virginia, just beyond the port area in Monrovia. It was there that Tolbert, as chairman of the Organization of African Unity, hosted the summit meeting of African heads of state. One estimate is that it took over $200 million to build the white elephant resort hotel and the 53 very posh chalets for heads of state adjacent to the hotel.[11] Add to this the construction of the airport terminal building, the lighting of the 60-kilometer road from Roberts Field to Monrovia, and the providing to each of the 53 delegations seven cars, color television sets, and other ''amenities.''

## The Rice Riots of 1979 and The Year of Ferment

It was an economic issue, however, rather than a strictly political problem that brought Tolbert's vacillation clearly into the open and began the ultimate unraveling of his power. I refer to the demonstrations and riots which occurred on 14 April 1979 in response to the announced 50 percent increase in the price of a bag of rice. Thus the groundwork for the popular acceptance of the coup of 12 April 1980 had actually been laid 364 days before the event. The Rice Riots clearly had raised the level of dissent to a transcendent level.

As was pointed out in an insightful and courageous statement before the commission of inquiry into the Rice Riots of 14 April 1979, the situation could have been avoided. Dr. Amos Sawyer—an associate professor of political science and dean of the Colleges of Social Sciences and Humanities at the University of Liberia and a key actor during the Year of Ferment—reminded the commission that government officials were aware of the devastating effect that a 50 percent increase in the price of the main staple of the Liberian diet would have upon the already impoverished family budgets. The average monthly income of urban Liberians was roughly $80. The new price for a bag of rice would have been $30. Although rice is grown in Liberia, the need for imported rice has grown steadily, accounting in 1979 for 25 percent of the 200,000 tons consumed. The reason is simple. Despite all Tolbert's rhetoric about the country being self-sufficient in food, there was little incentive for the tribal farmer to grow rice. Unlike the export crops that the "honorables" grew on their absentee-owned farms (such as rubber, cocoa, coffee, and other export crops), rice was not a subsidized crop for producers. The price, moreover, had been set artificially low by the government. Because the government had discouraged cooperatives as being potentially political, and government-sponsored marketing arrangements had not been created, the tribal growers had no alternative but to sell their rice at drastically reduced prices to Lebanese merchants, from whom they would have to buy the same rice back at inflated prices during the "hungry months." Thus, beyond growing enough rice for the immediate family, most growers had turned to other cash crops or to employment in the enclave economies to pay their taxes and to meet other needs. All of this, Dr. Sawyer insisted, was known to government economists.

Having made the first mistake of ignoring their own economists, the government made the second mistake of not anticipating that some form of public reaction was inevitable. What the Tolbert regime had seriously underestimated was the ability of dissidents within Liberia to organize significant and sustained opposition to any governmental policy. The True Whig Party had been accustomed to monopolizing the political scene since the 1870s, and thus the organization of returned students from overseas, lower income Americo-Liberians, educated tribal youths who resented the continuing power of traditional chiefs, and other dissidents was not taken seriously by any but the most conservative of the "Old Guard." Thus the Movement for Justice in Africa (MOJA) and the Progressive Alliance of Liberians (PAL) (discussed in the next chapter) were taken as temporary aberrations which would disappear once the leaders had been co-opted into the existing system. The miscalculation was quickly apparent when the Progressive Alliance decided to capitalize upon the rice issue and called for a mass protest march on 14 April 1979. The government panicked, banning the projected protest march and threatening to take severe action against demonstrators.

The PAL demonstration, consisting of over 2,000 unarmed students and other citizens, took place as planned despite the government's deployment of soldiers and police along the main route of march. Tanks were placed menacingly at major intersections. Although the soldiers apparently restrained themselves in the face of this confrontation, the Monrovia police lost control and after tear gas had failed to disperse the marchers, they began firing indiscriminately into the crowd. This action so outraged the marchers, as well as others not directly involved, that there ensued a day of uncontrolled rioting and looting. The shops of Lebanese merchants, who were felt to be directly responsible for inflation in Monrovia, and others were singled out as targets. Most significant, however, was the fact that somewhere between 40 and 140 students and others (depending upon which estimate you accept) had been killed and an additional 400 persons were wounded in the day's events. So alarmed was the Whig leadership that Tolbert—as Siaka Stevens of Sierra Leone had done previously—called upon President Sékou Touré of Guinea to dispatch Guinean troops to restore order. To many Liberians the most terrifying memory of the Rice Riots was the sight of Guinean MIG fighters making low passes over the disturbed area. The situation was so out of hand that a number of observers were convinced— in retrospect—that any determined group of protesters could that day have easily stormed the Executive Mansion and brought about the fall of the Tolbert regime almost a year earlier than the April 1980 coup. Tolbert, it was reported, was in a state of hysteria.

Instead of acknowledging its role in precipitating the 1979 Rice Riots (other than by rescinding its order increasing the price of rice), the Tolbert government began a massive roundup and detention not only of PAL leaders but of many other political dissidents as well. The writ of habeas corpus was suspended. Some 33 of the several score arrested were charged with "treason and attempting to overthrow the government"—charges which carried the death penalty or long years in prison. The University of Liberia was ordered closed once again. Various other measures were taken under Emergency Powers legislation. It was a full three weeks before the 700 Guinean troops were returned home. The lesson of the Rice Riots was, however, clear for many. It had demonstrated the vulnerability of the government and the fact that even a loosely organized but determined opposition could capitalize upon events to challenge the regime. April 14, 1979, marked the beginning of the end. Out of the dust of that day, two civilian opposition groups could be identified as rivals to the regime, and a third force—the military—was beginning to gather political momentum in the wings.

# XII.

# The Political Challenge to the Whig Regime

Even before the Rice Riots of 14 April 1979, Tolbert and his advisers had been put on notice that the currents of dissent ran deep in Liberian society. Instead of addressing dissent in a creative way, however, Tolbert became increasingly ultra-sensitive to personal criticism, and when the prospect of formal opposition to the True Whig Party emerged, he wavered aimlessly between conciliation and repression. The president, however, increasingly moved in the direction of repression: journalists and pamphleteers were prosecuted, universities were closed, political opponents were jailed, and troops were increasingly used to put down labor disorders. Tolbert seemed unable to please anyone for very long in the last two years of his rule, and general dissatisfaction greeted his efforts to placate various contending forces simultaneously. On the one hand, Tolbert was mindful of the legitimate demands of younger Liberians, both tribal and Americo-Liberian, for more significant participation in the ossifying True Whig Party. Tolbert's international image, moreover, required that he give these aspirations serious attention. On the other hand, his main base of support, the Whig gerontocracy and in particular the leaders of the Masonic Order, were alarmed by the rapid pace of change and insisted that Tolbert deal harshly and convincingly with dissent. Tolbert's "sincerity of the moment" created a universal impression of weakness and vacillation. Concessions to reformists one day would be withdrawn the next day in a stemwinding speech intended to arouse the flagging spirits of the party faithful.

Tolbert and the Old Guard Whig leadership had great difficulties in adjusting to the idea of sustained, organized opposition to continued settler domination of politics. In addition to the repeated grants of authority given to the president by the Legislature to deny the writ of habeas corpus in "emergencies," other steps were taken in the 1970s to set limits on strikes by students, labor unions, and others; to impose burdensome restrictions on the conduct of public meetings and marches;

and to limit the ability of new organizations to recruit members. Increasingly the terms "treason" and "sedition" were redefined to include almost any unauthorized discussion of public issues and any other act that could be interpreted as an encouragement of sectionalism or tribalism "with intent to divide the country."

Despite the hostility to organized dissent, when the dust of the 1979 Rice Riots had cleared, it was apparent that there were at least two civilian dissident organizations which had been strengthened rather than weakened by government measures in dealing with the crisis. Their leaders had been energized and their membership augmented. The third opponent—the military—still remained inchoate as a challenging group, yet the signs regarding their hostility to the regime had also emerged on the day of the demonstrations, and it was doubtful they would long remain in the wings.

## The Progressive Alliance of Liberians

The first of the two civilian groups was the group that had sponsored the demonstrations, the Progressive Alliance of Liberians. It had been organized in the early 1970s by Liberian students in the United States who had become dissatisfied with the slow pace of change at home, with the cult of personality which dominated Liberian politics during the Tubman and Tolbert era, and with the low esteem in which Liberia was held by other Africans. Under the leadership of Gabriel Baccus Matthews, a graduate of City University of New York, PAL had developed a kind of pragmatic African socialism, reminiscent of the agrarian socialism of Julius Nyerere. It was to be, according to Matthews, "revolutionary but not Marxist," and organized according to African principles and values. PAL's main recruiting targets were students both at home and abroad, low-income and unemployed workers in Monrovia, and the small rural cultivators. The leaders of PAL articulated a message which blended an emphasis upon a return to traditional values of cooperation with an insistence of greater distributive justice in Liberia's cash economy. On the face of it, PAL's programs seemed to demand reform of the system— "consciousness raising"—rather than the dismantling of the existing economic structures. It wanted, for example, greater processing in Liberia of the products produced by the foreign concessionaires. Its greatest ideological stance came in its adamant opposition to the more invidious class and caste distinctions which had in economic terms actually been intensified under the Tolbert regime. PAL tactics varied from open confrontation over issues and events to a studied determination to challenge the True Whig Party at the polls in peaceful competition.

In the Year of Ferment between the Rice Riots and the April 12 coup, PAL leaders and the Tolbert regime engaged in a bizarre sort of chess game. Although Matthews denied that any "plea bargaining" had taken place (he insisted that he was merely being practical in recognizing that he was dealing with a superior, ruthless force!), it did appear that a deal had been made. In return for the release of the Rice Riot detainees, PAL's leadership promised to refrain from overt acts against the government. The timing of the deal was critical. As the pamphleteer Albert Porte had pointed out, it would have been a great embarrassment for Tolbert—

who, as incoming chairman of the Organization of African Unity, was hosting the OAU in Monrovia in June 1979—to have so many political prisoners in the stockade at Barclay Training Center. Thus, in traditional Liberian political style, Matthews wrote an abject letter of apology to Tolbert from his prison cell. Responding in the same quaint style, Tolbert in due course (and in advance of the OAU meeting) "extended the hand of forgiveness" by declaring a general amnesty for those imprisoned in the aftermath of the Rice Riots.

With the OAU meeting out of the way, however, PAL decided to capitalize upon the strength it had acquired through its demonstrated ability both to challenge and to negotiate with the Tolbert government. Despite the fact that Liberia under Whig leadership was a de facto one-party state, PAL elected to register as a legal political party. It intended not only to contest the mayoral elections of 1979 and the national legislative elections of 1981, but to prepare itself for the 1983 presidential campaign—especially since Tolbert had in public indicated that he would not be a candidate to succeed himself. Although appearing to welcome the prospect of a political opposition party, Tolbert nevertheless permitted one of his lower-level judges to block PAL's efforts to meet the legal requirements for registration. When PAL threatened to demonstrate in the streets, Tolbert once again backed down and in January 1980 accepted the fact of recognition. As the newly renamed Progressive People's Party (PPP), Matthews and his colleagues proceeded to precipitate a further crisis. There is speculation as to whether the PPP's action was a calculated effort to hasten the pace of political change or whether it was a spur of the moment decision of Matthews to placate his own followers who were hungry for concrete, immediate results to sustain their enthusiasm for PPP. In any event, during the course of a late evening rally on 7 March 1980 Matthews urged the assembled to march on the Executive Mansion for an audience with Tolbert. The latter happened to be up-country at the time. Failing to have the instant audience, Matthews then called upon the country to observe a general strike the next day to force Tolbert's resignation from the presidency instead of having to wait until 1983.

Tolbert's reaction was no doubt predictable. Instead of resigning, he denounced the PPP leadership in scathing terms and declared, in effect, "that he was tired of being Mr. Nice Guy." Tolbert stated that he intended to be

tough and mean and rough from now on. I want to show you that this is the time to carry out the law of this country to its fullest. If in the past I have been lenient, I want the people to forgive. I am not going to be lenient with them anymore . . . and I know I am steady on the rock because I have the support of the Liberian people.[1]

That "support" was indeed well orchestrated, as wave after wave of delegations from various branches of the True Whig Party came to the Executive Mansion from the far corners of the Republic. Some of the petitioners demanded the full penalty of the law for those accused of treason; others sought the banning of the PPP; and still others demanded that Liberia declare itself a de jure one-party state under True Whig leadership. The Legislature passed similar resolutions, and the Old Guard seemed to take aim at the University of Liberia and any other potential sources of challenge in its demand for adherence to a hard line. Tolbert did ban the PPP and called for the detention of the PPP leadership on charges of treason or sedition. Thirty-eight dissidents were arrested or voluntarily turned themselves in, and they remained in prison until they were released during the early hours of the April 12 coup. In one of those diabolical symbolic twists of which True Whig leaders were often capable, the treason trials of Matthews and others were to commence on April 14, the anniversary of the Rice Riots. In still another ironic development, among those to be prosecuted by the overly zealous minister of justice, Joseph Chesson, was one Chea Cheapoo. The latter had once been considered a "ward" of Chesson and had adopted his surname until his disaffection with the settler aristocracy had led him to join PAL. On the day of the coup, Cheapoo left his prison cell to become the new minister of justice. On that same day his former patron, Joseph Chesson, was arrested and was later executed on the beach, along with twelve other Whig leaders.

## The Movement for Justice in Africa

The second civilian opposition to Tolbert had, almost until the eve of the April 12 coup, insisted that it wanted to avoid involvement in "class politics," hoping to achieve its goals of a changed society by other means. The Movement for Justice in Africa was started in 1973 by professors and students at the University of Liberia and appealed to middle-class persons of both tribal and settler origins. Its prime mover was Dr. Togba-Nah Tipoteh, American-educated (Ohio University, Ohio State, and University of Nebraska), who had once been a professor of economics at the University of Liberia. Tipoteh, who resumed his Kru name upon returning home, had a "revolving door" career in the Tolbert government, where he had several times been appointed and subsequently dismissed from government posts. Two professors of the Political Science Department (a group that Tolbert on several occasions took pains to castigate for its "unhealthy agitation") were also MOJA leaders: Dr. Amos Sawyer, who was previously mentioned, and Dr. H. Boima Fahnbulleh, Jr., the son of the former ambassador, Henry Fahnbulleh, who had been imprisoned for sedition by the Tubman government. In the long run MOJA probably sought a more dramatic restructuring of Liberian society and a more significant redefinition of national culture than was true of PAL. Its program included nationalization of major economic enterprises, confiscation of the illegal land holdings of the Whig oligarchy, and punishment of corruption. MOJA attempted, however, to remain a movement rather than a party. It hoped to effect change by calling public attention to corruption and other situations needing reform, by engaging in strikes or work slowdowns where necessary, and by direct action which would present demonstrable alternatives to the status quo. Since it sought mass support, its public programs and publications were presented in clear simple English.[2]

MOJA leadership was very careful to avoid provocative challenges to the Tolbert regime. Instead, MOJA attempted to be "more Catholic than the Pope" in dealing with Tolbert's own call for reforms. For example, since Tolbert had attempted to assume the mantle of continental leadership in the struggle for southern African liberation, MOJA not only applauded his efforts but organized seminars, film series, letters to the editor, and public discussion on South Africa. Most pointedly, the discussion of these films explicitly focused on the squalor of South African slums, the caste relationship between a settler minority and the indigenous majority, police brutality, the ban on effective trade unions and cooperatives, and other types of injustice. Implicitly, the target of the discussion was contemporary Liberia. Thus, MOJA emulated the tactics of pre-1789 French dissidents who escaped the heavy hand of the censor by appearing to criticize a distant "Persia" while in fact they were criticizing their own society.

Also taking Tolbert's rhetoric at face value, MOJA pressed for increased rice and other food production and a self-reliant economy—two persistent Tolbert themes. MOJA, through its sister economic organization, Susukuu (a combination of two traditional institutuions, the *susu*—a savings and loan group—and *kuu*—the traditional agricultural work group), attempted to make the Liberian small businessmen and craftsmen "self-reliant" by organizing them into craft companies. The Susukuu received grants from the Canadian University Service Overseas, the Dutch agency for cooperation with nongovernmental development organizations (NOVIB), and the consortium of German church organizations (EZE). Later the Liberian government secured a loan of several million dollars to begin a small-scale enterprises funding agency. With respect to food production, MOJA organized an agricultural cooperative in one of the less developed counties, Grand Gedeh. Completely bypassing central government officials as well as traditional paramount chiefs, the leaders of the MOJA cooperative decided to elect their own officers and determine their strategy. They chose to concentrate efforts on increased rice production and to do so by emphasizing traditional labor-intensive techniques rather than machine cultivation. To avoid the Lebanese middlemen, the cooperative further elected to undertake all phases of production, from planting, to harvesting, to milling, to marketing. They directly solicited and received support from church groups and international donor agencies, including the Swedish, Canadian, and American aid missions. Indeed, the cooperative was so successful in increasing the yield per acre that they were able to undercut both the Lebanese and the Americo-Liberian buyers in selling rice directly to neighboring communities. They even rented the milling facility to adjacent villagers. The overwhelming success of this independent action so threatened the equanimity of the Whig elite and the co-opted chiefs that during the second year government officials took various legal actions to interfere with the harvesting. Although the rice crop did spoil, MOJA lawyers took their case to an honest woman judge who found in favor of the cooperative society in a damage suit against the county superintendent and other officials. The judgment, curiously, came just a short time before the April 12 coup and provided further evidence of the vulnerability of the regime.

Not content with challenging the social and economic order, MOJA, in a reversal of strategy, chose to confront the regime on more overtly political matters as well. MOJA, for example, had labored hard after the Rice Riots to bring about the release at least of non-PAL leaders who had been jailed. More significantly, MOJA leaders took note of the constitutional provision for independent electoral challenges being permitted under the law. Instead of waiting till the presidential elections of 1983, MOJA leaders in August 1979 persuaded Dr. Amos Sawyer of the University of Liberia to run as an independent candidate in the November mayoral race in Monrovia. This would be the first challenge to the Whigs in over twenty years. So enthusiastic were the crowds which turned out for the campaign tours of the popular Dr. Sawyer, and so vigorous were the students and others in challenging the "graveyard" voters on the official registration list, that the Whig leadership was thrown for a loss. The slated Whig candidate, Francis (Choo-choo) Horton, by contrast was running a very lackluster campaign on the assumption that the official True Whig candidate always won. In a spate of indecision, the Whig leaders first indicated that the largely neglected property qualifications for suffrage would be vigorously enforced; next, they attempted to delay the holding of the Monrovia election; and finally, in the face of definite electoral defeat, they postponed the mayoral elections until June 1980. Once again, the power of the settler oligarchy had been challenged and found wanting. The scare that the Sawyer candidacy had engendered among the Whig hierarchy was evident in Tolbert's annual address to the Legislature in January 1980, in which he stressed the need to introduce change into the political order. Youth, he insisted, had a right to legitimate participation. He accordingly asked the Legislature to drop the property qualification and remove any other barrier to full adult participation in elections. His subsequent reactions in March to the efforts of the PPP to organize and recruit members once again constituted second thoughts on his part.

## The Politicization of the Military

The military challenge, the third line of political opposition to emerge during the Year of Ferment, became clearly visible only in the early morning hours of April 12. I, among other observers of the Liberian scene in the 1960s, had speculated that the military could be one of the potential forces for change which might confront the settler aristocracy.[3] It was felt that the most likely dissident sector of the military might be the officer class. This educated guess was made despite the fact that the division between officers and enlisted ranks very neatly paralleled the settler and tribal cleavages within the greater society. This prophecy seemed about to be realized in the alleged coup in the last year of Tubman's rule when the principal officer charged had the highly symbolic name of General George Toe Washington. He had been appointed chief of staff of the armed forces in 1965. Despite his Kru background, he had been raised in an Americo-Liberian environment and thus identified with the settler community. If there had been in the Tubman era or in the early years of the Tolbert administration any significant disaffection on the part of the Americo-Liberian officer class, it would have arisen from the new demands for professionalism within the army. There had been a rising emphasis on efficiency and technical performance, which had been imparted in officer training programs in the United States, which contrasted sharply with the casualness and blatant inefficiency of the Liberian governmental system. The developing professionalization of the police and the military elsewhere in Africa did raise the spectre that the demands for political power-sharing which accompanied professionalization could occur in Liberia as well. By the time of the 1980 coup, after all, a majority of the states in Africa had experienced at least one successful military intervention, with a majority of that number experiencing their second or more military coups.

Indeed, given the high cost of military technology and equipment, the corruption of the political system in Liberia had threatened the economic support for continued modernization of the military. As recently as March and April of 1980 it was still thought by some Whig leaders that it might be the officer class who would strike first against the Tolbert regime. The leaders of MOJA, for example, had vigorously complained that the Tolbert regime had been arresting officers who had appeared sympathetic to PAL/PPP leadership and their own efforts at reform.

The enlisted ranks—some five to six thousand strong—were not regarded as an effective fighting force. Size and efficiency of the military component, however, have not always been a factor in political intervention in Africa. Indeed, nowhere in Africa during the colonial period was the army larger than necessary for the maintenance of public order, and the forces were shifted about to suit the occasion. Nor did the military's lack of training in the art of governing in postindependent Africa prevent it from wresting control from civilian politicians. Indeed, the very fact that the military was overlooked as a factor of political consequence (as had been the case in both Nigeria and Ghana before their respective 1966 coups) was in itself an index of the low status of the army in postcolonial Africa and its low esteem in the minds of politicians, journalists, and scholars alike. This attitude increased the feeling of alienation from the system at both officer and enlisted levels.

This African-wide phenomenon certainly was the case as well in Liberia, where the military tended to be viewed with contempt, both by the Americo-Liberian military brass as well as by the tribal communities to which they were posted. Military personnel were invariably strangers to the area they served, since the army followed the deliberate practice of avoiding potential ethnic conflicts of interest. In the early days of the Liberian Frontier Force—as the army had been called—soldiers received low pay. In certain cases where the officers or the civilian district commissioners had a practice of "eating" the salary money, the troops were expected by their officers to compensate by living off the local community with impunity. In later years, as their tribal sons and brothers became involved in the enclave economy or became students at the University of Liberia or Cuttington College, soldiers found themselves in conflicting roles. Increasingly they were compelled to oppose their fellow tribesmen and kinsmen, as the Tolbert regime contributed to the politicization of the military by using soldiers to put down dissent on university and school campuses and to break up strikes of urban and agricultural workers. It was reliably reported that during the Rice Riots of 1979 the military in Monrovia had refused to fire on the demonstrators because they sympathized with the plight of their own relatives and friends. It was the police who actually panicked and killed the demonstrators. Finally, there was evidence in the months preceding the 1980 coup that military personnel (both officers and noncommissioned officers) and civilian dissidents were pursuing parallel lines of protest. The troops received far less prestige and far less compensation than did the civilian bureaucrats and politicians; yet they bore the brunt of civilian hostility when they were employed in domestic crises which should have been resolved by the politicians through negotiation, not through the use of force.

Party leaders elsewhere in Africa, recognizing the potential threat posed by the military to civilian rule, employed various techniques designed to keep the military "on tap rather than on top." In Guinea, for example, Sékou Touré put his army to work in community development schemes when he was faced with the mass return of pensionless veterans following the rupture with de Gaulle in 1958. Nyerere, following the army mutiny of 1964, created a citizens army, which was to become an extension of the Tanzanian African National Union and a positive instrument for carrying out his policies of "self-reliance." In Uganda under the first Obote government, the leadership attempted (unsuccessfully, it turned out) to emulate the British colonial predecessors by using ethnicity as an element in control. Obote relied heavily on his own less-modernized Nilotic peoples of the north as the significant element in the armed forces, hoping thereby to stay the political ambitions of the more advanced Baganda and other Bantu groups.

Before 1908 the Americo-Liberians relied upon either foreign assistance or hastily organized "home guard" units to defend the settler communities against tribal attacks.[4] The home guard units normally consisted of an Americo-Liberian officer in the militia who recruited his troops from among the poorer class of Americo-Liberians, tribal wards, and friendly tribal persons whose "loyalty" to the Americo-Liberians had been demonstrated. Once the threatening situation had abated, the organization largely dissolved. In 1908, however, the menacing posture of both France and Britain along Liberia's frontiers convinced the Liberian government that it should regularize its system of control over the people in the border areas, and the Liberian Frontier Force was established to carry out police, customs, and other functions in the hinterland.

As long as the Liberian Frontier Force remained small and its mission was limited to the control of poorly organized and poorly armed tribal rebels, it was a sufficient structure of support for the Whig aristocracy. The officer class, drawn almost exclusively from the Americo-Liberian group or from tribal elites with firm links to the ruling group, was selected largely on the basis of patronage. It was thus a group that was generally "satisfied" with the existing distribution of political power within Liberian society. The general lack of professional training did not give the officers any motivation to alter an inefficient political system in the way that the technologically concerned officer groups have done in many Asian and Middle Eastern states. Equally satisfied with the status quo were the tribal people recruited to serve in the ranks. The low salary was more than compensated for by the authority of the uniform and the carte blanche that members of the Frontier Force had in exploiting the communities in which they had been stationed. It was a matter of policy not to post an enlisted man to his home area, and thereby the army avoided possible conflicts of loyalty. It also, thereby, removed many social restraints on bad behavior.

The Liberian elite felt, too, that they had been able to control the tribal enlisted ranks by engaging in a finely tuned game of ethnic stereotyping and segregation within the armed forces. In my discussion in 1960 with the secretary of defense, for example, he commented quite frankly that the Loma, the Bassa, the Kpelle, the Kru, and others were assumed to possess distinct cultural traits which made them best suited for specific roles as fighters, cooks, carriers, clerks, and the like. Incidentally, he suggested that the Krahn—of which Master Sergeant Doe and many of his coup colleagues are members—"make excellent musicians." (Undoubtedly, many Liberians must have felt that certain Krahn "made beautiful music" the morning of April 12.) In addition to stereotyping, the assignment of soldiers to units tended for the most part to follow tribal lines, which made it difficult for dissidents to form cross-tribal alliances.

Obviously, as the modernization of government and the economy proceeded, some ethnic groups were more heavily siphoned off into the enclave economy and government than were others. Thus, the maintenance of ethnic balancing within the armed forces had been significantly eroded. One clue regarding the growing politicization of the armed forces came during the 1979 Rice Riots, when the soldiers failed to join the police in the assault on the demonstrators and were even charged with participating in the ensuing rioting and looting. Their dignity, moreover, had been affronted by the calling in of Guinean troops to handle the riots.

In the two decades preceding the 1980 coup, various security situations made new demands upon the military (which had been restyled the National Guard in 1962). The presence of a large number of aliens throughout the hinterland in con- nection with the expanding economic and educational enterprises as well as the problems of illicit diamond and gold mining operations increased the training needs with respect to internal security. (Ordinary police functions have now been assumed by the Liberian National Police Force.) External threats, real or imagined, intensified demands for the more rapid professionalization of the armed forces. Indeed, several times before Tubman's rapprochement with Sékou Touré of Guinea, rumors ran through the streets of Monrovia that Guinean forces had marched across the border and claimed Nimba Mountain. Finally, Liberia's new role in intra-African politics affected its military preparedness. Liberia's debut in that role during the Congo crisis of 1960 showed in a rather embarrassing way the inadequacy of the Liberian troops' training. Since that experience the Liberian government had been more receptive to the suggestions for training made by the United States military mission. Gradually the military structure was reorganized along more professional lines and modernized in many respects.

Professionalism, however, threatened old political practices. The military lead- ers, as well as the American donors, were becoming increasingly annoyed with the illegal use of soldiers and military equipment for the cultivation of crops and for road construction on the farms of "honorables." The spectre of military intervention itself was raised in February 1963, when the head of the National Guard, Colonel David Thompson, and others were arrested—according to the official announce- ment—to forestall an alleged coup. Colonel Thompson was reported to have said that "if only 250 Togolese soldiers could kill President Olympio and overthrow his government, an army of 5,000 in Liberia can do wonders."[5] Again, during the unrest following the labor strikes of 1966, Tubman dramatically announced that a foreign power (never named) had attempted to bribe army officers to stage a coup during the president's pending health leave in Switzerland.

A number of reported coup attempts—whether real or imaginary—occurred with almost predictable frequency during the remainder of the Tubman period and throughout the Tolbert era as well. One manifestation of the plot syndrome came in March 1968 with the arrest of Henry Fahnbulleh, Sr., a prominent Vai, who had been serving as Liberian ambassador to Tanzania and Kenya. The treason trial, which led to his conviction and imprisonment for twenty years at hard labor, was given shrill coverage in the Liberian press. It was alleged that Fahnbulleh had plotted in East Africa to have Chinese guerrilla-warfare experts smuggled into Liberia and had planned to infiltrate subversive agents into Monrovia's radio stations to facilitate his seizure of power. Contradictory statements by students and others to the prosecution's charges during the trial constituted, in the memory of long-time observers, the first case of open criticism of President Tubman. Indeed, students who attended the trial were warned that they were guilty of disloyalty in their cheering of the defendant and booing of the prosecution witnesses. It was apparent that the government was alarmed, even though Tubman in a press conference attempted to attribute student unrest around the world—during the Vietnam era—to the fact that "mothers these days have stopped breast-feeding their babies. They begin feeding babies with cow's milk as soon as they are born. Thus, they develop a cow's instinct." Fahnbulleh was also charged with having written the Nigerian ambassador indicating that "one fine day, aborigines like our counterpart, the gallant Ibos, will rise up against their reactionary minority clique to regain their fatherland." Purportedly another letter went to the Israeli ambassador accusing the Liberian government of signing a secret agreement with the American government to deport fifty thousand Black Muslims to Liberia. The letter supposedly stated that "African states which maintain ties with your Zionist government are colonial stooges and lackeys, especially so our own Liberian government."[6]

More direct efforts to implicate the military in plots against the Whig regime began to occur with greater frequency at the very end of the Tubman presidency. One celebrated case—referred to previously—led to accusations being made against the Army Chief of Staff, General George Toe Washington. He had been accused in October 1970 of an assassination attempt against his designated successor and the new secretary of defense. Another coup attempt, which was allegedly directed against President Tolbert and his two brothers in 1973, implicated the assistant minister of defense and two army officers. This was reported to have been inspired by Kru dissidents—one of the tribal groups which had longstanding grievances against the Americo-Liberians. Curiously, even when the series of reported coups led to convictions, invariably the "guilty" parties were subsequently pardoned. The trials constituted warnings to potential dissidents.

Violence had always been just below the surface in maintaining the settler/tribal relationship during the First Republic, but incidents of sporadic resort to violence seemed to have been escalating during the two decades prior to the 1980 coup. It was clear the rapid urban growth, the expanding economy and its associated greater freedom of movement, as well as increased enrollments in public schools had strained the Whig control apparatus to its limits. The reaction of the regime tended increasingly to be both swift and ruthless in putting down dissent. Despite the potential threat posed by the military, the response of the Americo-Liberians was to make the army more and more indispensable to the functioning of the political system. Use of military forces in resolving worker unrest, student strikes, and other domestic crises became often the first rather than the last resort on the part of the regime. Emergency powers given Tubman during the Firestone strike of 1966 authorized him to increase radically the size of the military in dealing with civil emergencies. Similar grants of emergency power were extended to Tolbert, virtually on an annual basis.

The importance of the military to the regime was underscored as well by the steps taken to establish the National Military Academy that the Legislature gave Tubman as a "birthday present" on his seventieth birthday. No attempt, however, was made to capture the political commitment of the professionalized officer class. The Whig regime was thus in danger of creating a political monster it could no longer control. On the other hand, little was done to reorganize the citizen militia, estimated at twenty thousand, which could have been an independent source of support for the Americo-Liberian class in a contest between the governing elite and the regular army. The militia (which is similar to the politically controlled National Guard in many American states) carried out its training program in a most lax and casual fashion. It was drawn largely from the ranks of the Americo-Liberian class and tribal persons who had long years of residence in the more urbanized area of the coast. It played no role at all, ironically, in the events of April 1980. Moreover, when the military did succeed in toppling the Whig regime, the coup leadership came from an unexpected quarter—enlisted personnel.

It was a commentary upon the fragile nature of the process of evolutionary change in Liberia during the First Republic that so much came to depend upon the force of personality of the incumbent president. Tubman and Tolbert alike had become the Grand Scenarist, attempting skillfully to manipulate and maneuver and, in the process, irreversibly alter the rules of the political game. For all of the authority that had been accumulating in the hands of the executive, neither Tubman nor Tolbert were dictators—rather, they could be considered the managing directors of an experiment in controlled change. At any particular moment, it was impossible for the president to stray too far from the interest of the Americo-Liberian group that constituted the president's primary constituency. Ironically, although the president could not fully control events or the settler group, he had become the Indispensable Man with respect to the survival of the caste relationship. When the president fell—as Tolbert did in the early morning of 12 April 1980—the entire structure of dominance fell with him.

# XIII.

# The 1980 Coup
## *Exhilaration and Trauma*

Several years after the 1980 coup there is still no authoritative and unchallenged version of the events that took place on the night of the eleventh and the early morning of the twelfth of April 1980. What was planned and what was accidental or happenstance remains a mystery. Rumors of impending coups had been circulating for over a month before the action of Master Sergeant Samuel Kanyon Doe and his fellow enlisted men (two staff sergeants, four sergeants, eight corporals, and two privates) materialized, but each version had a different group identified as the challenger to the regime of President William R. Tolbert. As suggested earlier, the arrest of both army officers and enlisted men during the month of March 1980 had heightened suspicions that a coup might come from that sector. Although most of the PAL/PPP leaders were in jail at the time, there were other civilian groups that remained potential challengers of the True Whig elite. The Movement for Justice in Africa, for example, had become increasingly assertive and its leaders had decided to follow PAL's lead and officially register as an opposition party. There were as well prominent people inside the government who were making Tolbert and his henchmen nervous with demands for moderation in dealing with political dissent. One of these was an original sponsor of PAL—the highly respected economist and former minister of finance Ellen Johnson-Sirleaf, who was destined to continue her vigorous role as conscience, critic, and dissenter during the tenure of Samuel Doe as head of state. Of even greater political significance at the time was the call for a repeal of the Sedition Law made by Tolbert's own son-in-law (and son of former President Tubman), Senator "Shad" Tubman, Jr.

Equally believable, however, were the rumors that it was the Old Guard of the True Whig Party that had elected to act, with or without the acquiescence of President Tolbert. They had already indicated their impatience with reform by balking at Tolbert's suggestion, a week before the coup, that the Legislature eliminate the property qualification for suffrage. It was strongly hinted that the Old Guard would wait before seizing power until Tolbert had left early the next week to preside over the independence celebrations in Zimbabwe in his capacity as chairman of the OAU. Many of the jailed dissidents firmly believed—and some of the coup leaders purportedly confirmed having seen the papers—that the execution orders for the PAL/PPP leaders had already been prepared by Justice Minister Joseph Chesson even before the April 14 trials were to have commenced.[1] Credence was given to the prospects of a right-wing coup by the increased displeasure voiced by House Speaker Richard Henries, Chief Justice James Pierre, and other extreme reactionaries regarding Tolbert's vacillation on the question of permitting a legal opposition, and on his handling of internal developments at the University of Liberia (discussed below), the loss of the court case brought by MOJA against the superintendent of Grand Gedeh County, and other threats to settler solidarity and control over the political system. It was believed that Henries and Reginald Townsend, the national chairman of the True Whig Party, were responsible for the steady procession of petitioners to the Executive Mansion demanding adherence to the hard line, and demanding the death penalty for the "PPP traitors." Chesson's Ministry of Justice had even put out inciteful "wanted" posters, offering cash rewards for the capture "dead or alive" of PPP leaders—an action that brought quick protest from Amnesty International.[2] Indeed, one prominent MOJA leader, Dean Amos Sawyer of the University of Liberia, was awakened during the early hours of April 12 and spirited away into hiding by his household staff, who were convinced that the reported shooting at the Executive Mansion was a right-wing coup.

How Tolbert happened to be at the Executive Mansion rather than spending his usual weekend at the family mansion at Bentol also remains a mystery. One version has it that the coup leaders had received inside help in tricking Tolbert to spend the night in Monrovia. A second version is that he and his very close associates spent long hours the night of April 11 debating who should be Tolbert's chosen successor in the 1983 campaign, and that consequently—as a matter of pure happenstance—Tolbert was too tired to make the journey to Bentol that night. Another question is why was the Executive Mansion so poorly guarded, given the tenseness of the preceding month. Finally, the details of how Master Sergeant Doe managed to make his way into the inner sanctum of the Executive Mansion remain unclear. Admittedly, being the senior noncommissioned officer in the Liberian armed services, he might have been too powerful to have been challenged by other enlisted men. Those who engage in "external conspiracy" theories suggest that his presence was "expected," since most of the direct participants in the coup were part of the U.S. Green Beret–trained force. Ironically that unit had been created a year previously to improve Tolbert's security following the breakdown in order associated with the Rice Riots of 1979. In any event, the seventeen coup leaders entered the Executive Mansion at approximately one o'clock in the morning and swiftly moved to kill Tolbert and twenty-six other occupants, most of whom were security personnel. Within hours, the new military leaders went on the air at government radio station ELBC to announce that "the Tolbert government is no more." A carnival atmosphere prevailed in Monrovia and the countryside throughout the long weekend.

There appears to be no corroborating evidence that the action by the military was coordinated with a parallel civilian conspiracy. Most of the PAL/PPP leaders were in jail. Nevertheless, the master sergeant, two staff sergeants, four sergeants, eight corporals, and two privates first class moved with extraordinary swiftness in establishing a new government. Styling themselves the People's Redemption Council—with echoes of Lieutenant Jerry Rawlings in Ghana—they posed as the "guardians of the revolution." Recognizing their own limitations, however, the PRC quickly set up a cabinet which consisted primarily of civilians. Samuel Doe, as the ranking noncom, remained in control as chairman of the military PRC. Sensing that power was equated with control over revenues, the military also retained most of the key "money" posts in the cabinet, such as finance, commerce, and postal affairs. Understandably, too, the civilian minister of defense was not expected to have more than nominal control over the internal affairs of the armed forces. The remaining cabinet positions, however, were distributed among a coalition of civilians, including four leaders of PAL/PPP, two from MOJA, and three holdovers from the Tolbert regime who also had solid linkages with the preceding Tubman era.

The formation of this coalition government accomplished another objective which has been an integral part of coups in other African and Third World countries: the release of political detainees of the preceding regime. Other parts of the scenario also fell quickly into place, such as the seizure of the instruments of communication, both to assert control over the reins of government and to undermine (or at least discourage) those who may have contemplated resistance to the new regime. The customary pledge with respect to an early return to civilian rule, however, remained somewhat vague and only implicit.

The most surprising thing about the action of Master Sergeant Doe and his colleagues was that this bold—but nonetheless isolated—act would have instantaneous effect throughout the length and breadth of the Republic. Some minor skirmishes of resistance did in fact occur here and there. On the whole, however, the balloon of Americo-Liberian power burst in one loud bang. The rejoicing in Monrovia and elsewhere was spontaneous and reflected the general relief that the oppression of the Whig aristocracy had come to an end. Undoubtedly, however, many of the people who had come down to Monrovia as loyal True Whig adherents several weeks before—demanding the banning of the PPP—were the very same people who now danced in the streets, celebrating the Doe coup. They were probably among those who cheered as the mutilated bodies of Tolbert and others killed on April 12 were taken through the streets of Monrovia on an open cart and dumped without sermon or ceremony in a swampy area adjacent to the city's Palm Grove Cemetery.

Obviously, not all Liberians were rejoicing. In addition to the twenty-seven killed on the twelfth, some ninety or more Tolbert officials in Monrovia and up-country were arrested (or had turned themselves in) and were placed in the same cells at Barclay Training Center that had only recently been vacated by the released leaders of the PAL/PPP. Many other officials—including some foreign heads of economic enterprises in Liberia—were placed under house arrest or told to "sit down small'' until their future had been determined. And many who were not killed or arrested suffered physical abuse at the hands of undisciplined and unrestrained troops. In addition to the arrests, there began a systematic "trashing" or vandalizing of the houses of many of the key leaders of the Tolbert regime, such as Speaker Henries, Justice Minister Chesson, Planning Minister Cyril Bright, and Foreign Minister Cecil Dennis. Most obvious of the physical targets were the various Tolbert family villas at Bentol. The vandalism extended to the level of stripping homes of everything, including light bulbs and toilet fixtures—anything not nailed down. Any parked car in Monrovia or up-country was a candidate for destruction or "requisitioning" by the military or by civilian looters. In addition, a small detachment of soldiers undertook an assault on the grandiose Masonic Temple which stands on the hill at Mamba Point. The soldiers not only ransacked the building but they also sought out the caretaker in his home at Caldwell and shot him.

Amid praise for the new Liberian leadership from some unaccustomed quarters—Libya, Ethiopia, Cuba, and East European states—there was either studied silence or outright protests from Liberia's more familiar friends and associates, such as the United States, Sierra Leone, Nigeria, and Ivory Coast. Criticism focused on the killings that had occurred on April 12 and concern regarding the fate of the ninety or more officials that were in detention. Ignoring the protests from abroad, the People's Redemption Council set up a special tribunal consisting primarily of military personnel to examine various charges of corruption and abuse of human rights leveled against the imprisoned Whig leaders. The "trials" by the Special Military Tribunal were not trials in the accepted use of that term. The accused were denied the right to counsel or access to their personal and official records about which they were being questioned. The proceedings were conducted in private. Although summary transcripts of the "trials" were released, they were not conclusive. The inquisitors appeared to focus upon several themes, among which official misdeeds and personal corruption were prominent. Invariably, the accused official was asked "Why did you permit Tolbert to abuse the rights and trust of the people?" There were recurrent suggestions that the Tolbert period was somehow an aberration from the positive reforms commenced under President Tubman. Routinely, as well, the accused disclaimed their involvement in corruption but acknowledged—almost as a litany—that the late president had lost touch with the people and had abused their rights.

The efforts to engage in at least a semblance of legality (however crude) were regarded both domestically and internationally as a sign that the PRC was ultimately going to approach the problem of justice and punishment in a logical, systematic fashion. Indeed, it was assumed to be in the best interests of the regime to keep the officials alive if for no other reason than to discover where all the hidden assets of the "honorables" were and what under-the-table deals had been made within the government or between government and foreign concessionaires. Although it was suggested that the younger dissidents in government—reminiscent of Madame DeFarge in *A Tale of Two Cities*—had already been compiling dossiers on questionable expenditures and "shady" deals, most observers tended to question whether the accounting of misdeeds had been very thorough or systematic.

There were other signals as well that the PRC was interested in an early reestablishment of order. The PRC in the days following the coup was urging that the recently ransacked shops "of our Lebanese friends" be reopened, that people return to work, and that even those business concerns of the deceased or imprisoned former leaders continue to operate—since they employed so many people and their products were needed. The Tolbert Mesurado Fisheries, for example, obviously fell into this category. In addition, to strike out against anomic acts of violence, the PRC televised the execution of three soldiers and a civilian who had been caught in the act of looting. Reminiscent of crises during the Whig era, a national week of prayer had been called for jointly by the clergy and by the political leadership.

That the government and the elite-owned businesses did begin functioning again so very quickly after the coup demonstrated three significant facts. First, it showed that the high-living absentee Americo-Liberian "businessman" and other officials were to a certain extent superfluous with respect to actual production and productivity. Second, it showed that the underpaid and less privileged managers, civil servants, and others—whether Liberian or aliens from the West Indies or other West African countries—were the ones who made things actually work in Liberia. And third, it demonstrated that perhaps the expanded educational programs of the Tubman-Tolbert eras had actually paid off in providing a pool of trained manpower. If so, it was regrettable that it took a bloody coup to provide the evidence.

*The Executions on the Beach*

The general euphoria domestically and the cautious optimism of the foreign diplomatic community regarding an orderly approach to reform and retribution took a sudden and dramatic turn ten days after the coup, with the decision of the PRC to execute thirteen of the ninety or so officials of the Tolbert regime. The international reaction was immediate and vehement, due primarily to the fact that the execution of the officials on the beach behind Barclay Training Center took place in the full view of invited journalists and in the full glare of television cameras. The somber significance of the event was almost lost in the face of the absurd and frivolous behavior on the part of the executioners.

Why did the executions take place? Until that point the PRC had appeared to be proceeding in an orderly and deliberate fashion in bringing the more than ninety arrested officials to trial on charges of corruption, abuse of human rights, and other offenses. Despite the summary nature of the "trials," they were in a sense traditional with respect to Liberian national politics in that they resembled the manner in which the Whig aristocracy treated political "offenders" even within their own ranks. That is, the accused would often "confess" to outrageous offenses, with the understanding that in due time the "hand of forgiveness" would be extended and he would be not only pardoned but permitted to return to government employment at an even higher level. This time, however, the confessions were tendered but the forgiveness was withheld.

It had earlier been expected that some harsh penalty—perhaps even the death sentence—would be brought against those who symbolized the worst aspects of the

Whig aristocracy. This would include Chief Justice James Pierre, the father-in-law of the late Stephen Tolbert, who was one of the most articulate hard liners over the years; the late president's other brother, Senator Frank Tolbert, who served as president pro tempore of the Senate and epitomized the personal corruption of the Tolbert family; Minister of Justice Joseph Chesson, a Robespierre-like figure in his relentless pursuit and persecution of political dissidents; and the most hated of all the Old Guard, Speaker of the House Richard Henries. Henries had a remarkable record of political survival during the forty years he served as Speaker, a fact attributable to his alleged knowledge of where every political skeleton in the system was hidden. He apparently used his knowledge of misdeeds within the system to blackmail others in the Whig hierarchy who disagreed with him. In addition to those four, some sources indicated that Reginald Townsend, the national chairman of the True Whig Party and Grand Master of the Masonic Order, for symbolic purposes, was on the "death list." In any event, it is firmly believed that the Special Military Tribunal had not brought in the death sentence for some of the lesser offenders and certainly not for Foreign Minister Cecil Dennis, whose primary offense was guilt by association with the late Stephen Tolbert.[3] It was assumed that, at worst, the remainder of the thirteen, as well as some of those still awaiting trial, might be sentenced to Belle Yella Prison in the interior, the odious Whig "correctional institution" from which most inmates were "corrected" out of existence. Although there might be some dispute regarding the verdict of the Special Tribunal, there is no doubt that the PRC itself decided that all thirteen Whig officials were to be executed (a fourteenth accused, with tribal antecedents, was spared).

Why did the People's Redemption Council appear to disregard the advice of its own civilian cabinet members and the warning of the international community? Lack of governmental experience, which made it impossible for them to anticipate the adverse international reaction, may be one explanation. Another rationale is that the basic insecurity of the PRC regarding its own power required that it do something which would convince not only other Liberians, but more importantly *itself*, that it was actually in control and that the all-powerful and oppressive Whig aristocracy had come crashing to a halt as a result of one good night's work. After all, if one had been convinced for decades that the settlers were an oppressive group that was firmly in control, had created an elaborate system of surveillance, manipulated resources, and had powerful friends abroad, then how could the action of seventeen enlisted men on the morning of April 12 bring about the total and instantaneous collapse of that regime's authority from one end of the Republic to the next?

Indeed, in the ten days following the coup there were frequent rumors of countercoups being mounted within Liberia and in the neighboring Ivory Coast. The latter country was particularly suspect, since the fugitive son of the late president, Representative A. B. Tolbert, was married to the neice (ward) of President Félix Houphouët-Boigny of the Ivory Coast. Although A.B. Tolbert was eventually discovered in the French embassy and forcibly removed, it was first thought that he had been beheaded the day of the coup. Later it was rumored that he had fled to the Ivory Coast. Suspicions about the Ivory Coast were increased when former

Vice-President Bennie Warner (who had been attending a conference of Methodist bishops in Nashville, Indiana, at the time of the coup) allegedly made a broadcast from Abidjan, stating that he was the constitutional successor to Tolbert and calling upon Liberians to mount a general uprising against Doe.[4] The PRC leaders seemed convinced that the surviving Whigs would call for and receive support from the Americans (who would want to protect their investments), from the Guineans (who had rescued Tolbert during the Rice Riots), from the Ivoriens, or from the Nigerian and other OAU leaders who had voiced their shock with regard to Tolbert's murder. One long-time observer of Liberian politics reported that Doe so feared a counter-coup during the first few months that he seldom would sleep at the same place two nights in a row.[5]

The feeling that the Doe government was under international quarantine was reinforced by the studiously cool official American treatment of the Doe regime, and by the successful efforts of Nigerians and other Africans to bar Doe and his Liberian advisers from attending scheduled meetings of the OAU, of ECOWAS (the West African Economic Community), and other African organizations. Foreign aid and new investment probes came to a halt. The International Monetary Fund and the World Bank imposed harsh terms in providing money that would permit the government to meet its payrolls. Collectively, these actions only intensified the regime's self-doubts. Thus, the executions could stand as a warning to potential counterrevolutionaries.

Much of the foreign criticism of the execution of the thirteen on April 22 focused on the manner in which it was carried out: the televising of the event, the carnival behavior of the troops, the disheveled appearance of those about to be executed, the absence of blindfolds, the unceremonious dumping of the bodies in a common grave, and the subsequent harassment of the widows of the deceased and other accused officials. To put this in perspective, only the televising of the event is novel to the Liberian scene. Under the long years of Whig rule, there was no international outcry (other than some occasional protests by Amnesty International) regarding the summary nature of trials in Liberia; the countless public beatings and executions; the dragging of accused political prisoners through the streets of Monrovia in chains or with ropes around their necks; and other deviations from humane treatment of the accused. Indeed, the very refusal of the PRC to turn over the bodies of the executed officials to their relatives had a certain symmetry with more recent Liberian history, namely the refusal of the Tolbert regime to turn over the bodies of the students and others killed in the Rice Riots of 14 April 1979. Indeed, the common graves of the victims of the April 12 coup and the April 22 executions are adjacent to the common grave of the April 14 rice demonstrators of the year before. Even the treatment of the widows of the deceased must be put in perspective. Often the abuse meted out by the wives of Americo-Liberian officials to servants or ordinary citizens was more cruel and unpredictable than the more predictable and limited abuse by the male officials themselves. Moreover, power in many cases went to a male official because of the relationship of his wife to a more prominent member of the settler oligarchy. Hence, by striking at a female, one was actually striking at her family patron.

## The Sober Reassessment

To an on-the-scene observer of Liberia in the immediate postcoup period, it was obvious that the events of 12 April 1980 were slowly being sorted in the weeks following the coup. There was an ecstatic rejoicing of many tribal people that a new order had arrived in which there would be a dramatic and immediate reversal of fortunes between the discredited Americo-Liberians and the oppressed tribal people. This was followed by a sober reawakening. "The head of the viper had been cut off," as one tribal elder put it, but the settlers' descendants still had better education, more sophisticated connections with the outside world, and a continuing hold on much of the wealth of the country. The Americo-Liberians were a divided group which ranged in attitudes from those who had a realistic fear for their lives and property to those—especially the younger element—who looked upon the coup as a way of liberating themselves from a social caste system in which they were the unwitting exploiters of their tribal fellows. Gradually an attitude of guarded sober optimism permeated the country. The tribal people could at least content themselves with the fact that a tyrannical system of rule had come to an end and that they no longer need feel ashamed of their tribal origins. For the Americo-Liberians who had not been arrested or had not felt compelled to flee, there was a feeling that things could be worked out and that all Liberians would be the healthier for it.

To the credit of the Doe regime in its early weeks, the coup was being calculatedly interpreted as a victory over an oppressive system rather than a triumph of one ethnic group or groups over another. The public, and in particular those in the media, were being admonished to avoid ethnic labels in referring to their fellow citizens. It was as if Africa's oldest state was seriously, and for the first time, addressing the question of national identity. It was doing so with a vigor not noticeable in the Unification Program of Tubman and Tolbert.

If people were relieved that the old system had been destroyed, the outline of the new political system was still somewhat slow in coming. Although a preliminary constitutional commission was almost immediately put to work (assisted by Tubman and Tolbert's former minister of foreign affairs, Rudolph Grimes), no explicit commitment was initially made either to hold elections or to return to civilian rule. Internationally the new regime was almost completely isolated from its traditional allies. Domestically, the various political forces seemed to be playing a waiting game, testing not only the goals but also the strengths and weaknesses of the vaguely defined political forces that had remained or had emerged following the coup and the execution of the thirteen on the beach.

Clearly, the military was dominant among the various contending forces. It had demonstrated this most effectively in that its action at the Executive Mansion on April 12 had brought about the collapse of Whig authority throughout the Republic. While many both inside and outside Liberia found the televised execution of the thirteen on the beach repulsive, that act alone clearly demonstrated that it was the seventeen-member People's Redemption Council that was in charge— particularly as the rumors persisted that the military had overruled the civilian cabinet members on that issue. Indeed, the omnipresent rifles, machine guns, and pistols on Liberia's streets, in its more expensive restaurants, at the post office, and in other locations during the early weeks gave evidence that power came from the barrels of guns. There were several questions, however, regarding the power of the military.

First of all, it was not quite clear whether the PRC would be able to exercise authority over the rank and file of its own army. Almost daily during the early period, the commanding general of the armed forces, General Thomas Quiwonkpa, had to issue orders relating to the "unrevolutionary behavior" of soldiers. The behavior referred to in the orders included extorting money from citizens; moving into the unoccupied homes of deceased former Tolbert officials; molesting foreign entrepreneurs, "which would drive away the people who are providing jobs"; arresting citizens without orders from higher authorities; and carrying loaded weapons in unauthorized areas. The PRC had attempted to use both the carrot and the stick to keep its troops in line. One of the first orders of the PRC, for example, had been to raise the minimum pay of soldiers to $250 a month (while leaving the minimum for civil servants at $200). In an effort to break the settler monopoly over officer ranks, moreover, there were a number of instant promotions of noncoms to the ranks of captain, major, and general. On the other hand, in addition to the public execution of three soldiers for looting, the PRC had sentenced an officer and eight soldiers to the much-hated Belle Yella Prison in the interior for molesting citizens. The PRC seemed intent upon dealing harshly with its own soldiers who undermined the revolution.

A second question relating to the power of the military was the problem of ethnicity within the army itself. Some observers had suggested that the constant exhortations to journalists and the broader public to avoid ethnic labels was in part a self-serving device on the part of the PRC. Contrary to the initial claim that the PRC was broadly representative of the country as a whole, its membership was drawn largely from the southeast areas such as Sinoe and Grand Gedeh counties, which are among the less-developed sections. The PRC was predominantly Krahn in terms of tribal origins, with a sprinkling of Kru, Gio, and Grebo. Significantly, the initial PRC included only three Loma (a fourth was later added) despite the fact that the Loma constitute the largest single ethnic group within the armed forces and are often regarded as "its best fighters," by those engaging in stereotypes. The "quiet word" on the streets and among the military was that the "Loma had *their* chance to bring down the government in the aftermath of the Rice Riots of 1979, but they muffed it!" The ethnic imbalance within the group that brought off the coup was perhaps understandable, given the ethnic segregation practiced by the Americo-Liberian leadership. Successful coup tactics, moreover, would seem to dictate that a conspiracy be limited to close, trusted associates. For the long haul, however, perceived ethnic imbalances within the PRC became a significant factor in frustrating the revolutionary process.

The third major question regarding the power of the military is whether the PRC possessed the confidence that it actually had that power as well as the ability to use it wisely on its own behalf and on behalf of the country. The lack of self-confidence could be significant in explaining the extended continuation of the 11 P.M. to 6 A.M. curfew for over two years. More important, it accounted for the televised execution of the thirteen officials on the beach despite the reported disapproval of civilian cabinet members and the earlier pleas of the Pope as well as the American, the Nigerian, and other governments to avoid "a bloodbath."

# PART THREE

Second Chance for Democracy
*Promise versus Performance*

# XIV.

## The PRC as "Balance Wheel"

The term "military government" is in many instances a deceptive concept, particularly when applied to Liberia and most African countries; for the seizure of state power by the military does not automatically clothe the sergeants, colonels, and even generals who precipitated a coup with the ability to govern effectively. Indeed, the history of Africa since the 1966 military coups in Nigeria and Ghana has confirmed this. In analyzing the performance of the political role of the military against that of the civilians whom they displaced, it is rare to find a situation in which *either* the military *or* the civilians alone govern and manipulate political power. The national political arena must be viewed as a complex set of relationships obtaining between, on the one hand, those who have the expertise and responsibility for protecting the society against both external and internal threats to its existence, and, on the other hand, those who have the talents and experience required to cope with the broad spectrum of concerns which any society normally expects its national elites to address. Even a society such as the Zulu under Shaka in South Africa during the nineteenth century had civilian specialists in traditional law, medicine, agriculture, and other fields, even though the values and interests of the military permeated so many aspects of Zulu society. Conversely, when contemporary Gambian leaders attempted to construct a civilian-dominated society which would dispense with the need for any army, they rudely discovered that the police—the one legitimate set of specialists in force and violence—had it within their power to challenge civilian leadership in the abortive 1981 coup.

Instead of the political relationship of the military and civilian leadership being viewed as an "either/or" proposition, the relationship can be better analyzed in terms of a series of models along a continuum in which the involvement of the military in the political process of a society is either minimized or maximized. Both are competitors for a claim on the society's scarce resources; both have a role to play in the health and survival of the society. At one end of the continuum, however, is the *civilian supremacy model* in which the role of the military is largely focused upon the task of defending the society against external threats. That model establishes that civilians, rather than the military, control decision making with respect to war and peace, the determination of the size and general shape of the military establishment, the methods of recruiting both officers and enlisted personnel, the allocation of major privileges and rewards within the service, and—of great importance—the allocation of government revenues for the funding of all military and paramilitary activities. The military becomes the specialist in the technology of warfare and is given some latitude—especially during wartime—in determining strategy and tactics for dealing with the external threat; in the training and disciplining of troops; and in other areas where the military leadership has greater expertise than civilians. Although the actual application of these aspects of the civilian supremacy model differs widely even within Western European democracies, the general adherence to these principles is essential. It is a model, curiously enough, which has been embraced in recent history not only by Western industrial democracies, but by most societies committed to a communist or socialist strategy of development. Even more ironically, it is the normative model accepted and proclaimed by most military leaders themselves when they undertake a coup against entrenched civilian political leaders. In the litany of coups one of the first explicit or implicit pledges made by an interventionist military cadre is a promise for an early return to civilian supremacy as soon as the situation which invited intervention has been rectified. Thus, this pledge becomes the standard against which the subsequent performance of the coup leaders is to be judged.

At the other end of the continuum is the *atavistic model*, in which the military not only attempts to become the focal institution for the society, but seeks to substitute its values, its interests, and its institutions for the civilian ones which previously prevailed. Thus, glorification of violence, heroism, blind obedience to authority, conformity, and other military mindsets are to prevail in the economic, social, religious, and other sectors beyond the military arena itself. The example of traditional Zulu society has already been cited, but for recent African history the efforts of Idi Amin in Uganda provide a good case to illustrate the atavistic model.

In between the two poles on the continuum are a series of ideal types which indicate variations in both the temporal duration and the complexity of the political intervention which the military has set for itself (or—in some cases—been asked to assume). The most limited of these interventionist models is one which I have labeled the *watchdog model*. This is a situation in which the military is constituted as the guardian of the existing "constitution" in the broadest sense of that term. The military only intervenes when the basic political ground rules of the society have been violated, and it continues to exercise an extraordinary political role until such time as the preexisting legitimacy of the system has been restored. In searching for an African example, the interventionist role of the Sierra Leone military in 1967–68 may suffice, even though the example is a far from perfect one. It took almost a year and a series of intramilitary coups for the Sierra Leone army to play the critical role in seeing that the opposition party of Siaka Stevens, which had won the 1967 election, was actually awarded the reins of government. At that point the military as a bloc withdrew to the wings and resumed its more minimal role as defender of the state against external threats.

The *balance wheel model* constitutes the next relationship on the hypothetical continuum, indicating a situation in which the persistence of disruptive forces or the destruction of the previous order does not permit a quick restoration of the status quo. Inasmuch as the military is reluctant to assume a more overt role in governing (or lacks the abilities and talents to do so), it provides the necessary order and stability which will permit the bureaucrats, the judges, the teachers, and other technicians to bear the major burden of fashioning a new and more workable political compact for the society. Again, when the balance wheel function has been performed, the military withdraws to the barracks. Conversely, in the event of failure on the part of the civilians to provide a new formula for national reconciliation, the military may find itself obliged to intervene further in the political process.

The more sustained and systematic involvement of the military in the act of governing—that is, performing functions normally left to experienced civilians—can be analyzed in terms of two diverging models. The more conservative of the two finds the military acquiring the necessary civilian skills or more closely supervising the performance of civilian technicians in the resolution of the basic economic, social, and other problems which beset and divide the country. Essentially, however, this *direct rule model* is largely a commitment to the restoration of the status quo but at the same time also recognizes that religious, ethnic, sectional, or other conflicts within the civilian leadership cadre prevent the latter from negotiating an acceptable settlement of a major constitutional crisis. Thus, the military, in a technocratic fashion, attempts to perform that task for the society. De Gaulle and his colleagues provided this model in France in 1958; and Gowan, Murtala Mohamed, and Obasanjo provided this model in Nigeria during the Biafran War, after the balance wheel model proved to be ineffective in resolving the issues of interethnic conflict and the more equitable national distribution of oil revenues.

The second, more revolutionary of the two models of actual government by the military is the *social transformation model*, in which the military attempts a dramatic overhaul of the fundamental values and institutions of the society on the assumption that the preexisting political system was woefully inadequate in addressing the real problems of the society. The withdrawal of the military, if contemplated at all, will only take place after an extended period. The earlier example of Atatürk in Turkey after World War I has African counterparts in the efforts of Muammar Qaddafi of Libya and Mengistu Haile-Miriam of Ethiopia to reshape drastically their respective societies.

### Model Options Considered by the PRC

The assumption of power by the People's Redemption Council in 1980 undoubtedly put the country into the mainstream of contemporary African politics. A majority of the new states of Africa have now experienced at least one successful case of military intervention. The Liberian military intervention, however, was supposed to be different. The longer history of civilian politics, the close economic and cultural links with the United States, and the large pool of individuals who possessed degrees in higher education from Liberian institutions or universities overseas seemed to guarantee the early restoration of a more solidly established system of civilian government. Helpful in this regard was the recognition by the military itself regarding its own limited talents in governing. The broad popular acceptance of the PRC as the savior rather than the destroyer of Liberian democracy seemed a further assurance of harmonious civil-military relations.

In analyzing the behavior, the policy pronouncements, and the attitudes of the Liberian PRC—and of Doe in particular—it is apparent that the regime either implicitly or explicitly considered several of the described models of civilian-military relationships between the 1980 coup and Doe's inauguration as president in 1986. Aspects of several models were detectable simultaneously; in other cases there was a progression from one distinct model to the next.

At the outset the PRC gave strong signals of a desire to pursue a radical social transformation model. Indeed, the use of the term "People's Redemption Council" was reminiscent of the efforts of Lieutenant Jerry Rawlings to revolutionize Ghanaian society during his first coup in 1979. In retrospect, however, a far more populist reading was undoubtedly given than was warranted to the official slogan of the Liberian military regime (adopted from the PPP of G. Baccus Matthews): "In the cause of the People, the struggle continues." Much attention was given in the European and American press to the fact that the Soviet ambassador was called in on the morning of the coup, without giving equal attention to the fact that the highest-ranking U.S. diplomat present in Monrovia was also summoned at the same time. There was also a focus upon several key civilian members of the new government who had been vocal about the need for "Third World solidarity" and Liberia's "nonalignment" in global politics. The immediate expressions of support for the PRC from Ethiopia, Cuba, the Soviet Union, and Libya, as well as several quick visits by Liberian officials to key capitals in this revisionist group, also were taken as signals of new directions in the Liberian state. Doe even sent some Liberians to Ethiopia for training in adult literacy and the government accepted a number of Libyan scholarships for Liberian students to go to Tripoli.

The ideological phase of the PRC coup, it turned out, was very short-lived. In coping with the economic problems (discussed later in this chapter) it became a stark fact of life that Liberia was too much a prisoner of its domestic economic past and its historic linkages with the West to pursue dramatic new directions. The PRC's enthusiastic constituency, which was discernible on the day after the coup, would have vanished quickly as the problems of poverty worsened under experimentation with untested ideological strategies. By 1982 the proponents of nonalignment in foreign affairs and a more radical approach to economic development had definitely lost out. This was graphically signaled by the execution of Doe's second-in-command, Major General Thomas Weh Syen, the most radical of the "revisionist" PRC membership, along with four of his colleagues. It was also signaled by the departure from the cabinet of the two most outspoken civilian advocates of new directions: Togba-Nah Tipoteh of MOJA and (albeit temporarily) G. Baccus Matthews of the PPP, who at that time was the foreign minister.

There were earlier indications, however, that a radical departure from past norms was being quickly shelved by the PRC in its new status reversal. Samuel Doe and other leaders of the PRC quickly took on many of the trappings of authority accumulated by the discredited Tolbert regime, despite the public claims of the military to seek a redistribution of power and privilege in the new society. Master Sergeant Doe soon gave up his modest apartment and moved directly into the Executive Mansion built by Tubman; Doe's wife took over Victoria Tolbert's Mercedes and police escorts for her trips to the supermarket; and schoolchildren were still required to sacrifice their studies in order to stand long hours along the highway awaiting the return of the head of state from his trips abroad. The newly appointed national and local officials continued to receive the sycophantic accolades and to be "gowned" in the traditional robes of authority by the rural delegations from about the country. The delegations undoubtedly consisted of the same people who only weeks before the 1980 coup had presented petitions and hymns of praise to the members of the Tolbert regime. It was early rationalized by the PRC that many of the trappings of authority from the previous regime would have to be retained to maintain the legitimacy of leadership. There is probably a great deal of truth to the statement that "the people expect this." What was lacking at the early stage of the revolution, however, was some indication regarding how a popular revolutionary group differs from an autocratic regime in terms of the flaunting of power and privilege.

It was not likely that the PRC could have opted for the watchdog model of civil-military relationships. Indeed, the events of April 1980 revealed that far more than cosmetic surgery would be required to overcome the deep social wounds in Liberian society. It was not a question of an early restoration of the status quo; what was required was the creation of a new sense of legitimacy, with an entirely new cadre of leaders drawn from the ranks of the previously untapped tribal majority as well as from among the ranks of disaffected Americo-Librians. The death, arrest, or flight into exile of so many Whig officials left a power vacuum. The destruction or truncating, moreover, of most of the dominant political institutions of the First Republic left Liberia in an almost rudderless condition. In the face of this destruction of the old regime, chaos seemed to be the only alternative to the stability the military alone seemed capable of providing. The old settler family networks were obviously undermined in terms of exercising political power, as were the social clubs that supported the True Whig leadership. More central to the collapse of the old order were the formal political institutions which had guaranteed settler corporate privilege (and the title of "honorable") during most of the history of the First Republic. The suspension of the 1847 Constitution challenged some of the basic assumptions of settler supremacy. The death, imprisonment, or flight of most legislators obviously put that institution out of operation for the time being. Similarly, the judicial system—which temporarily ceased to function—was reconstituted as a series of "people's courts" with the appointment of a mix of judges with tribal as well as Americo-Liberian backgrounds, operating under the authority of the Special Military Tribunal.

Even more critical in terms of limiting the intervention to a watchdog model was the collapse of the political system. The True Whig Party, which was formed in 1869 and had not lost an election since 1877, was perhaps shattered forever, its leading patrons dead or headed for prison. Other parties—including those represented in the coalition cabinet—were placed in limbo until the new constitution had been promulgated.

Another institution with distinct political overtones was also dealt a near mortal blow at the time of the coup—the Masonic Order, which served as a semireligious, semipolitical guardian of Whig privilege. One experienced a strange feeling in the weeks following the coup in passing the Masonic Temple high above Mamba Point in Monrovia. The now-sacked edifice stood silent, its windows and doors ajar, the big wrought iron gate around the courtyard standing half open, and not a soul was in sight on what had been its once well-manicured grounds. The temple appeared to be totally irrelevant to the new Liberian society. Yet, at the same time, the vacated building seemed to pose the lingering menace to future trespassers that might be attributable by a Gola or a Mende tribesman to the wounded spirit protecting a desecrated sacred grove of the Poro secret society.[1] The Masonic Order's power may have been diminished, but few would risk fate by further abusing it. Over time the perceived spiritual threat would diminish, for in my subsequent trips to Monrovia it was readily apparent—from the makeshift curtains and drying clothes that fluttered in the broken windows of the Masonic Temple—that it had become squatters quarters. But predictions regarding the permanent demise of the Masonic Order itself proved to be premature. Doe, in a calculated gesture to win the support of the Old Guard Whigs in his 1985 presidential campaign, suddenly reinstated the Masonic Order as a legitimate organization.

In addition to the military's new enjoyment of privilege, the constant appearance of machine guns and rifles in public places in the wake of the coup became, more than anything, demonstrable proof of the military's new power and prestige and its sheer enjoyment of that power. Indeed, it was the blatant display of instruments of violence that convinced many internal and external critics that an atavistic model (as delineated above) was the new civil/military relationship being actively pursued. For military coup leaders who had only recently claimed an identity with "the common man," the members of the PRC had become uncommonly wealthy in a very short span of time. As a corporate group, moreover, the military had come to exercise a far greater claim to Liberia's scarce resources than was thought possible in the past. The PRC worried that this new privilege could be jeopardized by an early return to civilian rule. In other terms as well, the military was attempting to substitute its values, heroes, and institutions for those of the broader civilian population. One of the most ominous of these atavistic tendencies—and one that persisted even after the new constitution had been promulgated in 1984—was the trying of civilians before the Special Military Tribunal and holding civilians accountable for civil offenses under the Uniform Code of Military Justice. Symbolism was also important in stressing the new pivotal role of the military in Liberian society. The statue of a soldier, with fixed bayonet, which stands in the middle of the road on Capitol Hill between the Executive Mansion and the Capitol is the most prominent and most frequently passed statue in the city.

The concerted efforts, however, of the PRC to substitute the red and white Redemption flag (which also contains a sketch of a soldier and other military symbols) for the traditional red, white, and blue national flag (with its single star and eleven stripes) failed miserably. Similar popular resistance was presented to the PRC's efforts to have Redemption Day (April 12, the anniversary of the 1980 coup) take the place of July 26—the anniversary of the settlers' declaration of independence from the American Colonization Society—as the most prominent national holiday. Finally, there was one atavistic effort of the PRC which has had serious fiscal implications as well as symbolic overtones. I refer to the minting of five-dollar Liberian coins featuring a replica of the military statue on capitol hill. The coins, derisively referred to as "little soldiers," have been as unpopular in Liberia as the Susan B. Anthony dollars were in America. The minting and mandatory circulation of the new Liberian coins constitute an ominous inflationary measure. True to one of the oldest "rules" of money and banking—Gresham's law ("bad money drives out good")—the year 1985 witnessed a serious shortage of American paper currency in Liberian banks and shops.

Rather than the watchdog, the social transformation, or the atavistic models of civil-military relationships emerging in the immediate transitional period, the predominant model which prevailed from 1980 to 1986 was clearly that of the balance wheel. The PRC, under the leadership of Master Sergeant Doe, had no intentions of immediately withdrawing to the barracks after the 1980 coup. On the other hand, they recognized that they lacked the talents to perform the broad spectrum of duties which the Liberians had come to associate with the national government. This was signaled early by the co-optation of a number of prominent Liberian civilians to undertake many of the responsibilities with respect to economic development, foreign affairs, health delivery, and other governmental functions.

One of the early hopeful clues regarding the intentions of the PRC to restore civilian rule was provided by Sergeant Doe himself. Despite the ample precedent provided elsewhere in Africa in the wake of military coups, Doe in the initial phase of intervention (and indeed during the first four years of the transitional period) studiously refrained from usurping the title of president. He relied instead upon the title of head of state when governmental responsibilities were involved. Although many of his PRC colleagues insisted upon their instant promotion to the now-vacated ranks of captain, major, or even general, Doe during the first year preferred to retain the modest title of master sergeant. Symbolically, of course, the use of the title perpetuated his links with the lowly enlisted ranks who effected the coup.

Regardless of his modesty with respect to titles, however, Doe rapidly shed the shy image initially manifested to the international press and began to enjoy the public accolades. As one long-term observer of Liberian politics commented, Doe found himself "taking regular lessons in English grammar and pronunciation, spending hours to know where Peking was and why despite her strong dislike for communism, the USA was friendly with Peking or having long briefing sessions on complicated problems involving the IMF and the World Bank. . . .''[2]

There was no indication during the initial period how the PRC operated internally, and whether Master Sergeant Doe was but first among equals or fully in charge. Among the Liberian masses, nevertheless, there seemed to be little doubt regarding Doe's immediate popularity in terminating a hated regime. He made himself visible in various quarters of Monrovia, but refrained from extensive touring of the interior or down-coast counties until power had been consolidated. Although the expatriate community made disparaging remarks about his command of the English language, they completely missed the point that he spoke the brand of Liberian English understood by the overwhelming number of tribal Liberians, and that a genuinely empathic bond between him and the urban masses had emerged in the aftermath of the coup. Similarly, the reported shock of Senegalese President Léopold Senghor upon seeing a head of state appear for an ECOWAS meeting dressed in camouflage fatigues and packing a sidearm failed to take into account that a significant power reversal had taken place within Liberia which required constant symbolic reinforcement. Sergeant Doe provided that. His humble Krahn background as son of a former army private and temporary schoolteacher, his birth in a small village (Tuzon) near Zwedru on the road to Ganta, his working his way through night school to the eleventh grade at Marcus Garvey High School, and his youth—in a society that venerates age—all symbolized the new priorities in Liberia. His home county, Grand Gedeh, is the least developed in the country, and the Krahn people have been among the least exposed to Western education and a monetized economy among the sixteen major ethnic groups in Liberia.

Indeed, if an election had been held in the immediate wake of the coup, many armchair strategists predicted that Samuel Doe could have won it hands down in view of his historic role in ending the Whig tyranny. But the ambition to govern as a civilian head of government at that time seemed to be far from his mind—as well as his capabilities. The task of governing (as noted in the next chapter) was to be left essentially to civilians. The more immediate balance wheel function, however, could only be provided by the PRC, and that was a monumental challenge. I refer to the restoration of public order—a direct responsibility of the PRC, inasmuch as it was the military itself that was one of the major contributors to the chaos. That instability in turn affected Liberia's second credibility problem: international acceptance of the Doe regime as the de facto government.

### Restoration of Public Order

In drawing up a balance sheet of the PRC's performance as a balance wheel in the post-Tolbert era, the analyst comes up with mixed results. The harassment of innocent citizens, confiscation of vehicles, and occupation of homes of former officials by enlisted personnel intoxicated by their status reversal in the wake of the coup cannot be expunged from the PRC's early performance record. Petty shakedowns of pedestrians and commuters became a form of institutionalized extortion at the hinterland highway checkpoints or during the urban evening curfew, a phenomenon that remained in force for almost two years, even though real security threats—whether external or internal—simply did not materialize.

Despite the aberrational beginning, and in spite of the resumption of lawlessness in the period following the 1985 elections, the PRC in the initial period of its rule did demonstrate a rather remarkable ability to restrain its own forces. A considerable measure of military discipline had been reintroduced by the end of the second year, due in part to the joint training exercises carried out with the U.S. Green Berets in 1981. An even more important factor was the popularity of the one member of the original PRC who managed to command the respect of both a broad spectrum of the civilian population as well as the military—the commanding general of the armed forces, Thomas Quiwonkpa, who later became Samuel Doe's conscience, his nemesis, and ultimately a challenger for power. Quiwonkpa was flamboyant, not averse to publicity, and was often regarded as the "strong man" in the PRC. The appearance of "headline grabbing" stemmed not only from his public insistence on the need to restore civilian rule but also from the fact that he had the unpopular task of attempting to keep the 5,000 or more rank-and-file troops from abusing their new political role in society. On the other hand, it is apparent that Quiwonkpa was the member of the PRC who most insisted upon the public "hearings" to determine whether the new civilian cabinet members were "free of Tolbert corruption." Quiwonkpa was able to accomplish the task of restoring discipline within the military because he was a "soldier's general." That is, he preferred to live in the barracks with his troops, drove his own jeep in his tours of the countryside, and avoided the sudden acquisition of new wealth (confiscated homes of the "honorables," Mercedes, and other signs of improved lifestyle) that had been the penchant of his colleagues in the PRC.

In any event, most analysts at the time credited Quiwonkpa for the fact that by the fall of 1980 weapons were once more being stored in the barracks and the more benign "walkie-talkie" had replaced the ubiquitous machine gun as the visible symbol of military authority. Occasional announcements from the army command indicated that sporadic cases of military extortion were occurring, but by 1982 the problem of the PRC controlling its own forces seemed to have been resolved. An even more tension-reducing factor was apparent in that the military by the end of 1980 felt more self-confident. It clearly enjoyed its new high status as reflected in the revised wage structure, in military sequestering of the OAU chalets and some recently completed housing estates, and in the appearance of uniformed enlisted men in hotels and restaurants where their presence in the past would have been challenged by a maître d'.

Even greater self-confidence on the part of the PRC regarding the restoration of public order was revealed in Doe's 1981 Christmas message, in which he announced the release of all political prisoners. At that moment, Liberia was one of the few African states that could make such a claim. The policy of reconciliation had been in evidence even earlier when the process of returning confiscated properties began, except for those belonging to officials executed during or just after the coup. Liberians who fled to exile abroad were encouraged to come home, and many did so. The PRC's emphasis on the point that the revolution was directed against a discredited political system, rather than against a class of people who could be ethnically identified, did much to restore confidence among those who wanted to make their contribution to a new Liberia. Equally reassuring to the Americo-Liberians, the changes in cabinet and other government posts by mid-1982 provided solid evidence of a commitment to bridge the gulf between Americo-Liberians and indigenes.

For the long haul the behavior of the troops was not the most serious problem with respect to the maintenance of public order. Rather, it was the behavior of the PRC internally, as well as its corporate ability to live up to the pledge to return the army to the barracks once civilian rule had been restored. Rumors and allegations regarding intramilitary plots have been as characteristic of Liberia as they have been with most African states. Military intervention almost inevitably breeds a series of coups based upon differences in ethnicity, ideology, ranks, age, and other factors which separate the entrenched top military leadership from internal military contenders. Until the Quiwonkpa abortive coup of November 1985, the more serious challenges came in the 1982 "conspiracy," which resulted in the secret trial and subsequent execution of Doe's second-in-command, Major General Thomas Weh Syen, and four other members of the PRC; and the split which came in November 1983 between Doe and Quiwonkpa, who was then the commanding general of troops. The internal problems of the PRC, however, will be dealt with in greater detail in a subsequent chapter.

## International Recognition and Economic Support

The restoration of public order was critical in other respects than the maintenance of political control within Liberia. Public order affected international acceptance of the regime, which in turn was directly related to the regime getting the foreign aid, investment, and trade needed for economic recovery and further development. Unlike most other coups in Africa, which brought about an almost immediate diplomatic recognition of the coup leaders by the governments of sister African states, the Doe regime in April 1980 appeared to be in danger of being treated like an international pariah. This stemmed in part from the relative popularity which Tolbert had enjoyed as the sitting chairman of the OAU. There was not, however, a universal quarantine of the PRC. Initially, the reactions of other states to the Liberian coup and its aftermath could be divided into four categories.

### THE TENTATIVE TILT TO THE EAST

In the long run undoubtedly the response which proved to be the least important to Doe's stability came from that group of states that had not been particularly friendly to Liberia in the past. These states not only immediately welcomed the collapse of the Tolbert regime and its "capitalist tyranny," but they even applauded the instability caused by the public execution of the thirteen officials on April 22. In this category belongs the Soviet Union, which had had several of its officials declared persona non grata by Tolbert in the months preceding the coup. A second state, Ethiopia, which had its own unenviable record of liquidating members of a former regime, made an ostentatious gesture of inviting the new Liberian foreign minister to visit the OAU headquarters in Addis Ababa after Liberia was denied entry to a meeting of the OAU in Lagos. Also in the list of radical states making friendly overtures were Cuba and the leader of the rejectionist camp, Libya. Although much attention was focused on the fact that the Soviet ambassador was called in by Doe on the day of the coup, the incident must be put in perspective. As noted earlier, the head of the American mission was also called in for consultation that day. Doe probably wanted to secure nonintervention by both superpowers. And finally, the threat of an abrupt "tilt" to the socialist bloc could not be taken seriously given the regime's economic problems and the economy's heavy orientation to the West and Japan. Indeed, many of the external alarmists who had predicted a "tilt to the East" had failed to take into account the long-term de-emphasis by Tubman and Tolbert of the special American linkage, which paralleled a strengthening of Liberia's relationships with other Western states, with its African neighbors, and with the Third World in general. This disengagement was initiated during the Tubman era but accelerated during Tolbert's quest for the 1979–80 chairmanship of the OAU. Libyans, Russians, Bulgarians, and others were already well established in Monrovia at the time of the coup.

In any event, doubts about a major reorientation of foreign policy under Doe had vanished by mid-1981. This was clearly signaled in the intracabinet and intra-PRC struggle in 1981, which culminated in the closing of the Libyan People's Bureau and a drastic reduction of the staff of the Soviet embassy, which had been growing steadily in the preceding years.

**THE TRADITIONAL FRIENDS**

The attitudes of the states that have long been considered friends or close associates of Liberia—and particularly those that have had substantial trade and investment relations—were more complex. With these states the regime had been caught in a vicious cycle relationship. The death of Tolbert and the others on the day of the coup brought forth public criticism of the scope of the killing and a consequent delay in extending full diplomatic recognition to the Doe government. This attitude by Liberia's former friends undoubtedly heightened the sense of insecurity on the part of the youthful and inexperienced PRC members. It may have been a contributing factor in the decision to televise the executions of the thirteen Tolbert officials. That action constituted a way of showing the world that the old regime was finished and that the PRC was in charge. The executions, however, had the reverse effect, in that they further aggravated the problem of international recognition. The new round of criticism and admonition regarding a "blood bath" intensified the psychological isolation of the Doe group. And still feeling paranoid about the prospects of a countercoup, the PRC retroactively sanctioned the 14 June 1980 storming of the French embassy by several officers who arrested the fugitive A. Benedict Tolbert.[3] Since the late president's son had boasted about being his father's successor, the capture of A. B. Tolbert had particular symbolic significance to the regime,

regardless of the international consequence. The United States attempted to keep
its note of protest about the incident low-key, but the European Parliament in
Strasbourg passed a resolution urging the nine members of the European Economic
Community to "review relations between the Community and the Liberian government in its capacity as a signatory of the Lomé Convention." This could have
serious ramifications, since earlier in 1980 Liberia had received over $10.2 million
in compensation under the treaty for losses in iron ore sales resulting from the steel
industry crisis in Europe.

Despite various reservations on the part of the major trade and investing states,
the West and Japan continued full diplomatic relations with the new regime. This
was certainly true of the United States, which not only had roughly $1 billion in
trade, banking, and investment interests in Liberia but also the largest contingent
of expatriates (an estimated 6,000 at the time of the coup). The American government, nevertheless, indicated its displeasure with the assassination of Tolbert, the
subsequent executions on the beach, and the assault on the French embassy. There
was also an orderly but staggered withdrawal of dependent wives and children from
both public and private American enterprises, including Christian missions. American AID assistance, which had amounted to $10.5 million in 1979, initially had
gone into a "slowdown" phase with little concrete discussion of new projects. As
one senior official put it to this author, "We cannot afford to be far ahead of the
African states—particularly Nigeria—on this issue." There were some gradual
positive signs of cautious support, however, such as the special visit of Assistant
Secretary of State Richard Moose early in June 1980 and the continued presence
of the Peace Corps at almost full strength. In general, however, Liberians both in
and out of government expressed great anxiety regarding their being "deserted by
our American friends." Several contacts expressed the view that the official American coolness "reflected a serious lack of understanding of the real nature of the
Whig oppression."

THE AFRICAN RESPONSE

In contrast to the diplomatic posture of the trading and investing states, the attitudes
of most of Liberia's African neighbors bordered on a de facto withholding of official
recognition. Although there were a number of bilateral visits and discussions between officials of the Doe government and government leaders in Nigeria, Ivory
Coast, and elsewhere, African diplomatic pressure was exerted within the context
of multilateral gatherings. The African Development Bank, for instance, canceled
its April meeting scheduled for Monrovia. The new foreign minister, G. Baccus
Matthews, was refused landing rights in Lagos by the Nigerian government when
he attempted to attend a special economic summit meeting of the OAU on April
25. Subsequently, the Liberian defense minister was not invited to a meeting of
defense ministers of the Economic Community of West African States on May 12.
The greatest blow, however, came when Master Sergeant Doe and his twenty-four-
person delegation were refused admission to the ECOWAS summit meeting in

Lomé, Togo, on May 27. Nigeria and the Ivory Coast had led the move against Doe, despite the fact that he had flown to Lomé as a guest on the private plane of President Sékou Touré of Guinea. The display of popular support in Monrovia upon Doe's return did not mask the fact that the regime had suffered a crushing diplomatic rebuff.

Private as well as official Liberians found this diplomatic "quarantine" of the Doe government difficult to comprehend. Several pointed out that, until now, it had become almost a cardinal rule among African states that new regimes would be quickly afforded diplomatic recognition no matter what the character of the leadership or how they came to power. Thus, the bloody military coups in Togo in 1963, in Nigeria in 1966, and in Ethiopia in 1974, or the deposing of Amin following the Tanzanian invasion of Uganda did not materially affect the question of recognition. Attitudes toward African heads of state have seldom been affected by the repugnancy of their domestic political behavior. Witness, in this regard, the elevation of Idi Amin to the chairmanship of the OAU during the height of his outrageous massacre of countless thousands of fellow Ugandan civilians.

The coolness of leaders of certain neighboring states was more understandable than the collective behavior of African heads of government toward Doe. The response of Siaka Stevens in Sierra Leone, for example, was comprehensible, since Stevens, too, had been faced with serious internal disorders, and much of the internal criticism of his government in 1980 paralleled that directed against Tolbert the previous year; much of the discontent focused on the lavish expenditures involved in Sierra Leone's hosting of the OAU summit meeting in July 1980. Another neighbor, Houphouët-Boigny of the Ivory Coast, as head of a very conservative capitalist-oriented society, could hardly have welcomed a revolutionary regime on his doorstep even if he had not had the personal connection with A. Benedict Tolbert, who was married to his niece (ward). The leaders of still other African states may have been alarmed by Doe's flamboyant statement on the morning of the coup that he would "not rest until every inch of African soil is liberated."

The more general withholding of African diplomatic acceptance undoubtedly stemmed from a reluctance to support a regime which had just assassinated one who had been perceived to be a very hard-working incumbent chairman of the OAU—no matter how unwarranted Tolbert's apparent popularity may have been. In addition, the coup came after a period of about twelve months in which the African political milieu had taken a decided turn for the better. To the relief of most African leaders, the unholy trinity of Idi Amin of Uganda, General Bokassa of the Central African Republic (formerly Empire), and Macias Nguema of Equatorial Guinea had been removed from the scene. Even more promising for democratic government in Africa, several major states—including Nigeria and Ghana—had witnessed a return to civilian rule. As President Sangoule Lamizana of Upper Volta stated after the Lomé snub of Master Sergeant Doe: "Everybody can change their regime, but the methods used in Liberia are a dishonor to Africa, and we wanted to show that." Lamizana, ironically, was no stranger to officially orchestrated violence. Finally, there was the obvious self-serving nature of the hostility of some

African leaders to the Doe regime: no regime, after all, looks forward to the prospect of its own physical demise in the wake of a successful coup. An example had to be made of Doe.

No matter what the rationale for the diplomatic quarantine, it did make the PRC's task of governing in Liberia all the more difficult. Liberian reaction to the diplomatic snub following the coup focused in particular on Nigeria, which had led the ostracism at the international meetings in Lagos and Lomé. Indeed, the intensity of bitterness toward Nigeria following Doe's return from Lomé in May caused many Nigerian businessmen in Monrovia to shutter their shops and leave town. It was only the cool counseling of Secretary of Education Fahnbulleh and Dean Amos Sawyer that prevented students from various high schools and the University of Liberia from marching on the Nigerian embassy. The feeling was that Nigeria was not only flexing its muscle as the "superpower" of West Africa but that it was acting hypocritically as well. After all, Nigeria at that point had not only had three coups (at least one very bloody) but had also undergone a three-year civil war because of its own interethnic hostilities. Thus, in addition to Liberia recalling ambassadors from the Ivory Coast, Sierra Leone, ECOWAS, and the Mano River Union, Nigeria was singled out for hostility following the closing of its embassy in Monrovia. Liberia withdrew its mission from Lagos in retaliation.

Friendship for the Doe regime, however, did come from one unexpected source; Sékou Touré of Guinea. Some Liberians suspected that it was decidedly self-serving. Sékou Touré, after all, had perhaps delayed the inevitable Liberian revolution by coming to the support of Tolbert during the 1979 Rice Riots. Touré, however, hoped to continue to have access to the free port of Monrovia and saw as well the possibility of exporting his iron ore and other commodities from eastern Guinea through the new Liberian port at Buchanan. Thus good relations were in Guinea's interest. A more charitable interpretation was that Touré remembered his own lonely days in 1957 when his defiance of France in securing Guinean independence had led many states to deny him recognition for fear of offending France.

Whatever the rationale, Sékou Touré was the first African head of state to invite Doe to visit him. Despite Touré's giving Doe a "Dutch Uncle" lecture on human rights and the need to be "honest and sincere in dealing with those you govern," this action proved crucial during the early difficult days of the regime. The Guinean diplomatic link later provided Liberia with an advocate in the delicate discussions with France over the incident at the French embassy and proved to be the significant key in reestablishing relations with Liberia's other African neighbors. Touré, for example, played a key role in arranging both the regional reconciliation meeting of the presidents of the Ivory Coast, Sierra Leone, Guinea, Togo, and Liberia at Abidjan on June 16, and a similar meeting in Doe's capital late in June, on the eve of the OAU summit meeting in Freetown. Touré's gesture ultimately brought diplomatic acceptance to the Doe regime. The resultant reduction of psychological tensions permitted the new government seriously to address its critical domestic problems. International recognition also provided the signal to the IMF and the World Bank that the Doe regime had at least the possibility of enduring until Liberia decided the exact nature of its future political, economic, and social system.

## NEW DIRECTIONS

Once it passed the initial hurdle of achieving basic de facto acceptance of the PRC, the new leadership in its quest for aid did undertake to search for a broader category of diplomatic relationships beyond the Western bloc. In seeking these new diplomatic and economic linkages in the Third World, the PRC looked to those states which not only were regarded as friendly to the United States but which often have had the means to provide forms of "South-South" aid. With this objective in mind, Sudan's President Jaafar Nimeiry was invited to Monrovia as an honored guest at the 1983 Redemption Day celebrations; Doe paid a state visit to Saudi Arabia in 1983; and an embassy was opened in South Korea. Until Liberia recognized Peking as the official government of China (paralleling a change in U.S. policy), the Taiwanese mission had been providing much-needed agricultural assistance.

The most dramatic development in expanding diplomatic horizons was the reestablishment of diplomatic links with Israel in August 1983. In undertaking this step, Liberia joined Zaire in breaking ranks on the linked "quarantine" of Israel and South Africa forged by the Arab and sub-Saharan African states between 1967 and 1973. Liberia's decision had been viewed by critics as toadying to the United States, but it could also be assessed in terms of Liberian as well as Israeli self-interest. Although Liberia has received roughly $46 million in repayable loans from Arab states, recognition of Israel would register Liberia's disappointment that it has had neither loans from the Arab fund nor concessions from OPEC states on the price of its imported oil. This flaw had been central to Liberia's balance of payments problems, to its recurrent oil and gas shortages, and to other problems of development. In contrast, Israel's technical assistance before the diplomatic rupture in 1973 was significant, and the benefits from the reestablished relationship ultimately included military assistance, technical training, new trade and investment opportunities, and development of transport.

Thus, by one means or another Doe was able to secure the diplomatic recognition which permitted the PRC to play what has been characterized as the balance wheel role. More importantly, with recognition came the financial support to keep the regime afloat. Unfortunately, "The Perils of Pauline" come to mind when one catalogs the dramatic shift of funds from one account to another and the quick assists from the International Monetary Fund or the U.S. government that have repeatedly been used to save the day for a government beset by recurrent payroll crises, fuel shortages, and threats of default on international loans. Yet the fact is that the PRC did manage to stay financially afloat during the critical years after the coup. In assessing the performance record of the government in dealing with the economy since 1980, moreover, we should not lose track of the fact that many of Liberia's problems of this decade derive from the excesses of the Tolbert and even the Tubman eras as well as from the drop in prices for the country's key exports.

# XV.

## The Path to Civilian Rule
### *The Hope for Democracy*

The decision of a military interventionist group to limit its role to that of a balance wheel does not automatically guarantee an early return to a civilian supremacy model, let alone a commitment to democracy. Recent Latin American history provides many cases of the military attempting to perpetuate itself in a balance wheel mode, while leaving taxation and other unpleasant and less popular tasks of government to civilians. The explicit rationale for such a strategy is that the continuing crisis within the society requires that the military play this extraordinary role. The unstated reason is that the military sees a continuing political role as the only way to guarantee both its newly found personal and corporate privilege and the future funding of the manpower and high-cost military hardware which it deems essential for defense. Against whom the society is defending itself is not always clear. A successor civilian regime would undoubtedly be responsive to broader public constituencies and would have differing priorities in the fields of health, education, and welfare. It might also pursue a more conciliatory foreign policy even against traditional "enemies." It was this situation, for example, which prompted the Ghanaian military in 1975 to attempt to institutionalize a "unionist" government in which the military would continue to share power even though the reins of government had been once more entrusted to civilians.

Doubts about the sincerity of even the explicit pledge to restore popular government come from the differing mode of operation of military and democratically inclined civilian elites. The military prides itself upon discipline, efficiency, management by objective, and relative conformity. It operates through hierarchies of command. Leaders in a democratic milieu, on the other hand, accept the "art of the possible" as being the end product of political action, expect negotiation rather than command decisions, and encourage diversity of both opinion and action. Unlike the military, which seeks quick resolution of conflict, civilian politicians in a democratic society expect that all political situations are open-ended and continuous rather than subject to closure. The military, moreover, relies heavily on the authoritative sanctions of force and ritual. Conversely, democratic elites regard force as the sanction of last resort and underplay ritual in preference to economic, educative, and group sanctions for legitimacy. Hence, the military, by disposition, is hardly a likely candidate for midwife in the birth or rebirth of democratic political systems. Indeed, the history of Africa both before and after the 1980 Liberian coup confirms this. The 1979 experiments in an orderly restoration of civilian rule in both Ghana and Nigeria had provided great hope for a remedy of this situation. Both, however, failed within less than five years of being launched.

The successful restoration of civilian rule requires a reaffirmation by civilians of their respect for the legitimate role of the military as the defender of the nation. It also mandates a reeducation by the military regarding the essentials of the civilian supremacy model and its value to the military itself. The successful restoration of civilian rule requires the creation of a process, with timetables and intermediate targets, the significant involvement of key civilians in the process, and the encouragement of a broad-based pluralism within society so that power will be distributed more widely throughout the community. Finally, the military can only succeed in restoring civilian rule if it seriously addresses—prior to turning over the reins of power—the long-term crises which beset the society and which invited military intervention. Indeed, during this transition period, it is the steadfastness of the military's commitment to a restoration of civilian rule that provides the military with its base of legitimacy among the populace in general.

Despite the tenuous nature of sound precedents elsewhere in Africa, there were relatively few Liberians I encountered during the early weeks following the April 1980 coup who doubted that Master Sergeant Samuel K. Doe and his colleagues had accepted the need ultimately to surrender the reins of power to civilian hands. Admittedly the PRC leadership failed to provide what has become almost a ritual during the early hours of coups in Africa, namely, an explicit pledge for an early restoration of civilian rule. This confidence in the intentions of the PRC was, nevertheless, detectable even among many who had had a close association with the discredited Whig regime and who had been particularly repulsed by the bloodshed which had accompanied the collapse of the First Republic. It persisted, moreover, even among the students and the younger professionals who nevertheless felt somewhat restrained by the PRC's ban on political discussion. Politics, after all, is the most fascinating indoor sport of most Liberians. The ban, however, did provide a beneficial cooling-off period which would permit the Liberian society not only to restore order but also reflectively to redefine its priorities in establishing a new political order.

The optimism regarding Samuel Doe's intentions persisted despite the fact that the PRC delayed a full year before setting the machinery in motion that would create the framework for a democratically elected government. Eight more months passed, moreover, before Doe established a target date for the transfer of power. Although the initial date of 12 April 1985—the fifth anniversary of the coup—was subsequently shifted in favor of January 1986, even that adjustment was not fatal to public trust. The delay could be sufficiently rationalized in terms of the technical difficulties encountered in just getting a reliable voters' roll established before new national elections.

Other than those who felt that the pressures for genuine democratic reform in the waning days of the Tolbert regime had actually been interrupted by the 1980 coup, there was a generally shared view that the restoration of civilian rule would take time. It simply could not be accomplished overnight.

### The Co-optation of Civilian Leadership by the PRC

What were the grounds for this optimism regarding the PRC's intentions? One sign, which was noted previously, was Doe's studious avoidance of usurping the civilian title of president in the seizure of state power. Even more reassuring—albeit implicit—evidence of the long-range intentions to restore civilian rule could be found in actions taken during the early hours following the coup. The fact that the PRC immediately tapped the talents and energies of prominent civilians in administering the country was a self-admission of the military's own lack of formal education and experience in governing. Master Sergeant Doe and his group—none of whom had even a high school education—recognized that their experience as privates or noncommissioned officers in the army had hardly prepared them for the art of governing a country.

Despite the absence of any hard evidence of collusion between the coup leaders and the civilian opponents of the Tolbert regime, the PRC managed to put together a coalition cabinet within 24 hours of the coup. This was taken as a sign that the military was determined to limit its intrusion into governmental operations to those areas that were most vital to security (defense and the police), to the maintenance of the "spirit of the revolution" (information), and to the management of the economy. Recognizing the importance of the Ministry of Finance, Major Perry G. Zulu—one of the few officers from the precoup period who was co-opted by the PRC—was given this portfolio. Zulu had a B.S. in business administration from the University of Liberia and had served as comptroller at the Ministry of Defense.

For the balance of the cabinet posts, the PRC co-opted as ministers representatives from the two major political groups opposing Tolbert—MOJA and the PAL/PPP—as well as two former True Whig Party officials who were more closely identified with the Tubman than with the Tolbert regime. The assumption was that Tolbert had corrupted the process of change which had been launched so promisingly under Tubman's Unification Program and his Open Door policy. The very insecurity of the PRC in the presence of their better educated and more articulate civilian colleagues, however, almost upset the good working relationship that had been established at the outset. Not quite confident in their own judgment regarding whom they had co-opted, the PRC insisted upon conducting public "hearings" to determine that the civilian cabinet members were not tainted by "Tolbert corruption." The PRC rejected the suggestion of G. Baccus Matthews, the minister of foreign affairs, that the military members of the cabinet ought themselves to be questioned in a like manner.

The civilian elements in the initial coalition consisted of four members of the PPP, three leaders of MOJA, and some holdovers from the Tolbert regime who had earlier expressed support for reform of the First Republic. Added to this was an assortment of civilians who had fallen from grace during the Tolbert era and were now called upon to accept advisory roles or sub-cabinet appointments. In the opinion of many observers, the PRC had chosen wisely. The civilian group was not only well educated but also articulate. Three characteristics stood out. First, the PRC had co-opted several key individuals in whom the international community presumably had confidence. Certainly, this included the PRC's adviser, Dr. Rudolph Grimes, the former foreign minister under Tubman and Tolbert. Also in this category was Ellen Johnson-Sirleaf, a former minister of finance, who would be invaluable in her position as head of the Development Bank in convincing the officials of the International Monetary Fund, the World Bank, and other agencies regarding the future stability of the revolutionary government. A second major characteristic was that many of the civilians had earned their political credentials as opponents of the Whig regime by having been "prison graduates." This included not only the PPP leaders, who were in jail at the time of the coup, but several MOJA leaders as well.

There appeared to be, furthermore, a conscious effort to recruit those with strong links to the Tubman regime as a method for "borrowing" legitimacy. This matched the very pointed questions put to the accused True Whig officials by the Special Military Tribunal regarding why they had permitted Tolbert to undermine the positive achievements in development and national integration made during the twenty-seven years of rule by William V. S. Tubman.

This treatment of the Tolbert era as an aberration from the Tubman reform period was clearly demonstrated by the PRC's retaining both Tubman's son-in-law, Gabriel Tucker, as minister of public works and Tubman's nephew, Winston A. Tubman, as UN ambassador (and later as attorney general). Most significantly, however, former President Tubman's son, Shad Jr., was not only permitted to return from a trip abroad but was given a key advisory role—albeit temporary. Thus, the revolutionary factors were partially balanced off with aspects of traditionalism and continuity. Although the military continued to hold the guns, it was the group of civilians who were to be crucial to the issue of whether the revolution could succeed in its positive goals of economic, social, and political development. Despite having been vetoed on the issue of the execution of the thirteen Tolbert officials on the beach, the co-opted civilians in the cabinet were permitted a wide range of authority in actually running the government.

The civilian component, however, was not a monolith. Some rivalry persisted from the days before the coup—particularly between PPP and MOJA leaders. The PPP not only had stronger representation in the cabinet, but as a bloc their revolutionary credentials were also stronger since they had to pay the price of imprisonment. Although the MOJA slogan, "Our eyes are open: the time of the people has come," was often employed by the PRC, it was the PPP slogan: "In the cause of the people, the struggle continues"—that became almost an official PRC signature for all edicts and pronouncements. Moreover, since many of the new regime's problems were so intertwined with the problems of international recognition and fiscal solvency, the role of Foreign Minister G. Baccus Matthews became very prominent, and it was felt that Master Sergeant Doe relied increasingly upon Matthews as his principal civilian adviser. It fell to Matthews to provide the public explanation to the Liberian people regarding the refusal of the Economic Community of West African States summit meeting to seat the Liberian delegation. Matthews had had prior diplomatic experience, and he demonstrated that his oratory could move people to action. In addition to Matthews, there were other members of the PPP in the new cabinet with strategic positions.

The MOJA component within the new government was also strong. Its leader, Togba-Nah Tipoteh, had early demonstrated his sympathies with his tribal rather than his Americo-Liberian links by dropping the name Rudolph Roberts and adopting his present Kru name. As a respected professor of economics at the University of Liberia, he gained a reputation as one who pressed hard for distributive justice as the only way of overcoming Liberia's vulnerability to neocolonialism. Tipoteh's role as minister of planning and economic affairs gave him a forum for introducing some of his innovative ideas, which were a blending of traditional and modern approaches to production. His task was an enormous one, however, for he had first to convince the international bankers and other foreigners who controlled the heights of the Liberian economy that a vigorous assault on the question of land tenure was not just long overdue but also vital for stability and that land tenure reform was not disruptive of public order. Significantly, although the Master Sergeant was rejected by his fellow heads of state at Lomé during the last week in May, Tipoteh had been working very effectively with his counterparts at Lomé for more than a week preceding the summit.

A second MOJA leader with a vital role to play in the new cabinet was Dr. Henry Boima Fahnbulleh, Jr., who was appointed minister of education. Fahnbulleh was a third-generation persecuted dissident. His maternal grandfather, whom I had interviewed in 1960, was a thorn in the side of Tubman and his predecessor, Edwin Barclay. Fahnbulleh's father was accused, on the basis of flimsy evidence, of treason while serving as Liberian ambassador to Kenya and Tanzania in the mid-1960s but was restored to respectability at the start of the Tolbert era. The viciousness of the prosecution of Fahnbulleh, Sr.—conducted by then-Attorney General James Pierre—had more than its fitting revenge in Pierre's execution on the beach on 22 April 1980. Fahnbulleh, Jr., himself had run afoul of Tolbert several times since taking a position in the political science department of the University of Liberia.

Fahnbulleh's role as minister of education was crucial at the early stages of the revolution despite his later falling out with Doe. Despite the successes of the Tubman-Tolbert educational efforts, the public schools were patronage-ridden and their clientele among the lowest-paid civil servants. Political pressures had kept the school curriculum oriented to legal studies, the clergy, and the classics and away from agriculture, business, medicine, and other fields needed for development. Efforts to present the tribal contribution to Liberian development in civics and history textbooks had been frustrated by the fact that the author of the standard required civics text was the wife of Speaker Richard Henries. Efforts to get "Liberianized" textbooks written and published in Liberia ran into the curious situation of President

Tolbert's daughter, Christine Norman, having a monopoly over the importation of textbooks into the country. Hence, the younger Fahnbulleh had a formidable challenge in helping build Liberia's new educational system.

And what of the holdovers from the previous Tolbert and Tubman regimes? Kate Bryant as minister of health and the only woman in the cabinet did represent the forward-thinking and outspoken critics of the Tolbert regime who worked for reform from within. The same applies to Mrs. Ellen Johnson-Sirleaf, the very gifted former minister of finance, who enjoyed the respect of IMF and World Bank officials.

The greatest question mark, however, concerned the pool of civilian talent from the past regimes which had not yet been tapped. Some of those awaiting sentencing or trial were regarded as beyond rehabilitation and some were sent to Belle Yella Prison. Others—once they had signed over their properties, as the thirteen executed on the beach were required to do—retired to private life.[1] But it is clear that the vast majority of civil servants who initially were dismissed constituted a pool of educated talent that the new regime could ill afford to ignore if it hoped to reshape the society in a constructive fashion. Unrestrained revenge would not solve the problems of unemployment, lagging international investment, and national integration. Fortunately, the PRC and their co-opted civilian colleagues recognized this. Some reduction, of course, in the scale of privilege enjoyed by the old elite had to be anticipated. There were, however, some bizarre efforts at "ritual" cleansing. Ellen Johnson-Sirleaf, for example, was summoned to the Executive Mansion several weeks after the coup. After being subjected to humiliation by being ordered to disrobe in front of her military inquisitors, and expecting brutal treatment, she was surprised to be asked to accept an important new assignment with the government! Many of the Liberian ambassadors—most of whom were left in peace—also had to undergo some type of "rehabilitation" before being assigned to other posts within the government. In any event the initial choices of the PRC helped restore some confidence on the part of the international community regarding the new regime. More importantly, it provided at least an implicit sign that the military had some commitment to civilian government and was not about to embark upon an Idi Amin-like atavistic plunder of society.

## Creation of a Constitutional Process

The pledge of the PRC to restore civilian rule only became explicit in Doe's speech on Redemption Day in 1981, the first anniversary of the April 12 coup, when he announced the creation of a National Constitutional Commission (Con-Com). Although the PRC would have a veto role over specific aspects of the proposed constitution drafted by the entirely civilian commission, the latter was to be given free rein to establish procedures for broad citizen participation in the process and for deciding what would actually go into the draft document. The integrity and independence of the commission was certainly guaranteed by the quality of the individuals selected by Doe. Although it was noticeably underrepresentative of women (only one of the twenty-five members), Con-Com did include in its membership a wide range and diversity of geographic, economic, professional, religious, and other interests in Liberian society. What gave the commission almost instant credibility, however, was the appointment of Dr. Amos Sawyer as its chairman. Widely respected and admired, Sawyer had been one of the more effective challengers of the Tolbert regime during the Year of Ferment preceding the coup. Con-Com also included a number of elder statesman who had established their credentials as advocates of democratic expression and had "paid their dues" in terms of imprisonment, outrageous fines, and other penalties at the hands of the Tubman and Tolbert administrations. Albert Porte, the inveterate pamphleteer, had been a thorn in the side of the last four presidents (as well as the PRC itself); Henry Fahnbulleh, Sr., a former ambassador, had survived a trumped-up charge of treason; and Tuan Wreh, a lawyer-journalist, had suffered repeated abuse for his exercise of free speech and press.

The broad mandate given to the commission permitted it—as a first step—to involve the public in a creative dialogue regarding the merits of the suspended 1847 Constitution. Although that constitution had often been attributed to the handiwork of Harvard University law professor Dr. Simon Greenleaf, recent historical studies have challenged this assertion, noting that many passages could only be the handidiwork of Liberian leaders themselves.[2] The publication of the suspended constitution in the *Daily Observer* oddly enough provided many Liberians with their first view of the document that had presumably governed their lives during the First Republic. It was a constitution that had often been honored only in the breach.

The commission literally took its show on the road and conducted a nationwide seminar on constitutionalism to get comments from citizens of every county regarding both reactions to the suspended constitution and suggestions for the new instrument of government. It performed a heroic service in soliciting advice, formalizing the issues for the public and itself, sifting through the contradictory suggestions, and putting forth a draft which—to a substantial degree—is the one accepted by the voters in 1984. Con-Com was also given carte blanche by the PRC in recommending procedures for the review of their draft document, as well as for a popular referendum on the constitution. The commission was specifically asked to create the electoral machinery for the registration of voters in advance of both the referendum and the national elections under the new constitution. These elections were originally set for the summer or fall of 1984 but were later delayed to the fall of 1985.

After almost two years of intense labor, Con-Com presented its draft document to the PRC for its commentary in January 1983. The commission had always felt that the draft, along with the PRC commentary, should be presented to a popularly chosen National Constitutional Advisory Assembly for a review. This second stage, it was argued, was essential in securing a broad base of legitimacy for the new political system. Equally important, the commission felt that a "second opinion"—from citizens not burdened by the plethora of detail the commission had had to consider—was important in "fine tuning" the draft document prior to its submission to a referendum.

## THE VOTER REGISTRATION CONTROVERSY

It was at this stage that the commission had its first major falling-out with Doe and the PRC. True, there had been earlier differences with Doe—particularly over the age requirement for the presidency, since a 35-year age minimum would have made Doe ineligible for the originally scheduled 1984 elections. Doe got around this barrier, however, both by extending the timetable of elections to 1985 and by handling his "age" problem in the ingenious manner discussed in the next chapter. The issue that cast most doubt upon Doe's commitment to democratic civilian government, however, was his initial objection to the creation of the Advisory Assembly and his reluctance to fund the task of voter registration. The registration lists from the Tolbert era were inadequate at best, actually fraudulent at worst. Many Liberians, particularly in the rural areas, had migrated from their home areas. The property requirement, moreover, had disenfranchised many. To start the task of compiling a reliable registration list from scratch would cost money. Doe ranted about the high estimates presented by the commission and even balked at its considerably scaled-down revisions which would tap the talents and time of students, public employees, and others in getting the job done on a volunteer basis or for token compensation. Doe insisted that the government simply could not afford a new expenditure item. He rejected, moreover, all proposals for citizen contributions to a registration fund, for a nationwide lottery similar to the one being used to finance the Ganta-to-Harper highway, and for any other alternative. At that point he virtually ordered Con-Com to limit its work to writing a new constitution. Some of the members persisted in exploring external support, however, and ultimately the British, the American, and other foreign governments contributed to this enterprise.

## THE ISSUE OF AN ADVISORY ASSEMBLY

The second major controversy with Doe dealt with the creation of the 59-member Constitutional Advisory Assembly which was to be elected to review the Sawyer draft. Doe's objection here also turned, at least in part, on the question of funding. Prophetically, the Assembly, once it met, was actually tied up over the petty issue of the size of its per diem. More fundamental, however, was Doe's fear that the elections for the Assembly, as well as its public deliberations, would constitute a violation of the 1980 PRC ban on political discussions, which he was not yet prepared to lift. It would also create another group of 59 civilian delegates with whom Doe and the PRC would have to contend.

Although Doe ultimately gave in to the concept of the Advisory Assembly, he never gave the members of the Sawyer Commission the appropriate recognition for their work. At one stage he actually became so enraged that he forbade the members of the commission to travel to Gbarnga in the fall of 1983 while the Constitutional Advisory Assembly was engaged in its deliberations. Even Con-Com's technical staff was excluded from contact with the Assembly. Why did Doe ultimately accept the concept of an Advisory Assembly? Most conclude that it was a response to pressure from those in his inner circle who argued that he could not afford to appear to obstruct the process of constitution-making so blatantly, since it would affect not only future private overseas investment but also the American and other governments which had from time to time bailed out the Doe government during its recurrent financial crises.

The Assembly was elected through a pyramid of electoral colleges, starting at the town or district level, with each of the nine counties being represented in rough proportion to its population. The Assembly included none of the members of the Sawyer Commission and had no leading representatives of either MOJA or the PPP. It included within its ranks various old stalwarts of the Tubman era, some aspiring young Liberian businessmen, a few paramount chiefs, and other rather "safe" political personalities. It operated under the chairmanship of Dr. Edward Kesselly, who possessed reputable academic credentials. Kesselly, whose parents were Loma but who also has family linkages with the large Mandingo group which forms a corridor from Lofa up into Macenta, Guinea, thus was identified with the interior rather than the Americo-Liberians at the coast. Many critics of the Assembly in its early stages felt that Doe had struck a deal with Dr. Kesselly, so that in return for doing the PRC's bidding Kesselly would be Doe's running mate in the presidential elections under the new constitution.

If the allegation was true, it was surprising then that the Assembly went about its task in an independent, businesslike fashion. Indeed, in order to involve even the barely literate in the process of constitution-making, the Assembly had composed a simplified version of its approved revised draft. For example, as a translation for "This Constitution is the supreme and fundamental law of Liberia and its provisions shall have binding force on all authorities and persons throughout the Republic," the simplified version read "This New Book is the big, big law that will control everybody . . . and any other law which does not agree with it is no law. . . ." The draft constitution was read in its entirety over the government radio station, ELBC, for the benefit of illiterates.

Despite the rather startling quixotic behavior of Doe in instructing the Assembly that they could do anything they wanted to do with the Sawyer Commission's draft— including scrapping the document entirely—the Assembly acted somewhat responsibly. They made few substantive changes in the tripartite division of powers among the executive, legislative, and judicial branches beyond recommending changes in the tenure of the president (from 4 to 6 years), senators (from 7 to 9), and representatives (from 4 to 6), making frequent elections less necessary. What the Advisory Assembly did drop with respect to structures of government were several innovative and creative agencies which would have provided greater protection for the individual citizens. One of these was the Claims Court, which would have permitted a citizen to hold government officials accountable for personal damages. Another was the office of Auditor-General, a quasi-independent official (immune from arbitrary impeachment proceedings) who would deal with the matter of public corruption. The Assembly also eliminated the Ombudsman Commission, which would have had broad investigative authority with respect to public misconduct and arbitrary treatment of citizens.

One clause in the Sawyer constitution which was offensive to the military was the provision which denied suffrage to members of the police and armed forces. Although intended to guarantee the civilian supremacy model, it had actually gotten by the Sawyer Commission without much serious consideration, on a day when there was a bare quorum present. The clause was both unnecessarily offensive to the military and perhaps far more restrictive of the civic rights of soldiers than democratic constitutions elsewhere in the world. The Assembly left the provision untouched, although curiously it did not appear in the published version of the draft submitted to the public in the July 1984 referendum. Beyond that, the Assembly did not tamper significantly with the strengthened civil rights guarantees in the Sawyer draft, which included the separation of church and state. Nor did the Assembly alter the limits on executive emergency powers or several other sections of the draft which Sawyer and his colleagues had viewed as dramatic improvements over the 1847 suspended constitution.

Finally, the Assembly let stand the clause that limits citizenship (as well as the corollary clause restricting land ownership to citizens) to persons "who are Negroes or of Negro descent"—a carry-over from the 1847 document. A racial clause does not necessarily make Liberia a racist society; rather, it is a recognition of the history of white colonialism elsewhere on the continent where a handful of Europeans came into control of a disproportionate share of the land. It also recognizes that Lebanese, Indians, and others have had de facto control over many sectors of the economy even without citizenship; if citizenship had been available to them, it was argued, most of the property in Monrovia would probably be in their hands. In any event, despite the preference of many Con-Com members to drop the clause, its omission could have led to the rejection of the entire constitution. Thus, political expediency prevailed.

**THE UNCERTAINTY OF THE REFERENDUM**

Once the Assembly had reached its decision and presented its work to the PRC, still further months of delay were to pass before the final draft was voted upon on 3 July 1984 by citizens over the age of 18. The referendum was presented on a take-it-or-leave-it basis. The delay may have been in part justified, given that voter registration had still not taken place. The latter task did not even get under way until May 1 and was done in such a haphazard fashion that it cast serious doubt over the validity of the registration list for the October 1985 elections. Many voters registered more than once, and quite a few registered for a county but not for a precinct. To make the point that the new draft of the constitution—as revised by the PRC—did not exclude the military and police from voting, Emmett Harmon, chairman of the Special Elections Commission, sent a registrar to the Executive Mansion to personally enroll the head of state as "Number One Eligible Voter in Montserrado County" (despite Doe's home county being Grand Gedeh).

The less than enthusiastic manner in which Doe presented the draft to the people prior to the referendum again casts doubt on his full commitment to the process. He indicated that the PRC would abide by the referendum even though the Assembly had ignored PRC proposals regarding terms of office, residency requirement for the presidency, and the formula for determining the number of representatives.

The real stinger came with the announcement by Commissioner Harmon on the very eve of the referendum that a favorable verdict would require a two-thirds vote of the estimated 977,826 *eligible* registered voters. Since the rolls were grossly inflated, and there was bound to be a low turnout during the period of heavy rains, this imposed an extraordinary burden on those who wanted the new constitution to pass. Indeed, if Doe and the PRC had been permitted to hold to that eligible-voter requirement, the referendum would have failed by 145,298 votes—even though the vote announced on July 20 was 510,113 in favor to a miniscule 7,771 opposed (with 14,759 abstentions and 4,248 questioned ballots).[3] Ultimately, Doe and the PRC properly concluded they had to accept the overwhelming expression of popular support. To save face, it was announced that the Special Elections Commission had miscalculated the number of eligible voters. The actual number of registered voters was estimated to be only 689,928—almost 300,000 less than the original figure! Doe had no other choice but to promulgate the new constitution.

## Creating the Foundations of Pluralism

Among other deficiencies of the First Republic in terms of achieving democratic norms was the low level of pluralism obtaining within the society. Not only was political party activity monopolized by a single dominant party, but many of the major structures which might have shared power in society with the True Whig Party found themselves subordinated to it. Interlocking directorates at the leadership level made the churches, educational structures, social organizations, and economic units appendages of the party rather than independent structures competing in the allocation of values for society. The prescriptions and proscriptions regarding membership in these structures, moreover, effectively precluded from participation members of the tribal majority in the hinterland. This obviated the possibility of transcaste crosscutting alliances based upon exposure to new forms of wealth, modern education, and other factors superseding the structures which were based on narrowly primordial attachments such as ethnicity, family, or geographic sectionalism.

For a healthy, vibrant, and innovative democracy, the existence of a great variety of outlets is necessary for the development of the broadest range of human talents within society. This stimulation of innovation in a democracy is encouraged by the formation of formal groups which provide emotional, financial, organizational, and other forms of support to those seeking to develop one aspect or another of their personalities. In the absence of any benign, all-knowing authority dictating what is or is not good for society, the "good" for that society is normally the end product of the competition among these groups for the resources of the society. Political parties serve as regulators of the competition among the groups. They do so by aggregating the diverse goals and means represented by these various and often conflicting demands in forming an acceptable governing coalition.

For societies in which the contest for scarce resources is limited to the military and a dominant political party, the prospects of the former subverting the latter are substantial. Stability requires the emergence of relatively autonomous economic, religious, and other groups if that society is to develop the full potential of its human and physical resources. It is not enough for the military to re-create a dominant party or even a limited series of competing parties before withdrawing to the barracks. What is required is that there be a series of strong, intervening counterforces which not only share societal power and influence as well as making independent demands upon the loyalties of the citizens in general, but also serve as potential mediators in the emergence of any future contest between military and party leaders. Otherwise a hastily contrived civilian supremacy model would be vulnerable to repeated military interventions in the future.

In many respects the developments in Liberia during the immediate post 1980 coup era were very promising in terms of the creation of a healthy pluralism within society. First of all, the Sawyer Constitution explicitly provided for the existence of political parties and political groups, since the "essence of democracy is the free competition of ideas."[4] Thus, multipartyism was to stand at the center of the new pluralist society. Some of the moves toward autonomy of interest groups evident during the PRC period were a continuation of trends that were already discernible at the very end of the First Republic. Pluralism had emerged almost in spite of the intentions of both Tubman and Tolbert to orchestrate the nature and direction of the changes which had accompanied economic growth, the Unification Program, and other developments.

The draft constitution, moreover, attempted to guarantee a wide measure of autonomy for new economic, social, religious, and other groups. Chapter 1, Article 14, for example, provided that "no person, while serving as the leader of any religious denomination or faith shall at the same time hold any political office." It was further stipulated that corporate bodies, business organizations, and labor unions are excluded from canvassing for political parties either directly or indirectly."[5]

JOURNALISTS AND A FREE PRESS

The existence of a free press is an indispensable ingredient in the attainment of a pluralistic society. Without the ability of individuals to express effectively their dissenting points of view on politics, religion, social arrangements, and other issues, the commitment to innovation and diversity remains a hollow promise. This requires at a minimum the means which will permit editors, publishers, and journalists to exist independently of the support which a government, a dominant political party, or a well-entrenched social or religious group could provide. It requires an attitude of mind on the part of both government and the public at large which allows for receptivity to unpopular and even unorthodox points of view. And it requires both specialized training and courage on the part of a working press, enabling it to walk the narrow line separating—on the one hand—dissent, vigilance with regard to the

public interest, and an unrelenting search for the truth from—on the other hand—
libel, sedition, and other threats to the integrity of honest men and to the survival
of a democratic society. The task is particularly difficult where the level of literacy
within society has—as President Stephen Yekeson of Cuttington University College
has estimated for Liberia—only been attained by 21 percent of the population. It
is even more difficult where the leadership is not only uncertain of its ability to
stay in power but also lacks the refinements of education and sophistication to be
able to withstand justifiable public scrutiny and even harsh criticism of its rule.

Liberia has had a long—but unfortunately intermittent—history of vigorous
reformist journalism emanating from the private sector. As noted previously, most
opposition newspapers invariably had a brief life limited to a few volumes or even
one or two issues. A few, like the Liberian *Herald*, launched during the tutelary
period under the ACS, survived for many decades despite its sometimes critical
posture toward the established political powers. There were others in this century
as well that survived for several decades. They were, however, the exceptions. The
lack of advertisers and other financial supporters, as well as the descending wrath
of government officials, quickly terminated the existence of a vigorous critic. Despite the glowing promises regarding freedom of the press made by Tolbert upon
his succeeding Tubman in 1971, the efforts at censorship during the last decade of
the First Republic became merely capricious rather than systematic. Some journalistic critics of the Whigs survived; others, such as the very courageous *Revelation*,
did not. One very persistent dissident did persevere, however—the inveterate Albert
Porte, who had been born in 1906 (and died in 1986). His long contribution to the
cause of freedom of speech and the press was recognized by the Doe regime through
his appointment to the Constitutional Commission in 1981. Since Porte's first assault
in 1929 against President C. D. B. King for his use of government funds to build
himself a private residence, Porte had been a thorn in the side of four Whig presidents. His pamphleteering was carried out on a shoestring budget, and his broadsides
appeared largely in mimeographed form. He frequently risked arrest and the banning
of his publication. Indeed, the million-dollar lawsuit that the brother of President
Tolbert brought against Porte in the early 1970s for his exposé of Tolbert family
corruption was undoubtedly one of the most serious threats to Liberian press freedom
in the country's history.[6] The lawsuit against Porte certainly gave pause to other
potential critics of the True Whig Party.

The apparent commitment of the PRC and the Doe regime to a relatively relaxed
climate of press freedom was in evidence during the first two to three years following
the coup—in spite of the continuing ban on political discussion, the occasional
banning of an edition of a newspaper, threats against editors and journalists, and
continuation of the Whig practice of subsidizing a government-owned press. With
respect to the last item, it was obvious in the early period of the PRC that the
government was not in the same firm control of its own official "mouthpiece" as
the Whigs had been of theirs. Journalists and editors of the *New Liberian* were on
several occasions reprimanded, threatened with arrest, detained, and otherwise harassed for publishing news that was regarded as offensive to the military or to
civilian members of government. The first PRC minister of justice, Chea Cheapoo,

for example, in April 1981 threatened the editors of the *New Liberian* for having repeated the comments of the independent *Daily Observer* regarding the misman-agement of affairs by the Justice Ministry. And it was the *New Liberian* on 3 April 1981 which quoted Minister Cheapoo (who, it should be noted—in fairness to the military—was a civilian member of the PPP, and not a military man) as saying: "You feel fine receiving government pay and doing nothing. . . . You have scored nothing because you failed to come out with an editorial to defend government." The editors and reporters of the *New Liberian*, nevertheless, persisted in their reporting of official corruption, shortages of school supplies, and other failings. The *New Liberian*, for example, was as vigorous in its reporting of the January 1982 sentencing of six student leaders to death by firing squad as was the independent newspaper. The *New Liberian's* editor-in-chief, J. E. Zehkpehge Bowier, insisted that they were not the "bootlickers" of government and that "in the service of national development, the mass media are agents of social change." Mr. Bowier insisted that under its present leadership, "the *New Liberian* . . . will not cower before any master nor bend to any threat . . . as watchmen, the media are the eyes and ears of the people."[7]

The latitude allowed both the government and the independent press in criticism of official policies and actions troubled many of the new military leaders. During the month from March 3 to April 3, 1981, there were sixteen articles that drew retorts from government officials. Admittedly, some were reactions to gross in-accuracies or failures of inexperienced reporters to check all sources before pub-lishing a story, but the government's reaction demonstrated extreme sensitivity to any overt criticism. This hostility was particularly noticeable with respect to the leading independent newspaper, the *Daily Observer*, but it applied as well to the eight or more weekly publications, such as the *Sunday People*, the *Liberian In-augural*, the *Sunday Express*, *We*, and *Weekend News*. Many of the weekly news-papers were started in the waning days of the Tolbert era, but their survival rate in 1980 and 1981 seemed to give hope for a more relaxed attitude toward the inde-pendent press. Although the weeklies survived largely on reporting of sports events and sensational coverage of cases of ritual murder or public hangings, they too increasingly turned to reporting on flagrant examples of official corruption.

Unlike the weeklies, issues of the *Daily Observer*, until its banning in January 1984, were read widely up-country as well as in Monrovia. Its editor, Kenneth Best, came by his advocacy journalism naturally, since he is a nephew of Albert Porte. During the first year or more following the coup, the journalists and editors of the *Daily Observer* dealt boldly with troubling issues in a balanced way, even at the risk of offending military and civilian officials. As Mr. Best noted in the presence of this writer, "Liberian reporters have to walk a tightrope in potential confrontation with government." What is needed is "not division," he stressed, but "unity with criticism." He acknowledged that many of the abuses on the publisher's side could be attributable to lack of professional training of journalists. "What we are doing now," he stated, "is not journalism, but survivalism." Despite the problems, Mr. Best insisted, "ultimately freedom of the press is not something that is given by government; it is taken!"

There were many instances during the first two years of the PRC government that demonstrated the vigor of Mr. Best's investigative talents. He harshly criticized the civilian members of the cabinet for having acquiesced quietly regarding their "induction" into the army (discussed in the next chapter). He risked both contempt of court and actual detention when he came to the defense in 1982 of University of Liberia student leader Commany Wesseh, who—despite his membership on the Constitutional Commission—had been arrested for criticizing the government. As Mr. Best's edition of 16 February 1982 pointed out, the PRC ban on politics and political criticism seemed to apply to everyone else in society except Doe and the PRC.

Despite the broad appearance of press freedom in Liberia (and this assessment would have to include the ready availability of foreign journals and newspapers in the several bookshops of Monrovia), many Liberian leaders and expatriates during the third year of PRC rule felt the tenor of press freedom had changed. Editors and journalists appeared to have taken seriously the veiled insistence of the minister of information that they be "critical in a constructive fashion." Reporting in both the *New Liberian* and the *Daily Observer* became less strident, and journalists seemed to be far more aware of the tightrope Mr. Best had referred to a year earlier. The full brunt of these official "instructions" only became apparent as the PRC entered its third and fourth year of governing.

THE EDUCATIONAL ESTABLISHMENT

Although education long had a high priority among the Americo-Liberians, this was not translated into prestige for Liberian teachers individually and corporately. While Liberian teachers did profit from the role models provided by European and American missionaries and by the members of the Peace Corps, there was an unintended depressing of both prestige and income for the teachers by continued reliance upon this external form of support. The University of Liberia and Cuttington College (later University) were similarly challenged by the expanded bursary program of the Tolbert government and by external donor agencies which tended to siphon off the best potential teachers (as well as the cream of the student body) for study abroad.

The expansion of the school system into the interior under the Tolbert administration and the insistence of overseas donors upon having primary and secondary education as well as undergraduate study provided "in-country" rather than overseas did much to improve not only standards of teaching but also the bargaining power of Liberian teachers. By the time of the coup, the National Union of Liberian Teachers was already beginning to flex its muscle with regard to low salaries, inadequate supplies, and delayed paychecks. Students as well at all levels were becoming increasingly politicized; strikes, followed by school closings, became as much a part of the school ritual as commencement exercises. The students in many respects felt that they were part of the "Doe revolution," by virtue of the impetus they provided to the drastic change which had come in the wake of the April 1979 Rice Riots. As Amos Sawyer suggested in his precoup study of student and non-student attitudes toward national development, students tended to be far more critical of the existing Whig leadership but at the same time more prone to identify in terms of the Liberian nation rather than their ethnic subgroup. They also assumed that they had a national mission and were more tolerant of others and convinced of their ability to effect meaningful change despite the entrenched position of the existing government.[8]

The one educational institution in particular that was assumed to be a factor in positive change in society was the University of Liberia. The reshaping of other institutions, the fashioning of a genuinely new national identity, and the development of innovative approaches to the crises of poverty, disease, and ignorance seemed to be appropriately the university's mandate. Yet this had not always been the case during its more than a century of existence. It was a political institution in the sense that it had long been the reserve of the privileged Americo-Liberian upper caste, and its faculty was far too heavily drawn from the ranks of Whig legislators and other politicians who regarded their university salaries as part of their unearned perks of office.

In the last decades of the First Republic, however, the university had lived down its reputation of being little better than a second-rate high school. Under Rocheforte Weeks and later Mary Grimes Sherman, it had become a very respectable institution in terms of the faculty it had attracted, the courage and articulateness of its students, the quality of its library collection, and the broadening of its offerings to include agriculture, forestry, and other development areas. Significantly, even prior to the April 12 coup, its faculty had started to win the battle of autonomy from the political power structure. Before the coup of 1980 the conservative politicization of the university was reflected in the fact that the president of the Republic served as the university visitor, and some of the oldest and most reactionary of the Old Guard Whigs constituted the Board of Trustees. It was with great difficulty that the university had gradually assumed the role of the independent conscience of Liberian society—for which, on a number of occasions, both Tubman and Tolbert had closed the university. It had, as well, developed a student newspaper which was courageous in its chronicling of the ills of Liberian society. The university had actually achieved one of its greatest victories in its struggles for political autonomy just a few days before the coup. In a serious challenge to one of the scions of the True Whig oligarchy (his father had once been chairman of the party), the president of the university had relieved Dean DeShield of the School of Agriculture of his administrative duties because of his abusive treatment of a driver. President Mary Grimes Brown Sherman had very respectable settler antecedents as a daughter of a distinguished chief justice, but she never concealed her tribal origins either. She was confronted in the incident by Speaker Richard Henries and the other trustees with the demand for Dean DeShield's reinstatement. On this issue President Sherman had the solid and outspoken support of her faculty. In a dramatic showdown involving Speaker Henries and others a few days before the coup, Tolbert surprisingly backed the administration and the faculty against the Whig Old Guard.

Like the churches, the University of Liberia from the 1980 coup until the crisis of 1984 (discussed in the next chapter) functioned without its direct linkages to the political system, since many of the former trustees were either dead or in exile. Inasmuch as the political connection was normally more a liability than an asset, the leaders of the university attempted to take advantage of this unique opportunity to shape their own environment in terms of the university's future relationship to the broader society. The attitude of many in the Doe government initially seemed favorable to the university's desire to be both relatively autonomous in terms of its own curriculum, staff, and modus vivendi and, at the same time, serve as a focal institution within the new Liberian society. Although some criticized Doe during the first few months because of his reluctance to visit the campus (which was literally only a stone's throw from the Executive Mansion), this may have been due to his sense of inadequacy, given his own lack of formal education. The more significant gesture came on the first anniversary of the 1980 coup, when he selected a Constitutional Commission which drew heavily for its membership from among the ranks of University of Liberia faculty and administrators, as well as former and present students. Thus, the University of Liberia at that point seemed destined to play a vital role in the new pluralism manifesting itself in Liberian society.

**RELIGIOUS STRUCTURES**

The Christian churches in the postcoup era were similarly undergoing adjustment to the search for a new national purpose. Although settler and tribal persons were nominally members of the same broad Christian fold, in Liberia they entered the Kingdom of Heaven in different chariots. Some of those chariots were distinctly ethnic in character, such as the Loma Church, the Bassa Community Church, and the churches which separated the more high-status Americo-Liberians from their "Congo" associates. Within the Americo-Liberian minority the religious distinctions were more finely tuned in terms of association with a particular cluster of key patrons. Many of the leading members of the cabinet, the Legislature, or the courts were also pastors of their churches or lay officials at some higher level in the church hierarchy. William Tolbert, for example, was regarded as the pastor of the Zion Baptist Church in Bentol, and for several years he had been president of the World Baptist Alliance. Vice President Benny Warner was the presiding bishop of the Methodist Church, and there were many parallel situations. With the collapse of the Whig power elite, many of the churches now were permitted to pursue more purely religious objectives without the external partisan political controls. The Methodists in particular found the political connection very much a double-edged sword, particularly after Benny Warner's clumsy radio address from Abidjan a few weeks after the coup, calling for a counterrevolution. Some Methodist missionaries in Monrovia were jeered, and it became necessary for the new government to issue the curiously worded announcement that "Methodists are also citizens of Liberia." The surviving Methodist Church hierarchy took immediate steps to divest Warner of his post as bishop and placed him in "involuntary retirement." As it developed, the liberation of the churches served to make them more vital forces in achieving new national goals.

On the other hand, the collapse of support from the political center also made the more politically active Christian churches vulnerable to challenges from Islam, from fundamental Christian sects, and from a rejuvenated set of Poro leaders. Islamic leaders, for example, became increasingly outspoken in their demands that the Christian bias of the suspended 1847 Constitution as well as the Legal Code must be altered in the new society in favor of a more eclectic religious approach. They succeeded in the first objective; the second remains to be accomplished. Certainly the prestige of Islam (the religious faith of many of the new military leaders) is attested to by the great mosque that was built in the heart of downtown Monrovia. Similarly, the fundamentalist and breakaway Christian churches also took on new strength in postcoup society, inasmuch as they too have a membership which consists largely of lower strata Americo-Liberians and recently urbanized tribal persons.

A renewed vitality, however, was also manifest among the main line Protestant churches, which had been recently liberated from their linkages with the leading politicians of the dominant Whig party. A similar assertiveness with respect to political issues, civil rights, freedom of the press, and other aspects of the norms of democracy became evident among the clergy of the Roman Catholic Church—particularly from Bishop Michael Francis, the first Liberian to hold that post. In a period when the PRC-declared moratorium on political discussion had effectively limited journalists, educators, businessmen, and others, church leaders were far less restrained in speaking out on abuses. It is difficult to reconstruct how this came about, but certainly a significant milestone in this new political independence of the churches was the speech of Bishop Alford Kulah of the United Methodist Church on the first anniversary of the 1980 coup. With Master Sergeant Doe and other members of the PRC seated on the platform behind him, Bishop Kulah, in a sermon entitled "Arms That Liberated Must Not Enslave Us," acknowledged that Liberians were very mindful of the inequities of the past under the Whig system of repression. But, he added, Liberians are

> looking ahead or in front of us. And what do we see? We see the Armed Forces of Liberia; we see men and women in arms, with weapons, marching up and down the streets of our towns and cities. We hear and see some soldiers harassing and intimidating innocent, harmless, helpless people. In front of us, we see some soldiers who have no respect for the poor, the rich, the educated, and the elderly.
>
> Master Sergeant, we, like the children of Israel, are afraid. Some of the rich who got their property through honest, hard labor are afraid that their homes will be taken from them without explanation or just compensation. The educated people are afraid that some PRC members are sacking well-educated people and replacing them with either half- or semi-educated people. To be educated in our country is now like committing a crime. It is true that the gun can win a war, but it cannot build a nation. It takes talented, dedicated and well-educated people to plan and develop a country. . . .
>
> The weapons that were meant to protect the Liberian people, the weapons that were meant to deliver the Liberian people, the weapons that were used to liberate and free the Liberian masses must never be used to enslave and destroy the Liberian people.
>
> [Let us hope] that our popular revolution headed by Master Sergeant Samuel K. Doe will never get to a place where the masses will regret that it ever took place.

The bold words of Bishop Kulah had an electrifying effect upon a populace that had grown weary of abuses by the military "in the name of freedom," and encouraged other clerics to begin speaking out. They also had their effect upon Doe, who a week later went out of his way to take a direct swipe at the clergy, urging them to "preach about Christ and lead their flock to the Throne of Grace rather than engage in politics."[9] Refusing to be silenced by the veiled threats of Doe, his justice minister, and other officials, the Christian leadership actually intensified their political assertiveness during the months preceding the 1985 elections. In addition to the collective denunciation by the Liberian Council of Churches regarding the continued use of PRC Decree 88A limiting political dissent, (see chapter 17), individual bishops and other clergymen criticized the Doe regime's handling of the 1984 military assault on the University of Liberia campus, the detention of political prisoners, delays in registering opposition parties, and other specific issues. Episcopal Archbishop George D. Brown spoke for his colleagues when he asserted in June 1985 that "politics cannot be divorced from the church." A month later, the popular pastor of the Providence Baptist Church in Monrovia, the Rev. Peter Amos George, insisted that the church would speak out against the evils of the state and society, even to the point of persecution. Bishop Ronald Diggs of the Lutheran Church during the critical period following the 1985 election rejected Doe's call for political neutrality on the part of clerics, stating that the Bible cannot be isolated from life, and that religious leaders have a mandate to speak out regarding all things that affect man. Nor was the political activism limited to the Catholic and mainline Protestant churches. The charismatic Mother Dukuly added her voice to the chorus of dissent, indicating that her "sermons come from God, and Doe will have to listen to what God is saying."[10] Wishing to demonstrate their even-handedness in this new assertion of political activism, three bishops conferred with opposition leader G. Baccus Matthews in late August 1985, urging that he and his people exercise restraint and patience in dealing with their great frustration over the banning of his political party by the Doe regime (see chapter 18).

**THE JUDICIARY AND THE LEGAL PROFESSION**

As was noted in chapter 8, the subordination of the judicial to the executive branch had been one of the dominant characteristics of the First Republic—particularly during the administrations of Tubman and Tolbert. The Supreme Court reached perhaps its nadir in the early 1970s when Chief Justice James Pierre presided over a libel case in which he rendered a decision in favor of his son-in-law, Stephen Tolbert, against pamphleteer Albert Porte. It was only during the waning days of the Tolbert era that signs of assertiveness were evident among Liberian judges, several of whom had rendered decisions which were adversely received by individual members of the "honorable" group or by the government. There was, for example, the celebrated case in which the interests of the MOJA cooperative, or Susukuu, were upheld against the combined interest of Whig politicians acting in their private and official capacities. The increased representation of educated tribal youths within the legal profession was also noticeable as the leading Monrovia law firms took on tribal "apprentices." Leading scions of the settler group were beginning to take cases which could seriously redresss the imbalance between Americo-Liberians and tribal groups within the national community.

Much of the progress in judicial independence and professionalism within the legal community, however, appeared to be undermined by some of the early actions of the PRC. Particularly threatening was the action which subordinated the civilian system of courts to the Special Military Tribunal. The latter did not limit its jurisdiction to the military, but summarily tried civilians under the Uniform Code of Military Justice. Even the pretense of due process was discarded in several celebrated cases—including the "trials" of the thirteen officials executed on the beach shortly after the April 12 coup.

Although somewhat delayed, the popular hostility to the Special Military Tribunal's taking jurisdiction over cases involving civilians and meting out sentences of death by firing squad had, by the second year after the coup, appeared to be achieving its goal of restoring credibility to the civilian judicial system. The fact that Head of State Doe had twice within 1982 been forced to reverse decisions of the Special Military Tribunal had been an embarrassment to the PRC abroad and had undermined its legitimacy at home. The first of these two incidents occurred in January with regard to the threatened execution of six student leaders, accused of treason for having attempted to organize student political parties. Doe, at the eleventh hour, was compelled to relent in the face of a massive outpouring by thousands of students, market women, and others who felt that they, too, had made the revolution of 1980 possible. The second incident occurred at the end of June, when the Special Military Tribunal—acting in what it regarded as a grant of power in PRC Decree 5—sentenced to death by firing squad two police officers and a civilian convicted in a bribery case. Since bribery is prevalent in the society, the verdict sent chills through the community. Actually, an almost Solomonic judgment by Doe may have made him a net winner in this case. The head of state decided that the execution should indeed take place but that the minister of justice would first have to find three honest policemen to serve as the firing squad. When the director of the police had to acknowledge that he could not find three such men, both he and the minister of justice were fired. Doe took this occasion to privately lecture the Special Military Tribunal about its political role. The almost immediate appointment, moreover, of the very respected Winston Tubman as minister was undoubtedly intended to restore the prestige of the civilian judicial process and to provide the Ministry of Justice with sufficient political muscle to thwart future usurpations of jurisdiction by the Special Military Tribunal. Winston Tubman is a nephew of the former president and had previously served for many years as Liberia's ambassador to the United Nations.

Although Doe persisted in his hostility to the legal profession and insisted as well that the judiciary was not necessarily an independent body, lawyers and judges displayed both commitment to principles and acts of courage during the two to three years preceding the 1985 elections. The Liberian National Bar Association, a few months before that election, pointedly reaffirmed its commitment to the independence of the judiciary after Chief Justice Gbalazeh—a Doe appointee—had taken Justice Minister Jenkins Scott to task by holding him in contempt of court and attempting to disbar him. And although it was not without ambiguity, the Supreme Court also under Gbalazeh attempted to remove itself from the legal obstacle course which the Special Elections Commission (chapter 18) had erected to prevent opposition parties from registering. Even more significant in that respect was the earlier action of Probate Judge Luvenia Ash-Thompson in telling several of Doe's partisan objectors to the registration of the Liberian Action Party in April 1985 that they were engaged in "nothing more than a legal mischief which . . . would result in upsetting and delaying the due process of law. . . ."[11]

## NEW ECONOMIC FORCES

The difficulties with respect to forming new economic groups in the postcoup era stemmed from the fact that Liberia has been a prisoner of its Whig past, in which politics took priority over independent economic activity. Opportunities for entrepreneurship were denied both tribal and settler Liberians. The major heights of economic change during the Tubman Open Door policy were commanded by Americans, Western Europeans, and other expatriates who controlled iron mining, rubber plantations, banking, shipping, and other significant activity. The Lebanese (more recently joined by Indians, Nigerians, and others) still control the significant commercial and transport enterprises relating to distribution of goods both at the coast and up-country. Mindful of the vulnerability of the Lebanese merchants during the 1979 Rice Riots, the PRC went out of its way in the postcoup era to reassure the Lebanese community that government had no intention of nationalizing their businesses. If expansion of an industry was compatible with the goals of the revolution, Doe stated, this would be allowed. While acknowledging the Lebanese role in providing needed food, clothing, and other commodities—as well as employment to Liberians—Doe and his officials nevertheless felt obliged to comment on the alleged price gouging, the rude treatment of Liberian employees and customers, and outright cheating by foreign merchants. The Lebanese were also criticized for their ability successfully to manipulate the political system in the past to circumvent immigration laws, statutes regarding ownership of reserved industries, and export controls. Lebanese as a group stood immediately in the path of quickest advancement for those Liberians who did possess a modicum of capital and commercial talents. This was true not only in retailing, but also in minor crafts such as barbering, tailoring, and the like. With their extended family connections, Lebanese were in control of the whole commercial nexus from production to wholesaling to retailing and thus were in better position to undersell a Liberian competitor or to engage in a more profitable barter arrangement.

Despite the limitations of the past, a new group of Liberian businessmen after 1980 had begun to emerge for the first time in the present century to complement the traditional Mandingo traders, who had long ago monopolized the trade in craft goods, works of art, and household wares. More recently the Mandingo shifted interest to the domination of the transport industry for transshipment of goods to the interior as well as monopolizing both the legal and the illegal trade in gold and diamonds (much of which had been mined in Sierra Leone). The new Liberian businessmen were in some cases the scions of well-connected Whig patrons who had been established in business during the Tolbert era, when appropriate governmental posts were simply not available. Other aspiring Liberian entrepreneurs were Whig politicians who had returned to Liberia after the PRC had cleared their names and promised the restoration of their confiscated properties—a gesture which applied to all but the Tolberts, Henries, and a few other families. These returnees, recognizing that politics was at least for the time being closed to them, made their former secondary concern their new primary occupation. Still a third category of businessmen appeared de novo in response to the vacuum created by the confiscation of the vast Tolbert family Mesurado Group of companies. Although the PRC had once contemplated running the Tolbert enterprises as parastatal institutions, it was clear that the government was unable to find the required managerial talents, and the properties were actually losing money for the government instead of turning a modest profit. In addition, the government lost potential tax revenues from the Mesurado companies if they remained parastatal.

The delay in making a decision about the fate of the Mesurado companies permitted a number of enterprising Liberians to take up the marketing of fish, timber, and the other products which were clearly needed to sustain the economy. Organizing themselves into the Liberian Business Caucus, these new business entrepreneurs were instrumental in the government's worldwide search for new sources of investment capital and trading opportunities. They also, however, became increasingly a thorn in Doe's side as they protested against the legal restraints upon business as well as the shakedowns by soldiers and corruption by officials which perpetuated Liberia's image as an unattractive place for foreign investment. They were also vigorous in their frequent public complaints that the PRC regime had perpetuated an old Whig habit of preferring to award government contracts to unqualified Lebanese and other foreigners rather than to competent Liberian businessmen.

What raised the ire of Doe, however, and demonstrated the loosening of the political links between the established government and the business community, were the political stances which the Liberian Business Caucus took as the electoral campaign of 1985 proceeded. Caucus leaders on a number of occasions expressed their concern about the banning of opposition party leaders, the forcing of public employees to join Doe's political party, and the arbitrary arrest and detention of civilians without due process of law.[12] Not content with public pronouncements alone, the acting chairman of the Caucus met with representatives of the four registered political parties a month before the 1985 election, to lend support to the demands of the opposition parties for a free and fair election—including the resignation of military and paramilitary personnel who were aspiring to political office, and the representation of all parties during the counting of the ballots.[13]

A similarly vital role appeared to be in store for the trade unions and the agricultural cooperatives after the 1980 coup. Both groups had been given only begrudging legal recognition during the Tubman and Tolbert eras.[14] Both, moreover, were saddled with restrictions on the way in which they functioned and the degree of autonomy they were allowed (the sons of both previous presidents, for example, were "elected" as heads of the national trade union movement). In the rural sector the MOJA-sponsored agricultural cooperatives, in particular, could be significant structures in meeting modern needs in a traditional fashion. They could attract people back to the land and resolve the food shortage in the country. Unfortunately, given the unstable nature of both the PRC leadership and the Liberian economy in the early phases of the postcoup era, the PRC leadership appeared to be reluctant to give free rein to labor and cooperative leaders who would be demanding an increasingly larger share of limited resources for their constituents.

The one lower echelon economic group, however, that had acquired political significance in the revolutionary ferment preceding the 1980 coup was the Liberian Marketing Association, which consisted primarily of women. Their turnout had swelled the ranks of the rice demonstrators in 1979, and of the crowds celebrating the 1980 overthrow of Tolbert. In 1982, when the PRC attempted to deal too harshly with student dissidents, it was the march of the market women on capitol hill that led Doe to reverse the decision of his own Special Military Tribunal. Thus, they were a force that Doe decided to reckon with, and he began a very carefully calculated strategy to win their support in his future campaign for the presidency. Curiously, Doe saw nothing inconsistent in his threatening the Liberian Business Caucus for having involved itself in political matters (suggesting that its members were violating the law by not devoting their time entirely to business matters) and his subsequent encouragement of the Liberian Marketing Association to come out in full force for a rally in behalf of candidates from his own political party. He declared 12 October as a national marketing holiday to encourage a greater turnout.

# XVI.

# Addressing the Long-Term Agenda

There appeared to be a growing consensus during the three years following the 1980 coup that the PRC, acting in consort with its civilian cabinet, could properly have pursued aspects of a Direct Rule model of military intervention in two key areas. This related to the resolution of items on the long-term national agenda which required immediate attention and could not be deferred until the restoration of civilian rule in 1986. The first issue was the matter of interethnic hostility; the second was the matter of economic development. On the first item, the PRC in its initial stages appeared to make some remarkable progress. With respect to the second, the record has been one of miserable failure.

### Redefining the National Identity

Over the long haul, one of the major tasks facing the People's Redemption Council and its coalition cabinet was the creation of a new national identity, while at the same time avoiding the interethnic bloodshed which has characterized the post-independence periods in the Sudan, Nigeria, Chad, and Uganda. The task of nation-building in the new Liberian society has been a formidable one. Not only has there been the overt as well as latent hostility between the Americo-Liberian minority and the tribal majority, but there are as well the variations in cultural and other norms that had been perpetuated within the heterogeneous tribal majority itself. Several things appear certain. First, the fashioning of new national norms has—as in most other areas of Africa—taken place within artificially created international boundaries. Second, the new national norms could not be a mere continuation of the previously imposed Americo-Liberian culture. Admittedly, that culture had been modified by settler adoption of some tribal aspects of diet, dress, speech, and art; nevertheless, the main thrust of integration during the First Republic was in the direction of acceptance of settler norms. In any event, on the social plane it had become increasingly apparent over the last two or three decades that there was a blurring of the once rigid lines separating Americo-Liberians from tribal persons. Marriage (not merely informal liaisons with "country wives") had become fairly common and socially accepted between those whose origins were primarily settler and those whose antecedents were considered tribal. The expansion of economic enterprises, the educational system, and governmental operations had—in spite of the fears of the True Whig Old Guard—brought settler and tribal descendants into more meaningful and lasting relationships. This was particularly true of the students who had gone abroad for study. They became part of the small, but growing, cadre of young professionals in the law, health services, journalism, engineering, and education who either shunned politics or opted politically with MOJA or PAL upon their return from overseas.

While far from cohesive, there emerge from within this cadre a common sense of class identity. They manifest a commitment to change and to the technology that they had been exposed to abroad and which they were convinced could make meaningful change possible in Liberia. The acceptance of the "work ethic" had rubbed off on them in Europe or America, and they were increasingly impatient with the outrageous corruption, the ostentation in life styles, and the formalism that had characterized the Old Guard in the True Whig Party during the last two or three decades of the First Republic. Although church membership remained important in terms of social linkages, this younger group was decidedly more secular in its approach toward problem solving. They worked hard; but they also wanted to enjoy life in the style to which they had become accustomed overseas—with television, sports, the conviviality of "the bar," and reading for pleasure's sake. Since education had brought about this restructuring of values and was central to the faith in technology, this new class placed a high priority on education for themselves, their children, and their country. Finally, there was a cosmopolitanism with respect to the world beyond Liberia. In the process of achieving this new class-oriented national identity, the end product was neither Americo-Liberian, nor Congo, nor tribal.

A similar class identity was developing in the urban environment among the lower echelon Americo-Liberians, the Congoes, and recent immigrants from the rural hinterland. This was occurring not only in Monrovia (which had attained a population of 166,000 at the time of the 1974 census and has been growing steadily since), but also in the other urban centers associated with the growth of the iron ore industry and plantation agriculture. By 1974 there were twenty-two urban centers having more than 6,000 inhabitants, and—in addition to Monrovia—Buchanan, Congo Town, Yekepa, Tubmanburg, Harbel, and Harper had exceeded 10,000 in population. With regard to political oppression at the hands of the dominant elite, many Americo-Liberian urban families shared the same fate of exclusion or discrimination meted out to tribal families.

However divisive the emergence of these new class identities within the ranks of the educated youth and the urban poor may have been, they did provide new crosscutting bonds which challenged the previous horizontal and vertical stratification of Liberian society along largely ethnic lines. Despite the blurring of the boundaries, however, and the emergence of new class identities within a national framework, at the end of the First Republic the distinctions between settler and tribal antecedents remained crucial to the issues of state power and the acquisition of significant wealth and educational opportunity. The rising young tribal lawyer, for example, seldom made it on his own; he succeeded by apprenticing himself to a Monrovia-based law firm. The dominant institutions in all phases of national society prior to 1980 were still settler in origin and settler-oriented and controlled. At least, that was decidedly the way things were until the coup of 12 April 1980.

April 12 did make a difference in settler/tribal relationships. Some of the settler-controlled national institutions have been irrevocably shattered, while others have perforce been substantially modified. In fashioning a new national identity, the PRC in its early beginnings seemed to engage in some selective, but nevertheless creative, social engineering in providing new symbols of unity, new heroes and devils, and in the reshaping of traditions that would have broad applicability across the settler/tribal divide. The task commenced early. The Masonic Temple, long a symbol of Whig dominance and mystery, was one of the first casualties. Similarly the statue of the "grey eminence," Speaker of the House Richard Henries, met an early demise, while curiously the statues of Tubman and even Tolbert remained as part of the historical record. The more serious task of rewriting the civics, history, and other textbooks to properly reflect the multicultural origins of Liberia was begun in earnest (and still needs to be fully addressed at this writing). It was certainly appreciated that cosmetic change was not sufficient, such as the renaming of the "Pioneer Room" at the Africa Hotel as the "Native Room." The flag, the motto ("The Love of Liberty Brought Us Here"), and even such holidays as Independence Day (July 26) and Matilda Newport Day had strong settler biases. And, while clearly beyond the scope of either domestic or international funding, the suggestion of Doe in mid-1982 that the capital of Liberia be relocated in the interior of the country constituted a symbolic gesture (paralleling a similar decision made by Julius Nyerere in Tanzania). It would have signaled a historic reversal of Monrovia's dominance of the tribal hinterland.

Several vital questions arose with respect to the forging of the new national identity. The first question related to the ability of the new political leadership to continue to present the revolution as an action against an invidious system rather than an action against an ethnic class. There were constant efforts from all quarters during the initial period of PRC rule to downplay ethnicity, particularly among the new officeholders who had experienced a dramatic status reversal. Army Chief of Staff General Henry Dubar, in March 1981, for example, criticized those in power who made pejorative reference to Americo-Liberians. Dubar stated that this is "the time the nation should be healing wounds by preaching freedom, liberty, justice, brotherly love, equal rights and the spirit of 'one for all and all for one.' " "Liberians," he argued, should "regard each other as Liberians."[1] The official pronouncements, moreover, were matched by significant statements from those who had earned their spurs in attacking the Whig regime. In a very penetrating editorial by Kenneth Best of the *Daily Observer*, the editor argued not only that there were many so-called Americo-Liberians who had endangered their lives for the common good of the nation, but that many "country people" had served the True Whig Party, changed their names, and "simply jumped on the Americo-Liberian bandwagon because it was a wagon that promised and gave economic prosperity. Those country people who refused to ride the wagon were left in the economic backwater."[2]

The co-opted tribal persons referred to by Kenneth Best included not only traditional chiefs and elders but also educated tribal youths who in recent years had apprenticed themselves to Monrovia-based lawyers or had become the managers of the expanding economic enterprises of the Tolberts and other Americo-Liberians.

There was a multipronged attack on the interethnic hostilities which had divided Liberia in the past. One effort consisted of an attempt to downplay ethnic identification. At the border crossing from Sierra Leone, for example, there was a huge sign reading: "No tribalism, no socialism." In state speeches, in homely skits acted out on radio station ELBC, and in other arenas Liberians were being admonished to refrain from inquiring into the ethnic identity of a countryman. "We are all Liberians," Chief of State Doe had insisted.

Another tactic in establishing a new national identity—which to a certain extent contradicted the preceding effort—resulted from a renewed pride among tribal persons in their traditional heritage. There were, for example, scattered legal notices indicating that "Lansana P. Joe is henceforth to be known as Lansana Ponteh Quillah." Suggestions were made in the public hearings on the proposed new constitution that internal political boundaries within the Second Republic take into account tribal identity and cohesion which had existed prior to settler rule. Emmanuel Gbalazeh, the chief of the People's Supreme Tribunal (the national supreme court), urged in 1981, moreover, that the lawyer apprentice system be reintroduced so that promising tribal youngsters could be admitted to the bar without having to be graduated from the University of Liberia Law School. It was argued by Gbalazeh that these youngsters better understood tribal law and would be more inclined to provide legal aid to poorer tribal people.

The most significant effort in dealing with interethnic conflict consisted of the attempt to amalgamate traditions and to reinterpret symbols and events in terms of a unified Liberian nationality. The "new nationalism" was to be one which neither ignored nor was unduly hostile to the settler contribution to Liberian national existence but which rather properly emphasized the values of the tribal societies that made up contemporary Liberia. Dr. Mary Antoinette Brown Sherman, president of the University of Liberia, and one whose antecedents reflect both communities, urged in a Redemption Day address in 1981 that the present period

> provides an opportunity to draw from our traditional institutions, culture and values
> to build the type of nation of which Edward Wilmot Blyden dreamed—a country with
> foundations rooted in African culture, institutions and values . . . (such values as)
> concern for human beings, solidarity of the family, group cohesiveness, cooperation,
> emphasis on responsibility and productivity.

Dr. Sherman stressed that nation-building is not the result of a single event, whether it be immigration, a declaration of independence, or a coup d'etat.

Only when people tend to use *achievement* criteria in evaluating job applicants, candidates for educational fellowships, or aspirants to political office would the full talents of the society be used in behalf of all. The continued use of *ascriptive* qualifications, such as ethnicity, sex, relative age, and other factors beyond the individual's control, would guarantee both strife and underdevelopment of Liberian society.

Closely related to this redefinition of nationalism and emphasis on achievement has been the question of the degree of latitude given to the various ethnic groups in revitalizing institutions or customs which had been subordinated or suppressed under the settler domination of national politics. The 1980 coup was being interpreted by some leaders of the Poro and Sande societies as a mandate for revitalization of secret societies among the Gola, Kpelle, or Mende. The co-opted appointed chiefs of the old system were being challenged by political leaders with more modern claims to authority and by those with more valid historic claims of a traditional nature. In more positive terms, a resurgence of ethnic pride at the local level had to be harnessed and channeled to provide the initiative to convert Tubman and Tolbert's rhetoric about the need for rural development into a political reality.

The third question related to the language of national politics, commerce, education, and cultural development. Although the Doe government in the early period had daily radio "commercials" that attempted to downplay ethnic differences, the pressure increased to expand the number of hours station ELBC broadcasted in tribal languages. Some of those pressures extended to the matter of primary instruction, the printing of government documents, and other areas. It must be recognized that the cost of multilingualism (or even the more extensive official use of Liberian English) can be enormous in a society with sixteen tribal languages and only limited resources. There can even be disputes regarding which version of Liberian English will become the "national" language. There is, first of all, the standard American English, which is the language of international diplomacy, employed largely by the newer breed of Liberians who have been educated abroad, at the University of Liberia, or at Cuttington University. Second, there is a version called "high Liberian," which is the flowery speech of the Americo-Liberian clergy, the old-line politicians, the lawyers, and others—marked by the characteristic of never employing one adjective when three or four will be much more impressive. Finally, there is the version of English that is understood by a far wider sector of Liberian society. It is a form of pidgin, which is highly functional and can justly claim to be the national language. While it may amuse foreigners and embarrass better-educated Liberians, it is, after all, the language of the masses. In this respect I am reminded of Mark Twain's response to an English critic of his American English: "Sir, there is no such thing as the '*Queen's* English.' The property has been turned over to a joint stock company, and the Americans hold most of the shares." The question in 1980 became, what use are the Liberians going to make of their property rights in the Liberian version of the English language? The fact that the draft of the new Sawyer constitution was published in both Liberian and standard American English provides a partial answer.

*Economic Development*

There was almost total agreement among both Liberian leaders and expatriates that the economic problems facing Liberia headed the priority list of major unresolved problems. There was need not only for immediate attention to some of the short-run crises but also for positive signals that the long-range problems were at least being addressed. In the absence of that the coup could very easily go through a rapid "circulation of elites," with the once enthusiastic supporters of the Doe regime switching their allegiances. Yet it was clear from the outset that the economic problems facing the PRC in 1980 were beyond quick and easy solutions. Thus, revolutionary momentum was in danger of being lost in the interim. Quite clearly the PRC needed time, first of all in dealing with the disrupted phases of the Tolbert economy. If the immediate chaos was not addressed there could be no serious discussion of new sources of foreign investment.

The greatest restraint on a drastic reformist revolution was the nature of the Liberian economy. Under Tubman's Open Door policy, the role of American, West European, Japanese, and other foreign investors and entrepreneurs increased enormously without the emergence of a Liberian cadre. The threat of confiscation or even the serious suggestion of a tilt toward the socialist camp might immediately have undermined the economic structure on which the military government survived. Even more threatening drastic solutions which might have been considered would have been the stiffened attitudes on the part of the International Monetary Fund, the World Bank, and other officials who formerly treated Liberia as a favored customer. Time has been important because Liberia is essentially a poor country. Although it has not been officially counted as a member of the "Fourth World"— that is, the poorest of the poor as defined by the World Bank in terms of survival at or below the subsistence level—in fact most Liberians are living close to the poverty line. The level of foreign concession activity has masked this fact in the past.

The immediate economic problem was how to face several somewhat conflicting constituencies simultaneously and have each of them come away contented. The urban unemployed, who were involved in the initial phase of the Year of Ferment— the Rice Riots of 1979—were already demonstrating at the Ministry of Labour, Youth, and Sports a month after the coup with demands for meaningful jobs with the Liberia-Libya Construction Company complex in Monrovia. The urban middle class and the civil servants, upon whom the PRC was depending for the remarkable continued functioning of government, would not remain supportive once it was apparent that no assault was being made upon the rising rate of inflation. Since the Tolbert regime had long deferred substantial increases in civil service salaries and perquisites, the bureaucrats were already expressing concern that the wealth previously monopolized by the Whig elite was not being more equitably distributed. They had waited far too long for the fulfillment of the promise that higher education would bring enhanced economic, social, and political standing. But how could the PRC meet the demands for new jobs, controlled inflation, and increased salaries in the urban sector while at the same time improving the lot of the farmer? The absence of subsidies for food crops, of property rights in land, and of adequate marketing arrangements not only had accelerated the withdrawal of farmers from the rural sector but had seriously aggravated the balance of payments problem.

Where were the extra resources for accomplishing this balancing act? One approach to the problem of additional revenues would be to reduce the "fat" in the national budget by recovering the national wealth that had been squandered by the globe-junketing and high living of the Americo-Liberian officials. A further suggestion was that the number of embassies in countries where Liberian interests were prestigious at best could be diminished substantially. The new Liberian press, moreover, had daily revelations of hidden True Whig governmental assets—such as the large number of "ghost" employees on government payrolls and the former payment of double salaries to legislators and other Whig officials. Finally, a vigorous attempt was being made to collect delinquent income taxes from individuals whose political status had insulated them from enforcement measures in the past.

While it is true that some additional government resources could have been recovered in this fashion, it was soon all too clear that only substantial international assistance would help save the day in the short run. The International Monetary Fund had already permitted the Doe government to utilize Liberia's special drawing rights to meet the first-month payrolls and had awarded Liberia $4 million in trust funds. The reserves at the end of May 1980, however, were dangerously low, and the IMF and other international banking agencies were becoming increasingly conservative until they ascertained the direction the new government was heading. The lack of international acceptance of the coup had decidedly complicated the economic standing of Liberia.

But what of the long-range problems? Undoubtedly the first priority was land reform, for this issue stood at the heart of the psychological and emotional as well as economic tensions between the settler and the tribal communities. The desire of settlers to acquire tribal land on a freehold basis—despite the absence of such a concept in tribal law and custom—was symptomatic of strained settler-tribal relations almost from the first day of colonization. The opening of the hinterland under Tubman's Open Door policy had not only brought in the foreign concessionaires interested in developing the iron and other resouces, but had also launched the systematic acquisition of vast holdings by the leading Americo-Liberian families. Under Tolbert this land hunger had reached monumental proportions. Whether true or not, it was popularly believed that President Tolbert and Speaker Henries owned nearly half of Bong County, and within the city of Monrovia, the Horton family owned most of the land on which the Bassa people lived.[3]

It was clear that land reform was crucial in giving the tribal cultivator either the security that the traditional tribal usufructory right of occupancy had given his fathers before him or the security that modern freehold tenure could provide. It was doubtful whether there would otherwise be any incentive to the farmer to make the investment in capital and labor needed to produce both the food crops required by the nation and the export crops needed to pay for Liberia's substantial imports. As noted previously, the alternatives to this were high prices for food, aggravated balance of payments problems, and—most important—the continued drift of rural cultivators to the foreign-owned mines and planations or, even worse, to the cities, where they ultimately swelled the ranks of the urban unemployed. Unless there were early indications from the regime that it had given the problem of land reform a high priority and had actually started work on a solution to the problem, the legitimacy of the revolution would soon be in question. Liberia did not need another donor agency "feasibility study"; what it needed was action now![4]

Indeed, the failure of the PRC government to deal quickly and definitely with the burning political issue of land reform was symptomatic of a cluster of problems. For there was not only the question of confiscation versus negotiated purchase of the vast estates of the Americo-Liberians in the hinterland, there was also the social and economic question of whether the lands should be put up for public sale, or returned to the traditional tenure system based upon usufruct, or whether there should be some combination of state and private ownership.

Beyond the social and political issues involved, the question of land ownership and management related to the problem of production. Liberia had to increase its domestic food production. At the same time, the decline in earnings from iron production during the current worldwide recession in the steel industry was matched by a decrease in rubber sales, related to the declining fortunes of the United States auto industry. Thus, the government logically should have felt compelled to take a more drastic role in encouraging a diversification of agricultural crops for export. Diversification and efficiency in land use took priority over the political and social aspects of land tenure.

In addressing the many economic problems, the PRC was restrained by the fact that the IMF and other banking interests assumed a conservative stance whenever the Liberian economists of the new regime started talking about achieving "a more equitable distribution of income and wealth." One area where this could come about quickly and with a measure of both social justice and fiscal responsibility was through tax revision. The enforcement of not only the national income tax, but even the collection of the water and other utility rates from the families of the "honorables" was nothing short of scandalous. Small wonder that, according to a 1979 survey, roughly 4 percent of the population owned or controlled 60 percent of the country's wealth. Indeed, the postcoup publication in the newspaper of names of persons who were delinquent in the payment of taxes—coupled with a threat by the minister of finance to turn those names over to the minister of justice for immediate prosecution—brought about a dramatic crush of leading Liberian families to pay taxes. On the other hand, the collection of hut taxes by the Whig regime had in the past been pursued with an unremitting passion. The inequity of the hut tax was that it often consumed roughly 50 percent of the cash assets of the tribal family. In addition to asserting the supremacy of the settler community, the hut tax also served as the "push" factor needed to get rural cultivators into the foreign-owned enclave economy or to seek wage employment on the rubber farms of the "honorables." In the absence of surveillance over the collection system, moreover, the hut tax provided individual Americo-Liberian hinterland officials with their own private reserve for exploitation, which then enabled them to have the financial resources required to advance up the political ladder in national politics. Thus the

PRC made an early decision to end this oppressive and regressive tax, as a stimulant to increased production and to the early entry of tribal cultivators into the more desirable income-tax-paying category.

The third economic reform had to do with educated manpower. In a remarkably courageous working paper prepared before the coup, Dr. Amos Sawyer of the University of Liberia noted that many deficiencies of the Liberian educational system continued to exist despite the substantial expansion in the scale of the educational enterprise during the Tolbert period.[5] Sawyer noted, for example, the 80 percent illiteracy in the country; the disproportionately low percentage (compared to a number of leading African states) of the national budget allocated to education; the geographical disparity between the facilities and teaching staff available at the coast (where the majority of Americo-Liberians lived) and those available in the tribal hinterland; the preference in funding of the private schools (where many of the leading Americo-Liberians were educated) over government schools; and the distorted direction of much of Liberia's educational system. With reference to the last point, Dr. Sawyer was criticizing the longstanding bias in both lower and higher education toward careers in the ministry, the legal profession, or politics, as opposed to the very recent orientation toward forestry, agriculture, engineering, commerce, and the other more development-oriented skills. The bias, moreover, was very much in favor of those skills needed for the foreign enclave economy rather than for the development of Liberia as a viable balanced economic system.

Indeed, the nature of that foreign enclave economy was the fourth area of economic reform which still had to be faced both by the new government as well as by outside economic and financial interests. The dialogue was already commenced in the postcoup era regarding the continuing role of the foreign entrepreneurs who controlled the plantations, mines, shops, and other aspects of Liberia's cash economy. Rash action by the Doe government, admittedly, could have undermined the confidence required by present and future foreign investors and businessmen as well as stiffening the backs of the representatives of the IMF and the World Bank upon whom the Doe government relied for solvency. Indeed, actions during the first ten days following the coup had seriously alarmed the foreign economic community. Shippers, for example, were reluctant to come into port during the first few days of the coup. Some Greek, American, and other shipowners were beginning to question the advantages of registering their vessels under Liberia's "flag of convenience." Some even threatened to switch their registration to Panama—thus depriving the new regime of a substantial source of revenue.[6] The Lebanese merchants only reluctantly reopened their shops, and it was rumored they were keeping exceedingly low inventories. The European and American managers of plantations and iron mines, moreover, were beginning to complain about the uneconomic effects of the curfew and about vigilante action by soldiers and others. Perhaps the most disturbing action of all, however, was the announcement by the newly appointed justice minister, Chea Cheapoo, in the early days of the coup that approximately twenty managers of foreign corporations were to be placed under house arrest. Although the order was swiftly countermanded by Master Sergeant Doe himself and although various steps were taken to reassure local businessmen (including in particular, the Lebanese), the signals Cheapoo's action sent to the business and financial interests were ominous.

Despite the delicacy of the foreign investment and trade situation, it was already clear to the more responsible foreign entrepreneurs even before the coup that there would have to be some "upping of the ante" if they were to continue their operations in Liberia. It could not simply be "business as usual." The Lebanese merchants, for example, who possessed the skills that many Liberians could most readily acquire, should have been funding the study of commerce and business administration in the secondary schools and the University of Liberia as well as taking on apprentices who would be prepared to engage in both wholesaling and retailing operations. The major concessionaires in the agricultural and mining sectors, moreover, were not as rigorous as they could have been in providing training programs for Liberians—particularly in the professional and highly skilled areas. Firestone, LAMCO, and others were slow to provide increased wages and social service benefits for employees and dependents.

Foreign corporations long resisted opportunties for greater processing of raw materials in Liberia itself. Certainly this action could have created greater employment opportunities, lowered the price of some consumer goods, and helped the balance of payments problem. Several Liberians openly complained about the fact that Firestone Plantations processed Liberian rubber into tires in Ghana! Finally, the foreign entrepreneurs had been slow with respect to "Liberianization" of major economic enterprises. No one was openly talking about confiscation or even "nationalization," but it was clear that the neocolonial relationship was a barrier to Liberians coming into control of their own destinies.

The last point leads into the fifth area of economic reform: the diversification of the economy. Whether Liberia could achieve a measure of industrialization was subject to question, since it possessed one of the ingredients—iron ore—but lacked the oil, coal, other sources of energy (uranium, hydroelectric power), and skilled manpower necessary to sustain major industrial growth. It could have achieved a modicum of light industrial development, however, through the *in situ* processing of raw materials. It could, moreover, give itself greater insurance against the downward trend in world prices for its two principal exports—iron and rubber—by pursuing a policy of diversification.

The final question to be addressed is one over which economists differ: namely, the significance of Liberia's continued use of the American dollar as its official currency. Some economic analysts would hold that this was a major factor in the initial success of the Open Door policy under Tubman and Tolbert, for it attracted foreign investors to a hard currency area. At the other extreme, some economists view this as a mark of total economic subservience of Liberia to the United States and lament the fact that it limited the ability of Liberian leaders to plan, to assess properly their actual balance of payments situation, and to retain capital within the country for further development purposes.[7] Still a third point of view is that the issue of currency is basically irrelevant and that there are far more serious problems relating to successful development, such as diversification of investment, retention of profits, and other factors.[8] The use of the American dollar has taken on added significance due to the Doe government's minting of five-dollar coins—derisively referred to as "little soldiers" or "Doe dollars." Since they are not acceptable on international markets and are not in fact U.S. dollars, they have literally driven the American five-, ten-, and twenty-dollar notes out of circulation. The American notes are either being taken out of the country or are stored away in mattresses or rafters. This has had a tremendous negative impact upon the commercial sector.

On a more positive note, one of the highest priorities for international assistance would be the completion of a thorough geological survey to assess Liberia's mineral potential. Without disparaging what had been done before 1980 by well-trained Liberian geologists, much still remains to be done, using the latest sophisticated technology. Moreover, instead of continuing the pursuit of rubber, rubber, and more rubber, there is no reason why Liberia cannot emulate its next-door neighbor, the Ivory Coast. The latter has developed markets for every conceivable temperate and tropical zone agricultural crop and is doing most of the processing in that country. Admittedly, this would continue the orientation of Liberia to external global markets, but it could be an effective hedge against world price fluctuation for any one commodity and would provide expanded employment opportunities for Liberians.

In all the discussion regarding economic reform following the 1980 coup, one thing remained unmistakably clear: Liberia's innovative options were severely restricted. This was reflected in some of the immediate postcoup actions, such as the public reassurance to overseas investors, to owners of ships registered under the Liberian flag (which provide a substantial portion of the Liberian government's revenues), to local bankers, and in particular to Lebanese merchants. It was also reflected in some longer-term policy commitments, such as the stated intention to continue the use of the American dollar as the official currency; the public pronouncements regarding the regime's embracing free enterprise; the promise not to make "structural changes . . . in the near or medium term"; the honoring of all foreign debts; the lifting of the postcoup currency regulations which limited repatriation of earnings; and the commitment to continuing the Open Door policy. If the regime had hoped to keep the allegiance of its various urban and rural constituencies, it had to acknowledge that *bold* assaults on poverty, redistribution of wealth, and other drastic restructuring would have to be deferred. The economic realities in 1980 were dominated by the fact that the preponderance of Liberia's trade and investment lies with the United States, Western Europe, and Japan. Any ideological "tilt" to the socialist camp or—even worse—to the rejectionist states, such as Libya, would have created an almost immediate flight of capital and employment opportunities.

Also, a positive note, it was apparent that the collapse of society predicted by those who witnessed the initial interethnic violence did not occur. The economy and the government continued to function, if somewhat precariously. Ironically, the people who were taking charge in Liberia were the tribal people and the lower income Americo-Liberians who were educated under the expanded program of education of the Tubman and Tolbert periods. The absentee landlords, the jet-setting international diplomats, and the central participants in the pageantry of Whig aristocracy were either dead or in exile. In retrospect, they seemed to be almost superfluous to the real revolution that had been taking place all along under the very noses of the settler elite.

# XVII.

# The PRC and the Assault on Democracy

The process of reestablishing civilian rule, though not without hitches and halts, was creatively conceived. The third week of July 1984 was to have ushered in a critical stage in its fruition. The week was to begin with the announcement on July 20 of the affirmative results of the July 3 referendum on the new draft constitution. The week was to culminate on July 26, the 137th anniversary of Liberia's declaration of independence from the sponsoring American Colonization Society, with the long awaited lifting of the ban on political activity. These were developments which led the *Times*, the *Guardian*, and the *Telegraph* in Great Britain and such papers as the *Washington Post* in America to hail Liberia's "first bold step towards civilian rule" and progress toward constitutional democracy. The perception abroad was that Doe was living up to his and the PRC's promise to relinquish the reins of political power and return to the barracks.

Unfortunately, even as the cheers were still echoing regarding the promulgation of the Constitution of the Second Republic and the lifting of the ban on political discussion, it was becoming all too apparent that Liberia's fledgling experiment with constitutional democracy was in grave danger of becoming a victim of infanticide. It was threatened with strangulation almost at the very moment of leaving the nest by the one man who had become popularly identified with its conception: Samuel Kanyon Doe. A well-orchestrated charade had been slowly developing. The events of the week of 20–26 July made it apparent that during the preceding year there were actually two contradictory dramas unfolding simultaneously, a play within a play, in the tradition of a Shakespearian tragedy. The broader play was the series of events described in the preceding two chapters which had enhanced the hopes for democracy. The play within the play was a series of parallel steps calculated to undo most of the good work of the preceding three and one-half years. This was Samuel Kanyon Doe's "second coup," striking at the very concept of constitutional democracy. It was not that signs of trouble regarding the democratic experiment had emerged overnight. Indeed, they had started to emerge almost a year previously in the conflicts over the Constitutional Commission and the Advisory Assembly. But until the last week in July 1984 there was still a glimmer of hope that the military would live up to its initial promise of new efforts to establish a Liberian democracy.

Although the nature of Doe's second coup will be dealt with in detail, an indictment of Doe, based upon words and actions during that critical week in July 1984, would consist of the following elements. Samuel Doe (1) engaged in the deception of asserting that civilian rule had already arrived, whereas the military was still firmly in charge; (2) revealed the outline of a personalized political movement that he had consciously constructed while all other participants had been meticulously restrained from engaging in political activity; (3) usurped the title of "President" (albeit as president of the Interim National Assembly); (4) declared his candidacy for the presidency while still in uniform; (5) revealed that he intended to monopolize patronage and other fruits of incumbency while forcing other aspiring politicians to resign from office; (6) intensified a systematic effort to harass, immobilize, and even arrest all potential political rivals; and (7) further entrenched the military in positions of authority while pretending to implement the restoration of civilian rule.

### USURPING THE PRESIDENTIAL TITLE

The one glimmer of hope that Doe would lead the troops back to the barracks had been his longstanding refusal to take the title of "President," despite the many African precedents. (One of Doe's 1985 state visitors, Colonel Lansana Conte of Guinea, for example, had immediately proclaimed himself president in the coup that followed within a week of Sékou Touré's death.)

During the early weeks and months following the 12 April 1980 coup, the designations "Head of State" or "Chairman of the PRC" were applied to Doe, but he preferred the simple title of Master Sergeant. The latter not only had a sentimental ring to it but it symbolized as well that the origins of the coup, as well as the beneficiaries of the revolutionary change, were to be those at the lower echelons of society. The usage persisted until it became more and more awkward within the PRC and the military generally to have a master sergeant outrank his former enlisted colleagues who had overnight become majors, colonels, and even generals. At that point—early in the second year in office—Doe "retired the rank" of master sergeant for the duration of the revolution and increasingly assumed the title of Commander-in-Chief while continuing to be referred to as Head of State and Chairman of the PRC. Significantly, about that same time, he began to appear less and less in public in his battle fatigues with the hand grenades at his belt. (It was this attire that so alarmed Léopold Senghor and some of the elder African statesmen when Doe attempted to take his rightful place as the Liberian representative at a meeting of the Economic Community of West African States a few months after the coup.) Increasingly, Doe began wearing the brightly colored, diaphanous flowing gowns of a traditional chief or the informal "swearing-in" suit that Tolbert had popularized in breaking with the more formal top hat and tails of Tubman and his other Whig predecessors in the presidency.

By the third year, Doe no longer complained that he longed to go back to his rural village and be a farmer, or that he would be pleased to serve out his days as a clerk to his clan chief. Rather, he answered queries about his future by declaring he would be pleased to serve his country in whatever way his successors would find most useful. Journalists who had covered Doe from the early days of the coup, when he had appeared to be shy and overwhelmed by the glare of publicity, detected a greater ease in dealing with the public and an improvement in his ability to deliver a speech. In more ways than one, he "grew with the job." Hence, although Doe celebrated his twenty-eighth birthday within weeks of the 1980 coup, by an accelerated process he celebrated his thirty-third birthday three years later! He claimed at that time that the press had mistakenly reported his age as twenty-seven at the time of the coup! Coincidentally, the revised version of his age made him eligible for the office of president under the revised timetable of the draft constitution, which would be in effect during the October 1985 elections.

Further progress in his attempt to project himself as a civilian head of state rather than a military leader came in his acceptance of an honorary degree from the National University of Korea in Seoul. From that point onward the press releases from the Ministry of Information and the government-controlled newspaper have used the preferred title "Dr. Doe." It seems not to embarrass him that it is not a real doctorate, for that too has a long history in Liberia, in Africa, and in the Third World generally. What did seem to irritate Doe and his PRC colleagues was that the University of Liberia had not conferred its traditional honorary doctorate upon him, as it had upon Tubman and Tolbert. The university, fortunately, had a good excuse. As University President Mary Sherman pointed out, the Board of Trustees had been suspended at the time of the coup, since many of its members had died or were in self-imposed exile; therefore it would have been illegal for the university authorities to confer such a degree on their own. After receiving the Korean degree, "Dr. Doe" regularly began to appear in a smartly tailored three-piece business suit and assumed the general demeanor of any other modern African head of state. The frail master sergeant became a rather paunchy bureaucrat.

Still, for more than four years he studiously avoided usurping the title of President, even though foreign journalists erroneously referred to him in that fashion. The illusion, however, was rudely shattered on the day after he announced the results of the referendum: Doe jumped the gun and gave himself the advantage of presidential incumbency by appearing to be already the elected president of a civilian government. His maneuver had three stages. First, the military PRC was dissolved. A few days later, however, Doe began to issue decrees ex post facto in the name of the defunct PRC, dealing with issues he had forgotten to cover prior to the PRC's dissolution. Second, although the members of the PRC—including Doe himself—had never resigned from the military, they were nevertheless absorbed into what was advertised as a civilian Interim National Assembly (INA), which included chiefs, businessmen, former ambassadors, and other civilians representing the various political subdivisions of the country. This body was to serve as a quasi-legislative assembly until the new Senate and House were elected in October 1985 and was to advise Doe on the transition. Significantly, there was no mention of a transitional Interim National Assembly in the new constitution, nor had the idea been discussed either by the Sawyer Con-Com or the Kesselly Consultative Assembly. It was purely an invention of Doe and the PRC. Nor was there a need for it.

The third element in the sleight of hand was the manner in which Doe managed to usurp of the title of President. Technically, Doe had named himself president of the Interim National Assembly, but the qualifying clause was soon lost as the government press proclaimed in banner headlines ''Doe to be Inducted as Prexy Today.'' Indeed, the sign over the entrance of the new market he was to dedicate following his induction to the new office proclaimed simply: ''Welcome President and Mrs. Doe.'' Furthermore, one of his assistants, Dr. Bernard Blamo, was designated as ''Minister of State for *Presidential* Affairs.'' When queried at a press conference regarding the choice of that title rather than ''chairman'' of the Interim Assembly, Doe incomprehensibly responded that ''it would not have been appropriate for the Assembly to be headed by a chairman, as is the PRC.'' He kept insisting, moreover, that he was the *elected* or the *selected* president of the Assembly. It is difficult to understand how this was possible. It was Doe (with or without his PRC advisors) who chose the members of the Assembly, and not the reverse. Indeed, the Assembly had never convened to elect its own officers, much less to name its president. The list of officers, including the president, was presented to them. The members of the Interim Assembly were actually sworn in *after* Doe and the other officers had taken their oath. He nevertheless has persisted in the charade of having been elected.

On the day following the lifting of the ban on politics, moreover, Doe at long last made explicit what many had taken to be implicit: he announced that he was a candidate for the presidency in the October 1985 elections. Doe thus repudiated the statement he had made only the previous day, that he was ''not interested in politics; the development of my country is my only concern.'' Assuming that there would be anyone left to provide a reasonable challenge, Doe was at that point able to enjoy all the advantages of patronage, control over the use of force, access to the media, and the other governmental props that could be marshaled in behalf of an incumbent officeholder. Evidencing his disdain for the very constitution-making process and the notion of the civilian supremacy model which he had set in motion, he did not bother to resign his post in the military before declaring his candidacy. He made his announcement from Camp Schieffelin in the presence of high-ranking officers.

On the face of it there was no democratic principle violated if a military officer presented himself as a candidate for office in an openly contested election. Nor should the citizens of a democratic state be denied the political services of one who had performed some outstanding feat in another capacity. There are both good and bad precedents of a military leader assuming the mantle of chief executive after guiding his country in the shaping of a new civilian constitution. George Washington, Atatürk, and Charles de Gaulle come readily to mind. Undoubtedly, many Liberians still viewed Doe's actions in ending the Whig oligarchy as well as his governmental experience of the past four years as credentials enough for high office. What many other Liberians objected to was that the action of Doe, in usurping the powers of an incumbent "president," reduced the possibility of a free choice in selecting a future chief executive. And that was what the new constitution was supposed to be all about.

## MONOPOLIZING POLITICAL DEBATE AND PARTICIPATION

The suspicion that the military itself had taken advantage of the four-year ban on political activity and discussion to consolidate its own political position and to immobilize or emasculate any potential opposition became explicit on 26 July 1984 with the formal lifting of the ban on political activity and discussion. The military seemed to be specifically concerned about the emergence of any contrary ideology.

Initially, the ban on politics could have been justified in terms of the understandable fear on the part of the PRC that remnants of the True Whig Party within Liberia would secure outside support in conducting a countercoup. It could also be rationalized in terms of not permitting any one organized group—whether MOJA, the PPP, or others—to take advantage of the period of political uncertainty and to prejudge the nature of the new constitution and political system. The early neutrality of the PRC seemed to be manifest by its inclusion of leaders of MOJA, the PPP, and those associated with the Tubman (but not the Tolbert) regime in a kind of coalition nonpartisan cabinet with the military. Until such time as the popular support of any or all of these groups could be determined in honestly conducted elections, the best Liberia could hope for was that the talents and experience of these prominent civilian leaders would be tapped for the transitional period. Indeed, they provided the PRC government with the legitimacy it otherwise lacked. The ban on political activity thus prevented the premature setting of the national agenda in favor of one ideological program over another.

Doe and the PRC indeed took an unusual stance to guarantee that the civilian members of the government would not take advantage of political office either in building personal constituencies or in using their positions to engage in public debate over new ideological directions in foreign policy or in the reshaping of Liberia's economic, social, and political institutions. On 26 July 1981, Doe introduced the novel device of inducting all civilian cabinet and subcabinet officers into the army, giving ministers the rank of major and deputy ministers the rank of captain. At least one leading cabinet member, Togba-Nah Tipoteh, who had been a founder of MOJA and was serving as minister of planning and economic affairs, took this as an effort to muzzle independent thought by subjecting civilians to military discipline. Indeed, when he refused to return to Liberia following a visit to the Ivory Coast (fearing political harassment by Doe), in keeping with military rather than civilian norms he was declared AWOL.

## CONTROL OVER IDEOLOGY

While Doe and his colleagues were excoriating members of the PRC as well as civilians such as Foreign Minister G. Baccus Matthews for suggesting new political directions (''alien ideologies''), it was apparent that Doe and the PRC collectively were going far beyond the maintenance of the ideological status quo in both foreign and domestic matters. Rather than merely rejecting the call for ''positive non-alignment'' of Liberia in African and world affairs, Liberia actually strengthened its links with the United States—a trend that was being steadily reversed during the latter days of the Tubman era and throughout the Tolbert administration. Given the absence of government assistance to the Doe regime from other Western powers, this closer link with the United States may have been for the PRC a matter of economic and finanical survival. Indeed, the United States had to be vigorously urged to step into the void at the time of the 1980 coup. Nevertheless, the PRC took other stances, such as reducing the size of the Soviet embassy staff in 1981, closing the Libyan People's Bureau, and rejecting Polisario's bid for recognition as the sole representative of the people in Western Sahara, which not only reversed shifts in foreign policy dating back to the Tolbert period but fell squarely into line with the official attitudes and politics of the Reagan administration. The most significant action in this respect was the 1983 resumption of diplomatic ties with Israel, which many external critics felt also coincided with American interests. Internally as well, the frequent statements of Doe and other PRC leaders regarding the commitment of Liberia to free enterprise, the rights of private property, and other capitalist norms suggested more than a ''go slow'' on consideration of alternative strategies of development.

Suspicions that the military intended to control ideological debate even after the new constitution came into effect were confirmed by the issuance of Decree 75A on 19 April 1984—a few months before the ban on political organizations was to be lifted. This decree empowered the Special Elections Commission to ''deny the registration of political parties or independent candidates whose members or officers at any time whatsoever have engaged in activities or have otherwise expressed converse and/or adverse ideological aims or objectives that are repugnant to our intrinsic values as a people and our republican form of government.'' The banning could be appealed to the People's Supreme Court, but its scope was so sweeping that it gave vast discretionary power to a small number of people to determine what was and was not proper ideology for Liberia. Although this decree was formally rescinded in July when the ban on politics was lifted, its portent was quite clear and the concept reemerged in 1985 during the process of registering parties for the October elections.

## CONTROL OVER POLITICAL RECRUITMENT

Beyond the PRC's preemption of the political stage in terms of ideology, a series of moves from 1982 onward resulted in the removal from office of most of the effective civilian participants in the government of the Second Republic who might have been viewed as opponents of Doe. Some of this came about from the shuffling of cabinet positions, which led some individuals to resign voluntarily from their new, but less attractive, offices. There were other instances of outright dismissals (in some cases with just cause, such as the removal of the sometimes erratic Minister of Justice Chea Cheapoo). There were also resignations of some civilians based upon policy disagreements, such as the departure of former Foreign Minister Henry Fahnbulleh, Jr., over the issue of diplomatic recognition of Israel. Finally—although it had serious implications beyond the actual number of individuals involved—there was the thirty-day ultimatum issued in April 1983 in which Doe demanded that any official who had intentions of running for office under the new constitution had to resign immediately from his current job with government.

Although the 1983 ultimatum was subsequently reversed, it did lead to the resignation of three very significant civilians: G. Baccus Matthews, former foreign minister who had subsequently come back into government as director-general of the cabinet; Oscar Quiah, managing director of the National Housing Authority; and Mr. Marcus Dahn, director for technical services in the Housing Authority. But the long-term implications were not lost upon the many more who did not resign but who nevertheless had hoped they would be eligible for political office under the new constitution. The decree served to more narrowly restrict public officials in the discussion of issues which might be considered "political," and the PRC itself monopolized the definition of what was *political*. Since government was the single most important employer in the country, the financial risks of running afoul of the PRC's ban were high indeed.

The preceding should not be interpreted to mean the PRC was unrelenting in its efforts to monopolize the political arena or that, in the early stages, there was a detectable and systematic plot to perpetuate Doe and his colleagues in political office. On the contrary, there were countervailing signals that the PRC was still sincerely committed to expanding the future base of political dialogue in Liberia and engaging in a policy of reconciliation. Evidence in this regard includes the offer to return the confiscated properties of most True Whig officials who had fled the country at the time of the coup. The only exceptions remained the properties of William Tolbert and Clarence Simpson, as well as the assets of the True Whig Party. Even former Vice President Benny Warner was extended executive clemency on 26 July 1984. In addition, the action of Doe in his Christmas message of 1981 in releasing the last of the four hundred political prisoners who had been held in Belle Yellah and other detention centers since the coup seemed also to be a gesture in the direction of letting old political scores be bygones. At that moment, Doe could rightfully claim that Liberia was one of the few African states without political prisoners. And one could point to the dialogue which was in fact taking place in public forums regarding the faults and virtues of the 1847 Constitution and the new constitutional proposals as evidence that the ban on political discussion was not total.

The evidence on the other side of the argument was nevertheless gradually mounting. Some of the old bag of tricks employed by the discredited True Whig Party were being employed anew by the Doe regime in dealing with political dissidents. "What the right hand giveth, the left hand taketh away" is an old Liberian political maxim. Private citizens or officials whose undivided loyalty to the regime was suddenly suspect found themselves charged with some gross criminal offense. One celebrated case was that of Hilary Dennis, former president of the Housing Bank, who was charged with having misapplied $1.9 million of bank funds after having previously defended himself successfully against a charge of having misused $2.9 million in bank funds. When he won the second case, there was no guarantee that his time and money would not be further exhausted in an appeal by the government to a higher court.

In some cases an official who had served the regime well was removed from office because he was assumed to be the "client" of a "patron" who had lost favor. During the disturbance of November 1983, two ambassadors-designate who were residents of Nimba County had their commissions withdrawn when their assumed patron, General Thomas Quiwonkpa, also from Nimba, fell out of favor with Doe and was forced to flee the country. Another case was Toye Bernard, a private legal practitioner from a prominent Americo-Liberian family, who made some offhand remarks in the spring of 1984 questioning the legal basis for the PRC's original confiscation of the properties of former Tolbert officials. Counsellor Bernard quickly found himself under arrest because his remarks had offended Doe and his colleagues.

The capricious enforcement of the law, moreover, such as the 1984 drive to collect $26 million in taxes and customs duties owed the government, was also used in a flexible fashion in dealing with political dissidents. One victim was Oscar Quiah, a founder of the PPP who had served the PRC as minister for internal affairs and later as managing director of the National Housing Authority until he resigned in the April 1983 ultimatum on political intentions. Quiah found his efforts in 1984 to establish a private business frustrated by the government's arbitrary action in insisting upon the payment of $127,771 in customs duties. In Quiah's case the payments were supposedly due on imported chickens and meat which had been allowed to spoil at the docks and which Quiah insisted were to be replaced by fresh produce from the supplier. The Doe government used the Quiah incident not only to put him in jail but to make a general case against aspiring civilian politicians. It is time, one of Doe's spokesmen said, for "those who want to be leaders of this country . . . to respect the law, be patriotic and show good examples by paying their taxes." The official went on to condemn the Liberian political culture which "permits many who want to continue receiving without giving." Despite special pleading, Quiah—unlike Toye Bernard—was not freed from jail in Doe's clemency action on Independence Day, 26 July 1984. He later saw the light, threw in his lot with Doe, and got himself elected secretary general of Doe's party. He is one of the consummate survivors.

**RESTRICTIONS ON FREEDOM OF THE PRESS**

Although foreign journalists made much of the conciliatory gesture that Doe extended in his 26 July 1984 speech regarding the Liberian press, the fact is that freedom of expression had a rocky history under the PRC. The Doe regime proved to be particularly thin-skinned with regard to any criticism of its governance. This sensitivity went beyond any desire merely to reduce political tensions during the period of transition. Press criticism of the military and editorial commentary on alternative paths for economic and political development were often regarded by the government as acts of disloyalty to the society itself. True, the PRC in that respect differed little from its Whig predecessors, who not only made life difficult for editors and journalists of independent newspapers but would have preferred to have government monopolize communications. During the Tubman and Tolbert eras, dissemination of news was dominated by government-owned publications such as the *Liberian Age* (1946–64) and the *Liberian Star* (1964–80) or by the *Daily Listener* (1957–77), the private plaything of an entrenched Whig politician, C. C. Dennis, Sr. Radio broadcasts, other than from the conservative Protestant Christian station, ELWA, and from a Roman Catholic–owned radio, were the monopoly of the government station, ELBC.

Unfortunately, for the history of freedom of the press under the PRC, the government scoldings, threats, and occasional fines which marked the early relationship between the PRC and the working press later turned to more serious forms of intimidation and harassment. These practices, which continued throughout the period before the 1986 inauguration included journalists being detained and held incommunicado without formal charges having been filed; trials of civilian journalists by a military court; and the banning of specific issues of the *Daily Observer* or *Footprints Today* which some government official had regarded as offensive.

The most frequent target of official PRC scrutiny was the *Daily Observer*. The efforts of Kenneth Best and his staff to meet government standards of "responsibility" never quite satisfied the Doe regime. After having had *Observer* reporters arrested for "offensive" articles and after having forced the paper to suspend publication on three occasions, the PRC intended its January 1984 banning of the *Daily Observer* to be permanent. The offense committed by the newspaper was that of publishing a front-page article on the demonstration by teachers who were owed several months' pay. (This situation with the teachers has continued to occur with distressing regularity.) The publication of the story, however, coincided with the state visit of Israel's president, Chaim Herzog. Since many associated with the *Daily Observer* had been critical of the renewed relationship with Israel, the prominent attention this newspaper gave the teachers' situation, while downplaying the Israeli linkage, was viewed by Doe as a calculated effort to embarrass his government. Instead of merely suspending operation of the paper, Doe proceeded to revoke its charter of incorporation. In challenging the PRC on that issue, the *Observer* won its case in a lower court, which once again demonstrated the independence of the judiciary. Doe's minister of justice, however, demanded that the decision be appealed to the People's Supreme Court. After a series of delays in hearing the case, the Doe government simply moved to have the decision on the case delayed to October 1984—three months after the ban on political discussion was to have been lifted.

The 26 July 1984 statement of Doe regarding his government's intention of dropping the appeals case against the *Daily Observer* was supposed to be a conciliatory gesture. Instead of immediately resuming publication, however, Kenneth Best and his colleagues elected to go slowly. They would not start printing the paper until they had secured guarantees that the suspension would not be repeated and that the newspaper would be absolved of any suggestion of wrongdoing in the events leading up to the court case. Best's caution was well considered, for Doe's lifting of the suspension was coupled with a warning that "government will not tolerate any attempts directed at character assassination, violence or the spreading of any lies by any individual or party."[1] Doe lamented that "many unfair articles have been written and published about the Liberian government by some journalists reflecting their own selfish motives." Rather than a freewheeling assessment of politics as it had developed during the period since the coup, Doe wanted to focus attention on the "discussion of the issues, defining the national role and direction, and the overall well-being of the Liberian people." The head of state ended with a veiled threat that the behavior of the people now "will determine whether the Second Republic will prosper or perish." His remarks were equally directed against the international press, which had, he insisted, "a moral obligation to promote international understanding and goodwill among the people of our world community." Thus Doe hoped that foreigners would cover Liberia "objectively"—that is, in a manner sympathetic to Doe.

The publication of the *Observer* was again halted in January 1985, for the fifth time since the 1980 coup, over the very trivial issue of the editor's giving greater front-page play to an article in which a labor leader asked for a repeal of the decree banning strikes than to a speech which Doe had given regarding local street vendors. The government insisted that the *Observer* was closed "indefinitely." Kenneth Best and his uncle Albert Porte decided to take legal action against the government for "wrongful closure." The justice minister's retort was that the *Observer* is opposed to the government, does not promote tranquillity, and does not "operate in the best interest of the society in which we live."[2] Thus the most eloquent voice of dissent was stilled during the remaining nine months of the electoral campaign. When Best boldly undertook to resume publication following Doe's inauguration in January 1986 (on the assumption that the new constitution and its guarantee of press freedom was now in effect), the *Observer* pressroom was mysteriously torched within hours of its reopening.

Even before the *Daily Observer* had resumed publication on 6 August 1984, the only other independent press of consequence at that time, *Footprints Today*, was experiencing similar harassment. *Footprints* had been launched as an independent triweekly paper and weekend magazine to fill the void left by the earlier suspension of the *Observer*. Although its editor insisted it would "not kowtow to the whims and caprice of anyone" in its pursuit of freedom of the press, it wanted to "avoid libellous and yellow journalism" (18 May 1984). Until the new constitution had been promulgated in July 1984, *Footprints Today* carefully avoided offending the government and was a courageous but nonetheless tepid substitute for the *Observer*.

On the day after Doe had himself named president of the Interim National Assembly, however, there was a very pointed editorial in *Footprints* regarding the role of the military in politics which began with the statement that, "in some countries, the career soldiers seized power perpetually and eventually formed political parties or movements to give their administrations some kind of constitutional image . . . " and concluded with the argument that "obviously the ideal situation should be that out-going military governments should be completely withdrawn from the politicking that prevails in their countries during the process of returning to constitutional rule."

Doe was reported to have been furious. The August 2 issue of *Footprints* appeared to Doe to be an oblique attack on his candidacy. First, the paper gave equal coverage to Doe's announcement of candidacy and to the announcement by Gabriel Kpolleh of his formation of the Liberian Unification Party. Kpolleh was once regarded as a quixotic schoolteacher whose candidacy no one took seriously. Indeed, some suspected at the time that his party would be permitted to run as a "shill" party, which would give the appearance but not the substance of a multiparty campaign. In retrospect this was unfair to Kpolleh.

Secondly, the editorial in *Footprints Today* admonished the country not to make the mistake of the past by creating a single-party system, which would permit dictatorship and the "subterfuge by one man or one political party to manipulate the Liberian people." The paper promised to be evenhanded in treating each party seriously. Finally, in the same issue a front-page banner headline story dealt with possible corruption in the Public Works Ministry's dealings with the Liberian Steel Products Corporation. Even before this issue hit the streets, however, president and publisher Momolu V. Sackor Sirleaf was detained, along with his sports editor, without formal charges being made or even reasons being given other than that the two were "helping with some ongoing investigations." The detention without formal charges persisted for fifty-five days despite a vigorous protest by some of Liberia's leading lawyers and businessmen.

Unfortunately the ordeal of the two *Footprints* journalists did not end with their release from jail. They were again arrested, in July 1985, when they had the temerity to bring charges for false imprisonment against the National Security Agency and Minister of State for Presidential Affairs Dr. J. Bernard Blamo. Blamo had formerly been president of the University of Liberia, and his faithfulness to Doe was rewarded by his being named minister for foreign affairs in January 1986. The two *Footprints Today* journalists were charged with "breach of security and criminal malevolence" for their action and were tried not by a civilian court but by the Special Military Tribunal. After spending over two months in the stockade, they were released at the end of September 1985 as part of a general amnesty in advance of the October elections. The harassment of the *Footprints Today* staff continued through the campaign, however, with members of the NDPL Special Task Force (see chapter 18) invading the premises and threatening to close down the paper after the election. To their credit, the editors continued to publish news on opposition party activities, thereby offsetting the virtual blackout of such coverage by the government-owned *New Liberian*.

It was apparent that Doe's sensitivity to press criticism extended beyond the Republic's boundaries. Rufus Darpoh, who had once been associated with the government's *New Liberian* and later with the *Observer*, was arrested in mid-June 1984 for having written articles critical of the Doe regime which appeared in the foreign press. It was only much later that the government acknowledged Darpoh's detention but refused to comment on reports that he had been assigned to hard labor at the dreaded Belle Yallah maximum security prison in the interior. This, however, had indeed been his fate, and pressure from the worldwide press community became a factor in his ultimate release six months later. Mr. Darpoh's saga did not end there. Upon returning to Monrovia he again attempted to capitalize upon his twenty-five years of experience as a journalist and helped found a new private newspaper, *Sun Times*, which along with *Footprints Today* attempted to fill the gap left by the *Observer*. By August 1985, Mr. Darpoh was once more in difficulty with the Doe regime. The reason was not—as the government spokesman insisted—because Darpoh had "sensationalized the news and inflamed the minds of the public" but rather because the *Sun Times* reported the news with far too great a concern for accuracy. The offending headline and article on 14 August quoted Doe's speech the preceding day in Nimba County in which he threatened to use military force against the "few Congo people who are against his government." The government did not deny the truth of the reporting—just the fact of reporting. After several days of interrogation of Darpoh, the paper was banned by the Interim National Assembly for a month and a half—being permitted to resume publication only two weeks before the election.

The ultrasensitive reaction of the Doe regime to unfavorable reporting pervaded various branches of government. The Special Military Tribunal in August 1985, for example, barred all journalists—independent as well as government employed— from covering the trial of Ellen Johnson-Sirleaf (see chapter 18), because of their "unprofessional, unpatriotic, and inaccurate" reporting on issues vital to the interests of Liberia. The wrath of Doe and effective manipulation of the news also extended to other news media as well. Government-owned ELTV, for example, had almost no coverage of candidates other than those associated with Doe's National Democratic Party of Liberia (NDPL). Following the coverage of electoral fraud during the October 15 balloting, the government brought pressure on ELWA, the Protestant-owned radio station, to remove its chief news editor, Joe Mulbah, who most foreign observers felt had been doing a balanced job of reporting.

Among the unforeseen developments in Doe's repression of the press, however, were the growing professionalism of the many young aspiring Liberian journalists and the support that detained journalists received from a variety of quarters. The international press community and Amnesty International seemed to display a far greater interest in abuses of the press under Doe than they had under the preceding Whig regimes. Internally as well, the Press Union of Liberia had become far better organized and courageous in challenging the government on its frequent violations of freedom of the press. They were joined in their efforts by church leaders and by such groups as the Liberian Federation of Labor Unions.

## CONFLICT WITH STUDENTS AND EDUCATORS

The partial nature of the lifting of the ban on 26 July 1984 was further evidenced by the general warning given by Doe that he expected "absolute discipline and responsible behavior on the part of every citizen." He singled out students and educators for specific admonition, for they had been most restless under the ban. The latter rightfully felt their actions and words had been crucial to the undermining of the True Whig system before April 1980 and that their quick acceptance of the coup gave the PRC the early legitimacy which made four years of military government possible. Faculty and administrators at the University of Liberia, moreover, were the largest single bloc in the Sawyer Constitutional Commission, and they insisted they had a vital stake in seeing the orderly return to civilian rule. Historically, the campuses of the University of Liberia and Cuttington University College had been regarded as the natural breeding grounds for future governmental leadership, and hence the students and faculty felt they had been unduly restrained by the four-year ban on politics. The narrow interpretation of "political" by the PRC, moreover, meant that any form of criticism of the Doe regime by the students was an occasion for quick retaliation. Various campuses had been closed several times since 1980 and student leaders had been detained and even threatened with death by firing squad.

Aside from political activities, educators at all levels had other reasons for becoming severely disaffected after the coup. While teachers and school administrators were able to observe the governmental outlays for new army barracks and equipment, new highways into the interior, and a new marketplace in Monrovia, as well as the continued expenditure on international representation, the national expenditures on education declined both relatively and absolutely after 1980. Far from getting the doubling of the salaries that the military received almost immediately after the coup (which, in fairness, may have been in part overdue), the already underpaid teachers had been among those in government employment who suffered the most under the January 1983 austerity measures. These measures resulted in monthly take-home pay being reduced 16.66 percent to 25 percent for all civil servants—depending upon grade. To complicate the problem, monthly payrolls for civilians in the government fell steadily behind. Checks for teachers for April 1984 were paid on June 1. On 25 July 1984, at the very hour when Doe was having himself inducted as president of the Interim Assembly, two blocks away teachers had gathered outside the Ministry of Education building to demand their May paychecks. The demonstration, which this author witnessed at the margin of the crowd, became ugly as teachers and sympathizers began to run down two of the main streets in downtown Monrovia, tipping over lottery booths and threatening to overturn cars. It was only after soldiers specially trained in riot control raced onto the scene with rifles at the ready that the crowd began to disperse. Later that morning the American embassy and the British once more came to Doe's rescue by promising to meet the payroll of teachers in Monrovia. Hence, the launching of Doe's new "civilian" transitional government was accompanied by violence.

Doe made it clear that although the ban on political discussion had supposedly been lifted in July 1984, he would not permit political activity, such as "distributing leaflets, inciting unrest or demonstrating," to take place on the campus of any educational institution. Not only did he threaten to hold school administrators directly responsible for any violation of his ruling, but any violator would also be "arrested and detained without trial until the process of constitutional rule is finalized," under a new PRC decree, 88A, issued on the day after the PRC had actually been dissolved.

Doe's statement alarmed all potential politicians, since it was patently at variance both with the idea of party politics and with the new constitution Doe himself had promulgated only six days before. If that constitution was now in effect, the freedom of expression of Article 15 and the right to a writ of habeas corpus and a speedy trial guaranteed under Article 21 were not to be denied. Moreover, as the editorial in *Footprints Today* pointed out on 3 August 1984 (two days after its publisher and an editor had been detained without charges), the movement for change had very strong roots on the campuses and "the role of students as a pressure group in national politics will remain significant as most of them at the college level meet the age requirements to vote." The editorial further noted that "students who are interested in national politics will find a means to participate in the political process off campus."

## THE ASSAULT ON THE UNIVERSITY

It was apparent that students would not be denied a place at the political table, and even before the lifting of the ban on political discussion on 26 July 1984, an anonymous group called REACT (Revolutionary Action Committee) was circulating leaflets on the campuses. One, appearing before July 20, warned the citizenry that Doe and the PRC would attempt to deny the victory of those favoring adoption of the new constitution. A second attacked the creation of the Interim Advisory Assembly with Doe as its "president," and called for vigorous action to guarantee civilian rule after 26 July 1984 when the ban would be formally lifted. Unfortunately, the call on the part of REACT for industrial and bureaucratic sabotage, military disobedience, tax strikes, and even death to paramount chiefs who supported the military appeared to substitute one form of repression and violence for another.

The incident that did afford the students a legitimate reason for protest was the arrest of Dr. Amos Sawyer, Dean of the College of Social Sciences and Humanities at the University of Liberia and chairman of the Constitutional Commission. Sawyer's offense was to take Doe's lifting of the ban on politics at its word and to state openly in a newspaper interview what many Liberians had been complaining about privately to this author. Sawyer asked why, if all public employees who were interested in forming new parties had to resign their jobs, did this not apply to Doe himself and his government colleagues who had been specifically assigned political duties in organizing Doe's National Democratic Party? Using Doe's own artful phraseology, Sawyer invited Doe to "take advantage of the privilege" of resigning that he had extended to others. This would, Sawyer stated, "allow the Head of State to promote his candidacy, spending full time campaigning, and bring vigor to our democracy." He also criticized the Doe party for jumping the gun in holding organizing meetings before the Special Election Commission had laid out the guidelines for political parties.

The Sawyer interview prompted Doe a few days later to cut short his two-week medical leave in West Germany and cancel his state visits to Austria and Romania. Immediately upon his return, Doe ordered the arrest of Sawyer as well as his faculty colleague in MOJA, Mr. George Kieh. Also arrested were Colonels Larry Borteh and Jerry Friday, two members of the defunct PRC who were supposedly linked to Sawyer. Doe then created the fiction of a plot in which Sawyer and his colleagues were allegedly attempting to oust Doe and establish by force a socialist government in Liberia. Significantly, rumors of a "fake plot" to give Doe the excuse for canceling the new constitution had been circulating in Monrovia for days before the Sawyer arrest. Sawyer and the others were to be given a "fair and speedy" trial on the charge of treason. Other Liberian People's Party leaders, including Dusty Wolokollie, who took over after Sawyer's arrest, were detained. Some LPP members went underground.

The reaction of the students was predictable. Dr. Sawyer's open lifestyle and his longstanding commitment to democratic, nonviolent processes made a mockery of the Doe charges. It was also recognized that if a person of his stature could be arrested, then no one in Liberia was safe from political harassment. At the start of the week students marched in town carrying a coffin labeled "Liberia's rights and liberties" and placards reading "Doe, Go in Peace," and "Rescind Decree 88A" (the order that permitted detention without trial until a new civilian government is chosen). To legitimize his actions, Doe convened the Interim National Assembly for its first official meeting since its creation a month earlier. Instead of engaging in even the pretense of seeking the members' advice, Doe proceeded to harangue his colleagues regarding the lawlessness on the university campus, located just across the street from the Capitol Building and the Executive Mansion. He berated not only the students but also the university administrators and the Faculty Senate, which had addressed a public letter to Doe demanding Sawyer's release. Then Doe abruptly adjourned the meeting and ordered the special riot troops to clear the campus.

The details of what actually ensued may long be shrouded in secrecy, for the military cordoned off the campus for five days, denying all requests of foreign diplomats and journalists to inspect the premises. Phone contacts between Liberia and the outside world were jammed by the government. The government acknowledged only that 74 persons were wounded but denied that any persons had been killed. Doe proceeded to remove from office all university administrators and appointed new administrators and filled the vacancies on the suspended Board of Trustees. Doe also fired all members of the Faculty Senate. Although the military had offered denials, many reports indicated that faculty and administrators were beaten and that the campus was pillaged. Most important, the secrecy of government actions gave rise to unconfirmed reports that a number of students had been killed and their bodies disposed of by riot troops the night of the military assault. That so many students were being reported missing by their parents suggested that the magnitude of the tragedy was staggering.

Despite such intimidation, Doe's critics did not remain silent. The opposition to Doe mounted and became more articulate. The first to respond to the university crisis were the bishops and other heads of the six major Christian churches in Liberia. In their capacity as the Liberian Council of Churches, the leaders sent a petition to Doe on the day of the assault on the university and had their statement read in churches throughout the country on the following Sunday. The church leaders urged the head of state to reduce what they called "the escalating tension" in the country by "redressing the damages already done." "None of us, Mr. Head of State," the petition read, "is able to assess the damage that can come from constant intimidation and an atmosphere of tension which is so prevalent in Liberia now." They demanded that the government stop arbitrary arrests, mysterious disappearances, and extralegal trials and that it rescind Decree No. 88A, which can "easily be used to plunge the nation into a reign of terror, a strategy used by past administrators." Doe left it to his minister of justice to respond to the religious leaders. On August 27, Doe began to parry a challenge from another quarter—the military. For, in addition to arresting two members of the former PRC, Doe turned upon his number one deputy, Major General J. Nicholas Podier, who, it was alleged, had been in consultation with Sawyer and his colleagues during Doe's absence from the country concerning a possible change in the top leadership. The arrest of Podier now left Doe the only survivor of the original core of PRC executive leadership. In typical Liberian style, the one who informed on Podier regarding the alleged conversations was also arrested: it was a double irony, for the informer, Counselor Isaac Nyeplu, Podier's uncle and a former minister of justice as well as more recently a member of the Special Elections Commission, had been a constant adviser to Doe.

As a consequence of both domestic and international pressure, Doe was obliged later in 1984 to backtrack. Realizing the case against Dr. Sawyer and others who had been arrested in early August was of very uncertain legality, Doe was compelled to release Sawyer and many of the others detained on political grounds. The military leaders, including General Podier, were released and retired from the military. The process of forming new political parties continued and hopes still lingered that the forthcoming national elections would ultimately provide Liberians with the fruits of their longstanding quest for democracy. At this writing, however, Doe has yet to have an impartial investigation of the military take-over of the university campus.

### The Flawed Delivery of the Second Republic

Having visted Liberia each year between 1980 and 1984, I found it patently clear that the popular climate had turned steadily against Doe and the PRC since the halcyon days following 12 April 1980. At the time of the coup, people in various ethnic groups, economic strata, and positions in society were personally supportive of Doe and confident that he was sincere about his commitment to an orderly return to civilian rule based on constitutional democratic norms. There was a feeling of togetherness, of participation in a noble cause. Sometimes their sentiments bordered on euphoria, even while noting the many obstacles. As late as 1983, confidence in Doe remained high. This continued despite mounting economic and financial difficulties and the growing feeling that rampant corruption by the military was creating a new order of privilege.

By mid-1984 the sense of mission and optimism had all but evaporated. Almost no one had anything good to say about Doe, and indeed, after the ban on politics had been lifted at the end of July, there was an outpouring of animosity toward the military and toward Doe in particular. His poor speaking ability was mimicked, his accumulation of personal wealth was compared to the abuses of the True Whig period ("Same Taxi, New Driver" was the popular slogan of the day), and his hypocrisy in calling for a return to constitutional democracy while doing everything possible to undermine that goal was derided. It was generally acknowledged that if Doe had kept to his initial word, the citizens of Liberia might of their own accord have made him the first freely elected president of the Second Republic. But that point had now passed. Liberians were glumly complaining that they had substituted one form of tyranny for another. Thus, as one MOJA leader said—borrowing the slogan of the old PRC—"In the name of the people, the struggle *must* continue."

# XVIII.

# The Resumption of Party Politics

### Reestablishing the One-Party System

Ironically the full impact of Doe's systematic exclusion of viable civilian opponents from government and his attempt to restrict and channel political dialogue during the postcoup era became even more pronounced and systematic in the weeks following the July 1984 promulgation of the new constitution. Instead of having a multiparty or two-party system, which the new constitution explicitly sought to encourage, Doe was attempting to reestablish Liberia as a one-party state.

The first aspect of this "grand design" became explicit the day following the announcement of the results of the July referendum. This was his actions in the preempting of the electoral contest for a new civilian government under the new constitution. Doe hoped to accomplish this by having a purportedly civilian government already in place and functioning fifteen months before the elections and eighteen months before the new civilian government of the Second Republic was to commence operations.

The use of the term "grand design" is justified. Indeed, more than six months before the promulgation of the new constitution, an article appeared in, of all places, the *Swazi Observer*, the leading paper of Swaziland, predicting that Doe would "soon dissolve the PRC, which the council members (on January 23) said he could do, and then head a transitional government charged with supervising the handover to elected politicians." Subsequently, "Doe would be nominated for the presidency by one or more newly formed political parties."[1] The article, based on the journalist's interviews with several prominent Liberians, quoted Amos Sawyer directly in noting with respect to Doe that, ". . . as the incumbent and with the assured backing of the military, it is possible that [he] could get elected."

## Charade of Civilian Government

The actual scenario as it unfolded in mid-1984 turned out to be a somewhat more elaborate scheme. For, in addition to dissolving the PRC (which nevertheless continued to function "from the grave," issuing decrees retroactively and continuing to have civilians tried by the Special Military Tribunal), Doe attempted to have a new civilian executive and legislature functioning in advance of elections. Although the fifty-seven member Interim National Assembly was not the bicameral legislature called for in the new constitution, it was assumed that many of those who were appointed to this ad hoc body would be the candidates who presented themselves to the electorate in October 1985, with all the advantages of incumbency.

The vice-president of the Interim Assembly, moreover, was afforded all the deference given to a vice president of the Republic. Dr. Harry Moniba, Liberia's ambassador to Great Britain, whether he liked it or not was the perceived running mate of candidate Doe for the fall 1985 elections. It was an astute choice on Doe's part. Having a doctorate in history from Michigan State University and the manners and articulateness as well as the overseas experience that one would associate with an ambassador to the Court of St. James, Dr. Moniba could be attractive to the better-educated coastal members of the old True Whig Party. And yet he was, like Doe, a person from the interior. As a Gbandi in ethnic origin and a graduate of Cuttington rather than the University of Liberia, Moniba was associated with the ethnic shifts in power that were supposed to have occurred with the 1980 coup. Unlike Doe, however, who was strongly identified with the Krahn and Grand Gedeh County, Moniba was a resident of Lofa County, from which roughly 60 percent of the armed forces come, and hence was reassuring to the rank and file in the military. In any event, Dr. Moniba was given a suite at the Ducor Palace Hotel, a set of bodyguards, a limousine with police escort, and other perquisites not previously made available to the officers of either the Constitutional Commission or the Constitutional Advisory Assembly. The notion that Dr. Moniba enjoyed something more than an honorific title was attested to by the steady stream of petitioners and well-wishers calling at his hotel suite (which was at the opposite end of the hall from the room my wife and I had briefly occupied as we prepared to leave Liberia).

Although the civilian members of the legislature-in-embryo outnumbered the remaining sixteen members of the PRC who were absorbed into that body, the very presence of the latter in the INA cast doubts upon the boast that this was a civilian institution in a civilian transitional government. The former deputy chairman of the PRC, General Nicholas Podier, was named the Assembly Speaker and the other officers of the Interim Assembly had close ties with the military. The civilians who were co-opted were substantially drawn from the ranks of the former Constitutional Advisory Assembly, which had been discharged when the new constitution was promulgated on July 20. One very obvious exception was the Advisory Assembly chairman, Dr. Edward Kesselly, who just before the July referendum had given an injudicious interview which appeared in the April-May issue of *Footprints Today*. Kesselly had suggested that violence is always associated with elections in Third

World countries, and, he added, "don't kid yourself, we will have violence. . . ."
It was for this reason, he argued, that Liberia needed longer terms for presidents
(six years rather than four), so that there would be fewer elections! He also managed
to take a swipe at the Special Elections Commission, and asserted that historically
senators are more responsible than members of the House. Doe's reaction was
instantaneous, and he charged the statement with demonstrating a "high level of
indiscretion and immaturity."[2] At that point, Kesselly's chances of being named
vice-president of the Interim Assembly apparently vanished.

The INA membership (unlike the Sawyer Commission) included no one who
was identified with MOJA or the PPP. Nor did it include anyone who was regarded
as one of the courageous independents or True Whig Party members who had braved
the wrath of the Tubman and Tolbert governments. Instead it consisted of women
(two only) and men who were traditional chiefs, former True Whig stalwarts who
had served in non-policymaking positions (ambassadors, district commissioners),
and conservative businessmen and lawyers who would probably have been in politics
were the ban on political activity not in effect. The popular characterization of the
group is that they were "survivalists," who opportunistically persevered no matter
what the top leadership and political mood of the day happened to be. This became
the nucleus of Doe's National Democratic Party of Liberia, which competed in the
1985 elections.

Prior consultation by Doe and the PRC with the potential members of the
Interim National Assembly was minimal. Indeed, one member admitted having first
heard of his appointment on his car radio while driving to work. Several privately
expressed great displeasure at the requirement that they quit their present jobs in
government or the private sector in order to take up their new assignments. Moreover, as the civilian members found to their distress, the military members did not
resign their commissions and were unwilling to sacrifice any "corporate interests,"
which included, among other things, most of the offices in the Legislative Building
that the Interim Assembly members were supposed to occupy. Civilians in the
Assembly felt they had been put on the spot and had no alternative but to accept
the dubious assignment. Only the minister of planning, the very competent Emmanuel O. Gardner, begged off appointment to INA by managing to persuade Doe
that he could serve the government more effectively by continuing his present post.

Doe very pointedly suggested that nothing should prevent the Assembly members from running for office under the new constitution. It was clear, however, that
they had no legitimate claim to office other than their linkage with Doe. The role
and function of the Interim Assembly was left purposely vague, and it was significant
that basic decrees issued in the ensuing weeks as well as significant personnel and
policy decisions were the handiwork of Doe alone without even the pretense of
consulting the Assembly. It was apparent that the Assembly was to perform the
same rubber stamp role the Legislature had done under the True Whig system.

### The Call to Duty—Doe's Constituency

With his incumbent government in place a full three days before the formal lifting
of the ban on politics on July 26, Doe quickly moved to put in place the other

elements in this scheme. It amounted to what many Liberians perceive to be a reinstitution of the monopoly that the True Whigs once enjoyed over the political process. The next step was also reminiscent of the traditional True Whig style of political behavior—namely, well-orchestrated calls from several groups for Doe to present himself as a candidate for president in the fall 1985 elections. The term "well-orchestrated" is used advisedly, since two of the groups involved had been the recent beneficiaries of Doe's patronage: the Liberian Marketing Association and the traditional chiefs.

## THE MARKETING ASSOCIATION

The Marketing Association, which claims a membership of over 300,000—mostly women—called for Doe's nomination twenty-four hours before the lifting of the ban on politics. This was on the day that Doe was dedicating a $1.7 million annex to the Rally Time Market on United Nations Drive and pledging his government to the construction of other market facilities. The market women were a group whose favor Doe had been cultivating from the earliest days, since it was apparent that their enthusiastic support following the April 1980 coup had been a factor in the quick consolidation of PRC power. On another occasion, moreover, they had revealed themselves as a potential threat to Doe: in January 1982, they had joined in the vigorous protest over the Special Military Tribunal decision to impose the penalty of death by firing squad on six student leaders from the University of Liberia, Cuttington College, and the Liberian National Student Union. The students had been convicted of "treason" for having violated the ban on political activities on the campuses. The fact that Doe at the last minute was forced to reverse the decision demonstrated the market women's continuing political clout. The July 1984 endorsement of Doe's candidacy by the leaders of the Marketing Association, however, did not suggest they were completely in his pocket as a constituency. The leadership suggested that if Doe did not keep his promises, they would have "no alternative but to use the veto power of Liberian womanhood," and noted that the association "could be more effective if they were permitted to run their own affairs without government direction."[3]

## THE TRADITIONALISTS

The second group to call for Doe's nomination, the traditional chiefs, had also been carefully cultivated, especially after some from Nimba County had protested the arrest and trial of General Thomas Quiwonkpa in November 1983. Doe's appeal to the chiefs took on particular significance for the future of Liberian politics since it further reinforced the notion that a "new tribalism" was emerging as a counterforce to the new class identities referred to previously. (See chapter 16.) This constituted a direct threat to those who were attempting to create a national identity which transcended ethnicity.

The elements of this "new tribalism" were discernible on the very day of the coup itself, when the quickly constituted People's Redemption Council had a disproportionate representation from the Krahn group in particular and the southeastern Liberian ethnic groups in general. The enlargement of the PRC to provide a better ethnic balance and the appointment of civilians representing a broad spectrum of Liberian society seemed to be healthy correctives to the Krahn dominance in the immediate postcoup period. Gradually, however, as the collective responsibility of the PRC gave way to decision making by the smaller Executive Committee, the narrow ethnic base of influence became more pronounced. And as MOJA and PPP civilians in the cabinet, in ambassadorial positions, and in other posts of responsibility were eased out of office or resigned, their places were taken by relatives of Samuel Doe himself or by other Krahn and members of southeastern tribal groups. It was not merely that the Americo-Liberian family network of the First Republic was being replaced by a Krahn-dominated network; it was also a diminution of the quality of performance. Many of the new appointees lacked the education, the governmental experience, and other talents required for the jobs they were filling. It was patronage by ascription in the crudest sense of the term.

The direct corollary to Krahn ascendancy in this "new tribalism," unfortunately, was that particular groups were again being singled out for abuse. There were, from 1984 onward, increasingly public references to "settling old scores with the Congo boys" (referring to Americo-Liberians and Congoes collectively). Even more the targets of hostility were the Gio and the Mano, several of whose leaders had played significant roles in the coup and in the early post-1980 governmental scene. But the dispute with Thomas Quiwonkpa in 1983, the presidential candidacy of Jackson Doe (no relative of Samuel Doe) in 1985, and the abortive Quiwonkpa coup a month after the elections actually led to physical assaults against Gio and Mano in their home area of Nimba County and elsewhere in the country.

Despite the fact that the Krahn leadership enjoyed a near monopoly over the use of force in Liberia, they were after all still a small group and short on talents in critical areas. They needed to reinforce their position of dominance not only by getting the assistance of the more educated tribal youth and the survivalists from the old Whig regime, but by putting together a broad coalition of rural tribalists. One way of doing this was to provide legitimacy to the demands for the creation of new territorial administrative units which roughly coincided with tribal or subtribal boundaries. Pressures in this direction had actually been developing for a long period, most markedly after Tubman's creation of new counties in the hinterland in 1964. The Constitutional Commission under Amos Sawyer had acknowledged the existence of such pressures but feared that the creation of such new administrative units along tribal lines would undermine the efforts to eliminate tribalism at the expense of a new Liberian nationalism. Indeed, it could encourage or reinforce historical intertribal rivalries and hostilities. Rather than risk offending the traditional chiefs and others who had petitioned the Con-Com on this matter, they decided that this was a "political" rather than a constitutional matter, and they passed it along to the future civilian government to handle.

Even before the new government was established under the Second Republic, however, new counties were created—Grand Kru at the coast and Bomi in the northwest area of Montserrado County—a concession to longstanding demands on the part of the Gola for ethnic recognition.[4] (See map 1.) Still other petitions to the PRC and even to the new Interim National Assembly were presented by River Cess Territory leaders, as well as jointly by the people of Bopolu and Gbama, each requesting county status designation. Citizens of Gbaepo and Webbo districts together with Jedepo chiefdom in Sinoe similarly requested county status. Ultimately River Cess was established as a county and the combined Marshall Territory and Gibi District were consolidated and given county status as Margibi County. This brought the number of counties to thirteen. Even under the new constitution, the creation of counties would not constitute a devolution of power from the central government, since Liberia is not a federal republic. County status along ethnic lines, however, was viewed by its proponents both as a device for focusing attention upon a particular people in their efforts to get needed development funds as well as a patronage device. Each new county had its set of administrative officers, senators, and representatives who could provide added income and prestige to local tribal personages.

Even more directly related to the "massaging" of the tribal chiefs were the introduction in 1981 of a communal farm program in the hinterland (providing additional sources of wealth to the chiefs) and Doe's renovation of the Native Mansion, a residence in Monrovia reserved for paramount chiefs and tribal elders when they are in the capital on official business. The cost of renovation of the mansion—during a time of austerity—was $156,000. Doe called all the chiefs to Monrovia in mid-July for the dedication of the refurbished building and encouraged them to stay on at government expense through the Independence Day celebrations. Pleased to be included in the official program, they performed well in "gowning" various ambassadors as honorary chiefs and—to the surprise of the foreign emissaries—urging them to give continued support to Doe now and in his future role as president of Liberia. Three days later the chiefs formally requested that Doe not return to the barracks in 1986 but retain the reins of leadership.

Finally, in an effort to appeal to traditional chiefs as well as to those ethnic groups in which Poro is operative, Doe in the latter days of the 1985 campaign had himself inducted into the Poro in the Kpelle area. Taking on the title of *Tarnue* (one of the ranks within Poro), Doe thereafter referred to himself as Head of the Supreme Council for Zoes in Liberia. As with Whig presidents of the past who engaged in such ritual, the knowledgeable authorities on the Poro could only be amused by Doe's presumption of any real power over the *zoes*.

Collectively, the creation of the new counties, the Krahn domination of government, the currying of favor among the traditional chiefs, the efforts to woo the leadership of the Poro societies, and the special targeting of the Gio and Mano cast serious doubts about the ability of a Doe-led government to accomplish Liberia's long pursued quest for democracy.

**THE POLITICIZED MILITARY**

It was Doe's endorsement by the military itself, however, that turned out to be the most crucial constituency support. The announcement of Doe's candidacy came on

July 28 at a closed meeting at Camp Schieffelin military barracks 18 miles outside Monrovia. It was made in the presence of the "top brass," indicating far more than the continued support the military might be expected to accord the leader of the 1980 coup. While the military had earlier called on Doe to run, this announcement demonstrated quite clearly that the new constitution, promulgated only the week before, was not being taken seriously by Doe or his colleagues. The military fully intended to be a significant factor in the politics of the Second Republic and claimed to do so "in the name of the people." Significantly, Doe did not resign his commission before making himself a candidate for the highest civilian office in the new government.

The military's endorsement was significant in several respects. First, it demonstrated the depths of the military's fear that an entirely civilian government under the Second Republic would be difficult to restrain in terms of seeking retribution against those military leaders who had committed personal abuses against private citizens or who had illegally accumulated vast amounts of land and other forms of wealth. On this point the Constitutional Commission had gone out of its way to reassure the PRC by including in the transitional provisions of the draft constitution a special section (Article 114) protecting personnel of the military government against future recrimination. No court or other tribunal could make any order or grant any remedy for actions taken by any member of the PRC government in carrying out its decrees. Similarly exempt from future judicial proceedings were all of the actions resulting in the overthrow of the Tolbert government, the suspension of the 1847 Constitution, the confiscation of property, and other acts associated with the 1980 coup and the establishment of the PRC government. Although actions taken under the cover of PRC decrees were protected, the illegal *private* actions of soldiers and others were not specifically protected from future retribution. And that is what disturbed many of the members of the military government who had engaged in extraordinary acts of "status reversal"—moving from the underprivileged to the privileged group almost overnight. Indeed, despite the several years of public scolding by former Army Commander General Thomas Quiwonkpa and other leaders within the military, the PRC members and other soldiers were still in May 1984 occupying the homes and farms of the former True Whig officials. This included the properties of many who had returned to Liberia in response to Doe's urgings that they come home without fear of retribution. Despite the dissolution of the PRC in July 1984, moreover, the Special Military Tribunal continued to pass judgment on nonmilitary personnel.

Second, the military endorsement of Doe's candidacy dramatized the way in which Doe alone had come to represent the military collectively in Liberian politics. Although the PRC had started as a mechanism of corporate leadership in which Doe was *primus inter pares*, Doe had emerged as the unchallenged maximal leader in symbolic if not real power terms.

That role was not achieved without great difficulty. Doe and the majority of the initial members of the PRC were either Krahn or originated from Grand Gedeh County in southeastern Liberia. The Krahn area is among the least-developed in Liberia in terms of education, economic change, and roads and other infrastructure.

Within the military the Krahn were not only far from being among the larger ethnic contingents (the Loma of Lofa County were long the backbone of the military) but they also had very low prestige in terms of the ethnic stereotyping that the Americo-Liberians had pursued in maintaining control over the army. Hence, if Doe and his colleagues were to remain in control of the military, the perception of ethnic even-handedness had to start with the PRC itself. One early step, as noted previously, was the expansion of the PRC from seventeen to twenty-eight members. A conscious effort was also made to promote to officer grade persons who were from other hinterland counties. Finally, the patronage system within the government proper— the awarding of ambassadorships, the assignment of deputy and assistant minis-terships—was broadened so that clients of non-Krahn within the military got their appropriate share of these rewards. It was apparent not only to observers but to the Liberians themselves that the Krahn dominated many of the crucial posts within the military, the postcoup government, and Doe's National Democratic Party of Liberia.

Overcoming ethnic rivalry within the military was only one aspect of the problem. The broader one was the enhancement of the status of the military within Liberian society. The military had been almost at the very bottom of the prestige ladder during the True Whig period. Doubling the pay of the military immediately after the coup and getting new barracks constructed dealt with some of the material aspects of the problem; other actions were intended to deal with the psychological aspects. The appearance of military uniforms in places previously associated with civilian political power did much in terms of massaging the egos of the formerly abused troops. The unveiling of a statue of a soldier at one of the key traffic intersections in Monrovia, its reproduction on the new five-dollar coins, and the renaming of bridges and streets for the new military "heroes" were also relevant in this regard. Two other early innovations emphasizing the military, however, were more coolly received by the civilian public. The first was the effort to substitute Redemption Day (April 12) for Independence Day (July 26) as the primary day of national celebration. This effort did not survive beyond 1981, when both days were given appropriate recognition. The second gesture was the attempt to substitute the Redemption Flag for the Star and Stripes as the national banner. The Redemption Flag imposes military symbols on a red banner containing a white outline map of Liberia. Civilians persevered in using the traditional flag as the primary banner of Liberian nationhood and independence.

DOE'S CONTROL OVER THE PRC

The emergence of Doe as the single most important actor in the PRC became explicit only over time. The first rupture in the efforts at collective leadership became public around Christmas 1981, when Doe announced the PRC's decision to abandon the supervisory committee system. The committee system granted each of the twenty-eight members of the PRC some responsibility in exercising supervisory respon-sibilities with respect to one or more of nineteen cabinet ministries and government agencies. Although it was designed to give the members of the PRC some experience in comprehension of governmental problems, in fact it created a shadow cabinet in which the chairman of the respective PRC committee was constantly counter-manding the decisions of both civilian and military cabinet officers with respect to policy matters, personnel appointments, and the general administration of the ministries. It was not only demoralizing to the ministers but also required that Doe constantly intervene to mediate disputes between the ministers and the committees.

Eventually the PRC was effectively reduced to an executive group of four or five who worked with Doe. One by one, however, these key players fell by the wayside. One of the first was Major General Thomas Weh Syen, the former deputy head of state and vice-chairman of the PRC who had differed with Doe over many policy issues. He and four other members of the PRC were charged in August 1981 with having plotted the assassinations of Doe, General Thomas Quiwonkpa, and General Nicholas Podier. After a perfunctory trial, they were executed by firing squad. The ranks of core leadership then remained fairly stable until October 1983, when Doe had a falling out with Quiwonkpa. The latter was popularly regarded within Liberia, and outside as well, as the only truly honest man of the PRC. It was he, more than any other, who insisted that the military reestablish order within its own ranks, that it cease the illegal acquisition of properties, and that it adhere faithfully to the pledge to return Liberia to civilian rule. Rejecting the lavish lifestyle that his fellow PRC colleagues had assumed, Quiwonkpa preferred to live at the barracks and refused to move to the Executive Mansion. Recognizing the growing affection for Quiwonkpa—in contrast to the diminishing crowds for his own ap-pearances—Doe created some trumped-up charges and had Quiwonkpa detained. The immediate protest from the chiefs and elders of Nimba County, from which Quiwonkpa came, as well as complaints from within the military itself, compelled Doe to permit Quiwonkpa to leave the country even though a mock trial of some of his close associates had attempted to discredit him. That left only General Nicho-las Podier, who had become the deputy Chairman of the PRC and deputy head of state following Weh Syen's execution, as a significant wielder of authority in behalf of the PRC. On 28 August 1984, in the circumstances discussed below, he too was arrested on charges of plotting against Doe. That left Doe the undisputed leader within the military.

## The Flowering of Political Parties

However significant Doe's initial electoral constituency may have been, it was still too narrow a base from which to launch a presidential campaign. Thus, Act Three of the drama began: the launching of a governmment-supported political party. Doe's decision, however, was not the only action taken with respect to formation of a political party; for the lifting of the ban on political discussion on 26 July 1984 had signaled the beginning of a virtual flowering of political parties whose leaders were eager to provide an alternative to Doe's National Democratic Party of Liberia.

The profusion of parties in Liberia emerging in the year preceding the 1985 elections was not a phenomenon unique to that country. In other states on the continent the resumption of civilian politics after an extended period of military domination of the state had manifested a similar splintering of the political spectrum along lines which followed ethnicity, regionalism, historic patterns of partisanship, ideological cleavages, or *personalismo* on the part of a given party leader. In Uganda in 1979, for example, the civilian group that was assembled by Tanzania to govern the liberated state after eight years of suppression of civilian politics under Idi Amin was severely fragmented. The instability with regard to the provisional presidency, programs for reconstruction, the nature of the electoral process and the new political system, and all other major issues was only temporarily interrupted by the electoral victory of Milton Obote in 1980. The latter event only papered over the schisms which had grown deeper during the period of exile when the partisans lacked the sobering responsibility of governing or providing constructive opposition criticism. Continued fragmentation was a factor in the re-intervention of the military.

A similar proliferaton of parties emerged in Nigeria at the end of the thirteen years of military rule, despite the efforts of the framers of the new constitution to downplay ethnicity by constructing an electoral system which required registered parties to have a broad national constituency in two-thirds of the states. The victorious presidential candidate had to receive one quarter of all votes cast in two-thirds of the nineteen states. Even with these provisions, more than a dozen parties were formed in 1978, although only five parties actually competed in the 1979 election and again in the 1983 contest.

Liberia lacked the Nigerian electoral mechanisms which would have reduced political party fragmentation along ethnic or regional lines. Indeed, it was only the arbitrary rules established by the Doe regime itself that reduced the 1985 contest to four parties. The actions of Doe's partisans eliminated not only the frivolous contestants but also the two parties that constituted the greatest challenge to Doe. The fragmentation of the opposition into potentially ten parties can be attributed to several factors, the most notable of which was the virtual monopoly which Doe's close associates enjoyed with respect to formulating foreign and domestic policies and laying the groundwork for an effective organization during the four-year ban on politics. Secondly, the transition from co-optation, to restricting policy debate, to outright exclusion or harassment of the PPP and MOJA leadership made it difficult for these leaders to test the waters with regard to their respective constituency or to patch up the personality, policy, and program issues which differentiated the two groups. The former adherents of the True Whig Party (which was specifically denied a place on the ballot) largely felt uncomfortable with both MOJA and the PPP and thus sought a new partisan home. Many of the Old Guard survivalists or their scion threw in their lot with Doe; the reformist wing preferred to continue what they had regarded as the transformation of Liberian society (which they claim was interrupted by the 1980 coup) by forming a new reformist party or parties. Finally, there were others who felt that the new constitution provided them with an opportunity to make a clean break with the past in terms of party structure and goals. In any event, considering the size of Liberia, the array of political parties which presented themselves for the 1985 electoral campaign represented an extreme case of political fragmentation for a Third World country.

## NATIONAL DEMOCRATIC PARTY OF LIBERIA

With himself as "standard bearer," Doe informed his cabinet on August 1 that he had created the National Democratic Party of Liberia (NDPL) to advance his candidacy for the presidency. Its cadre of leadership consisted, for the most part, of the members of the recently appointed Interim National Assembly. As noted earlier, the Assembly included not only the entire PRC but a number of civilians who had indicated their explicit or at least tacit support of Doe's leadership. Notably absent from that body were any political leaders previously associated with MOJA or the PPP—although Oscar Quiah of PPP later "recanted his past sins" and took on the task of organizing the NDPL as its secretary general. In addition to the Assembly, the NDPL included a number of educated persons of tribal background, most traditional chiefs, and a number of strong supporters of the discredited Tolbert regime. The NDPL leadership also drew into its net several civilians and military leaders who had served in executive, ambassadorial, and other roles in early phases of the PRC rule. The prominence of the Krahn and other ethnic groups from Grand Gedeh County (Doe's home area) was evident not only in the leadership of the party but in terms of its later electoral support.

The party platform of the NDPL formulated in September 1985 went out of its way to commit itself to capitalism—as a way of distancing itself from what it regarded as the socialism of the UPP and the LPP (which both of the latter denied). This was essential since many of the civilian members of the Interim Assembly, who formed the bulk of the NDPL's cadre of leadership, were former politicians or their offspring who had turned to their families' secondary interests in transport, merchandising, banking, or planting during the postcoup ban on politics. These were the "survivors" in Liberian politics, who had over the years managed to be conservatives or reformists depending on the current political climate. Unlike the other parties however, the NDPL was obligated to have a specific plank in its party platform guaranteeing the well-being of all army personnel. Given its rural tribal constituency—particularly in the least-developed of counties, Grand Gedeh—the NDPL was also obliged to make extended reference to improving agricultural production and rural developments among its key concerns.

## UNITED PEOPLE'S PARTY

Not unexpectedly, within six hours of the lifting of the ban on politics, several voices of the recent political past were also heard from. The first to announce a challenge to the National Democratic Party of Liberia was G. Baccus Matthews, leader of the suspended Progressive People's Party, who announced the formation of the United People's Party (UPP). Matthews hoped the UPP would achieve a broad national consensus, appealing to the old PPP, the more liberal-minded of the former True Whig Party adherents, former MOJA members, the urban poor (who would remember Matthews's role in the 1979 Rice Riots), and those people who had been apolitical in the past. The United People's Party would not, Matthews stressed, be ideological or dogmatic, but would relate to the changed realities of Liberia. Using neither the old True Whig Party caucus method of selecting candidates nor the presumed Doe method of handpicking candidates, Matthews wanted a party primary in about six months' time to pick all candidates—including the presidential standard-bearer. Matthews hoped the public would judge him and his colleagues on the basis not only of what the PPP had done in the streets, fighting the True Whigs, but also the performance of Matthews and other PPP leaders in the PRC government.

Matthews's programs and politics as leader of the United People's Party were not sharply divergent from those he had urged upon the public in his leadership of the Progressive People's Party in the last year of the First Republic. These included protection of human rights and civil liberties, improved health and literacy programs, greater distributive justice, and national unity. In a pointed rebuttal to the UPP's detractors, the General Policy Statement of the UPP (which was distributed in July over the objections of the Special Elections Commission) disclaimed any commitment to a specific ideology. Indeed, the statement insisted that the UPP was committed to capitalism, but a capitalism in which Liberians rather than foreign entrepreneurs were the most prominent group of capitalists!

LIBERIAN PEOPLE'S PARTY

Since its credentials as an opponent of the Whig aristocracy were as valid as those of the former PPP, it was not long before the leaders of the Movement for Justice in Africa also reasserted themselves on the political scene. Their acting chairman, Dr. Amos Sawyer, announced on August 3 the intent to create a new party, the Liberian People's Party (LPP), which would forge a broad base, including professional and business people who were convinced that something had to be done to restore the government's integrity. Amos Sawyer acted in the absence of the nominal chairman of MOJA, Togba-Nah Tipoteh, who had remained in exile following his earlier resignation from the cabinet in his capacity as minister of planning. The LPP meant its appeal to reach beyond the upper and middle classes to market women, farmers, teachers, students, and common workers. Sawyer insisted that the party's structure, the delineation of issues, and the selection of candidates should be the results of decisions made by a cross-section of the future membership. At that time Sawyer wished only to indicate a firm intention of the LPP to compete in the forthcoming elections, as he believed that broad-based participation at this stage was essential to prevent "our evolving democratic process from being stampeded out of existence or transformed into a charade."

Moreso than most of his colleagues, Sawyer appeared to be more deeply committed to the democratic process than to his own political ambitions. His statement before the Election Commission in February 1985, when he was presenting the credentials of the Liberian People's Party, are indicative of this. In his speech, Sawyer stated:

You have a tough job gentlemen, and we hope you have the will and strength to do it properly. There are certain guidelines which the Liberian people have already given you. You will do well to heed them. First, the Liberian people have made it clear that they want a genuine return to civilian rule through a democratic process. They do not want "guided democracy", "selective democracy" or "martial democracy". They want "one person, one vote democracy". Second, they want a multi-party democratic process. There must be more than one political party participating in the democratic process and any attempt to avoid this will be totally contrary to the will and desire of our people, and will therefore be considered unpatriotic. The people of this country require that you treat all parties fairly. If dropping leaflets from the air is acceptable, then distributing leaflets on the ground should also be acceptable.[5]

## LIBERIAN UNIFICATION PARTY

One of the surprising developments was the attention given to, and the sustaining quality of, another early announced party, the Liberian Unification Party. The LUP was the brainchild of a former high-school principal, Gabriel W. Kpolleh. Kpolleh had attracted headlines previously when he responded to Doe's demand in the spring of 1983 that all civil servants who intended to run for office in the future should resign from government. Doe attempted to assure Kpolleh that the order did not apply to public-school teachers, but Kpolleh persisted in his ambitions. The LUP had the stated intention of being the party of "the masses, the privileged, the underprivileged, the rich and the poor, the old and the young." While some of Kpolleh's detractors criticized the LUP for the vagueness of its platform goals, he did go beyond lofty commitments to "national unity, stability, a fair and just democracy, and security of life and property." Indeed, his economic program was more specific than most in that he openly committed himself to free enterprise, achievement of Liberian self-sufficiency in food production and raw materials, the revival of the industrial economy, and an emphasis upon both health and education as essential ingredients in modernization.

But Kpolleh did appear to be quixotic, for example, when he threatened to "crush anyone who dares run against me."[6] Subsequently, when the leaders of the major opposition parties were being detained and threatened, Kpolleh remained unmolested by the Doe regime. Some Liberians speculated that he represented the "buffoon" factor—that is, the kind of harmless opposition party that Tubman had liked to encourage in order to maintain the appearances of a two-party system. Kpolleh's was the last of the four surviving parties to raise the $50,000 cash deposit and the property valuation statement of at least $100,000 needed to qualify for registration. Rumors persisted that Kpolleh had been given the funds by Samuel Doe, just to keep him in the race—as a "thank you" for Kpolleh's remarks made at the Executive Mansion after Doe had survived an alleged assassination attempt in April 1985.[7] Given the performance of the Liberian Unification Party in the October elections and Kpolleh's subsequent courageous actions, the charges of collusion with Doe seemed unwarranted.

MINOR PARTIES—THE "ALSO RANS"

As it turned out, neither the United People's Party nor the Liberian People's Party was actually permitted by the Doe regime to compete in the 1985 elections, for reasons which will be indicated later. There were as well a number of other groups within the pool of eleven potential parties which announced for the elections but which lacked the financial wherewithal and constituency support to qualify for registration as a legitimate party. This group included, for example, the small group behind Wade Appleton, a prominent Monrovia lawyer. Appleton infuriated Doe when his group declared themselves as the Convention Democratic Party (CDP), which was bound to be confused with the name of Doe's party. Appleton was quoted as having said that he wanted a party that would prevent Liberia from going socialist. The list of "also-rans" also included the National Integration Party (NIP), which was guided by Counsellor J. Leveli Supuwood and other Monrovia-based lawyers. NIP may have been able to muster the required $150,000 deposit, but as a matter of principle its leaders challenged the authority of the Special Elections Commission (SECOM) in formulating such rules of participation. Supuwood insisted that this was a form of "property qualification," which had echoes back to the old True Whig days, and was contrary to the spirit of the new constitution.

In any event, whether because of difficulties in raising the deposit or because the potential membership favored the better-organized parties, there were in all five minor parties that failed to meet the 1 March 1985 deadline for filing. This included the Convention Democratic Party and the National Integration Party, as well as the People's Liberation Party (PLP) of Mrs. Hawa Clement Danquah, the First All-Integrated Republican Party (FAIR) headed by Edwin Dunbar, and the Labor Party (LP) of Joseph W. Nimley.

LIBERIAN ACTION PARTY

The party which in the October 1985 elections proved to have the greatest base of popular support was one of the last to be organized and registered. The Liberian Action Party (LAP) undoubtedly secured a broader base of support because of the difficulties which some of the other opposition groups—particularly Baccus Matthews's United People's Party and Sawyer's Liberian People's Party—were encountering in clearing the various registration hurdles. And it secured electoral support in 1985 which would have been fragmented among several parties. The Liberian Action Party included in its leadership some former MOJA leaders, but it drew substantially from those who were considered the liberal reformist wing of the True Whig Party and had actually challenged Tolbert publicly on some of his principal policies and programs. Typical of the latter category was S. Byron Tarr, who had been a strong supporter of Amos Sawyer in his 1979 mayoral electoral bid. It also included Ellen Johnson-Sirleaf, the former minister of finance, as well as several professionals who had suffered imprisonment and other forms of harassment under either Tubman or Tolbert for their dissent—as had, for example,

Tuan Wreh, who became the general chairman for LAP. The party's main base of support were professionals, middle-class businessmen (many reformist politicians of the Tolbert era, who were now pursuing their secondary interests in business), teachers, and a number of lay leaders in the Catholic and mainline Protestant churches. Seeking to rise above possible identification as a settler-based party, and instead present the image of "reconciliation," the standard-bearer chosen for the 1985 election was Jackson Doe (no relative of Samuel Doe). Jackson Doe was a Gio (Dan) from Nimba County who had links with the Americo-Liberian group by virtue of having been raised in the household of a former distinguished chief justice of the Supreme Court, Louis Grimes. Jackson Doe had represented his home county in the House of Representatives (1967–72) and in the Senate (1975–80). His "bridge" credentials were evident in the fact that he had served as vice national chairman of the True Whig Party, but not without a challenge at the time of his appointment from the Old Guard within the Whig hierarchy who feared the popularity of a tribal man within the essentially settler party.

The LAP platform consciously sought a government of national unity that would transcend past partisan affiliations on the part of its supporters. In the forefront of its platform or goals, LAP took a liberal position on freedom of speech and the press, public access to officials, and the professionalization and regular compensation of the civil service and security personnel. The LAP also committed itself to expansion of free enterprise, and reduction of government intervention unless directed to the Liberianization of the economy; greater attention to rural development (at the expense of more urban public housing); and respect for, as well as professionalization of, the role of traditional authorities in the hinterland. It wanted also to reverse the flight of both capital and educated talent from Liberia which had emerged since the coup.

**UNITY PARTY**

The last of the four parties which competed in the October elections was the Unity Party, (UP) which had been organized by Dr. Edward Benyah Kesselly of Lofa County. Kesselly had many things going for him as a party leader and presidential candidate. His educational background, which included degrees from the University of Chicago and the University of Manchester, as well as his governmental experience as a cabinet member (Information, Cultural Affairs and Tourism; Posts and Telecommunications; and Local Government) made him an attractive candidate to the intelligentsia and to the middle-class Americo-Liberians. On the other hand, his Loma parentage and Mandingo family links, plus the fact that his father had once served as the commanding general of the armed forces under Tubman, made him attractive both to the tribal sector generally and particularly to the Loma, the largest ethnic group within the military. He had gained invaluable name recognition during his service as Chairman of the Constitutional Advisory Assembly—and might have been Doe's running mate had he not made some embarrassing public statements (discussed in Chapter 15).

The goals of Kesselly's Unity party were not radically different from those of the Liberian Action Party. One of the points of emphasis, however, did appeal to the growing business classes within both the Americo-Liberian and tribal sectors, namely, the insistence that many of the public corporations should be "privatized" to ensure maximum efficiency and production for the society as a whole.

# XIX.

# The 1985 Electoral Campaign

The analysis of the details of the 1985 electoral campaign is important to our understanding of why the legitimacy of the Second Republic is under challenge at this writing. But the events and mechanisms analyzed here are not *sui generis*. Indeed, they fit into the greater mosaic of post-independence politics on the African continent in general and of the Third World beyond Africa. The Liberian example of an entrenched military's efforts to "civilianize" its top leadership and to launch a dominant political party under the control of the military has echoes in Zaire, Burkina Faso, the Central African Republic, and elsewhere on the continent. The intervention of the military, moreover, to thwart the outcome of a freely contested election has African (Sierra Leone, 1967), Latin American (Dominican Republic, 1979), and other Third World parallels. Indeed, the Liberian election of October 1985 provided the U.S. congressional observer team with almost a clinical case of what they might anticipate in the Marcos-Aquino contest in the Philippines three months later.

## NDPL and the Advantages of Incumbency

Even before the emergence of the eleven political parties, it was soon evident that the 1985 election was not to be a contest among equals. This was apparent in terms of control that any incumbent regime enjoys with respect to the flow of information. As the government of the day, Doe and his colleagues in NDPL controlled the *New Liberian* daily, the government-owned radio and television stations, and other media outlets. Indeed, the bias in the government-owned media in favor of coverage of NDPL candidates and activities became so outrageous in the closing days of the campaign that the leadership of Liberian Action Party felt obliged to make a public protest. Even if the media had not been to a considerable extent government-owned, the *Observer, Footprints Today,* and other privately owned papers as well as the two private radio stations (ELWA and the Catholic station) out of sheer news value had honestly to give the edge to the Interim National Assembly, the now-defunct PRC, and other government officials simply because they were the incumbents. They had greater ability to make things happen. And so it was that the announcement of the formation of the National Democratic Party of Liberia should have had greater attention when it was established.

Beyond information, Doe and his cohorts early made it patently clear that they intended to enjoy the advantages of incumbency with respect to officeholding and the prerequisites of patronage. At the August 1 meeting, Samuel Doe gave all cabinet officers and deputy and assistant ministers one week "to exercise the privilege" of resigning from government if they expected to participate in the formation of competing political parties. Only those who identified with his policies and programs would be permitted to remain in his government. In a veiled threat he warned against "deceitfulness on the part of any individual who may want to play 'two-handed games'."[1]

One individual who was removed from a position of responsibility because of his lack of enthusiasm with respect to joining the NDPL became Samuel Doe's most vigorous challenger: Jackson Doe, who had served as head of the National Port Authority until his unceremonious removal without the benefit of explanation.

Control over the bureaucracy became even more blatant as the electoral campaign proceeded and Samuel Doe's colleagues gradually came to sense that they could indeed lose in a free and fair election. Crassly, a week before the October 1985 election Doe instructed all government workers that they had to prove that they had been NDPL members if they were to retain their posts after the election. "The real meaning of democracy," Doe asserted, "is to give jobs to somebody who can promote you." Curiously, he indicated that he did not regard this as either nepotism or tribalism. Even earlier, the courts and Doe's executive branch were busy removing from government jobs all candidates of parties other than the NDPL. One of the senatorial candidates of the Unity Party, for example, was instructed by Chief Justice Emmanuel Gbalazeh to resign from his post as stipendiary magistrate in Kru Town. No NDPL candidate, however—including those who were members of the Interim National Assembly, the rump assembly—was compelled to resign despite frequent complaints on this point from the opposition party leadership. With respect to the military as a political group, it was not until the very eve of the election (long after opposition candidates and sympathizers had been forced to give up government employment) that SECOM Chairman Emmett Harmon announced that all soldiers who had been nominated by political parties to run for office must resign their commissions. Harmon never made it clear whether this ruling applied to Samuel Doe himself. Indeed, with increasing frequency Doe—the nominally civilian head of the Interim Assembly in the transition to civilian rule—appeared in public in full combat gear, sporting the five-star-general insignia that he had unilaterally awarded himself. It was only belatedly as well that Harmon's Special Elections Commission ruled that soldiers should on election day vote in mufti and avoid carrying weapons near the polling booths.

In addition to direct patronage links, the NDPL monopolized government revenues as well as other weapons in attracting adherents and in holding potential dissidents in line. Thus, a week before the election, Samuel Doe used the power of the purse to advantage by suddenly reversing the practices of the past few years with respect to the payment of teachers. At least in Monrovia, Margibi, and other nearby areas, teachers received a portion of their long-overdue monthly paychecks as well as the withheld transportation allowances. Indeed, at that time the delay in payments had forced the long-suffering teachers to go on strike, refusing to meet their classes to prepare students for their final examination until the teachers had received their arrears payment. As the head of the union stated in traditional Liberian fashion, "Empty rice bags can't stand up."

Doe also used government funds (although he claimed it was his personal savings) to placate another hostile constituency, the students. Various schools were suddenly given funds for scholarships. In particular, the once besieged campus of the University of Liberia experienced a visit from Doe, who contributed $100,000 to needy students—a gesture which he insisted was "humanitarian . . . . and not intended to win him popularity or votes." He also took advantage of the offer of clemency to Ellen Johnson-Sirleaf, who had been convicted of sedition in September, to release a number of students who had been detained under the notorious Decree 88A.

Doe also used the advantage of incumbency which came through the NDPL's monopoly over legislation during the transitional period. Just before the election, for example, Samuel Doe promised labor union leaders that his new government would seriously consider dropping the PRC Decree 12, which forbids strikes. Earlier Doe made one of his infrequent visits to Firestone Plantations to hear labor grievances, and subsequently dismissed his labor minister in a grandstand play, charging him with negligence in protecting the welfare of plantation workers. In an obvious appeal, moreover, to the Old Guard of the True Whig Party, in April 1985 Doe lifted the 1980 ban on social clubs and fraternal associations, including the Masonic Order, which had been a primary instrument of Whig political control during the First Republic.

The incumbent government's monopoly over the awarding of contracts and other benefits to members of the business community had already paid off in securing the affiliation of a number of politicians-turned-businessmen to the Doe cause. Several members of the Interim Assembly more than took advantage of the "mutuality of interests" by securing enormous credits from the Liberia Produce Marketing Corporation or concessions with respect to petroleum supplies, overlooked tax payments, and loans from the Liberia Petroleum Refining Corporation. When, at the insistence of the International Monetary Fund and other external advisors, the Doe government began to crack down on offenders and defaulters with respect to the numerous parastatals, the dragnet drew in officers of government close to Doe, members of the Interim Assembly, and a number of nongovernmental NDPL leaders. High on the list was Kekura Kpoto, the first national chairman of the NDPL, who owed $448,000 to the petroleum parastatal and an additional $1.5 million to other parastatals and government departments. Four other members of the Assembly—who could not be prosecuted because of their membership on that rump parliament—were Archibald Bernard, Jeffrey Gbatu, Phillip Deah, and John Bar-tuah. Conversely, the Liberian Business Caucus, which had been vocal in criticizing Doe's violations of civil rights, coercion of public servants to join the NDPL, abuse of the courts, and other obstacles to a speedy return to civilian rule, found themselves lamenting the virtual scrapping of the Liberianization policy with respect to business. More and more government business and contracts were being directed to Lebanese and other foreigners in a fashion reminiscent of the old True Whig strategy.[2]

In dealing with potential threats from the business community, the incumbent party also had a number of negative weapons in its arsenal. Doe's control over the Ministry of Justice and the courts permitted him to alternate between imposing or relaxing legal pressure against possible dissidents, thereby keeping them in line. Criminal charges, for example, were quietly dropped against erstwhile opponent Chea Cheapoo despite the magnitude of his alleged theft. Even more significant was the case of Oscar Quiah, discussed below. The politician-turned-businessman-turned-politician is a remarkable case of the co-operation of an opponent who went on to become the secretary general of the NDPL during the election campaign. A parallel case of politicial-turned-businessman-turned politician was Quiah's col-league, Kekura B. Kpoto, who became the national chairman of the NDPL.

Finally, one of the special advantages enjoyed by the incumbent party in a transition phase of politics is the ability to establish and enforce the electoral law. As one opposition candidate wearily complained during the long-drawn-out struggle to secure official registration for his party, "it is difficult to find ourselves in a game in which the referees are also players." The creation of the Special Elections Commission was not without precedent, given the history of the First Republic, and it was actually provided for in Articles 99 and 100 of the Sawyer draft con-stitution presented to the Liberian electorate in the 1984 referendum. Unfortunately, however, even before the 1985 campaign had commenced, the Doe-appointed SECOM had demonstrated its penchant for mischief. In the 1984 referendum on the constitution, for example, its first major error was to hold a referendum before there had been a proper voters registration list. Second, despite any prior consultation with Con-Com or the Constitutional Advisory Assembly, SECOM Chairman Harmon had decided that a majority of all registered voters would have to approve of the draft constitution before it could be adopted. (See chapter 15.) Only public protest compelled Doe and his commission to reverse themselves on this.

Under the manipulative hands of Harmon—a scion of the old settler elite, and a lawyer with much governmental experience in both the Tubman and Tolbert administrations—SECOM managed to use the tactics of delay and obfuscation to the fullest in preventing a number of parties from being registered. At each stage of the game, only the NDPL went through the hurdles without serious challenge from SECOM. The other parties either failed to qualify as officially registered participants, or, if they did qualify, they could either face the prospects of having that registration taken away from them or be confronted with a multitude of barriers to their functioning effectively in the same fashion as did the NDPL.

Instead of SECOM being either a nonpartisan or even a broadly representative body, membership was by appointment of the standard-bearer of one party only— the NDPL. Samuel Doe undoubtedly relied on advice from Harmon, and only bona fide NDPL supporters were selected for SECOM. Doe also unilaterally and without public explanation removed SECOM members who gave signs of being sympathetic to the registration efforts of any of the opposition parties. At one critical stage, midway in the registration process, the entire membership of SECOM changed, with the exception of its chairman. Indeed, although the new constitution explicitly directs that the membership of the Elections Commission be nonpartisan, that concept is alien to Doe: if you are not with him, you must automatically be considered "anti-Doe." At one point the partisan nature of SECOM was crassly revealed when the brother of Bai Gbala, the deputy secretary general of the NDPL, was named to the commission after the removal of several members who had demonstrated fair-mindedness in their treatment of several opposition parties.[3] It was this partisan institution, therefore, which determined which organizations would get through the registration process. In the absence of registration, all canvassing for votes, nomination of candidates, distribution of party literature, and any other form of participation in the October election campaign subjected the participant to criminal prosecution. The Special Elections Commission itself enjoyed judicial powers to find party leaders "in contempt of SECOM" and to fine the organization—as they did in the case of Baccus Matthew's United People's Party in April 1985.

The leaders of the five opposition parties that had survived several hurdles hoped that they could make common cause with the NDPL leadership and circumvent SECOM's taking total charge of the electoral process to their detriment. To the surprise of many observers, they succeeded in convening an all-party conference (including the NDPL) on 5 July 1985 to review all issues relating to a restoration of civilian rule. The UPP, LAP, and LPP leaders had taken the initiative, and it was felt that this conference could help moderate the level of rhetoric and action in opposing one another as well as explore areas of mutual cooperation. The discussion went remarkably well and it was decided that a second round of talks should be held. It was quickly realized by the NDPL, however, that continued cooperation would lead to its sacrificing the advantage of incumbency. At that point George Boley, Bai Gbala, and other NDPL leaders staged a well-publicized walkout. In any event, four of the parties (the LUP did not sign the final statement) set forth what they considered the ground rules for free and fair elections. This included equal access of the parties to public facilities and to government-controlled services such as radio, TV, and newspapers; absence of molestation of partisans and campaigners; excluding the flow of aliens from across the borders during the campaign; and party representation at the polling booths and during the counting of ballots. The four party leaders, however, could not establish a meaningful dialogue with SECOM regarding this agenda for a free and fair election.

### Coercion of the Opposition

The all-party conference was quite correct in anticipating that the Doe regime would not only continue to use the "carrot" but would increasingly resort to the "stick" in eliminating or emasculating their potential opposition. Indeed, in the period since the alleged lifting of the ban on political discussion in July 1984, the regime continued to resort to the hastily implemented Decree 88A which gave the Interim Assembly and the Doe party leadership a monopoly with respect to determining what was considered fair political comment and what, on the other hand, could get one labeled seditious and thus liable to extended detention without formal charges being leveled against one. If a trial was held (mostly as a consequence of overseas pressure), civilians were invariably tried by the Special Military Tribunal. One outrageous instance of this was the incarceration of the LPP's deputy chairman, Dusty Wolokollie, on 28 August 1984 for protesting the arrest of Amos Sawyer. He was ultimately tried and acquitted on 7 June 1985, only to be arrested on 18 July and detained for a further six weeks.

THE FISCAL REQUIREMENT

An additional mechanism designed to weaken formalized political opposition was devised by Doe's handpicked Special Elections Commission: a financial requirement was imposed upon any group seeking to register as a bona fide political party. On the face of it this seemed to be a straightforward and neutral mechanism. The posting of money or a surety bond to prevent frivolous participation in electoral campaigns has longstanding precedent in Great Britain and other Western democracies. The purpose of elections in a democratic society, after all, is to provide the electorate with alternative choices among leaders who are serious of purpose and have some demonstrated capacity to lead the people and organize a government. The electoral process should legitimately narrow the range of choice, not expand it ad infinitum by catering to the vanities of individuals who lack any credible constituency. In the Liberian case, however, one party—Doe's NDPL—had a distinct financial advantage, since it could tap at will the resources of government or pressure government employees for contributions to meet the unusually high deposit of $50,000 in cash and $100,000 in bonds or property. Private Liberians would find it difficult to quickly come up with that kind of financial backing. There was also the potential for harassment in the government attempting to investigate the source of any unusually large private contribution to a potential party. The financial requirement was an effective device used by SECOM in almost immediately eliminating five of the more spurious parties; but one of the last to secure the required registration funds, the Liberian Unification Party of Gabriel Kpolleh, turned out to be one of the four that actually competed and did secure a good share of the vote in certain constituencies during the October 1985 election. Finally, there was the "Catch 22" situation which only the NDPL was able to circumvent. I refer to the constant insistence by SECOM that no group of citizens could legally act as a party and start recruiting members or raising funds until it had been officially registered by SECOM. Yet, until it was an official party, few voters would want to contribute funds to get the group officially registered!

## LEGAL OBSTACLES

The second line which the Special Elections Commission devised to harass the opposition to the NDPL was the series of legal obstacles which either SECOM or the Doe-controlled courts employed in delaying or outright denying registration to the parties. The NDPL was the only party which cleared all hurdles without serious objections being entertained by SECOM. On the other hand, spurious charges were permitted to be lodged by NDPL partisans against the membership petitions of the five viable challengers when the latter presented their party applications. As an example of the extreme harrassment, the initial challenge to the Liberian Action Party's credentials occurred early in 1985. It was not until the very eve of the elections—after the case had been heard by SECOM, the Probate Court, and the Supreme Court—that the challenges were dismissed. In the interim LAP lost precious time needed not only to campaign but to present candidates for each of the constituencies in the House and Senate. An even longer delay confronted the Unity Party of Dr. Edward Kesselly, which had to cool its heels for eight months before securing official clearance from SECOM, because of outrageous charges filed by unnamed NDPL adherents in Bomi County regarding the validity of the UP's list of registered supporters. It was a war of attrition that the nit-picking Emmett Harmon played to the hilt, finding technicalities, devising and revising rules as he went along, and not even bothering to mask his partisanship.

## UNDERMINING OPPOSITION LEADERSHIP

A third line of assault was even more insidious than the legalistic hurdles. This was the undermining of the potential leadership cadre of the opposition parties. One sub-theme in this regard was the wooing away of opposition leaders through enticement. Oscar Quiah, Jr., for example, who had been a long-standing colleague of Baccus Matthews in the former Progressive People's Party and was slated to be secretary general in Matthews's United People's Party, suddenly found his numerous and enormous financial difficulties with the government over the payment of customs duties quietly resolved. Quiah very quickly "got religion" and opted for membership in the NDPL. His reward for the switch was to be named director-general of the Civil Service Agency, which gave him tight control over NDPL use of government patronage. Subsequently, he was elected as secretary general of NDPL, where he used his PPP experience in party organization to the advantage of NDPL. He also became—in the view of opponents—the "hatchet man" for Doe in the campaign.

If outright seduction of opposition leaders was insufficient, these leaders in many instances found themselves and their families subjected to harassment. Amos Sawyer, for example, had his house sprayed with gasoline and torched. Both he and Baccus Matthews were involved in a series of strange auto accidents. Other opposition leaders were subjected to arrest and detention on trumped-up charges. For example, following the alleged 1985 assassination attempt against Doe (on what skeptics quickly noted was April Fools' Day), Baccus Matthews of the United

People's Party, Edward Kesselly of the Unity Party, and Tuan Wreh and Harry Greaves of the Liberian Action Party were arrested, detained for a week, and subjected to public humiliation as well as destruction of their property. The alleged assassin, Lt. Col. Moses Flanzamaton, in his carefully coached interrogation, named the four leaders as co-conspirators. Realizing the flimsiness of the "evidence" and its numerous internal contradictions, the Doe government was forced to release the party leaders, and then proceeded to "convict" and speedily execute Flanzamaton by a secret firing squad (thereby eliminating possible embarrassment for the Doe group). No apology was extended to the four opposition leaders, and Doe suggested that "it would appear logical that aspiring politicians, in some instances may be connected with plots."[4]

In addition to the outright jailing of Amos Sawyer in August 1984 before the military storming of the University of Liberia campus, Sawyer and Edward Kesselly, the leader of the Unity Party, found themselves politically sidelined by Doe's declaring that the former chairmen of the Constitutional Committee and of the Constitutional Advisory Assembly, had not settled their financial accounts with the government at the end of their tenure. Since in Sawyer's case the accounts had been closed almost thirteen months previously and he had hired an independent auditor to go over the books of Con-Com at that time, the partisan nature of the charge was patently obvious. Indeed, the government did not actually announce the findings, which lifted the suspension order and cleared Sawyer of any wrongdoing, until three weeks after the October election. Kesselly had been cleared earlier and did run for the presidency on the UP ticket.

Even more personally vindictive was the continuing battle that Doe and the NDPL had had with Ellen Johnson-Sirleaf, the former minister of finance and an organizer of the Liberian Action Party. Indeed, the longstanding vendetta persisted well into the period following Samuel Doe's 1986 inauguration as president of the Second Republic. What precipitated the NDPL harassment was a speech which Johnson-Sirleaf had made in Philadelphia, Pennsylvania, on 6 July 1985 before a group of Liberians studying in America. Her speech—copies of which were immediately transmitted back to Monrovia—candidly and caustically analyzed the problems which Liberia had faced politically, socially, and economically since the coup. The one phrase which nettled the PRC was her statement that when "I look at the many idiots in whose hands our nation's fate and progress have been placed . . . I shake at the unnecessary and tremendous cost which we pay under the disguise of righting the wrongs of the past." Her indictment of the PRC government on the grounds of tribalism, nepotism, corruption, and incompetence led to her being placed under house arrest upon her return to Liberia and being charged with "sedition, criminal malevolence, and violation of sections 88 and 94 of the Uniform Code of Military Justice." Despite the international outcry, she was convicted on 13 September by the Special Military Tribunal and sentenced to ten years imprisonment at Belle Yellah Prison. Again, in the curious style of Liberian politics and justice, she thanked the court for having given her the chance to defend herself and then directed a plea to Samuel Doe for clemency. Ten days later—in response to overt U.S. congressional pressure, threatening to cut off U.S. aid—she was given clemency by Doe and released along with other political prisoners. Upon release, Ellen Johnson-Sirleaf began campaigning for one of the Senate seats from Montserrado County. She had been nominated as an LAP candidate several days earlier while still in prison. Despite the statement of Justice Minister Jenkins Scott challenging the legality of her candidacy, her victory was one of the few that SECOM dared not suppress in the fraudulent electoral count in October. The harassment of Ellen Johnson-Sirleaf was resumed, however, in the aftermath of the Quiwonkpa abortive coup of November 1985, and she remained in jail until June 1986.

DISQUALIFYING THE OPPOSITION

The legal harassment of political opposition leaders was complemented by a fourth, more ironic weapon used to discredit and disqualify opponents. This tactic was specifically employed against the two party leaders who had the strongest popular bases of support, G. Baccus Matthews and Amos Sawyer. Having with great struggle overcome the financial obstacle in the registration process, the United People's Party and its leader, G. Baccus Matthews, were declared by action of the Interim National Assembly at the end of August to be ineligible to participate in the election campaign, "because of espousal of and involvement in ideologies foreign to Liberia." The UPP's registration bonds and checks were returned to the party by SECOM, and its program was described by Harmon as "not only alien but detrimental to the peace and stability of the nation."[5] A parallel banning of the Liberian People's Party and of Amos Sawyer had taken place a month earlier for allegedly the same reasons: "strange and foreign ideologies against our most tested and matured of life [sic]."[6] Thus, Matthews, who had provided the groundwork for the easy acceptance of the 1980 coup and had twice served in highly significant posts in the Doe government, as well as Sawyer, who was one of the key framers of the new constitution under which the elections were being held, were barred from participation! The accusation against Matthews, brought by John Bartuah of the Interim Assembly and the NDPL, was particularly harsh, charging that Matthews was "a socialist and . . . trained saboteurs to engage in seditious activities against the state." Ironically, given the basis of legitimacy of the 1980 Doe coup which the 1979 Rice Riots had provided, Matthews and his cohorts were accused of criminal responsibility for the Rice Riots of 1979. The Assembly itself took this action because the Supreme Court—in a rare display of independence—had refused to take action on a spurious complaint brought earlier by Bartuah against Matthews.

The disqualifying of the two most popular challengers to Samuel Doe and of their respective parties was clearly not in accord with the new constitution, which in theory at least came into existence when it was promulgated in July of 1984. Nowhere in the document are the words "socialism" or "capitalism" expressly mentioned. It is ideologically neutral with regard to economic systems, although there are references to economic values, institutions, and policies. Registration of parties under the new constitution is only denied under Article 83 to "parties or organizations which, by reasons of their aims or the behavior of their adherents, seek to impair or abolish the free democratic society of Liberia or to endanger the existence of the Republic." No matter the "unconstitutionality" of the action by the Interim Assembly, its decision sidelined the two most effective campaigners against Doe. Sawyer remained in Monrovia, virtually under a form of house arrest, until early 1986. Matthews remained silent during the campaign and left Liberia following the elections and remained in America during the subsequent period undergoing medical treatment.

INSTITUTIONALIZING VIOLENCE

The crudest line of assault on the opposition parties came with respect to NDPL adherents as well as Doe-appointed officials themselves physically harassing both the leaders and the rank and file members of the opposition parties and obstructing the performance of local chapters of the Liberian Action Party, the Unity Party, and the Liberian Unification Party (particularly in the rural constituencies, but this also occurred in Monrovia). Two senatorial candidates of the opposition parties were so badly beaten that one of them, the UP candidate from Bong County, withdrew from the race. The second, the LAP candidate from Grand Gedeh, Doe's home area, courageously chose to continue the fight. Among the more publicized cases of physical abuse was the assault on a special emissary of Counsellor Emmanuel S. Kormah, vice-presidential candidate of the LAP; the emissary was beaten by soldiers and then stripped, bound by ropes, and left for dead ten days before the election. The LAP national chairman, Tuan Wreh, who had suffered much physical abuse under Tubman, was on several occasions during the transition period to civilian rule publicly humiliated by security forces and thugs associated with the NDPL.

There may be some truth to the charges that NDPL stalwarts also suffered physical and other forms of abuse at the hands of the opposition parties in areas where they were far stronger than the NDPL. The difference was that the NDPL had the total resources of government—including the military and the police— available to recruit partisans to their cause. Especially significant was the role of the Youth Wing of the NDPL—the so-called Special Task Force. This was a group of roughly 9,000 largely urban unemployed youngsters (as well as a number recruited from Sierra Leone) organized by the NDPL chairman, Kekura B. Kpoto. There were numerous reported instances from around the country of violence perpetrated by the Special Task Force, as well as by soldiers, in the weeks preceding the October election. Despite NDPL Secretary General Quiah's insistence that the Special Task Force was not armed, on 3 October the offices of *Footprints Today* were stormed by thirteen burly young men wearing NDPL t-shirts who threatened with chains and batons to destroy the offices and equipment "if the paper does not stop publishing bad things about us."[7] During the campaign the Special Task Force disrupted opposition rallies and ransacked houses of non-NDPL leaders in the hinterland. In addition to these party-associated groups, local Doe-appointed officials used or abused their official powers to obstruct the opposition. Even SECOM recognized, for example, that the activities of the superintendent of Grand Gedeh County, Colonel Johnny Garley, were blatant in his harassment of Grebo and other non-Krahn voters. SECOM had publicly to order him a week before the election to release all UP and LAP leaders and followers whom he had arrested and to cease the illegal searches of their homes. Opposition candidates had been beaten and their lives threatened by soldiers acting on the instructions of the superintendent in Doe's home county.

## OBSTACLES TO OPPOSITION CAMPAIGNING

Doe also made it difficult for opposition candidates to campaign in their home areas, by requiring that parties must first secure permission to do so from the Ministry of Internal Affairs and the local superintendent. As a consequence, public facilities were in most instances reserved for NDPL use only, and permission to campaign was denied to the LAP, UP, and LUP local chapters even when meeting on private property. A simple gathering in Kakata for local Unity Party supporters to welcome their candidates was broken up by order of the superintendent on the grounds that it constituted a "secret" meeting. In another instance, the Liberian Action Party was required to forgo any campaigning in Margibi County on the day that Samuel Doe would be passing through the area.

Some indication of the potential for violence in the election was the statement of Justice Minister Jenkins Scott, a week before the election, suggesting that any presidential candidate who felt he needed police protection could get it. "Of course," he added, "if I were any of them, I would not ask for protection because this is my country . . . a peaceful country governed by law under which every citizen is given equal protection in accordance with the law." And the candidate would have to give "tangible reasons" why he needed the protection.[8]

Of a more general nature, the threats to the general public made by Doe's colleagues regarding the outcome of the election also cast a pall over the campaign. At the outset of the actual campaigning in mid-August, Defense Minister Major Gray D. Allison (a close advisor of Doe and one of the few who had continued in the cabinet in one capacity or another since the coup) warned that the Liberians should "not take the army for granted." He indicated that "as long as you want to bring chaos in this country, we will break you down, no matter who you are."

On election day itself, Colonel Harrison Pennue, one of the original seventeen participants in the 1980 coup and a member of the Interim Assembly, gave a radio interview in which he stated that if any party other than NDPL won, he was prepared to overthrow it within three days. In the interview, which was broadcast repeatedly that day over the government radio station, Pennue said in pidgin English: "Who want to win, I am not dead. I will overthrow you. I still a leopard. When we started 1980 nobody asked us to vote. We did it ourselves. We know we will win."[9] Next day he claimed he was "misquoted"! An embarrassed Doe regime attempted quickly to disavow the statement and put distance between itself and one whom his colleagues had often called "one of the crazies in our midst."

## Manipulation of the Electoral Rules of the Game

Having succeeded in narrowing the field of opponents to the NDPL, the Special Elections Commission next attempted to manage and manipulate the rules of the election itself. In this it found itself in a confrontational position with the three opposition parties and even with respect to NDPL on one issue—the counting of the votes. The first debate turned on the question of who were bona fide candidates and who were properly registered voters. With respect to the latter, the opposition complained in mid-September that despite SECOM's intention to have a list of qualified voters available 75 to 90 days before the election, no voter role had yet been compiled a month before the election, thus giving the opposition little opportunity of challenging the authenticity of the list.

The question of who would be legal candidates also troubled the opposition—particularly the Liberian Action Party and the Unity Party, which had only secured recognition a little over a month before the election. Since the parties were required to submit their list to SECOM, there was the implied threat that the commission could remove "unqualified candidates." Obviously this category already included G. Baccus Matthews, Amos Sawyer, and Ayun Cassell (a former member of the Interim Assembly, removed for reasons which were not made public at the time of his banning in May 1985). But the more critical issue was the senatorial candidacy of Ellen Johnson-Sirleaf, who had been convicted of sedition. Although she had been given clemency, Attorney General Scott attempted to force SECOM to declare her ineligible. On that point the Doe regime failed, and perhaps it made it easier for all other candidates to be accepted, whether or not they had served time in prison on political charges. She campaigned with vigor. Then, after having frustrated the three opposition parties in registration, Bai Gbala, NDPL campaign manager, criticized the challenging parties for not having compiled their candidate list after consultation with people all over the country.

A second issue related to the date of the elections. Originally the elections were to be held in two stages, with legislative contests to take place on 8 October, followed by the presidential election on 5 November. On the grounds that it would be far less expensive (and suspecting that legislative losses by NDPL in the Senate and House would make it more difficult for Doe to capture the presidency), the Interim Assembly, in a surprise decision, chose to consolidate all elections on 15 October. The UP, the LUP, and the LAP all found themselves at a severe disadvantage because of the interminable and protracted struggle over securing official registration. The Liberian Action Party, in particular, had less than six weeks to hold a convention, nominate candidates, clear them with SECOM, and campaign. Hence the LAP leaders' requested that the combined elections be delayed to 19 November to give it sufficient time to field candidates for every office. This request was speedily denied, with Harmon suggesting that it was up to LAP to act with dispatch and not waste further time arguing for an extension! The best that the LAP and the UP could do was field a list of 73 candidates for the 90 legislative seats (26 senatorial and 64 representative positions).

A third issue dealt with the presence of international observers at the Liberian elections. Jackson Doe—recognizing the advantages to the opposition—contended that it would be a "fraternal" gesture to invite observers from democracies elsewhere, and it should not be resented by those in Liberia who were committed to democracy. Kesselly of the Unity Party went even further and insisted that it seemed to be mandated since the United States in particular not only had provided $350,000 toward the electoral process but at that moment was bound by a "sense of the Congress" resolution which had linked continuation of U.S. aid to Liberia's performance in the area of civil rights and the holding of free and fair elections. Kesselly also noted that in spite of the history of Liberian independence, it has been almost a century since Liberia had had a genuinely effective multiparty system and thus it would profit by the presence of friendly international observers.

On this issue, however, Samuel Doe and his colleagues were adamant that having official observers would constitute a violation of Liberian sovereignty—even though journalists and other unofficial observers were welcome. Justice Minister Jenkins Scott insisted that "Liberians must be left alone to decide for themselves the leadership they want."[10] In hindsight, key U.S. senators and representatives on the respective foreign policy committees of Congress appreciated that their failure to insist on official observer status was a critical error (and one which they did not repeat when it came to the Philippines elections three months later). Failure to send official U.S. observers complicated the task of holding Samuel Doe and the NDPL accountable with respect to implementing the congressional resolution.

A final issue relating to electoral procedures turned out to be the most critical, namely, whether party representatives were to be present both during the actual polling and—most important of all—during the counting of the ballots. It appeared that the SECOM chairman's pronouncement on 8 September that parties would not be able to participate in either function caught even the NDPL leadership off guard and immediately prompted a caustic dissenting opinion from Doe's justice minister, Jenkins Scott. Ultimately Harmon backtracked with respect to party representation at the polling stations, but he proved to be unyielding regarding the counting of the ballots. Based upon a total misconception of the process of ballot counting in Western democracies, Harmon insisted that party representation violated the secrecy of the vote; it left SECOM "with nothing to do"; and it was contrary to the model of the United States, "where the Federal Elections Commission counted the ballots while invited guests stood outside and observed through a window." Above all, he insisted, it impugned the integrity of the Special Elections Commission itself, whose members, after all, "would be acting under oath."

The opposition party leaders were quick to point out that Harmon's ruling violated even the electoral law promulgated a year previously by the PRC in advance of the referendum on the constitution. Even the NDPL representative at the SECOM meeting was not mollified by Harmon's simplistic justifications. So heated did the controversy become after the meeting that the Unity Party, the Liberian Action Party, and the Liberian Unification Party on 26 September issued a joint communiqué threatening to boycott the elections if they could not have party representatives present at both stages in all constituencies where they had fielded candidates. Harmon vacillated for close to two weeks; the NDPL leaders alternatively "lamented" and chided the opposition for their threatened boycott; ultimately internal and external pressure forced the SECOM chairman to capitulate. But he did so in his characteristic fashion by insisting that party representatives had to observe the ballot count from a distance of 25 feet! Realizing that they could observe nothing from that distance—particularly at night when the ballot count would commence—Albert Porte denounced the move as contrary to the spirit of the election law. The controversy persisted another five days before Harmon conceded that a 15-foot distance might be more reasonable. The boycott was thus averted.

## Election Day 1985

When election day arrived, on 15 October, it was hailed by Samuel Doe as a historic event, and he congratulated the Liberian people on their orderly exercise of their democratic right and their peaceful conduct in putting a cap on the five and a half year process of restoring civilian rule. These sentiments were echoed by the U.S. State Department spokesman on the day of the election and—incredibly—were still the persistent line of Assistant Secretary of State Chester A. Crocker almost two months after the event. Speaking before the Senate Subcommittee on African Affairs in December 1985 (where this author was one of the other expert witnesses), Crocker stated that "election day went off very well, indeed. There is now the beginning, however imperfect, of a democratic experience that Liberia and its friends can use as a benchmark for future elections—one on which they want to build."[11] Crocker was almost effusive in calling this a "rare achievement in Africa and elsewhere in the Third World," since more than one party had competed and newspapers had covered the activities of all parties.

To a certain extent, these analyses were correct—but *only* to a certain extent. The popular enthusiasm was certainly there, with an estimated 900,000 out of an estimated 2 million citizens actually registered, with somewhere between an estimated 520,000 (by SECOM's count) to 800,000 (an unofficial count) voters actually exercising their right of suffrage. People had started lining up hours before the polls opened, and many were obliged to stand in long lines in the hot sun for six or seven hours awaiting their turn to vote. And yet it was the consensus of journalists and other observers that through most of the day good humor prevailed in most constituencies. Indeed, the massive turnout compelled SECOM to extend the poll closing hour from 6 P.M. to 11 P.M. Despite the bitter controversy that had raged for months between SECOM and the opposition party leaders, most reporters commented on the competency of the SECOM staff in the actual conduct of the election. The staff had obviously profited from their eighteen months of training and particularly from the "dry run" the year previously during the referendum on the constitution. Indeed, one of the disruptive incidents that day was in reality an exercise in democracy—namely, the near riot which occurred at the City Hall voting place when several of Doe's cabinet ministers and other officials attempted to break into the queue to cast their ballots. Out of respect, people had earlier let Samuel Doe cast the first ballot of the day at the booth set up on the steps of City Hall, but the later intrusion of his cronies brought forth the complaint that this was no time ''for big shot business since this was a national holiday.'' It took three hours to restore order, but the principle of equality had prevailed.

The enthusiasm, euphoria, and initial reports of generally good conduct aside, it became increasingly apparent as the day wore on that irregularities—if not outright fraud and coercion—had occurred. The reported incidents may have been, as the NDPL spokesmen immediately pointed out, abuses committed by the other three parties in constituencies where they were strong. But few observers agreed with Chester Crocker's blithe generalization that there were ''irregularities on all sides'' (a kind of evenhandedness in dealing with abuses by right-wing dictatorships which the Reagan administration repeated in the case of the fraudulent Philippines elections in January 1986). Clearly the weaponry of abuse was stacked heavily in favor of Samuel Doe's party, and they were not about to surrender the advantages of incumbency lightly. Much of the reported abuse on election day focused on the military itself. Not only were there numerous reported cases of intimidation by soldiers, some of whom compelled people in rural constituencies to shout out their electoral choices as they dropped their ballots into the appropriate boxes. Even more surprising were the polling booths which were set up at Barclay Training Center and other military installations which had not been officially listed as polling stations. There were frequent reports at the military bases of multiple voting, of children casting ballots along with their parents, of failure to ink the hands of military voters to prevent multiple voting, and of the barring of civilian opposition party observers from the military stations. Few objective observers were willing to accept the explanation of Francis Horton, the vice-chairman of NDPL, that his party ''had nothing to do with the army; they are not in fact official partisans of the NDPL.''[12]

Even earlier, there were reports that the Special Elections Commission had ordered many more ballots from the London printer than there were registered voters. There was also the ruling by SECOM that no provision would be made for absentee ballots (on the assumption that those in exile were opposed to Doe), which was a blow particularly to the LAP. There was the further problem that the parties had only a little more than a week to examine and challenge the accuracy of the voter registration list rather than the ninety days which SECOM itself had established. Finally, some of the ballots were reported to have photographs of Samuel Doe imposed upon them, as a way of guiding the illiterate voters in their choice. Harmon refused to probe any of the alleged abuses of NDPL; instead his public comments focused on alleged abuses by the three opposition parties.

### The "Slow Count"

Egregious as some of the electoral violations on election day may have been, they were relegated to the sidelines in the wake of the controversy over the counting of the ballots. Although SECOM insisted that it was to have total control over the process, it could not prevent optimistic speculation and less-than-scientific polling techniques crowding it from center stage. An NDPL official was one of the first to engage in premature announcements by claiming victory for his party in six of the thirteen counties. Action Party leaders, using the American technique of "exit poll samples," countered with reports that NDPL was losing badly all over the country, including Doe's home county of Grand Gedeh. Many voters, LAP spokesmen stated, had come out of the polling stations in Monrovia shouting "Action—Kokolioko," the slogan for his party.

Once the counting of ballots had commenced in earnest late that evening and early the next morning, it was apparent that the exit poll predictions of the Liberian Action Party were proving to be highly accurate. The tally sheets being tabulated by the party representative observers showed that the LAP was forging ahead in both the presidential and the legislative races in all but Bong County (which found the Unification Party in the lead), Grand Gedeh (where Doe's NDPL was well ahead), and two counties in which there were seesaw struggles taking place, between the NDPL and Kpolleh's Liberian Unification Party in Margibi County, and between the NDPL and Unity Party in Bomi County. No clear cut results, however, were in from Lofa, where Dr. Moniba was expected to pull the NDPL ahead, or from Sinoe. In fact so confident were the various sources of information of an LAP landslide that an American journalist, Chuck Powell, who was intervewed on BBC, stated categorically that reliable reports suggested a 60 percent landslide victory for the Action Party over all competitors. The next day, Secretary-General Byron Tarr of the LAP upped the figure to 70 percent. Both of these estimates were quickly denied by the minister of information, but there tended to be a measure of accuracy to the reports, given the response of the government to the actions of one member of SECOM, Emmanuel Shaw. Shaw had circulated several of the tallies which had been signed by party representatives who had witnessed the counting of ballots, and they confirmed the Liberian Action Party's general lead. He was arrested and charged with sedition.

Three weeks later—after much controversy—the LAP's "authentic results," based on reports from poll watchers from all parties (including the NDPL), indicated that the LAP had taken eight countries, the NDPL took Grand Gedeh, the LUP took Bong County, with no reliable count from either Lofa or Sinoe counties. What percentage of votes each party got will probably never be known, inasmuch as the counting of ballots was interrupted by Harmon after his visits to a few polling stations had indicated conclusively that the elections were going badly for Doe's party. Using various arguments to justify his actions, he halted the count in the early hours of October 16. His action was based on his claims that the party representatives had failed to observe the 15-foot rule on observation; that lower echelon workers in SECOM had been bribed by the LAP to falsify the results; that government officials, NDPL workers, and others had been harassed by the LAP and other party representatives during the ballot count; that the party representatives had violated their pledge not to reveal vote counts prematurely; and that the opposition parties had given too much assistance to illiterate voters in terms of steering them away from the NDPL. Not only was the counting interrupted, but ballot boxes from all over the country were ordered to be transported to the government's Unity Conference Center on the outskirts of Monrovia. And adding still another bizarre chapter to an already impossible saga, ballots were to be counted by an ad hoc committee of fifty citizens handpicked by Harmon. Despite the absence in law or precedent, Harmon insisted that the committee was nonpartisan, broadly representative of the country as a whole, and included representatives of the journalistic, religious, and business communities. There was an immediate denial from leaders of the Liberian Press Union, the Council of Religious Leaders, the Muslim Council, and the Business Caucus that there had even been consultation with their respective organizations, let alone selection of members to serve on the ad hoc committee. Instead of being broadly representative of the country, twenty of the fifty members were from Grand Gedeh, nineteen of whom were Krahn. There was no membership from the three opposition parties, but two senior aides to Doe as well as wives and other relatives of cabinet members and members of the Interim Assembly could be identified in the list—people who had openly supported the NDPL. None of the ad hoc committee members had any demonstrated experience in electoral procedures.

The arbitrary actions of the Elections Commission were immediately given legal reinforcement by the threats of Justice Minister Scott to prosecute anyone who made public comment on the "slow count" until it had been officially completed, reviewed by SECOM, and validated by the Interim National Assembly. Samuel Doe threatened with twenty-five lashes anyone who insulted him or his officials. To guarantee that there would be no credibility given to challengers, the count was to take place in secret.

Getting the ballots from remote polling districts took time. There were many reports by citizens of finding burned ballots strewn along highways in Margibi and other counties. The procedures for transporting ballots to Monrovia invariably involved entrusting them to the care of one of Doe's county superintendents. There were other strange developments regarding counting procedures. For example, it took almost a week to count the estimated first 45 percent of the ballots, then suddenly the remaining 55 percent were counted in three days.

Predictably, when the "official" results were announced on October 29, Samuel Doe had eked out a 50.9 percent victory in the four-way race for the presidency. His party, the NDPL, took 21 of 26 seats in the Senate and 51 of the 64 seats in the House of Representatives. Harmon—claiming no remorse of conscience—said the vote count "was directed by the hand of God." The battle over the election, of course, was far from over. Four days earlier Jackson Doe of the Liberian Action Party had delivered a lengthy and very eloquent speech to his supporters, which many regarded as his "victory speech." The full text was published in the independent press on the day that SECOM announced the electoral "results." On these very shaky grounds the Second Republic was about to be established.

# XX.

# Challenges to the Legitimacy of the Second Republic

On 6 January 1986 Samuel Kanyon Doe was inaugurated as the first civilian president under the Constitution of the Second Republic. The day which was to have signaled a milestone in the history of Liberia's long quest for democracy had arrived. Yet, instead of it being the day of celebration and rejoicing that had been anticipated during the more than five and a half years of transition from military to civilian rule, it was a somber day indeed. The honored guests (including a pointedly low-level official delegation from the United States) and even many of those who had voted for Doe and the NDPL realized that the election of the preceding October had not been a fair one. The challenges to the legitimacy of the Second Republic had been immediate once the election "results" had been announced by SECOM on 29 October, and they became bloody and filled with acrimony in the ensuing two months leading up to the inauguration.

Few Liberians or outsiders had been deceived by the announcement on 29 October 1985 that Doe had won the presidency by a margin of 50.9 percent. Admittedly, it was not the usual 90-plus percent that most autocrats in the Third World invariably award themselves in carefully controlled elections, but it was explainable in the Liberian context. First of all, it would not have been sufficient to have achieved a mere plurality over his three opponents, since under the new constitution a majority vote is required. A runoff a week later between the two leading candidates (neither one of which may have been Samuel Doe) would have permitted the opposition to consolidate their strength. On the other hand, to have claimed a victory of 80 or 90 percent would have been so far from the realm of the believable that Samuel Doe would have been laughed out of court. Hence the finely tuned results of 50.9 percent cleverly gave the appearance of a hard-fought campaign which had nevertheless produced a clear democratic majority for Samuel K. Doe. Few—other than the U.S. Department of State—bought that argument.[1] The NDPL, through its agent

SECOM, was not as prepared to be so generous with the opposition, however, when it came to allocating seats in the Senate and House of Representatives. Doe's 51 percent electoral majority was mysteriously transformed into control of 84 percent of the legislative seats by the NDPL.

There were clear indications that the NDPL was aware of the public's awareness of the fraud. On the night the results were announced the government—in what must have been a tongue-in-cheek explanation—forbade demonstrations, "out of fear that the jubilation might get out of hand." It was almost three days, moreover, before Doe ventured to appear in public, and at that it was in the relative security of the Executive Mansion grounds before NDPL partisans. At that point, having run roughshod over the opposition, Doe then had the temerity to appeal to the three defeated parties to "bear patience," because, as he put it—in reference to his new term of office—"six years is not too much." Arrogant in his triumph over his opponents, he called for a government of national unity in which all Liberians would forget the past and work for the reconstruction of the country. As a first step, the opposition should accept the seats they had been allotted in the Legislature "for the good of the country." "I have nothing against anybody," he stated, "and I stand ready to work for generations yet unborn." Once again, being his own worst enemy, however, Doe's efforts at conciliation were balanced off with threats to those disgruntled elements (particularly in the business community) who might compel him reluctantly to heed the anxious demands of those who cry "No more elections."[2]

## Challenging the Electoral Results

The proposal for a government of national unity under the NDPL's leadership was rejected in turn by the leaders of each of the opposition parties. This was quickly followed on 5 November by a joint LAP, UP, and LUP communiqué which provided a detailed and thoroughly documented "indictment" regarding the activities of SECOM, the military, and the NDPL partisans during the campaign. Despite the presentation of their complaints to the registrar of SECOM being publicized in all three independent newspapers (*Footprints Today, Sun Times*, and the *Daily Star*), Emmett Harmon once more engaged in the formalism reminiscent of his True Whig past by "categorically denying that SECOM had received any official complaints of electoral violations." He did so, it turned out, because the registrar had not been officially authorized to receive such documents; and the registrar's transgression in accepting the documents had led to his dismissal!

The next challenge to the legitimacy of the electoral results came with the individual and collective decision of the opposition parties to forbid their party candidates from assuming the legislative seats which SECOM had conceded to them. It was argued by the leadership of the three parties that acceptance of the seats would compromise the will of the people, legitimize the fraudulent election tactics and results, relegate the opposition to a position of subservience, and mortgage the sovereignty of the Liberian people to the personal ambition of the candidates who had been given the token seats.[3] Refusal to accept the seats took on added significance following the arbitrary arrests and detention of party leaders after the November 12 coup attempt in which former general Thomas Quiwonkpa challenged the Doe regime. The boycott of the Legislature became an additional form of protest to the detention of opposition leaders. To the chagrin of the NDPL leadership, which wished to maintain the facade of a multiparty system without the substance, the threatened boycott could have presented them with the one-party state they secretly desired but could not afford to have—given their dependence on American and other foreign aid. Thus, they alternatively threatened, lamented, and cajoled in an effort to frustrate the efforts at solidarity on the part of the opposition. The bizarre minidrama within the broader controversy over opposition seating focused on Ellen Johnson-Sirleaf, who even SECOM had to acknowledge had won one of the senatorial seats for Montserrado County. Since Johnson-Sirleaf had recently been convicted of sedition, the justice minister protested her election and the immigration commissioner denied her an exit visa for a proposed trip to the United States after the election. She steadfastly refused, however, to take the seat in the Senate and thus created an embarrassing dilemma for the NDPL.

The legislative boycott was further complicated by the *volte-face* on the part of the Christian church leadership with respect to the elections. Episcopal Bishop George Browne and others had been highly critical of the Elections Commission and Doe during the campaign preliminaries, and several religious leaders had stridently denounced Emmett Harmon and SECOM for having failed the Liberian people through their mishandling of the election and the ballot counting. In the face of the potential breakdown in order which the legislative boycott presented, however, several clerics pointedly reminded the opposition partisans that "corrupt elections are part of our national history; we cannot change them no matter how hard we try."[4] One who was particularly vigorous in urging the LAP, UP, and LUP to forget the past was Peter Amos George, pastor of the Providence Baptist Church. Pointedly, Samuel Doe switched his membership to George's church several days after the delivery of the sermon.

The legislative boycott also split the leadership ranks within the three opposition parties. Despite the official stance of the executive committees of the three parties, threatening to expel any "selected" candidate who accepted his or her seat, James Kaihoun, a LUP House candidate from Margibi County was the first to break ranks. Ultimately, by February 1986, thirteen of the eighteen non-NDLP candidates had accepted their legislative posts. The acrimony within the parties was deep—particularly on the part of the leadership that had been detained without charges after the November 12 Quiwonkpa attempted coup. They felt a keen sense of betrayal. Their anger was in particular directed against Tuan Wreh, the national chairman of the Liberian Action Party, who had considerably advanced the fortunes of his party in the campaign and who had strong personal credentials as a victim of Whig oppression. But his constant tergiversations with respect to the rejection or acceptance of his senate seat from Grand Kru County and his conflicts with his LAP colleagues made him a tragicomic figure of considerable dimension. The videotaped meeting between Wreh and Samuel Doe and his colleagues found him literally groveling and asking forgiveness for "the poor country boy that he was." Although his formal expulsion from the Action Party was later reversed, he was nevertheless stripped of his chairmanship of the party. Thus, each of the thirteen non-NDPL members of the Legislature was compelled to serve as an independent rather than a representative of the party that had elected him.

The first stage of the domestic challenge to the NDPL's claim that it was ushering in Liberia's first real experiment in democracy came to an abrupt halt on 12 November 1985. The Quiwonkpa attempted coup not only failed to accomplish its ultimate goal, but it further frustrated the ability of the opposition groups to sustain a concerted and unified attack on the legitimacy of the Second Republic.

## The Quiwonkpa Abortive Coup

Most coups and attempted coups in Africa are led by personalities who are relatively unknown to the general public, and hence if the coup is regarded as a "popular" one, it is largely because of the very unpopularity of the regime which is being displaced. In that sense, the attempted coup of 12 November 1985 was significantly different. The man who undertook the strike against the regime "that stole the election" was well known within the ranks of the military as well as among the civilian population in general. Thomas Quiwonkpa was one of the original PRC members who had carried out the coup of 12 April 1980. Early, however, in his role as commanding general of the army he had distinguished himself by his stern measures in restoring order to troops who had lost discipline in the aftermath of the coup and were attempting to bring about an instant "status reversal" by seizing the vehicles, homes, and other properties of the wealthier class. Quiwonkpa had managed to put distance between himself and his fellow PRC members by remaining a "soldier's soldier," avoiding the ostentatious lifestyle and the acquisitions of wealth that had characterized the PRC in general. He preferred to live at the barracks and to drive himself in a jeep. Of equal importance, he had endeared himself to a broad spectrum of the civilian populace by his constant haranguing of his colleagues regarding official corruption and his insistence that there must be no significant deviation from the timetable for reestablishing civilian rule. When his conflict with Samuel Doe over the latter issues led to Quiwonkpa's removal from office in November 1983 and his eventual exile in America, he had become almost a legendary figure, viewed by many Liberians as a healthy alternative to Doe in presiding over the transition to civilian rule. In the interim since his flight from Liberia, he had been receiving high school and college education in America and had largely remained silent except for an interview he gave to a London-based journalist early in 1985.

Thus, in the midst of the postelection despair, the announcement in the early morning hours of 12 November over the Liberian broadcasting system that "patriotic forces under the command of General Quiwonkpa had toppled the Doe regime" was greeted with unrestrained jubilation. Pictures of Samuel Doe were stripped from the walls, and a holiday atmosphere prevailed in Monrovia and other centers, with demonstrators carrying huge posters with enlarged photographs of Thomas Quiwonkpa. The sincerity of the response is perhaps attested to by the depth of mourning that greeted the failure of the coup and the death and mutilation of the coup leader himself a few days later. Even the full-page ads which merchants, party sycophants, and others took out in the local press congratulating Doe on his success in putting down the coup almost reverently referred to the coup leader as "the Former Late Commanding General Thomas G. Quiwonkpa." Sermons in the churches later that week were as much eulogies for Quiwonkpa as they were the prayers of thanksgiving for Doe's survival that Doe had intended them to be when he called for a special day of prayer.

The failure of the coup demonstrated that good intentions and popularity are not sufficient to topple a regime that has become well equipped to monopolize the use of force in society and that has become pleased with the enjoyment of the perquisites of power. Delay in establishing total control over the communciations system was one of the fatal flaws in the coup attempt: Doe was able to counter Quiwonkpa's early morning victory claim with an announcement later in the day that he was still in charge. This caused many of the civilian revelers to have second thoughts about pressing their assaults on the homes and persons of officials and the NDPL party leaders. Even more important, it led many of the potentially mutinous army troops who were emotionally committed to their old commander to back off from supporting what could be a losing cause. The second fatal flaw was the reluctance on the part of Quiwonkpa to "go for the jugular vein" and carry out a frontal assault on the Executive Mansion itself. This gave Doe time for his Krahn-dominated Executive Guard and for the First Infantry Battalion to arrive from Camp Schieffelin to put down the revolt. Quiwonkpa and his handful of co-conspirators had spent a good part of the day sitting around or rushing back and forth across town in efforts that were meaningless relative to the main objective of eliminating Doe's base of military support.[5]

Had Quiwonkpa succeeded in his efforts and had he been correctly quoted as pledging to maintain order for a brief period of three months before turning over the reins of power to Jackson Doe and the Liberian Action Party (which most observers had judged to be the real winners of the October elections), then the long-sought objective of democratic rule in Liberia might have been achieved. But failure of the coup attempt created a whole new set of problems, not the least of which were complications in Liberia's foreign relations. Since the Quiwonkpa forces were correctly perceived as having come from Sierra Leone, where they had been re-cruited and trained, relations between Liberia and Sierra Leone were severely strained. The border was—as Doe announced—"permanently closed"; the Liberian secretary general of the Mano River Union was recalled; and the level of hostile rhetoric between the leaders of the two states escalated. It was also charged that the Ivory Coast had been a source of recruitment for rebels. Even more significant than Doe's quarrel with his two neighbors, the extent of involvement in the Qui-wonkpa coup by the United States, Doe's primary source of economic assistance, became and continues to remain suspect. The role that American military and political advisors to Quiwonkpa had played in the United States, in Sierra Leone, and in Liberia itself with respect to the coup has never been fully explicated. The part that Israeli intelligence played in alerting Doe or the First Infantry Battalion with regard to the Quiwonkpa coup also remains uncertain. It surely had implications for Israel's long-range efforts to achieve diplomatic recognition elsewhere in Africa, and also cast further doubt about the relationship between America and Israeli intelligence linkages, which had been compromised by the Jay Pollard spy case in the United States.

Important as the foreign implications were in the long run, the failure of the coup created far more serious problems for Liberians themselves. The odious—and much abused—curfew was reintroduced, as were roadblocks on the up-country highway. The fact, moreover, that Quiwonkpa had indicated that he was not interested in power for himself but wanted to turn over the reins of government to the NDPL opposition gave Samuel Doe all the excuse that he needed to immobilize the leadership of the opposition parties. Although the Liberian Action Party was the primary target, with Jackson Doe, Ellen Johnson-Sirleaf, and others being detained without charges well beyond the inauguration, the leaders of the Unity Party and the Liberian Unification Party were also taken into "protective custody" for several weeks until Samuel Doe was convinced that they posed no direct threat. Samuel Doe also used the occasion to institute a ban on the Press Union of Liberia, the National Union of Liberian Teachers, the National Student Union, the Liberian Business Caucus, and other groups that had been critical of him in the past. His assaults on the news media, moreover, included not only threats to the independent newspapers but the arrest and death (many critics have labeled it officially sanctioned murder) of Editor-in-Chief Charles Gbenyon of govermment-owned radio station LBS, who had unfortunately been at the station during Quiwonkpa's initial announcement of the coup.

Ironically, one of the unanticipated consequences of the coup's failure was the erosion of the very unity and discipline within the military ranks for which Quiwonkpa had once been applauded. Many troops who had been at the Barclay Training Center (one of the few installations the rebels had captured) were held for trial. Others within the army who were Gio (Dan), the ethnic group from which both Quiwonkpa and Jackson Doe came, were subjected to harassment. And at the top level, General Morris Zaza, who had succeeded Quiwonkpa in November 1983 as commanding general, was subjected to a public trial because of his alleged involvement in the coup attempt. Others appointed by Quiwonkpa to posts within the military before 1983 were also purged. But worst of all, the once disciplined troops resorted to the extortion and harassment of civilians that had characterized their behavior in the wake of the 1980 coup. Not only active opposition leaders, such as Byron Tarr, but also respected civilian elder statesmen, such as Rudolph Grimes, were physically abused by troops and their properties destroyed. Krahn soldiers, moreover, in one of the worst manifestations of the "new tribalism" (see chapter 18) were given almost carte blanche to carry out a brutal campaign against the Gio and Mano areas of Nimba County, where the support for Jackson Doe and Quiwonkpa was the strongest. Charges of ethnic genocide toward the Gio were being raised against the Krahn within the military. Although the government tightly controlled movement along the major roads leading into the area, reports of whole villages being destroyed by undisciplined Krahn troops continued to filter down to Monrovia.

It was obvious during the attempted coup that Samuel Doe lacked broad-based civilian support and that the military displayed not loyalty, but rather a "wait and see" attitude toward the Doe regime during the Quiwonkpa coup. It was equally apparent, however, that Doe had the necessary armed support required to stay in power. Thus, the most serious consequence of the Quiwonkpa affair is that it demonstrated that hopes of a military solution to the Doe dictatorship had been preempted for a considerable time to come.

### The External Factor: "The Special Relationship"

Quite apart from whether it was in the best interest of the American or the Liberian people, one consequence of the 1980 coup and its aftermath was that the long-standing "special relationship" had become intensified during five and a half years rather than weakened. The efforts of the Tubman and Tolbert regimes to diminish that relationship had been welcomed by Washington, which had many more interests in Africa to be served now that independence had come to some forty-five states in the sub-Saharan region (see chapter 9). The 1980 coup terminated those efforts to reduce the American dominant presence, as West Europeans and others who had previously engaged in expanding trade, investment, and economic aid relationships with Liberia increasingly tended to regard that country as "an American responsibility." From an initial reaction of surprise and horror to the events of April 1980, the United States reluctantly took on the task of bailing out the very fragile regime from its deepening problems of international debts, inflation, trade balance deficits, and meeting government monthly payrolls. From a level of $20 million in aid in 1979, by 1985–86 the level of U.S. aid had grown to $90-plus million. Roughly half a billion dollars over a five-year period had been a major factor in keeping the Doe regime afloat. The United States provided over $14 million annually for military training, facilities, and other forms of assistance—much of which may have been needed to improve the prestige of the Liberian military as a corporate group and to make it a "satisfied" element in a future civilian-dominated society.

As long as the PRC and Doe remained committed to a program of democratic reform, that aid was welcomed by a broad spectrum of Liberian society. It was, moreover, regarded as an acceptable financial burden by those in the U.S. executive and legislative branches who wished not only to preserve the American economic, diplomatic, and other links with Liberia discussed in earlier chapters, but also to encourage a model of successful transition from military to civilian rule that other African and Third World states might emulate. The Department of State and the Congress seemed to be prepared to overlook the initial bloodletting, Samuel Doe's idiosyncrasies, his rude treatment of key U.S. officials, and his abuses of the civil rights and liberties of Liberians. There was a strong feeling that everything would come out all right in the end; that the elections would be held on schedule; that more than one party would compete; and that a civilian government would take over in January 1986.

Even during the assault on the University of Liberia campus in August 1985, the U.S. government did not ruffle official feathers and hence made no effort to secure an independent assessment of the loss of life and abuses of human rights. Aside from minor public chastising of the Doe regime for its sins of omission and commission in the restoration of civilian rule, it was not really until the arrest of Ellen Johnson-Sirleaf and other opposition leaders in August 1985 and until rumors began to surface regarding a proposed cancellation of the October election that the State Department sent out a special envoy to Monrovia to express Washington's concern with the progress of restoring civilian rule. Congress went even further and in August passed a resolution directing the administration to withhold 1985–86 economic aid unless Liberia's performance on human rights had improved.

The State Department, however, always appeared to be reluctant to press the significant advantages the United States enjoyed by virtue of providing roughly one-third of the annual revenues needed to keep the Liberian government operative. The Reagan administration always overreacted to charges by Doe of superpower intervention and to Doe's hysterical counterthreats, which took such quixotic forms as dispatching Foreign Minister Ernest Eastman to Libya and Algeria in September 1985 or widely deviating from U.S. policy by diplomatically recognizing Polisario in the Western Sahara conflict. Conversely, the Reagan administration appeared to be easily mollified by such action as Doe's recognition of Israel in 1983 or the breaking of relations with the Soviet Union in 1985—which demonstrated Doe's "anti-communism," an important symbol to Reagan. American timidity was difficult to understand. There was, after all, no need for the United States to engage in a policy of "constructive engagement" *à la* South Africa, since it was not a question of intervention ("the U.S. *had already* intervened by continuing to feed our monster," one Liberian opposition leader said to this author). And there was no basis for assuming that Doe could easily find a surrogate patron who would provide the military hardware and economic assistance at the same level as had the United States.

U.S. support of the Doe regime from 1980 to 1984 could have been fully justified as being in Liberia's and America's interests. But like the British colonel in *Bridge Over the River Kwai*, the State Department appeared to be psychologically incapable of making a radical adjustment as the situation and circumstances dramatically changed. The United States continued throughout the time of difficulties in 1985–86 to provide the formalities that are so dear to the heart of the Liberians— such as the warm words of praise and assurances of continued economic support when the new U.S. ambassador presented his credentials; Reagan's congratulatory messages to Doe after the October election and following the failure of the Qui-wonkpa coup attempt; and the dispatching of an official delegation (albeit it at a lower level) to the inauguration of Doe. On the other hand, the Department of State, and even the Congress, avoided doing those things which would have signaled deep concern and displeasure, such as sending an official observer team to Liberia during the elections; protesting the banning of the two most effective opposition parties and their leaders; establishing independent sources of information regarding violations of human rights at the University of Liberia or in Nimba County in the aftermath of the Quiwonkpa coup attempt; or protesting the interruption by SECOM of the ballot counting.

When Chester Crocker or a State Department spokesman did comment on developments, it was often in a way that undermined the effectiveness of the opposition to Doe. The suggestion following the election and the Quiwonkpa coup attempt, for example, that there were injustices *on all sides* was an effort at even-handedness that simply belied the case. The insistence that the opposition after the election ought "to get on board" despite the irregularities not only was insensitive but it really denied the validity of a multiparty as opposed to a single-party system. Urging the Doe regime to have speedy, civilian trials in which due process was observed failed to address the fact that subjecting to the harassment of a trial those who had not committed any conceivable crime was in itself a denial of due process. Moreover, characterizing the shift in ballot counting procedure as a "shortcoming" ignored the fact that it was fatal to the process of fair and free elections. And Crocker's willingness to regard the ad hoc ballot count committee as representing "various walks of life" ignored the highly partisan nature of that group and its narrow Krahn base. Furthermore, criticizing the opposition leaders and citizens in general for disseminating unsubstantiated rumors about the numbers of persons killed or other atrocities committed overlooked not only the fact that the Doe regime controlled the flow of information but that the U.S. government made no independent efforts to secure information which would have challenged the rumors. Finally, the Liberian opposition has been furious over Crocker's understatements, such as his assertion that the Doe government "clearly has not fully met our high standards for democratic and human rights practices"; that "it would have been better if all political parties which wanted to campaign had been allowed to do so"; or "credit here should be given for Doe's decision to go through with the return to civilian rule on schedule." Most Liberians would disagree with Crocker's optimistic assessment that the election was "a benchmark on which to build." Finally, Liberians were offended by Crocker's summary remarks before a congressional subcommittee that "there is in Liberia today a civilian government based on elections, a multiparty legislature, a journalist community of government and nongovernment newspapers, an on-going tradition among citizenry of speaking out, and a new constitution that protects their freedom."[6]

As in a number of other contemporary cases, it has been both houses of the U.S. Congress, rather than the State Department, that demonstrated the courage to demand that U.S. aid to Liberia be linked to human rights performance and the establishment of a democratic political system. Unfortunately, the virtually unanimous resolutions of the Senate in December 1985 and of the House of Representatives in January 1986 were nonbinding. An administration which insists upon executive branch preeminence in the field of foreign policy formulation resents being challenged by both Republicans and Democrats in the two chambers on a wide range of issues and areas (Philippines, South Africa, Central America, Angola, and the Middle East). The Liberian people thus became the unwitting victims of domestic political sparring in the United States. Rather than using the congressional resolutions as leverage, the Department of State subsequently indicated that it planned to continue providing aid—albeit at a reduced level of $65 million for economic assistance and $4.7 million in military aid. Even later—after a high-level State Department mission to Monrovia had yielded no substantial concessions on political reconciliation—the Agency for International Development extended an additional $11 million in food assistance. Fulfillment of democratic objectives and human rights seemed to have been replaced by Crocker's new standard of aid: "Doe seems to have the power to govern."

## Internal Challenges to the Second Republic

The failure of the Quiwonkpa coup reduced the prospects of a challenge to Doe occurring from within the ranks of the military, and the policies of the Reagan administration gave every indication of continued support for Samuel Doe no matter how diminished his base of domestic support had become. He was—according to Assistant Secretary of State Chester Crocker—the effective government and consequently the only one with which the United States could deal in pursuing its varied interests. This made it apparent that it would be the Liberians themselves who would ultimately have to prove themselves capable of bringing to fruition their long-pursued quest for democracy. The strategy and tactics employed by Samuel Doe and the military-civilian coalition which made up the NDPL had eroded the legitimacy of the regime prior to the elections: the forcible fashion in which Doe had dealt with the Quiwonkpa coup demonstrated that it was far from an authentic vehicle for the realization of democracy.

### THE ECONOMIC CHALLENGE

The failure of the Doe regime was everywhere in evidence, but it was the economic instability that proved to be the most critical, since it not only affected the Liberian people on a day-to-day basis but it undermined the confidence that the Doe regime had enjoyed earlier in the eyes of its overseas financial supporters and investors. The shortage of (or even absence of) rice and other basic commodities in the marketplaces of Monrovia was a recurrent phenomenon; petrol shortages had been experienced on almost a regular monthly basis; and teachers and other public servants (with the exception of Doe's own personal Executive Mansion forces and the Krahn-dominated First Battalion, which had been a factor in putting down the Quiwonkpa coup) had gone unpaid from October to mid-March. The latter situation had led to a teachers' strike, which in turn precipitated a student demonstration on March 18 that turned into a riot in which brute force was employed before order was restored. Unemployment, particularly among the youth of Monrovia, had reached crisis proportions. There was, furthermore, a continuing outflow of educated talent to America, Europe, and other African states despite the efforts of the Immigration Department to deny exit visas and passports to Liberians. New investment prospects—other than a few American firms—had evaporated. The Liberian five-dollar coins (reportedly between 20 to 40 million dollars worth had been minted since 1982) had driven American paper currency from the banks, commercial houses, and marketplaces and were being deflated to half or less the value of the American dollar.

But like Nero during the burning of Rome, Doe spent between one million dollars (the government's admission) and seven million (the popular estimate) on Doe's inauguration. Two international actions, however, both reflected and further aggravated the economic situation. The first was the decision in January by the International Monetary Fund declaring Liberia ineligible to use the special drawing rights and other resources of the Fund because Liberia had defaulted in payment of the $70 million interest on its more than $900 million international indebtedness. This forced the Doe regime in February to reduce all government jobs and salaries by 25 percent and to begin consideration of privatizing a number of the parastatals (telephones, petroleum refineries, produce marketing, the airline, and other enterprises), although it was questionable whether there would be any buyers. The second international challenge came—as indicated earlier—from the United States Congress, with resolutions in each Chamber linking continued economic aid to performance in the areas of civil liberties and political democracy. Although the resolutions were nonbinding, the State Department was politically obliged to reduce if not withhold some of the funds which had kept the regime afloat. It was clear that simplistic responses by Samuel Doe similar to those undertaken in the past by Tubman and Tolbert would not suffice.

**THE POLITICAL CHALLENGE**

Politically as well, Samuel Doe found himself in an expanding quagmire of his own making. The few conciliatory gestures toward the opposition were—in the traditional style of Liberian politics—often canceled out by being coupled with outrageous threats. And the gestures were tendered with such bad grace that they were invariably rejected. A day after the announcement of the election results, for example, it was rumored that Gabriel Kpolleh would be offered the post of minister of education (which was the usual "token" job for tribal persons in the Tubman and Tolbert cabinets). This was immediately recognized as a device for undermining Kpolleh's credibility and dividing the opposition ranks. When Doe did get around to offering that post at the time of the cabinet reshuffle following the inauguration, it was extended to Mary Grimes Brown Sherman, the former president of the University of Liberia. The latter had been removed from office by Doe in August 1984, and detained for several weeks without formal charges after the Quiwonkpa coup of November 1985. She first heard of Doe's cabinet offer over the radio, without prior consultation. She forthrightly rejected the ill-tendered offer. A similar rejection awaited Doe with respect to subcabinet positions which he offered to two of the officers of the Unity Party and the Liberian Action Party.

Admittedly some cabinet reshuffling during the inauguration and two months later did help remove some of the less competent members of his administration (such as his cousin, G. Alvin Jones, from the Ministry of Finance), several who were abrasive factors in international dealings (such as Foreign Minister Ernest Eastman), or those who had aggravated relations between Doe and the opposition, the independent press, and other private groups (such as Information Minister Carlton A. Karpeh). Emmett Harmon, moreover, was replaced by Isaac Randolph in the reconstituted Elections Commission. Nevertheless, the three most strident and acerbic members of his team remained: Jenkins Scott at Justice, Gray Allison at Defense, and Edward Sackor at Internal Affairs. Doe, moreover, violated the constitutional separation of powers by forcing out Chief Justice Emmanuel Gbalazeh, who had from time to time exercised judicial independence.

The opposition response to Doe's calls for reconciliation was not what he had anticipated. Indeed, Samuel Doe found himself hopelessly incapable of responding creatively and unequivocally to the almost spontaneous exercises of democracy which suddenly began to emerge shortly after the inauguration. Efforts to take the new constitution at face value were evidenced by both private individuals and groups. Many of the latter had been banned during the last several months of the Interim Assembly transitional regime and in the wake of the Quiwonkpa coup. Without apparent coordination, it began to be asserted with increasing vigor that 6 January had indeed meant something for democracy after all. With the full implementation of the new constitution, it was contended that all of the arbitrary bans on political and other forms of behavior introduced by the PRC or the Assembly had become null and void. The civil and political rights which the constitution guaranteed were now assumed to be in effect, superseding previous arbitrary restraints.

Examples of this spontaneous assertion of liberty included Amos Sawyer's announcement on 24 January that his arbitrary banning had ended with the introduction of the new constitution (about which he could speak with authority), and he was free to travel abroad—which he did. The Press Union of Liberia in late February indicated that it would meet, since the constitution guaranteed free association, and they were quickly followed in this regard by the National Teachers Union, which had also been banned following the Quiwonkpa coup. Not to be outdone, G. Baccus Matthews' United People's Party (during his continued absence in the United States) announced that it was resuming operations, since the Interim National Assembly ban was no longer in effect. Kenneth Best in a brief ceremony at the offices of the *Daily Observer* announced on 4 March 1986 that the frequently banned paper would once again resume publication after a thirteen-month suspension. Dissent regarding the validity of PRC decrees and Interim Assembly actions came, however, even from within the ranks of the NDPL. In April the members of the Doe-controlled Legislature began to challenge the legitimacy of the Assembly action during 1985 which would have permitted foreigners to own real estate in Liberia. Since this had been forbidden under the constitutions of both the First and the Second Republics, it was insisted that Articles 91 and 92, requiring a popular referendum to amend the constitution, were now in force and mere action by the Legislature was not sufficient.

The most dramatic challenge to the validity of PRC decrees and Interim Assembly actions came from those who were most versed in the significance of law and constitutions—namely, the legal profession. Starting in January 1986, interviews with some of the leading Monrovia members of the Liberian Bar Association stressed the fact that organic law is superior to all other actions and decrees, and the independent courts were required to declare actions in conflict with the supreme law of the land as invalid once the new constitution came into effect.[7] With encouragement from two visiting lawyers from the Washington-based International Human Rights Law Group, the Liberian legal profession homed in on two particularly egregious violations of the new constitution—the detention of individuals without formal charges being filed and the absence of guarantees of speedy trials in civilian courts.

The initial reaction of the Doe partisans to this developing scenario of taking the Constitution of the Second Republic at face value was predictable. Justice Minister Jenkins Scott in February flatly stated that all former PRC decrees were in force and people would be prosecuted under those decrees until the Legislature had expressly changed them.[8] He and the information minister specifically warned the Press Union of Liberia not to hold a meeting while still under an Assembly ban. Even earlier, Doe's newly appointed chief justice, James Nagbe, insisted that all the previous decrees and acts remain in effect until each is specifically challenged in court—a very elaborate procedure in moving from martial law to civilian rule. In effect the Doe regime took the position that the constitution was subordinate to military decrees, legislative acts, and judicial decisions.

On the plane of action, moreover, the regime alternated between a gesture of conciliation one day and either an act of obstinacy or outright resort to force on the next. For example, the Doe government on 5 March acceded to demands lifting the ban on the Press Union of Liberia and three other associations; yet they continued to lecture the press about covering so much political news ("cover murder, theft, and other human interest material," the new information minister told the journalists). It was also clear that on the same day that the ban on the Press Union was lifted, young thugs of the NDPL Special Task Force were responsible for the torching of the *Daily Observer* pressroom hours after Kenneth Best's decision to renew publication. The three-day strike by the other independent newspapers in sympathy with the *Observer* (with the refusal of newsboys to sell the government *New Liberian*) only brought forth additional government threats.

A balancing of conciliation and threats also came when Jackson Doe and several others who had been retained in the wake of the Quiwonkpa coup were released from jail on 12 February while the regime persisted in the persecution of Ellen Johnson-Sirleaf, formally charging her with treason. Instead, moreover, of taking steps to alleviate the deplorable situation faced by the teachers who had gone on strike in March over their salaries being four months in arrears, the government humiliated the head of the union, undermining his leadership, and broke up a demonstration on 18 March of students who were demonstrating in support of their striking teachers. Special riot police predictably turned the peaceful student demonstration into a riot. Far too often, the recurrent verbal harassment of journalists, church leaders, businessmen, educators, and others invariably carried the implied threat of resort to naked force. These actions caused a downward spiraling of popular support for the Doe regime, and the application of force telegraphed in no uncertain terms the fragility of Samuel Doe's base of authority.

## THE EMERGENCE OF THE GRAND COALITION

Still, it was reasonable for Liberians and friends abroad to ask what were the democratic alternatives to the Doe regime. The opposition to Samuel Doe was fully aware of the enormous advantages that the NDPL enjoyed when the ban on politics was supposedly lifted in July 1984; yet in their eagerness to make up for lost time and to serve special interests they proved to be incapable of consolidating their ranks and making a concerted effort to dislodge Doe in the October 1985 election. Throughout the electioneering period, it was apparent that unity of action and purpose had a far lower priority than personality conflicts, subtle nuances in programs and policies, historic memories, and regional or ethnic differences.

Ten fragmented parties could not constitute a democratic alternative to one-party rule, nor can five, the number of opposition parties which were still in the political arena three months before the October elections, or four, the number actually on the ballot. Even though the unofficial tallies seemed to make it quite clear that the Liberian Action Party had garnered most of the votes before the ballot counting was stopped by SECOM, neither the Unity Party nor the Liberian Unification Party would commit itself publicly to those results. If one candidate emerged with an actual majority in the ballot count preceding the intervention by SECOM, it was not because of courage on the part of the opposition to set aside their differences; it was the action of SECOM and the Interim Assembly in disqualifying the two significant challengers—the United People's Party and the Liberian People's Party—whose followers had no other option than to support the Liberian Action Party. If there had been a mood to organizationally consolidate their opposition to the NDPL, the arbitrary treatment of the leaders of the three opposition parties after the Quiwonkpa coup cast a severe pall over any such suggestion.

What ultimately galvanized the opposition parties into a determined effort to coordinate their dissent and participation in multiparty politics under the Second Republic was a series of indications that a one-party state was about to be formalized. An early signal came from the traditional chiefs, who presented Doe with a petition three days after the election asking that the one-party state be instituted. While some explained the petition away as an expression of self-interest (the chiefs were not looking forward themselves to having competition in the forthcoming chieftaincy elections), the fact that it was actually passed along by Doe to the Legislature for consideration suggested that far more was involved.[9] At about the same time, a rumor surfaced—attributable to remarks made on 10 January by Oscar Quiah, the secretary general of NDPL—regarding a possible military coup. The rumor involved an alleged plot linking opposition party leaders to Libya and Cuba. The "fake coup," as it came to be called by Gabriel Kpolleh and others, was allegedly to provide the NDPL with the pretext for the arrest of opposition leaders and the institution of the one-party state.

Although each of the opposition parties had previously come forth with creative proposals for adjusting to the realities of the Second Republic under Samuel Doe, it was Gabriel Kpolleh who was credited with the initiative in launching a Grand Coalition. Such an alliance would provide a formal structure for closer cooperation not only among the three parties that had competed in the October 1985 elections, but among other parties as well. Very quickly, the United People's Party, which had declared its intentions to resume operations in spite of the ban imposed by the Interim Assembly, was made a formal member of the Grand Coalition. This was a calculated defiance by the Grand Coalition of the Doe regime's efforts to prevent the UPP from having a formal meeting and its continued placing of barriers in the path of G. Baccus Matthews's returning from the United States. In mid-March 1986 the opposition leaders had met and presented a plan of action for reconciliation under the new constitution. It called for an admission of past sins on the part of all, the release of all political prisoners, and a continuous dialogue among the NDPL and the Grand Coalition on the basis of equality rather than as lords and serfs. The dialogue was to lead to the creation of a Provisional Council of twenty-six, representative of all the parties and the military and reflecting the various regional and other interests in Liberian society. The Provisional Council, under a leadership of its own choosing, would then organize and conduct elections within one year, with the elections being closely observed by reputable local groups (the Liberian Council of Churches, the Press Union of Liberia, the National Muslim Council, and the Bar Association were suggested) and external agencies (the United Nations, Amnesty International, the World Council of Churches, and others). Members of the Provisional Council would be expressly barred from standing for office, to avoid conflicts of interest.

The determination of the Grand Coalition to proceed was evidenced by their willingness at long last to make choices in terms of leadership. Gabriel Kpolleh (ironically, given the earlier suspicions regarding the seriousness of his political independence from Samuel Doe) was named president, with Jackson Doe and Edward Kesselly—the standard-bearers of the Liberian Action Party and the Unity Party—being named first and second vice presidents, and Wesley M. Johnson (in the absence from Liberia of G. Baccus Matthews) named as third vice president. Roman Catholic Archbishop Michael Francis, chairman of the Liberian Council of Churches, undertook to serve as mediator between the Grand Coalition and Samuel Doe.

To the surprise of almost no one, the initial reaction of the Doe government and the NDPL leadership was negative. His acceptance was conditional: the Coalition leaders would have to meet with him in the Poro sacred bush outside Gbarnga where he had recently been given the Poro title of *Tarnue*. Since the meeting date suggested by Doe was Good Friday, the affront to the Catholic Archbishop mediator and to the Liberian Council of Churches was patently obvious. Next, the chairman of the permanent Elections Commission made threats that the Grand Coalition was an illegal party ("subversive and dangerous to the security of the state"), that it had not been registered, and, moreover, that participation in the Coalition threatened the withdrawal of registration previously granted to the three parties that had been on the ballot in October 1985. The justice minister charged that the Grand Coalition was an attempt to "polarize our people to destroy or undermine the basic economic and political fabric and thereby frustrate all efforts to bring about a true democracy."[10] Beyond rhetoric, however, the Doe regime set up a commission to investigate the charges of a plot against the government, and in the process arrested Gabriel Kpolleh at the end of April on the charge of sedition and forced his supporters to post a staggering $20,000 bond for his release. Jackson Doe and four others were informed by security officials that they had been "blacklisted" by the Justice Ministry with respect to travel outside Monrovia.

## The Dual Scenario

In the face of the worsening economic crisis and the organized challenge of the opposition party leadership, Doe employed a strategy that had served him well during the process of restoring civilian rule: he resorted to a dual scenario (see chapter 17). On one level the scenario was clearly designed to placate and persuade the external sources of economic and financial support upon whom his regime had become rigidly dependent. The IMF, the World Bank, and the United States government needed positive reassurance that Doe was not only going to put his economic house in order but that he would meet their minimum expectations with regard to human rights, democratic performance, and the restoration of the political stability required for economic growth. On the second level the scenario was directed internally to those who increasingly threatened to undermine his control over the Liberian political system and to endanger the new-found privilege of the military and his Krahn-based constituency in postcoup Liberia.

### THE HIGH ROAD

This level of the dual scenario had both an economic and a political phase. The economic phase included the previously mentioned austerity measures introduced in response to the January decision of the IMF to deny special drawing rights for Liberia. It was followed a few months later by a "Green Revolution" campaign, echoing the earlier programs of Tolbert to cope with the fact that imports of food were radically affecting the balance of payments situation for Liberia. Unfortunately, the food campaign provided few incentives to cultivators, and it tended to concentrate on frivolous issues, such as threatening cabinet ministers with the loss of their jobs if they failed to take two weeks off from their official duties to work on their respective farms.

More serious was the move in May to introduce severe external controls over the Liberian economy. To the surprise of many—given Liberia's humiliating history of international receivership in the period between 1871 and 1924—the Doe government requested the World Bank, the IMF, the European Economic Community, and others to take a more direct role in supervising revenue collection and government spending.[11] Liberia also made an initial payment of interest due on American loans, inasmuch as the threatened default had provided legal obstacles to the continuation of U.S. aid. And to put a new face on Liberia's resolve to give serious attention to its economic crisis, Robert Tubman was brought in to replace the lackluster partisan who had previously held the post of finance minister. Tubman— as a second cousin of the former president—not only had the magic name, he had degrees from Harvard and the London School of Economics as well as significant experience with several international economic agencies. This was a sharp contrast with Alvin Jones, Tubman's predecessor, whose only qualifications for the job were that he was a cousin of Doe and had been a treasurer for the Episcopal Church. Doe's emissaries, moreover, made a pointed appeal to Israel for further aid to offset the loss of the substantial support the Saudi and Kuwaiti governments had provided prior to Liberia's diplomatic exchange with Israel. Finally, Doe's July 26th Independence Day speech constituted a very frank admission of the depth of corruption and mismanagement under the PRC and the transitional government.

The political phase of the "high road" scenario was marked, among other things, by Samuel Doe's surprising acceptance of the offer to meet with the leaders of the Grand Coalition at the home of Roman Catholic Archbishop Michael Francis on 5 May. The high road also included the government's release on 6 June of the thirty-four political leaders (including Ellen Johnson-Sirleaf) who had been detained in the period following the abortive Quiwonkpa coup. The latter action brought forth the anticipated notes of praise from the World Bank and from the U.S. Department of State. Once again Doe's political prisoners had served a useful role as "hostages" in securing continued external economic support after their release.

## THE LOW ROAD

The complementary and more negative scenario focused almost entirely on the political activities of the Doe regime. It was manifest by the fact that the release of political detainees in June did not include the formal withdrawal of treason charges against several in the group, nor did it completely restore their civil rights and liberties. There were still restrictions on their giving interviews or addressing meetings; they were not permitted to leave the confines of Monrovia—let alone get permission to travel abroad; and they found themselves harassed by the youth wing of the NDPL and government officials. Indeed, the continued persecution of Ellen Johnson-Sirleaf (including the ransacking of her home and an alleged threat on her life by Senator Kekura B. Kpoto, the chairman of the NDPL) forced her in September to flee the country for the United States.

Equally ominous was the hardening of the NDPL stance against the Grand Coalition. Although Samuel Doe did attend the May 5 meeting with the opposition leaders at Archbishop Michael Francis's home, it was clear at the end of the day that Samuel Doe saw no reason at all why he should sacrifice the advantages of being the incumbent president to the uncertainties which would befall him, the Liberian military, his colleagues in the NDPL, or the Krahn group under the provisional government advanced by the Grand Coalition. Under these circumstances, he said in his report to the Legislature, the "attitude on the part of opposition leaders would appear to create some difficulties for us to continue this discussion in good faith. For certainly, we cannot subscribe to actions which tend to undermine the constitution of our nation.'' He did not attend the second (and final) meeting between the NDPL and the Grand Coalition under the sponsorship of the Liberian Council of Churches.

On the contrary, the next several months were characterized by a continually escalating campaign by the Doe regime to destroy the opposition to the NDPL and make reconciliation virtually impossible. The chairman of the Elections Commission intensified his threats to decertify the three opposition parties that had participated in the 1985 election. Next, the minister of justice—with the ultimate support of the Supreme Court—denied the Grand Coalition the right to hold a mass political rally. The vestige of a once-vigorous independent press was threatened, moreover, with prosecution if it gave any detailed coverage to the Grand Coalition leadership— particularly the demands that Liberia hold new elections and that people boycott the government-owned *New Liberian* and the government radio station. Doe personally got into the act on 25 June by indicating to the Liberian Council of Churches that its proposed agenda for future discussions was biased and thus its role as mediator was no longer required.

Particularly irritating to Doe was the statement of Gabriel Kpolleh that ''there can never be peace among politicians in the country until re-elections are held.''[12] By mid-July, the Supreme Court was once more brought into the scenario, when Chief Justice Loke Nagba found the leaders of the Grand Coalition guilty of contempt for referring to themselves as members of the Grand Coalition—since it was not a political party recognized by the Elections Commission. The action may have been prompted by rumors that the three parties were about to formally merge under a single banner. Since Kpolleh, Jackson Doe, and Edward Kesselly steadfastly refused to pay the $1,000 contempt fine, they were arrested in August and quickly flown to the notorious Belle Yellah military security prison in Lofa Country—a violation of the constitution on several counts. Doe then took the extraordinary step of asking the Legislature to keep the men in jail for twenty-five years and deny them a future role in Liberian politics. Not only was Samuel Doe's action a threat to the judicial process, but, if the Legislature had acted, it would have produced a bill of attainder as well as an ex post facto law—both of which are prohibited under Article 21 of the constitution.

A chorus of protest arose not only from the expected sources, such as the opposition parties, the Liberian Council of Churches, the legal profession, and the business caucus, but also from those Samuel Doe had come to regard as his constituency, namely the market women. There was also outrage expressed in international quarters to the imprisonment of the three leaders. It was only the payment of the fine by several Liberian clergymen that brought the release of the three opposition standard-bearers.

Nowhere in the proceedings did Samuel Doe or his cohorts acknowledge that they had in so many ways violated both the letter and the spirit of the new constitution and revealed their contempt for political dissent. Undaunted, moreover, the Elections Commission almost immediately after the release of Jackson Doe, Kpolleh, and Kesselly renewed the charges that the certification of the parties should be reversed because of their collaboration in the Grand Coalition.

Thus, at this writing the struggle to attain the full promise of democracy for Liberia and Liberians has reached an impasse. The impasse is one which prompted a longstanding friend of Liberia to lament:

> political leaders both within the government and in the opposition are in the midst of a political quagmire which keeps them from taking effective action. If they cannot respond to the legitimate needs of the people, spontaneous violence might erupt and an entirely new leadership might evolve. What political orientation such a leadership might follow is open to speculation.[13]

The same student of Liberian politics predicted that the impasse could not persist:

> It seems likely that soon there will be a changing of the guard in Liberia. This could come violently through another internal army-led coup, from the outside by Qadafi-backed Liberian exiles or from a Dan (Gio)-led guerrilla war against the Krahn-dominated Liberian army. Or the change could also come peacefully through a negotiated settlement between Doe and the coalition of the combined parties which have demanded new elections.[14]

In any event, it appears that the decision ultimately lies with Liberians to accomplish their quest for a democratic society.

# NOTES

### Acknowledgments

1. Formerly the American Universities Field Staff.

## I.

1. World Bank, *World Development Report*, 1985 (Oxford University Press, 1986), passim.
2. Elliott Berg Associates, *Final Report: The Liberian Crisis and an Appropriate U.S. Response* (Washington: U.S. AID, February 1982), p. 4.
3. Robert W. Clower, George Dalton, Mitchell Harwitz, A. A. Walters, et al., *Growth Without Development: An Economic Survey of Liberia* (Evanston: Northwestern University Press, 1966).
4. Considerable help in drafting was provided by a Harvard law professor, Simon Greenleaf.

## II.

1. Philip D. Curtin, *The Atlantic Slave Trade: A Census* (Madison: University of Wisconsin Press, 1969), and the confirmation of Curtin's estimates by Paul E. Lovejoy, *Transformations in Slavery: A History of Slavery in Africa* (Cambridge: Cambridge University Press, 1983).
2. F. A. J. Utting, *The Story of Sierra Leone* (London: Longmans, 1931), pp. 31–35.
3. For an excellent treatment of the Spanish experiment in what is today Equatorial Guinea, see Ibrahim K. Sundiata, "The Fernandinos: Labor and Community in Santa Isabel de Fernando Poo," Ph.D. in History, Northwestern University, 1972.
4. One of the more interesting historical studies of the efforts to colonize Liberia is contained in P. J. Staudenraus, *The African Colonization Movement, 1816–1865* (New York: Columbia University Press, 1961). The standard work on the legal, constitutional, and historical background of the Liberian colonial period is Charles H. Huberich, *The Political and Legislative History of Liberia*, 2 vols. (New York: Central Book Co., 1947). The Huberich work brings together some of the most significant documents of the pre-1847 period and contains interesting biographical sketches of the pioneers. Aside from its almost exclusive concern with the colonial period, its main limitation is its formal legalistic approach to so exciting a topic.
5. Tom W. Shick, *Behold the Promised Land: A History of Afro-American Settler Society in Nineteenth-Century Liberia* (Baltimore: Johns Hopkins University Press, 1980), p. 13.
6. Staudenraus, *African Colonization*, pp. 19–22.
7. See Samuel E. Morrison, *"Old Bruin," Commodore Matthew C. Perry* (London: Oxford University Press, 1968).

8. Apart from the general studies, certain works are useful for the understanding of the colonial period, including Jehudi Ashmun, *History of the American Colony of Liberia from December 1821 to 1823* (Washington, D.C.: Day and Gideon, 1826); Ralph R. Gurley, *Life of Jehudi Ashmun, Late Colonial Agent in Liberia* (Washington, D.C.: J. C. Dunn, 1835); William Innes, *Liberia* (Edinburgh: Waugh and Innes, 1831); Archibald Alexander, *A History of Colonization on the Western Coast of Africa* (Philadelphia: W. S. Martien, 1846); J. H. T. McPherson, "History of Liberia," *Johns Hopkins University Studies in Historical and Political Science*, 9th ser. (1891), 479–540; and Charles I. Foster, "The Colonization of Free Negroes in Liberia, 1816–1835," *Journal of Negro History*, Vol. 38 (Jan. 1953), 41–67.

9. Jo M. Sullivan, "Mississippi in Africa: Settlers Among the Kru, 1835–1847," *Liberian Studies Journal*, Vol. 8 (1978–79), pp. 79–94.

10. Dwight N. Seyfert, "The Liberian Sailing Navy, 1821–1892," *American Neptune* (January 1978), pp. 52–61.

11. See Huberich, *Political and Legislative History*, I, II, *passim*.

12. Harrison Akingbade, "Liberia and the First World War, 1914–1926," *A Current Bibliography on African Affairs*, Vol. 10 (1977–78), pp. 243–258.

13. Sierra Leone Archives, Confidential letter of Governor Probyn to Lord Elgin, 28 May 1906. Letter box, no reference number.

14. For the most comprehensive treatment of the subject, see Ibrahim K. Sundiata, *Black Scandal: America and the Liberian Labor Crises, 1929–1936* (Philadelphia: Institute for the Study of Human Issues, 1980).

15. See Shick, *Behold the Promised Land*, 122–134, *passim*.

16. Other listings of immigrants, by name, occupation, origin, and other data, are contained in Shick, *Emigrants to Liberia—1820 to 1843: An Alphabetical Listing* (Newark, Del.: Liberian Studies Association, 1971), Research Working Paper, No. 2; and Robert T. Brown, *Immigrants to Liberia, 1843 to 1865: An Alphabetical Listing* (Newark, Del.: Liberian Studies Association, 1975), Research Working Paper No. 7.

17. Staudenraus, *African Colonization*, p. 32.

18. General studies which deal with Liberian history (and contain contradictory statements of fact) are Frederick A. Durham, *The Lone-Star of Liberia* (London: E. Stock, 1892); Sir Harry Johnston, *Liberia* (2 vols.; London: Hutchinson, 1906), Vol. I; Frederick Starr, *Liberia* (Chicago, 1913); Reginald C. F. Maugham, *The Republic of Liberia* (New York: Charles Scribner's, 1920); Henry F. Reeve, *The Black Republic* (London: H. F. and G. Witherby, 1923); Raymond L. Buell, *The Native Problem in Africa* (2 vols.; New York: Macmillan, 1928), Vol. II, 704–890. The Johnston volume, despite its innuendo, is particularly good on the nineteenth-century republican period. Starr's primary asset is his analysis of the early twentieth-century political behavior of the Liberians, which reveals the historical depth of current practices. More superficial but nonetheless informative on the first two decades of the present century are the Reeve and Maugham studies. The work by Buell constitutes one of the best, albeit brief, treatments of the period from the founding of the settlements to the establishment of the Firestone Plantations Company in the 1920s. Finally, for historic purposes, reference should be made to J. Büttkofer, *Reisebilder aus Liberia* (Leiden: E. J. Brill, 1890), which is a description of geographic and ethnographic expeditions to Liberia in 1879–1882 and 1886–1887.

19. Staudenraus, *African Colonization*, p. 109.

20. Methodists, Baptists, Congregationalists, Episcopalians, and Presbyterians dominated at the outset. The Lutherans, who are strong today, did not arrive until the American Civil War. The various Pentecostal groups, who now rank second only to the Methodists, did not appear until the beginning of the twentieth century. The Roman Catholics had a late start in the last quarter of the nineteenth century and had to abandon their mission temporarily before resuming work in earnest in Maryland and Montserrado counties in 1906.

21. For further documentation of this conclusion, see M. B. Akpan, "The Liberian

Economy in the Nineteenth Century: The State of Agriculture and Commerce," *Liberian Studies Journal*, Vol. 6 (1975), pp. 1–24.

22. Shick, *Behold the Promised Land*, pp. 27–28.

23. Akpan, "Liberian Economy," pp. 17–24. The early agricultural and commercial developments of the colony and Republic are very well described in George W. Brown, *The Economic History of Liberia* (Washington: Associate Publishers, Inc., 1941).

24. Dwight N. Seyfert, "The Origins of Privilege: Liberian Merchants, 1822–1847," *Liberian Studies Journal*, Vol. 6 (1975), pp. 109–128.

25. For a detailed critical analysis of the distinctions between Americo-Liberians and others—particularly in regard to the Grebo area—see Jane Martin, "How to Build a Nation: Liberian Ideas About National Integration in the Later Nineteenth Century," *Liberian Studies Journal*, Vol. 2 (1969), pp. 15–42.

26. Liberian scholars themselves have attempted to reconstruct their history: see Hannah A. Bowen Jones, "The Struggle for Political and Cultural Unification in Liberia, 1847–1930," Ph.D. thesis in History, Northwestern University, 1962; and Bowen Jones, "The Republic of Liberia," in Jacob Ajayi and Michael Crowder, eds., *History of West Africa*, Vol. 2 (London: Longman Group, 1974), pp. 308–343. One of the earliest studies by a Liberian is Thomas McCants Stewart, *Liberia, the Americo-African Republic* (New York: E. O. Jenkins, 1886). One of the most frequently cited works is Abayomi Karnga, *History of Liberia* (Liverpool: D. H. Tyte, 1962), which makes some original contributions but borrows heavily from the works of Johnston and other scholars. Two textbooks by Liberian political leaders were used in civics courses: Ernest J. Yancy, *Historical Lights of Liberia's Yesterday and Today* (rev. ed., New York: Jaffee, 1954), and Richard and Doris Henries, *Liberia, the West African Republic* (New York: Jaffee, 1958). In terms of understanding the process of political socialization and Tubman's Unification Policy, they are highly informative for what they did not say, as well as what they did say. The Yancy and Henries volumes served as required civics books in the Liberian schools, despite the fact that almost no attention was given to the contribution made by tribal people to modern Liberia, and certain historic events were glossed over or omitted entirely.

27. Svend E. Holsoe, "A Study of Relations Between Settlers and Indigenous Peoples in Western Liberia, 1821–1847," *African Historical Studies*, Boston, Vol. 4 (1971), pp. 331–362.

28. M. B. Akpan expanded upon the suggestion in some of my earlier writings comparing Liberia to South Africa in his "Black Imperialism: Americo-Liberian Rule over the African Peoples of Liberia, 1841–1964," *Canadian Journal of African Studies*, Vol. 7 (1973), pp. 217–36.

29. *Narrative of a Journey to Masardu, the Capital of the Western Mandingoes* (New York: S. W. Green, 1870).

30. Seymour and Ash penetrated the northeastern sector of Liberia and are referred to in the Royal Geographical Society *Proceedings*, IV, No. 4 (1860).

31. See Holsoe, "The Manding in Western Liberia," *Liberian Studies Journal*, Vol. 7 (1976/77), pp. 1–12. For a more general treatment of the Manding, see Carleton T. Hodge, ed., *Papers on the Manding* (Bloomington: Indiana University Research Center for the Language Sciences, 1971).

32. Only nine African states, including neighboring Sierra Leone, are smaller.

# III.

1. Editor-in-Chief Zehyu B. Wuduogar, *PRC Newsletter*, No. 2, Vol. 3 (April 1982), p. 1.

2. John H. Atherton, "Early Economies of Sierra Leone and Liberia: Archaelogical and Historical Reflections," in Vernon R. Dorjahn and Barry L. Isaac, eds., *Essays on the*

*Economic Anthropology of Liberia and Sierra Leone* (Philadelphia: Institute for Liberian Studies, 1979), pp. 27–45, *passim*.

3. Yves Person, *"Les Kissi et leurs statuettes de pierre dans le cadre d l'histoire ouest-Africaine," Bulletin de l'I.F.A.N.*, Vol. 23, series B (1961), pp. 1–57.

4. Svend E. Holsoe, "Economic Activities in the Liberian Area: The Pre-European Period to 1900," in Dorjahn and Isaac, eds., *Economic Anthropology*, pp. 63–78, *passim*.

5. Andreas Massing, "Materials for a History of Western Liberia: The Belle," *Liberian Studies Journal*, Vol. 3 (1970–71), pp. 173–206; see also Ronald W. Davis, "Historical Outline of the Kru Coast, Liberia, 1500 to the Present," Ph.D. dissertation in History, Indiana University, 1968; and Davis, *Ethnohistorical Studies on the Kru Coast* (Newark, Del.: Liberian Studies, 1976).

6. See Massing, "Materials for a History of Western Liberia: Samori and the Malinke Frontier in the Toma Sector," *Liberian Studies Journal*, Vol. 8 (1978–79), pp. 49–68; and "Materials for a History of Liberia: Kai Lundu, Mbawulume and the Establishment of Interior Rule in Western Liberia," *ibid.*, pp. 95–115.

7. Linguists, missionaries, and others classify ethnic groups in diverse fashions. One count places the number of tribes at twenty-eight. The sixteen enumerated in the Census of Population of 1962 and that of 1974 are indicated in table 3. The "alien African tribes" in the table include 5,166 Fanti, most of whom are coastal fishermen and consider themselves citizens of Ghana.

8. See Holsoe, "The Cassava-Leaf People: An Ethnohistorical Study of the Vai People with Particular Emphasis on the Tewo Chiefdom," Ph.D. dissertation, Boston University, 1967; and Raymond Smyke, *Massaquoi of Liberia*, manuscript (Algonac, Michigan: Reference Publications, c. 1986).

9. Jane Jackson Martin, "The Dual Legacy: Government Authority and Mission Influence Among the Glebo of Eastern Liberia, 1834–1910," Ph.D. dissertation in History, Boston University, 1968.

10. George E. Brooks, *The Kru Mariner of the Nineteenth Century: An Historical Compendium* (Newark, Del.: Liberian Studies Association, 1972); and *Yankee Traders, Old Coasters, and African Middlemen* (Boston: Boston University Press, 1970). See also Davis, *Ethnohistorical Studies*, *passim*.

11. Warren L. d'Azevedo, "A Tribal Reaction to Nationalism," 3 parts, *Liberian Studies Journal*, Vol. 1 (Spring 1969), pp. 1–21; Vol. 2 (1969), pp. 43–64; Vol. 3 (1970), pp. 99–116; see also d'Azevedo's "Continuity and Integration in Gola Society," Ph.D. thesis in Anthropology, Northwestern University, 1962; and d'Azevedo, "Uses of the Past in Gola Discourse," *Journal of African History*, III (1962), 11–34.

12. Holsoe, "The Manding in Western Liberia: An Overview," *Liberian Studies Journal*, Vol. 7 (1976–77), pp. 1–12.

13. See James L. Gibbs, Jr., "The Kpelle of Liberia," in Gibbs, ed., *Peoples of Africa* (New York: Holt, Rinehart and Winston, 1965), pp. 197–240; Gibbs, "Some Judicial Implications of Marital Instability Among the Kpelle," Ph.D. thesis in Anthropology, Harvard University, 1960; and Richard W. Fulton, "The Kpelle Traditional Political System," *Liberian Studies Journal*, Vol. 1 (October 1968), pp. 1–18.

14. d'Azevedo, "Tribal Reaction," Part I, Vol. 1 (Spring 1969), pp. 8, 16.

15. Massing, "A Segmentary Society Between Colonial Frontiers: The Kissi of Liberia, Sierra Leone and Guinea, 1892–1913," *Liberian Studies Journal*, Vol. 9 (1980–81), pp. 1–12.

16. Holsoe, "The Condo Confederation in Western Liberia," *The Liberian Historical Review*, 3 (1966), 1–28.

17. Joseph Greenberg's classification in 1963 designated all of the languages of the area as Niger-Congo. They were subdivided into three genetic subfamilies: West Atlantic (Gola, Kissi), Kwa-speaking Kru Branch (Bassa, Dei, Grebo, Kru, Belle, Krahn), and Eastern and Western branches of the Mande-speaking Peoples (Western: Manding, Vai, Gbandi,

Kpelle, Loma, and Mende; Eastern: Gio, Mano). See Greenberg, "The Languages of Africa," *International Journal of American Linguistics*, XXIX, No. 1, part two (1963), 8.

18. Benjamin C. Dennis, *The Gbandes: A People of the Liberian Hinterland* (Chicago: Nelson-Hall, 1972), pp. 14–22.

19. In presenting the material in this chapter, I have drawn heavily upon the Ph.D. dissertations of James Gibbs on the Kpelle and Warren d'Azevedo on the Gola, as well as other writings of these scholars. I have also used extensively the published works of the late George Harley, of George Schwab, Svend Holsoe, and other ethnographers. The Bureau of Folkways of the Liberian Department of the Interior has issued a series of tribal studies compiled by students of anthropology. Despite the Americo-Liberian social bias there is much information in *Tribes of the Western Province and the Denwoin People* (1955); *Traditional History, Customary Laws, Mores, Folkways and Legends of the Vai Tribe* (1954); and *Traditional History and Folklore of the Glebo [Grebo] Tribe* (1957). The authors of the government monographs are not identified in the publications but they are conceded to be largely the work of Bai T. Moore.

20. David Blanchard, "The Development of Small Agriculture in Liberia," U.S. AID, Monrovia, 31 July 1967, pp. 6–7 (mimeographed); see also Blanchard, "The Impact of External Domination on Liberian Mano Economy: An Analysis of Weber's Hypothesis of Rationalism," Ph.D. thesis in Economics, Indiana University, 1973.

21. Perhaps the most outstanding of the earlier students of Liberian tribal organization was George W. Harley, whose "Notes on the Poro in Liberia," *Papers of the Peabody Museum*, XIX (1941), and "Masks as Agents of Social Control in Northeast Liberia," *ibid.*, XXXII, No. 2 (1950), are essential reading for the understanding of tribal politics. Additional material by Harley appears in George Schwab, "Tribes of the Liberian Hinterland," *ibid.*, XXXI (1947). See also William E. Welmers, "Secret Medicines, Magic, and Rites of the Kpelle Tribe in Liberia," *Southwestern Journal of Anthropology*, V (1949), 208–243.

22. Kenneth Little, "The Political Function of the Poro," *Africa*, Vol. 35 (October 1965), 349–365; and Vernon Dorjahn, "The Initiation of Temne Poro Officials," *Man*, Vol. 61 (Feb. 1961), 36ff.

23. For some insightful comments on the local nature of the Poro among the Kpelle, see Beryl L. Bellman, *The Language of Secrecy: Symbols & Metaphors in Poro Ritual* (New Brunswick, N.J.: Rutgers University Press, 1984).

24. Caroline H. Bledsoe, *Women and Marriage in Kpelle Society* (Stanford, Cal.: Stanford University Press, 1980).

25. Harley, "Masks as Agents of Social Control," pp. x–xi.

# IV.

1. The racial and class divisions within Liberia are dealt with by Johnston, Karnga, and other historians cited previously. An earlier scholarly appraisal of the Americo-Liberians that largely avoids adverse conclusions is Richard P. Strong, ed., of Harvard African Expedition of 1926–1927, *The African Republic of Liberia and The Belgian Congo* (2 vols.; Cambridge, Mass.: Harvard University Press, 1930). Of quite another character is the highly critical evaluation of Liberian manners, morals, and politics contained in Elizabeth D. Furbay, *Top Hat and Tom-Toms* (Chicago: Ziff Davis Publishing Co., 1943), which has been banned in Liberia. Most revealing of all, perhaps, is the self-analysis conducted by some of Liberia's leading political, social, and religious leaders and set forth in John P. Mitchell, ed., of United Christian Fellowship Conference of Liberia, *Changing Liberia: A Challenge to the Christian* (Switzerland, 1959).

2. Wolfe M. Schmokel, "Settlers and Tribes: The Origins of the Liberian Dilemma," *Boston University Papers on Africa*, Vol. 4 (1969), pp. 153–173.

3. Further support for this conclusion is contained in Jane J. Martin, "How to Build

a Nation: Liberian Ideas about National Integration in the Later Nineteenth Century," *Liberian Studies Journal*, Vol. 2 (1969), pp. 15–42.

4. David Brown, "On the Category 'Civilised' in Liberia and Elsewhere," *Journal of Modern African Studies*, Vol. 20 (June 1982), pp. 287–303.

5. Jehudi Ashmun, *Journal*, 21 August 1821, in American Colonization Society 6th Annual Report, Appendix, p. 30; cited in G. E. Saigbe Boley, *Liberia: The Rise and Fall of the First Republic* (London: Macmillan Education, 1983), pp. 23ff.

6. Peter J. Murdza, *Immigrants to Liberia, 1865 to 1904: An Alphabetical Listing* (Newark, Del.: Liberian Studies Association, 1971), L. S. Research Working Paper No. 4.

7. For the discussion of some very recent Black American migration to Liberia, see chapter 7.

8. Liberia, Department of the Interior, *Annual Report*, 1959–1960, pp. 26–27.

9. An example from the Tubman period of this occurred in Tchien District (Department of the Interior, *Annual Report*, 1955–1956, p. 15, and *Annual Report*, 1956–1957, p. 16).

10. Liberian *Code of Law*, Sec. 83.

11. Difficulties encountered by Liberian officials in controlling access and in collecting the taxes, fines, and levies which were to regulate contact are documented in M. B. Akpan, "The Liberian Economy in the Nineteenth Century: Government Finances," *Liberian Studies Journal*, Vol. 6 (1975), pp. 129–161.

12. Cf. Yekutiel Gershoni, "The Paradox of Church-State Relations in Liberia, 1847–1930," *Liberian Studies Journal*, Vol. 10 (1982–83), pp. 67–82, passim. See also Jane J. Martin, "The Dual Legacy: Government Authority and Mission Influence Among the Glebo of Eastern Liberia, 1834–1910," Ph.D. dissertation in history, Boston University, 1968.

13. Thelma Awori, "The Revolt Against the 'Civilizing Mission': Christian Education in Liberia," in Edward Berman, ed., *African Reactions to Christian Missionary Education* (New York: Teachers College Press, 1975), pp. 116–133.

14. See *Liberian Code of Laws of 1956* (Ithaca, N.Y.: Cornell University Press, 1957), title 15, ch. 12C, secs. 301–303.

15. The Secretary of the Interior (later restyled Minister of Internal Affairs) generously made available to this writer the typewritten and mimeographed copies of the "Decisions Rendered by the President of Liberia on Administrative and Other Matters Heard and Determined in His Several Councils of Chiefs." These are important to the understanding of the Tubman Unification Policy and clarify many provisions of the *Liberian Code of Laws of 1956* regarding the administration of the interior. Also helpful in this latter respect was the mimeographed copy of the "Revised Laws and Administrative Regulations for Governing the Hinterland, 1949," which differ in certain marked respects from the *Code* provisions.

16. For an interesting summary of administrative policies and practices in the interior, see Monday B. Akpan, "The Practice of Indirect Rule in Liberia: The Laying of the Foundations, 1822–1915," in Eckhard Hinzen and Robert Kappel, *Dependence, Underdevelopment and Persistent Conflict—On The Political Economy of Liberia* (Bremen: Übersee-Museum, 1980), pp. 57–168.

17. Ibrahim K. Sundiata, *Black Scandal: America and the Liberian Labor Crises, 1929–1936* (Philadelphia: Institute for the Study of Human Issues, 1980).

18. For an excellent background discussion of the crisis, with a different perspective, see Raymond L. Buell, *Liberia: A Century of Survival, 1847–1947* in University of Pennsylvania Museum, *African Handbook*, No. 7 (Philadelphia: University of Pennsylvania Press, 1947).

19. For some interesting comments on labor recruitment practices in the 1960s, see the interviews reported in Robert W. Clower, George Dalton, Mitchell Harwitz, and A. A. Walters, *Growth Without Development: An Economic Survey of Liberia* (Evanston, Ill.: Northwestern University Press, 1966), pp. 296–298.

20. For a remarkably thorough coverage of the Tubman program, see F. P. M. van der

Kraaij, *The Open Door Policy of Liberia: An Economic History of Modern Liberia*, 2 vols. (Bremer, West Germany: Bremer Afrika Archiv, 1983).

21. Clower, Dalton, et al., *Growth Without Development*.

22. George G. Parker, "Acculturation in Liberia" (Ph.D. thesis in Religion, Kennedy School of Missions, Hartford Seminary, 1944), p. 261.

23. Perhaps the most reasonably objective study of the company's activities is Wayne Chatfield Taylor, "The Firestone Operations in Liberia," *United States Business Performance Abroad*, Case Study No. 5 (New York: National Planning Association, 1956). A very interesting treatment of the Firestone loan of 1927 is contained in Frank Chalk, "The Anatomy of an Investment: Firestone's 1927 Loan to Liberia," *Canadian Journal of African Studies*, I (March 1967), pp. 12–32.

24. Although numerous newspapers have been published in Liberia during its history as a colony and republic, political and financial considerations usually gave them brief lives. Files are either incomplete or nonexistent with respect to many of them. A discussion of newspaper sources covering the early period is found in Charles H. Huberich, *The Political and Legislative History of Liberia* (2 vols.; New York: Central Book Co., 1947), II, 1682ff.

25. See Mitchell, *Changing Liberia*, p. 17. The Conference included among others the Secretary of the Treasury Charles Sherman and Doris Banks Henries, the wife of the Speaker of the House. Mitchell later became Secretary of Education.

# V.

1. See Hans Dieter Seibel and Andreas Massing, *Traditional Organizations and Economic Development: Studies of Indigenous Cooperatives in Liberia* (New York: Praeger Publishers, 1974).

2. Dew Tuan-Wleh Mayson and Amos Sawyer, "Labour in Liberia," *Review of African Political Economy*, Vol. 14 (1980), pp. 3–15; and Nii K. Bensi-Enchill, "Development Problems in Putu Chiefdom," *West Africa*, 25 Feb. 1980, pp. 344–346.

3. H. W. Yaidoo, " 'Susu' in Liberian Society," *The Liberian Economic and Management Review*, Vol. 4 (1976/1977), pp. 81–92. *Susus* are often found among market women, but they are not limited to that group.

4. Mayson and Sawyer, "Labour in Liberia," p. 12.

5. "Complaints Presented by the I.C.F.T.U., the I.F.P.A.A.W., and the M.I.F. against the Government of Liberia," Case 506, International Labor Office, *Official Bulletin*, L., No. 3 (July 1967).

6. Mayson and Sawyer, "Labour in Liberia," p. 11.

7. *Ibid.*, pp. 7–8.

8. Dwight Seyfert, "The Origins of Privilege: Liberian Merchants, 1822–1847," *Liberian Studies Journal*, Vol. 6 (1975), pp. 109–125; Seyfert, "The Liberian Coasting Trade, 1822–1900," *Journal of African History*, Vol. 18 (1977), pp. 217–233; and George W. Ellis, "Political Institutions in Liberia," *American Political Science Review*, V (1911), p. 216.

9. See Rodney Carlisle, *Sovereignty for Sale: The Origins and Evolution of the Panamanian and Liberian Flags of Convenience* (Annapolis, Md.: Naval Institute Press, 1980).

10. Carlisle, "Liberia's Flag of Convenience: Rough Water Ahead," *Orbis*, Vol. 24 (Winter 1981), pp. 881–891.

11. Mayson and Sawyer, "Labour in Liberia," p. 6.

12. Frederick Starr, *Liberia: Description, History and Problems* (Chicago: by author, 1913), pp. 210–211.

13. John P. Mitchell, ed., *Changing Liberia: A Challenge to the Christian* (Switzerland, 1959), p. 51.

14. *Ibid.*, p. 7.

15. *West Africa*, 25 April 1964.

16. Colin Legum, ed., *Africa Contemporary Record*, 1972–73 (London: Rex Collings, 1973), p. B642.

17. Mayson and Sawyer, "Labour in Liberia," p. 4.

18. T. H. Bonaparte, "Multinational Corporations and Culture in Liberia," *American Journal of Economics and Sociology*, Vol. 38 (July 1979), pp. 237–251.

19. Ronald F. Storette, *The Politics of Integrated Social Investment: An American Study of the Swedish LAMCO Project in Liberia* (Stockholm: Alb. Bonniers boktryckeri, 1971).

20. Robert W. Clower, George Dalton, Mitchell Harwitz, and A.A. Walters, *Growth Without Development: An Economic Survey of Liberia* (Evanston: Northwestern University Press, 1966), p. 275.

21. Legum, ed., *Africa Contemporary Record*, 1970–71, p. B388.

22. Liberian Department of State, Bureau of Information, "National Unification" (May 1954), p. 11.

23. Accounts of the trial of prominent persons who were implicated in the plot against Barclay are contained in the 1940 issues of the *African Nationalist* (Library of Congress microfilm.)

24. Gail Stewart, "Notes on the Present-day Usage of the Vai Script in Liberia," *African Language Review*, VI (1967), 71–74.

25. Two surveys of educational endeavors during Liberia's first century as a colony and republic are Thomas Jesse Jones, *Education in Africa* (New York: Phelps-Stokes Fund, 1922), and Allen W. Gardner, *The Trustees of Donations for Education in Liberia: A Story of Philanthropic Endeavor, 1850–1923* (Boston: Thomas Todd, 1923). The impact of education upon both tribal and settler culture was analyzed during the period between the two world wars in James L. Sibley, *Liberia—Old and New* (Garden City, N.Y.: Doubleday, Doran, 1928), and in the postwar period by Thomas Hodgkin, "Education and Social Change in Liberia," *West Africa*, Nos. 1907–1911 (Sept. 12-Oct. 10, 1953). An interesting analysis of the problems of vocational training is contained in Alvin I. Thomas, *Technical Education in Liberia* (Columbus: Epsilon Pi Tau, 1961). A more comprehensive coverage of the educational needs of Liberia in terms of its internal and external commitments was prepared for Education and World Affairs of New York in 1965, by the Study Committee on Manpower Needs and Educational Capabilities in Africa. Its fifth report deals with *Liberia: Study of Manpower Needs, Educational Capabilities and Overseas Study*.

26. *Listener Daily*, 16 Feb. 1963, pp. 1, 10.

## VI.

1. The origins of political controversy and the emergence of political parties in Liberia as a whole and Maryland County in particular are traced in S. W. Laughton, "Administrative Problems in Maryland in Liberia, 1836–1851," *Journal of Negro History*, XXVI (July 1941), 325–365.

2. Charles H. Huberich, *The Political and Legislative History of Liberia*, Vol. 1 (New York: Central Books, 1947), pp. 670, 728–729, 841–842.

3. Frederick Starr, *Liberia* (Chicago, 1913), p. 90.

4. For an official version of the attempt, see Liberian Information Service, *The Plot That Failed* (London: Consolidated Publications, 1959).

5. *Liberian Code*, title 12, Ch. 8, sec. 216.

6. For a brief survey of the Liberian press, see Henry B. Cole, "The Press in Liberia," *Liberian Studies Journal*, Vol. 4 (1971–72), pp. 147–156; and Esuakema Udo Oton, "The Press in Liberia," *Journalism Quarterly*, Vol. 38 (Winter 1961), pp. 209–212.

7. Mr. Porte's writings include "Glimpses of Justice in Liberia," "Our Constitutional Rights," "A Few Articles Refused Publication By Our Newspapers," and "A Little Child Shall Lead Them—A Tribute to Maryland County."

8. The voice of the opposition to Tubman is partially expressed in a rather pitiful article by the 1951 unsuccessful candidate, Dihdwo Twe, "Liberia: An American Responsibility," *Annals of the American Academy of Political and Social Science*, 282 (July 1952), 104–107.

9. Reginald Townsend, ed., *President Tubman of Liberia Speaks* (London: Consolidated Publications, 1959), p. 99.

10. *Liberian Age*, 17 June 1960, p. 1.

11. *Liberian Code*, title 13, sec. 12.

12. *Liberian Age*, 3 March 1961, p. 4.

13. *African Nationalist*, 8 Nov. 1941, p. 3.

14. *Liberian Age*, 6 May 1959, p. 1; *Daily Listener*, 21 Feb. 1959, p. 1 and 24 Feb. 1959, p. 1.

15. Liberian Information Service, *The Plot That Failed*.

16. *Daily Listener*, 27 Feb. 1959, *et seq*.

17. *African Nationalist*, 8 Nov. 1941, p. 1.

18. The Convention of 1959 elected Senator Edwin Morgan as national chairman, Wilkin Tyler as vice national chairman, Postmaster-General McKinley DeShield as general secretary, and former Secretary of the Treasury William Dennis as general treasurer. Tyler succeeded Morgan as chairman; James Greene, who later became vice president, succeeded Tyler, and Reginald Townsend, who held the post under Tolbert, succeeded Greene.

19. *Liberian Age*, 3 Sept. 1962, p. 7.

20. *Daily Listener*, 27 Feb. 1959, p. 1; *Liberian Age*, 2 March 1959, p. 1.

21. *Daily Listener*, 4 March 1955, p. 1.

22. *Liberian Age*, 27 Feb. 1959, p. 1; 2 March 1959, p. 1; 13 March 1959, p. 10; and *Daily Listener*, 3 March 1959, p. 1.

23. Raymond Buell, *The Native Problem in Africa* (New York: Macmillan, 1928), II, 712.

24. Doris Duncan Grimes, "Economic Development on Liberia" (M.A. Thesis, New York Univerity, 1955), p. 6.

## VII.

1. The Liberian Census of 1974 indicated that there were 21,365 alien residents in the country. They came primarily from the following countries: Guinea (26,337), Ghana (8,068), Sierra Leone (6,440), Lebanon (3,430), the United States (2,399), and several West European states (4,101).

2. J. Gus Liebenow, "Liberia," in Gwendolen M. Carter, ed., *African One-Party States* (Ithaca, NY: Cornell University Press, 1962), p. 369.

3. Raymond J. Smyke, "Massaquoi of Liberia, 1870–1938," *Geneve-Afrique*, Vol. 21 (1983), pp. 73–105; and Smyke, *Massaquoi of Liberia* (Algonac, Michigan: Reference Publications, c. 1986).

4. *West Africa*, 7 Oct. 1967.

5. *Ibid*.

## VIII.

1. *Liberian Code of Laws of 1956*, title 27, ch. 3, secs. 52–57.

2. 12 Aug. 1960, p. 3; 6 May 1960, p. 11.

3. See Albert Porte, "The Observance of President Tubman's Birthday in Liberia," Monrovia, October 1965, mimeographed.

4. *West Africa*, 26 Oct. 1963.

5. The criticism of Stephen Tolbert was contained in Porte, "Liberianization or Gobbling Business?" (Crozierville: published by the author, 1974, mimeographed).

6. *Daily Listener*, 10 Feb. 1959, p. 1.

7. *Daily Listener*, 2 July 1962, p. 3.

8. *Liberian Age*, 21 Dec. 1962, p. 2.

9. Cornell University Press has been publishing two series on behalf of the Liberian government. Both are the products of the Liberian Codification Project under the direction of Professor Milton R. Konvitz. The first is the series of *Liberian Code of Laws of 1956* (1957–58). The second is the multi-volume *Liberian Law Reports* (1955–62), which contain the decisions of the Supreme Court from 1861 onward.

10. Republic of Liberia, "Annual Report of the Attorney General," 1959–1960, App. B; *Liberian Age*, 31 March 1958, p. 4.

11. See Parker, "Acculturation in Liberia," p. 270.

12. Anthony J. Nimley, *The Liberian Bureaucracy: An Analysis and Evaluation of the Environmental Structures and Functions* (Washington, D.C.: University Press of America, 1977).

13. The problems of administration within Liberia can be discerned from an examination of the annual reports of the heads of departments, which are remarkably frank in their self-criticism. A scholarly monograph dealing with the problems of local administration in Grand Bassa County is J. Genevray, *Elements d'une Monographie d'une Division Administrative Liberieenne* (Dakar: IFAN, 1952). A lighter but nonetheless informative treatment is the sketch of hinterland administration in Gbarnga District in "Our Far-flung Correspondents: Tubman Bids Us Toil," *New Yorker*, Vol. 33 (11 Jan. 1958), 72–91.

## IX.

1. See D. Elwood Dunn, *The Foreign Policy of Liberia During the Tubman Era, 1944–1971* (London: Hutchison Benham, 1979).

2. *New York Times*, 24 March 1957.

3. Hassan B. Sisay, *Big Powers and Small Nations: A Case Study of United States–Liberian Relations* (Lanham, Md.: University Press of America, 1985), p. 183.

4. *U.N. Yearbook of International Trade Statistics*, 1951–1982.

5. Nnamdi Azikiwe's *Liberia in World Politics* (London: Stockwell, 1934), which is a more contemporary indictment, echoes the criticisms expressed by Dr. Edward Wilmot Blyden.

6. See Christopher Clapham, *An Essay in Comparative Politics: Liberia and Sierra Leone* (New York: Cambridge University Press, 1976).

7. D. Elwood Dunn, "Anti-Colonialism in Liberian Foreign Policy: A Case Study," *Liberian Studies Journal*, Vol. 4 (1971–72), pp. 47–66.

8. J. Gus Liebenow, "Which Road to Pan-African Unity? The Sanniquellie Conference, 1959" in Gwendolen M. Carter, ed., *Politics in Africa: 7 Cases* (New York: Harcourt, Brace and World, 1966), pp. 1–32.

9. For a fuller discussion of this problem, see *ibid*.

10. For an informed discussion of this, see Dunn, "The 1975 Vorster Visit to Liberia: Implications for Free Africa's Relations with Pretoria," *Liberian Studies Journal*, Vol. 10 (1982–83), pp. 37–54.

## X.

1. Jerry L. Prillaman, "Integration of Tribal Courts into the National Judiciary of Liberia: The Role of the Local Courts Advisor," *Liberian Law Journal*, II (June 1966), pp. 43–67.

2. *West Africa*, 1 Feb. 1964, p. 120.

3. Fletcher Knebel, *The Zinzin Road* (New York: Doubleday, 1966).

4. *West Africa*, 27 Jan, 1968, p. 89.

5. *Africa Report*, XII (May 1967), p. 52.

6. The basic constitution was drafted with some assistance from Professor Simon Greenleaf of Harvard University. Its description of the structures of government, the distribution of powers, and the Bill of Rights is modeled after the United States Constitution of 1787, as amended.

## XI.

1. Elliot Berg Associates, *The Liberian Crisis and an Appropriate U.S. Response* (Washington, D.C.: U.S.AID, 1982), p. iii.

2. The impact of urbanization on social and cultural values is brilliantly handled in Merran Fraenkel, *Tribe and Class in Monrovia* (Oxford: Oxford University Press, 1964). A more recent analysis which demonstrates structural continuities in beliefs and institutions among one group of immigrant groups to Monrovia—the Kru—is dealt with in Lawrence B. Breitborde, "Structural Continuity in the Development of an Urban Kru Community," *Urban Anthropology*, Vol. 8 (Summer 1979), pp. 111–130.

3. Robert W. Clower, George Dalton, Mitchell Harwitz, A. A. Walters, et al., *Growth Without Development: An Economic Survey of Liberia* (Evanston: Northwestern University Press, 1966).

4. Berg Associates, *The Liberian Crises*, passim.

5. Clower, Dalton, et al., *Growth Without Development*, p. 94.

6. *Ibid.*, p. 77.

7. *Ibid.*, p. 33.

8. *Ibid.*, p. 67.

9. *Ibid.*, p. 95.

10. *Ibid.*, p. 33.

11. "Machet" in *West Africa* (23 July 1979), p. 1299.

## XII.

1. Quoted by Kayode Awosanya, "How the Liberia Time Bomb Exploded," in *The New Nation*, Vol. 3, No. 13 (1980), pp. 5ff.

2. For interesting interviews with dissident leaders, see *West Africa* (18 February 1980), pp. 291ff.

3. See J. Gus Liebenow, *Liberia: The Evolution of Privilege* (Ithaca: Cornell University Press), pp. 107–111.

4. H. O. Akingbade, "The Role of the Military in the History of Liberia, 1822–1947," Ph.D. dissertation in history, Howard University, 1977.

5. *Daily Listener*, 6 Feb. 1963, p. 1; and subsequent issues.

6. *West Africa*, 16 March 1968, p. 324. See also *West Africa*, 6 July 1968, p. 791, and 20 July, p. 847.

## XIII.

1. Quoted by Kayode Awosanya, "How the Liberian Time Bomb Exploded," in *The New Nation*, Vol. 3, No. 13 (1980), pp. 7ff.

2. *The New African* (May 1980), p. 26.

3. The question of whether Dennis had, or had not, sought asylum at the American Embassy on the 12th stirred a congressional inquiry in Washington and led to a review of American policy on the right of asylum.

4. There was also grave concern regarding the actions of a Major William Jarbo, who

had attempted to mount a countercoup. Jarbo was ultimately shot as he attempted to escape to Sierra Leone in a canoe on the Mano River.

5. J. Pal Chaudhuri, "An Analysis of the Recent Developments in Liberia," *Liberia-Forum*, Vol. 1 (1985), pp. 45–54.

## XIV.

1. The Poro is a male secret society which operates within the Gola, Vai, Dei, Kpelle, Mende, and several other tribal groups in Liberia and Sierra Leone. The Sande is the female counterpart. The rituals and sanctions of Poro within each of these ethnic groups take precedence over all secular associations and institutions. The council of Poro elders, meeting in the sacred grove, has the power of reversing decisions of secular chiefs and can even depose them or render them ineffective. The council had the power of life and death over members who violated its secrets, and the initiation of young men into the Poro constitutes their entry into adulthood.

2. J. Pal Chaudhuri, "An Analysis of Recent Developments in Liberia," *Liberia-Forum*, Vol. 1 (1985), pp. 45–54.

3. The late president's son had taken refuge in the French embassy three days after the coup. He apparently divulged his own whereabouts because of his insistence on making frequent telephone calls from the embassy guesthouse. He was charged with corruption and treason. He was sent to Belle Yella Prison in the interior and was subsequently shot by a member of the PRC "while trying to escape."

## XV.

1. Apparently the only one who refused to sign was Justice Minister Chesson, who was reported to have stated that he was convinced the PRC would kill him anyway, so why make it easy for them.

2. Robert T. Brown, "Simon Greenleaf and the Liberian Constitution of 1847," *Liberian Studies Journal*, Vol. 9 (1980–81), pp. 51–60.

3. *New Liberian*, 23 July 1984.

4. Chapter 8, Art. 77.

5. Chapter 8, Articles 81 and 82A.

6. Albert Porte, "Liberianization or Gobbling Business?" (Crozierville, September 1974).

7. Editorial: "Journalists, Not Bootlickers," *New Liberian*, 19 February 1982.

8. Amos Sawyer, "Social Stratification and National Orientations: Students and Non-students in Liberia," in John N. Paden, ed., *Values, Identities, and National Integration: Empirical Research in Africa* (Evanston, Ill.: Northwestern University Press, 1980), pp. 285–304; and Sawyer, "Social Stratification, Social Change, and Political Socialization: Students and Nonstudents in Liberia," in Paden, *ibid.*, pp. 305–320.

9. *Sunday People*, 19 April 1981.

10. *Footprints Today*, 28 October 1985.

11. *West Africa*, 29 April 1985, p. 734.

12. *West Africa*, 15 April 1985, p. 734.

13. *Footprints Today*, 19 September 1985.

14. See Dew Mayson and Amos Sawyer, "Labour in Liberia," *Review of African Political Economy*, Vol. 14 (1979), pp. 3–15.

## XVI.

1. *Daily Observer*, 20 March 1981.

2. 17 March 1981.

3. "Statement by the Liberian National Student Union," in *The Republic of Liberia News*, press release of the Liberian Embassy in Washington (May 6, 1980).

4. See various publications of the Goverment of Liberia (Monrovia), including Land Reform Commission, *Guidelines for Drafting of Land Tenure Decree* (1981); Land Reform Commission, *Summary Report* (1982); and Ministry of Agriculture, *Liberia's Agricultural Development: Policy and Organizational Structure* (June 1980/May 1981).

5. Amos Sawyer, "Imbalances of Educational Opportunities and the Implication for National Development," *Liberian Education Review*, Vol. 1 (May 1980), pp. 25–48.

6. Rodney Carlisle, "Liberia's Flag of Convenience: Rough Waters Ahead," *Orbis*, Vol. 24 (Winter 1981), pp. 881–892.

7. Robert E. Miller, "The Modern Dual Economy: A Cost Benefit Analysis of Liberia," *Journal of Modern African Studies* (May, 1971), pp. 113–121; and Robert L. Curry, "Liberia's External Debts and Their Servicing," *ibid*. (December 1972), pp. 621–626.

8. Maynard Geoffrey, "The Economic Irrelevance of Monetary Independence: The Case of Liberia," *Journal of Development Studies* (January 1979), pp. 111–132.

## XVII.

1. *Footprints Today*, 27 July 1984.
2. *Ibid.*, 15 April 1985.

## XVIII.

1. "News in Depth," *The Swazi Observer*, 31 January 1984.
2. *Footprints Today*, 8 June 1984.
3. *New Liberian*, 26 July 1984.
4. Warren d'Azevedo has written a manuscript on this matter.
5. *West Africa*, 18 February 1985, pp. 306–307.
6. *Mirror*, 28 July 1984; *Footprints Today*, 30 July 1984.
7. *Footprints Today*, 29 May 1985.

## XIX.

1. *New Liberian*, 2 August 1984.
2. Sebastian Cole, "Liberia: Doe's Capitalist Rivals," *Africa* (September 1985), p.10; *West Africa*, 15 April 1985, p. 734.
3. *West Africa*, 8 April 1985, p. 657.
4. *Footprints Today*, 9 April 1985.
5. *New Liberian*, 27 August 1985.
6. *Footprints Today*, 7 August 1985.
7. *Footprints Today*, 4 October 1985.
8. *Footprints Today*, 25 September 1985.
9. *Footprints Today*, 16 October 1985, p. 1.
10. *Footprints Today*, 26 August 1985.
11. U.S. Department of State, Bureau of Public Affairs, "Recent Developments in Liberia," *Current Policy* No. 773.
12. *The Mirror*, 19 October 1985.

## XX.

1. Chester A. Crocker, "Recent Developments in Liberia," U.S. Department of State Bureau of Public Affairs, *Current Policy*, No. 773 (10 December 1985).

2. *Footprints Today*, 1 November 1985.

3. *Sun Times*, 6 November 1985.

4. *Footprints Today*, 4 November 1985.

5. For fuller descriptions of the events of 12 November and thereafter, see *Africa Now*, December 1985, pp. 7–17; Larry James, "Quiwonkpa's Fatal Gamble," *Africa Report*, January-February 1986, pp. 47–49; and various issues of *West Africa* during that period.

6. Chester A. Crocker, "Statement before the Senate Subcommittee on African Affairs," 10 December 1985; and "Statement before the Joint Session of the Subcommittees on Africa and on Human Rights and International Organizations of the House Foreign Affairs Committee," 23 January 1986.

7. *Footprints Today*, 31 January 1986.

8. *Footprints Today*, 27 February 1986.

9. *Sun Times*, 20 January 1986.

10. *Sun Times*, 12 April 1986.

11. *West Africa*, 26 May 1986, pp. 1093–1095.

12. *Daily Star*, 27 June 1986.

13. Rev. Thomas Hayden, "The Liberian Impasse," *About Liberia*, No. 29, May 1986.

14. Rev. Thomas Hayden, editorial submitted 18 April 1986 to the *New York Times*.

# INDEX

Agriculture: importing of food, 2, 167–68, 171, 241; need to diversify, 62, 242; tribal, 72; extent of work force in, 166–67; subsistence nature of, 167; role of export sector, 167–68

Aliens: and development, 67, 78–81, 133

American Colonization Society: origins of, 12–13; official and private support of, 13–16, 18; Agents of, 14, 20; and Plan of Civil Government, 88–89

Americo-Liberians: percent of population, 3; origins of, 19–20; relations with ACS Agents, 20–21; adjustment of, to African environment, 21; attitudes toward agriculture and commerce, 21, 22, 75, 78; vocational preferences of, 22, 23, 156; norms of, dominant in First Republic, 48, 67

Anderson, B. J. K.: visit to Musardu, 26

"Back to Africa" schemes, 12

Bar Association, Liberian, 231, 309

Barclay, Arthur: background of, 50, 110, 117; and Indirect Rule, 54–56; attempt to control successor, 98

Barclay, Edwin: background of, 50; and League of Nations inquiry, 58–59; campaign against Tubman, 93

Bassa: deeding of land by, 16; early migration of, 31; location of, 34; role in settler economy, 35

Bentol, 121–22, 170

Best, Kenneth. See Press, *Daily Observer*

Blyden, Edward Wilmot, 50

Bureaucracy: inefficiency of, in First Republic, 129–33; patronage recruitment of, 131–32

Businessmen: rise and fall of, during nineteenth century, 75–77; links with political elite under Tubman, Tolbert, 76–78; reemergence of, since 1980 coup, 232–34, 281

Cabinet: ethnic representation in, during First Republic, 113; background of, 114–15; in initial PRC government, 214–17; major changes by Doe in 1985–1986, 307–308, 313

Cape Mesurado, initial landing at, 16

Caste relationship: nature of, during First Republic, 3–5, 24, 48, 50–55

Chiefs, traditional: authority in tribal society, 40–42; role in tax collections and labor recruitment,

55, 57; election of, 125; post-1980 political role of, 267–68

Christian churches: and education, 53, 68–69; as bulwark against Islam, 53–54; interference with Poro, 53; role in Grebo resistance, 53; attitudes of Americo-Liberians toward missionaries, 53–54; and social change, 68–69 *See also* Religion

—Baptist: 81, 228

—Episcopal: 53, 68, 81, 82, 230, 299

—Council of Churches: 262, 311, 313–14

—Lutheran: 54, 68, 230

—Methodist: 53, 68, 81, 82, 228, 229

—Presbyterian: 81, 82

—Quaker: 13, 22

—Roman Catholic: 81, 229, 311, 313, 318n20

—Syncretistic: 72, 82, 230

Citizenship: extension of, to tribal persons, 47; racial criteria for 67, 102, 221; linked to land tenure, 308

Civil/military relationships, 197–99

Civilian rule: commitment by PRC to restore, 7, 213–18

Class identity: emergence of, 236

Clan, as political unit, 41–42

Coleman, W.D.: interior policies of, 28, 91, 98

Communications: and social change, 69

Concessions: role in development, 79; threats to, after coup, 243–44

Condo Confederation, 37, 42

Congoes: origins, status of, 12, 19, 22, 23, 49; treatment of, by settlers, ACS Agents, 49; changed status of, 112–13

Constitutional Advisory Assembly, 218–21

Constitutional Commission: creation of, 217–18; obstacles to functioning of, 219; review of work, by Advisory Assembly, 219–21

Constitution of 1847: origins of, 89; 1980 suspension of, 201; review of, 218

Constitution of 1984: vote on, 221–22

Cooperatives: Tubman's opposition to, 72

Counties: changes in boundaries of, 64–65, 103–105, 130, 156–57; expansion of administrative offices in, 130; and tribal divisions, 268–69

Coup of 12 April 1980: events surrounding 3, 184–88; popular reaction to, 3, 5, 191–93, 213

Crocker, Chester: views of 1985 election and coup attempt, 203–204, 305–306